John Urquhart

**The Inspiration & Accuracy of the Holy Scriptures**

John Urquhart

**The Inspiration & Accuracy of the Holy Scriptures**

ISBN/EAN: 9783742810069

Manufactured in Europe, USA, Canada, Australia, Japa

Cover: Foto ©Lupo / pixelio.de

Manufactured and distributed by brebook publishing software (www.brebook.com)

John Urquhart

**The Inspiration & Accuracy of the Holy Scriptures**

# THE
# INSPIRATION & ACCURACY

OF THE

# HOLY SCRIPTURES.

BY

JOHN URQUHART

(Editor of "Word and Work" and of "The King's Own"),
And Author of "What are We to Believe"? "What is the Bible"? &c.

---

London:
MARSHALL BROTHERS, KESWICK HOUSE, PATERNOSTER ROW.

E. Goodman & Son,
Phœnix Printing Works,
Taunton.

# PREFACE.

A FEW prefatory words may help the reader of the following pages to see the writer's purpose. It seemed to me essential to ascertain, first of all, what the *Scriptural view* of inspiration is. How did inspired men regard the words which they and others have handed on to us, and, above all, how did our Lord receive them? A clear and full answer to that question is the need of the hour. Once got, it would settle this controversy for many. There is still loyalty enough in the Christian ranks to go anywhere with Jesus, and to separate from everything that would separate from Him. The first part of the present volume is an attempt to meet this want.

The second part answers another question. We want to know something of the other party to the controversy. "The higher critics" demand the surrender of our "traditional beliefs," and ask us to gratefully receive from their hands a "reconstructed" Bible. Who, then, are those new masters in Israel? Whence are they? What is their aim, and what has been their history? "The Genesis of Rationalism," which forms the second part of the Book, contains a reply.

One section more appeared to be necessary. Criticism has reached certain conclusions regarding various Books of Scripture. The older narratives are declared to be mere legends, and the history generally is described as tradition tinctured by the time when it was put into writing. Certain Books of the Old Testament are said to fall below even this low level. They are declared to be fictions, the soothing epithet "pious" being generally added, the representation being that evil was done by the writers that good might come! All these conclusions are placed before the public as genuine scientific discoveries.

Now, in the strangest fashion, facts have been brought to light, which enable us to put those statements to the proof. Parallel records in the history of Ancient Persia, Assyria, Babylon, Palestine, and Egypt have been recovered. These have poured a flood of light upon the Scripture, verifying many of its narratives, explaining many of its allusions, and settling the age of disputed Books. The third section of the present volume, brings these resources to bear upon the questions regarding *Esther* and *Daniel*, two Books which criticism has condemned with the utmost confidence.

Archdeacon Farrar's work on *Daniel*, which was published as this Book was passing through the press, is noticed in the appendix.

JOHN URQUHART.

April 8th, 1895.

# CONTENTS.

## BOOK I.
### THE SCRIPTURE DOCTRINE OF INSPIRATION.

| | | PAGE. |
|---|---|---|
| CHAPTER I. | THE CUSTOMARY VIEW OF THE BIBLE ... | 9 |
| ,, II. | THE VIEWS OF THE APOSTOLIC CHURCHES REGARDING INSPIRATION ... | 20 |
| ,, III. | WHAT THE SCRIPTURES CLAIM FOR THEMSELVES: 1. *The Witness of the Old Testament* ... ... ... | 32 |
| ,, IV. | 2. *The Witness of the New Testament* | 50 |
| ,, V. | 3. *The Witness of the New Testament* (Continued) ... ... ... | 60 |
| ,, VI. | OUR LORD'S ENDORSEMENT OF THE OLD TESTAMENT SCRIPTURES | 73 |

## BOOK II.
### THE GENESIS OF RATIONALISM.

| | | |
|---|---|---|
| CHAPTER I. | THE PRE-REFORMATION PERIOD ... ... | 93 |
| ,, II. | ,, ,, ,, ,, (Continued) | 104 |
| ,, III. | THE REFORMATION ... ... | 116 |
| ,, IV. | DECAY AND DOUBT ... | 131 |

|        |                                                                                  | PAGE |
|--------|----------------------------------------------------------------------------------|------|
| CHAPTER V. | THE BEGINNINGS OF ENGLISH RATIONALISM                                        | 145  |
| ,, VI. | CONTINENTAL PREPARATIONS FOR THE RATIONALISTIC HARVEST                           | 156  |
| ,, VII. | RALLY AND DEFEAT                                                                | 165  |
| ,, VIII. | THE RISE OF GERMAN RATIONALISM                                                 | 176  |
| ,, IX. | BLIGHTED HOPES                                                                   | 191  |
| ,, X.  | DEEPENING DECAY.—*The Rise of the Higher Criticism—Eichhorn and Paulus*         | 206  |
| ,, XI. | DEEPER DEPTHS: *Astruc, De Wette, and Strauss*                                   | 219  |
| ,, XII. | THE LAST STATE WORSE THAN THE FIRST: *Vatke, Graf, Kayser, Kuenen*              | 240  |
| ,, XIII. | PRESENT POSITION OF RATIONALISM: *Wellhausen, Reuss, Ritschl, English Criticism* | 254  |

# BOOK III.
## CRITICAL RESULTS TESTED BY MODERN DISCOVERY.

| CHAPTER I. | THE TEST OF CRITICISM: *Champollion; Grotefend; Sayce on the Minute Accuracy of Scripture* | 273 |
| ,, II. | THE BOOK OF ESTHER: *Absence of the Name of God; Who was Ahasuerus? Xerxes' Feast* | 288 |
| ,, III. | XERXES AND ESTHER | 310 |
| ,, IV. | FURTHER CONFIRMATIONS OF ESTHER | 325 |

## Contents.

|  |  |  | PAGE. |
|---|---|---|---|
| CHAPTER V. | THE BOOK OF DANIEL: *Its Portraiture of Nebuchadnezzar* ... ... ... ... | | 340 |
| ,, VI. | ALLUSIONS TO BABYLONIAN COURT OFFICIALS AND COURT CUSTOMS | ... | 359 |
| ,, VII. | BABYLONIAN NAMES—NEBUCHADNEZZAR'S DREAM—THE TWO LANGUAGES OF THE BOOK—A SEVENFOLD TEST | ... | 376 |
| ,, VIII. | THE WISE MEN OF BABYLON ... | ... | 391 |
| ,, IX. | NEBUCHADNEZZAR'S GOLDEN STATUE | ... | 404 |
| ,, X. | THE GREEK INSTRUMENTS MENTIONED IN DANIEL ... ... ... | ... | 419 |
| ,, XI. | BABYLONIAN TRAITS IN DANIEL ... | ... | 439 |
| ,, XII. | NEBUCHADNEZZAR'S MADNESS | ... | 456 |
| ,, XIII. | WHO WAS BELSHAZZAR? | ... | 477 |
| ,, XIV. | BELSHAZZAR'S FEAST... | ... | 501 |
| ,, XV. | DARIUS THE MEDIAN... | ... | 521 |
| ,, XVI. | THE VISIONS OF DANIEL ... | ... | 533 |

## APPENDIX:

| ARCHDEACON FARRAR ON DANIEL | ... | 553 |
|---|---|---|

# THE INSPIRATION AND ACCURACY

OF

# THE HOLY SCRIPTURES.

## CHAPTER I.

### The Customary View of the Bible.

IT is abundantly evident that the time has come when the question of the Inspiration of the Bible must be re-investigated. It is necessary for all parties. Those who believe most firmly will still have difficulties to meet and questions to answer, and these cannot be met and answered without inquiry and consideration. Those who are troubled cannot be reassured by mere authority: they need the assurance of conviction. Those who have surrendered the old belief will not be led back, unless it can be shown that former convictions were parted with under misconception, that supposed arguments were fallacies, that imagined difficulties were only obscurities which fuller knowledge is clearing away, and that the positive evidence in support of the old belief is simply overwhelming.

The task of this re-investigation will no doubt command the service of abler pens than mine; but in this great struggle each must do his part. In the day of battle, the lad, who only guides a battalion through vale or forest that it may take its appointed position, performs no mean service. If I merely help to make a place where others will smite the darkness with force and skill, it will be no trouble to me that the honours of war are given to those who have won the victory. There is one thing, however, which I trust will mark this attempt of mine. I hope to be guided by perfect honesty and straightforwardness. The reader and I shall look at this matter broadly and fearlessly. We shall listen to what is to be said for and against. We shall shirk no difficulty; and we shall decline to skirt a "dangerous" place, merely because the ice seems weak, and because people weighted with a theory may easily fall in. If there is a weak place, or a difficulty, we shall go right up to it, and see just what it means.

In this inquiry we shall have to find answers to three questions. The ordinary view is attacked. To understand this matter rightly, we have to inquire what the ordinary view is. Unless that is thoroughly done we may be led astray by misconceptions, and find that our reasonings are vitiated and our labour lost. This must clearly, therefore, be our first inquiry. We shall (1) ask what the ordinary view of the Inspiration of the Bible is, and whence it has come—in other words, what is generally said about the Bible, and who first said it.

## The Customary View of the Bible.

We shall then listen to its assailants, and ask (2) on what grounds this view is rejected; and finally, having heard and considered all that is urged on the other side, we shall (3) inquire whether any positive evidence can be brought forward in favour of the ordinary view. Treating the matter in this exhaustive, and, we trust, impartial fashion, we shall hope to arrive at some clear and satisfactory conclusion.

There is one epithet commonly applied to the ordinary opinion regarding the Bible which I refer to at the outset, because it may occasion a certain amount of unworthy and harmful prejudice.

It is said to be "traditional." Well, there are many things "traditional." The Copernican theory of the motions of the heavenly bodies has long ago become "traditional." We all believe in it, though not half a dozen men in this generation may have taken the trouble to test and prove it. It has been handed down to us; it gives what seems a simple and satisfactory explanation of the movements of the earth and of the heavens; and we consequently accept it willingly and gratefully. It will not trouble us much, should it be called "the traditional view." That it is "the traditional view" might be regarded, on the contrary, as something in its favour. It could hardly have endured so long, under the close and continued inspection of modern science, unless it had much to support it. It is quite true that there have been hoary traditions that have been burden and confusion to men; but, on the other hand, there is nothing so "traditional" as truth. The whole body of knowledge and discovery becomes "traditional." There is not a single science, or art, or manufacture in the world that is not governed by tradition. We may, therefore, discharge this term of whatever offence it has seemed to impute to the ordinary view, and we may use it freely to designate the long-continued belief of the Christian Church regarding the Scriptures.

What, then, is "the traditional view," which not very long ago ruled unquestioned in the churches of this land, and which to-day, for hundreds of thousands, is bound up with Christianity itself? The reply can be given fully only in the two words— Verbal Inspiration. But here again we have to guard against misconception. Opponents of this view run away with the inference that verbal inspiration must imply that the words were *dictated* to the inspired writers. The belief is, therefore, labelled "a mechanical theory," and is frequently at once thrown aside with contempt. Those who act in this way have no idea that they are doing injustice to the ordinary view; but such is, nevertheless, the fact. The presence of the word "inspiration," ought to have prevented them confounding it with dictation. The merchant does not inspire his clerk when he dictates to him. Dictation excludes the possibility of inspiration as completely as anything can. "Verbal Inspiration" merely intimates how far inspiration has gone, and that it has extended to the *form* as well as to the *substance* of the divine message. *Verbal Inspiration* implies no

## The Customary View of the Bible. 13

theory whatever as to *the mode* of inspiration; it only defines *its result*. It tells *what* we have in the Bible; not *how* it has been given. It is a rational answer to a natural and urgent question. We place the Bible in some man's hands, telling him that it is God's message to him, and that it has been given by inspiration of the Holy Spirit. He asks us in what sense he is to understand our statement. Does the inspiration extend only to the *purpose* of the Book? Were the writers prompted to undertake this varied service, and then left to find their own arguments? The ordinary view replies that the miracle of inspiration has gone further than that: the arguments were the result of the illumination and direction of the Spirit of God, co-operating with and informing the mind of the writer.

"Well, then," he replies, "you have taken me so far; but there is something more I wish to know. Did the Holy Spirit inspire the thought and leave the writers to find out, and to write down, what *words* they pleased? Are the *thoughts* inspired, but the *words* not inspired?" To this the ordinary view replies that the miracle of inspiration has gone further still. Thought is defined by words. *Perfectly* clear thought is wedded to the words which express it—to these very words and to no other. The Spirit of God is Light. The Spirit's thought is perfect in its clearness, and it is sharply defined, therefore, in its expression. Into the clearness of this thought the mind of the writer came, and he was "borne along" into its clear expression. The words, as they fell on the page one by one, were each like an added ray of light, and all of them bound together formed the beam which scatters the darkness. *The mind of the Spirit is expressed in the words of the Scriptures as they were originally given.*

That concluding phrase, "as they were originally given," is sometimes treated as if it cast a doubt upon the Scriptures as we now have them. How little ground there is for *that* misunderstanding we shall see by-and-bye. The Christian Church has not always had the apostolic autographs. Even in the apostolic age it was only the Churches to which they were specially sent that had these. But the Churches of Christ have always had the original Scriptures. They have possessed the Old and the New Testament in a form which the fullest investigation has never challenged in any important point. Meanwhile, I repeat that "Verbal Inspiration" defines the extent of inspiration, but says nothing as to the mode in which the Spirit of God operated. It expresses the result, but ventures no theory as to the process. It tells us that the inspiration of the Scriptures is such that it has left its clear impress upon *the words* of the Book, and that these words are what they are, and their very arrangement is what it is, in order that in them the mind of the Spirit might be clearly and fully declared.

*How* the Spirit of God has operated to give us a Book reliable in every word it has never concerned Christian men to say or even to know. A few have ventured upon *theories* of inspiration; but the mental gymnastics, which we dignify by the name of metaphysics, have never been popular. The intellectual tight-rope, on which one has to balance oneself by the adroit use of definitions, has few attractions for the multitude. And the popular instinct has been fully justified by the barrenness of the results. The intellectual Blondins of our race have gone to the end of their slim and aerial pathway and found—nothing. There has been much ingenuity but small enlightenment. We find ourselves on solid ground when we speak of *what* the Spirit of God has given us: the moment we talk of *how* the Spirit of God operated to give us an absolutely accurate Book we have ventured out upon the air, and the only result that can be looked for is a fall: When one asks *how* the dead are raised, Paul's reply begins with the significant words, "Thou fool!"

I have now to answer the second part of our question—whence has this belief come?

Webster, in the first edition of his Dictionary, defines inspiration as "The supernatural influence of the Spirit of God on the human mind, by which prophets, apostles, and sacred writers were qualified to set forth Divine truth *without any mixture of error.*" That was Webster's judgment of the meaning which the term bore when applied by Christian men to the Bible. The Archbishops and Bishops of the Church of England, in a united protest addressed to Bishop Colenso, in 1863, said: "All our hopes for eternity, the very foundation of our faith, our nearest and dearest consolations, are taken from us, *if one line of that Sacred Book be declared unfaithful or untrustworthy.*" If any further confirmation is needed that this has long been the customary view of the Bible, it will be found in the confessions of those who attack the doctrine of Verbal Inspiration. They speak of it as "the ordinary view." When they attack it, and endeavour to show that it is overthrown by the alleged existence of errors in the Bible, they are perfectly aware that they are saying or writing what will offend the vast majority of Christian people. They take the position, not of those expounding a belief which is in possession, but of those who set forth a belief which has got to make its way. They allow their beliefs to be named, without protest or offence, "the new views." They are the confessed champions of "the New Theology." Behind all these admissions lies the consciousness that, to the Christian community of our time, the Bible is, from beginning to end, the faultless Word of the faultless God.

The truth of that admission will be felt by everyone. The attitude of Christian men towards the Bible is that of absolute trust and of deepest veneration. There can be no question as to how the teachers in our Sunday-schools have regarded it. They teach the children to look upon it as *God's Book*. Rightly or wrongly, they always speak of it as standing apart from all other literature; and the reason which they assign for this unapproached excellence is that, while other books proceed from men, this has come from God. If we enter our churches and chapels, and ask how the Bible is regarded there, we have the same reply. The words of this Book are approached, expounded, and applied to the conscience and the heart as the very words of God.

I do not cite this belief as an argument, though it is only fair to note in passing that it ought, nevertheless, to have some weight with us. Multitudes of these are men who do not revere the Bible merely because they have been taught to do so. They know it. They have read it again and again. They have taken it line by line, and word by word. They have studied it as men have never studied any other book. They have ransacked every realm of knowledge, that they might shed light upon the Bible. They have translated it into the language of almost every nation and tribe which we have come into contact with. They have done more. They have never tired of translating its thought into sermons, addresses, tracts, treatises, and books. It has been made the light of their thought, the joy of their heart, the guide of their life. They have lived on the Bible and for the Bible.

If men exist, therefore, who ought to be able to give an opinion as to what the Bible is, these are the men. *They* have found no fault with the ordinary view. Their conviction of its truth has deepened. Their working hypothesis—that the Spirit's mind is to be reached by the clear understanding of *the words* of the Bible and by a full and even childlike acceptance of them—that working hypothesis has been neither abandoned nor modified; it has been established, and has become an unquestioned article of faith. If we inquire into the opinion held in past times, the answer is the same. The Churches of Christ have been disturbed and rent by great controversies; and in every one of them the Bible has been their only confidence. The Churches have said: "There is one court to which this cause must be carried; the Word of God must say with which side lies the truth, and on which side lies the guilt of error." And so, in every controversy, disputants have concerned themselves with the statements of Scripture. They have taken their stand upon sentences, and phrases, and words. Faith in the Bible, as being in its every utterance the Word of God, has been as marked a characteristic of the heretics as of the orthodox. Both parties may have been wrong in thus unanimously and unquestioningly ascribing Divine authority to the Bible; but there can be no doubt as to the fact that, through all the controversies of the Churches, this Divine authority has been ascribed to the Bible. Let men say what they will about "the absurdity" of Verbal Inspiration, no one can deny that every creed in Christendom has been hammered out upon that anvil. Controversy has circled round the meaning of a single word, round the force of a preposition or a particle, round the presence or the absence of a single letter. No one thought of rebuking this as a piece of Christian Rabbinism. There was, on the contrary, in the breast of all alike, a supreme conviction that, when the correct phrase was ascertained, and when the meaning and force of every word, however small, was apprehended and fixed, then the mind of God was known. Each word, it was evidently believed, was charged with Divine intention. The notion was that the word was there because God had willed it should be there, and that it was placed there so that it might more fully disclose His mind and will. Again, I say, that I have no desire to settle this question by counting votes, or to smother inquiry under an overwhelming weight of merely human authority. I am ready to grant, for the sake of argument, that this opinion *may* be a huge blunder; but we cannot be blind to the fact of its existence and of its long-continued power. The working hypothesis of all Christian study of the Bible, and the common ground of all Christian controversy and of all Christian teaching, has been for generations, and still is, that the Scriptures *in their words* convey with intention and precision the mind of God. In other words, to use a well-known phrase, the common basis of study, teaching, and argument has been belief in the "Verbal Inspiration" of the Bible.

## CHAPTER II.

### The Views of the Apostolic Churches Regarding Inspiration.

WE have now seen what the ordinary view of the Bible is and has long been. But we have still to push our question home—whence did this view come? It is the "traditional belief," but how old is the tradition, and from whose hands did the Churches originally receive it?

It might, for example, be imagined that this veneration for the Bible is nothing more than a remaining rag of the superstitions which were wrapped about the human mind as it lay in the tomb of the Middle Ages. It will be interesting, then, to go back to a still earlier time, and to ask what the Christian Church thought of the Bible during the first three centuries of our era. This will take us into the very age when the various writings of the New Testament were finding their way from city to city, and from land to land among the disciples, and when the Old Testament was also handed on to them by the Apostles of the Lord. How did these early Christians regard the Old Testament and the

## The Views of the Apostolic Churches.

New? Were they received as something entirely different from ordinary literature, and as clothed with Divine authority? Were they all received as alike inspired? Or did these early believers make distinctions between the Old Testament and the New: between one book and another: or between one part of a book and another part of it? Did they distinguish between "degrees of inspiration," or did they with simple confidence accept the Bible from beginning to end as the faultless and errorless, the fully-inspired and authoritative Word of God? By tapping in this way the stream of Christian opinion, we shall be able to determine whether "the traditional view" runs back to the Middle and earlier ages right up to Apostolic times.

In an appendix to Bishop Westcott's "Introduction to the Study of the Gospels," will be found an admirable summary of the views held by the leading writers of this period on the inspiration of the Scriptures. It may be well for me to confine my quotations to those given there. They will in this way be more easily verified, and the reader will have the assurance that their correctness cannot be questioned.

I begin with Origen, whose career as a Christian teacher in Alexandria, the Egyptian capital, began with the opening of the third century, and continued for fifty years. He was born in the year 185 of our era, and died in 253. His writings are marked by great independence of thought, and by that unfortunate tendency to the mysticism of the Neo-Platonists which marred the whole of Alexandrian Christianity. But, as regards the Authority and inspiration of the Scriptures, nothing could be more explicit or more in harmony with the universal belief than his statements. " Truly," he says, " it is most evidently preached in the churches that the Holy Spirit inspired each of the saints, prophets, and apostles, and that the same Spirit was present in those of the old time as in those who were inspired at the coming of Christ;" for " Christ, the Word of God, was in Moses and the Prophets . . . and by His Spirit they spake and did all things." " He assumes," says Bishop Westcott, " that 'the records of the Gospels are oracles of the Lord, pure oracles as silver purified seven times in the fire' (Psa. xii. 6), and that there is a meaning in their minutest details, while they are without error, inasmuch as we believe ' that they were accurately written by the co-operation of the Holy Spirit.'" "There are many sacred writings," he says, "yet there is but one Book. All the writings breathe the spirit of fulness, and there is nothing, whether in the Law or in the Prophets, in the Evangelists or in the Apostles, which does not descend from the fulness of the Divine Majesty. Even at the present time the words of fulness speak in Holy Scripture to those who have eyes to see the mysteries of heaven and care to hear the voice of God."

There is much in Origen's writings that seems to contradict this testimony. Speaking, for example, of apparent discrepancies in the Gospels, he says

## The Views of the Apostolic Churches. 23

that "if one were to set them all forth, then would he turn dizzy, and either desist from trying to establish all the Gospels in very truth, and attach himself to one . . . or, admitting the four, grant that their truth does not lie in their corporeal forms." The true explanation, namely, that the variations are in line with the prevailing purpose of each gospel, was then unknown. But here and elsewhere we meet with these inequalities and inconsistencies in Origen's works which have marred what otherwise would have been the richest contribution to early Christian literature. It is enough for our present purpose, however, to note that his attitude towards the Scriptures was one of absolute reverence. "We must read them," he tells us, " with attention, yea, with great attention, for it is needed in reading the divine writings, that we may not speak or form notions about them rashly." We must read them with reverence, "for if we use great care in handling the Sacred Elements, and rightly so, is it a less offence to disregard the Word of God than His Body?"

Clement of Alexandria, whose disciple Origen became, lived and laboured at the end of the second century, and within 100 years from the death of the Apostle John. He speaks of God using the inspired writers as His flute, His harp, His temple. Thus the foundations of our faith rest on no insecure basis, "for we have received them," he says, "from God through the Scriptures, of which not one tittle shall pass away without being accomplished, for the mouth of the Lord, the Holy Spirit, spoke it;" "and we have believed on Him through His voice; and he that believeth on the Word knoweth that the thing is true, for the Word is truth; but he that believeth not on him that speaketh disbelieveth God," for he disbelieveth "that which hath been spoken by the Holy Spirit for our salvation." Rejecting the Scripture—the written Word—is to him the rejecting of the Holy Spirit. "Some," he says, "patch together divers fabrications and falsehoods that they may seem to reject the Scriptures—that is, the Holy Spirit—with a show of reason."

Cyprian, Bishop of Carthage, suffered martyrdom in the year 258, after having held his bishopric ten years. He speaks of "the Divine Scriptures." The books of the Old and New Testaments are "the fountains of Divine fulness, from which the Christian must draw strength and wisdom." They are the "foundation of our hope, the bulwark of our faith, the support of our hearts, the guide of our path, the safeguard of our salvation." They are "the precepts of the Lord." "I know," he says, in reference to his attempt to encourage those likely to suffer martyrdom, "that the intricacies of human speech must be removed, and only those things set down which God says, and by which Christ exhorts His servants to martyrdom." Here the words of Scripture are distinctly ascribed to God and to Christ.

Tertullian had a varied experience. His earliest surviving work was written in the year 197, his last

## The Views of the Apostolic Churches. 25

in the year 213. Towards the end of his life he joined the sect of the Montanists. " On one point," says Westcott, " it has been well observed, Tertullian never doubted. Whether Catholic or Montanist, he still maintained alike the Inspiration of the Old and New Testament Scriptures. Whether he be writing to the heathen, the heretics, or the orthodox, he expresses the same belief in the same unwavering language. He tells us, in his noble Apology, that ' God sent forth from the first men, who, by their justice and innocency, were worthy to know God and to make Him known, and filled them to overflowing with the Divine Spirit;' and so gave us a written Testament that we might more fully and more deeply learn of Him, and of His counsels, and of His will. Nor does he scruple to call these books the ' writings ' (litteras Dei), and the ' words of God ' (voces Dei), which the Christian studies for warning or remembrance, and to which he looks as the food of his faith, the spring of his hope and the bulwark of his trust."

In a fragment attributed to Caius, a Presbyter at Rome, about the year 210, there is a significant outburst. The followers of Artemon made a boast of "correcting" the Scriptures, and this writer exclaims: "How great is the daring of their error cannot be unknown even to themselves; for either they do not believe that the Divine Scriptures were spoken by the Holy Spirit, and are unbelievers; or they hold themselves wiser than the Holy Spirit, and we must say they rave." Here it is assumed that to change a word was to alter the Spirit's work. The words of the Bible were therefore regarded as the words of God.

We draw nearer to the Apostolic age as we listen to Irenæus, who was Bishop of Lyons in 177. He had been a disciple of Polycarp, who had sat at the feet of the Apostle John. His writings are based upon a clearly defined belief in the full inspiration of the Scriptures. He says: "All who foretold the coming of Christ received their inspiration from the Son;" for "how could Scripture testify, as it does, of Him alone, unless all things had been revealed by one and the same God through the Word to believers?" Referring to the Evangelists, he says: "After that our Lord rose from the dead, and they were clothed with the power of the Spirit from on high, they were filled with a perfect knowledge in all things." Consequently, "they were beyond all falsehood." And again, "The Scriptures are perfect, inasmuch as they were uttered by the Word of God and His Spirit."

The nearer we come to the Apostolic times, the testimony to the fullest possible inspiration of the Scriptures, and their immunity from all error, becomes ever clearer. Theophilus, Bishop of Antioch from 171 to 183, says: "The words of the Prophets are the words of God." "The contents of the Prophets and the Gospels are found to be consistent, because all the writers spake by the inspiration of the one Spirit of God." He also quotes an injunction of St. Paul as an utterance of "the Divine Word."

## The Views of the Apostolic Churches. 27

Athenagoras addressed his Apology to the Roman Emperors in the year 168. He takes so high ground in his representation of the Scriptures that he seems to shut out the action of the sacred writers' own individuality. He says: "While entranced and deprived of their natural powers of reason by the influence of the Divine Spirit, they uttered that which was wrought in them, the Spirit using them as its instruments, as a flute-player might blow a flute." I have said, he *seems* to shut out the writers' individuality. But this may be only in appearance. The flute has its own sound, the trumpet another, and the harp one that resembles neither. There may, therefore, be place for the individuality of the writers of Scripture even under this figure; but there can be no mistaking the fulness of the inspiration here assigned to the Scriptures. The Christian, he says, "gives no heed to the doctrines of men, but those uttered and taught by God."

Justin Martyr suffered martyrdom in the year 164, and began to defend Christianity by his writings in 141 A.D. He gives us a most welcome glimpse into the practice of the churches in those early times. He says: "As Abraham believed on the voice of God, and it was reckoned to him for righteousness, so do the Christians too believe on the voice of God, which has been addressed again to them by the Apostles of Christ, and proclaimed by the Prophets . . . whose writings—the memoirs of the Apostles, or the books of the Prophets—are read each Sunday in the public assembly;" for "we have been commanded by Christ Himself to obey not the teaching of men, but that which has been proclaimed by the blessed Prophets, and taught by Him." He says also: "We must not suppose that the language proceeds from the men who are inspired, but from the Divine Word which moves them." The doctrine of "Verbal Inspiration" was never more clearly taught than in that last utterance.

Ignatius takes us right into the Apostolic times. He was Bishop of Antioch in the year 70, and 45 years afterwards sealed his testimony with his blood, being torn to pieces by wild beasts in the Amphitheatre at Rome in 115 A.D. He speaks of himself as having received at least one direct communication from the Holy Spirit, and thereby testifies to the reality of the Spirit's gifts conferred by Apostolic hands. But he places the writings of the Apostles on a higher level than the communications which he himself received. He says: "I do not give you injunctions as Peter and Paul; they were Apostles, I a condemned man." He calls upon them to "love the Prophets," and says that the Christian "who possesses the Word of Jesus s truly able to hear even His silence." The reader will notice the expression, "The Word of Jesus," used as a name for Scripture. He also writes that Jesus "was the subject of their (the Prophets') preaching, and the Gospel is the perfection of immortality," thus binding together the Old and the New Testaments as the one Word of God.

Polycarp was burned to death at Smyrna about

167 A.D. Some have placed his death as early as the year 148. When questioned and pleaded with by the Roman Pro-consul, he confessed himself a Christian of 86 years' standing. This brings us to the year 81, according to one date, or to the year 62 according to the other. But we have positive and direct testimony that he had been a disciple of the Apostle John. Irenæus, who knew him personally and who was brought up at his feet, tells "how he related his conversation with John and others who had seen the Lord; and how he related their sayings, of what he had heard from them concerning the Lord." This testimony brings us, therefore, quite into the Apostolic period. We anxiously ask, then, how the contemporaries of the Apostles regarded them and the writings, both of the Old and of the New Testament, which they have written or handed on to us. Does nearness show us a diminished sense of the authority of the sacred writers and of their words? Or is the reverence for both, which we have seen to be a characteristic of the first centuries, merely a prolonging of what was experienced in the Apostolic time? The answer, already given in the writings of Ignatius, is confirmed by the short epistle of Polycarp. He speaks of the New Testament writings as "the oracles of God," and says that "neither he nor any like him is able to attain perfectly to the wisdom of the blessed and glorious Paul." He "trusts that his hearers are well versed in the sacred writings," alleging at the same time Psa. iv. 4; Ephes. iv. 26. "Indeed," says Westcott,

"the words and spirit of the New Testament seem to be inwrought into the mind, for though he only once mentions the name of the sacred writer whom he quotes, there appear to be in his short epistle more than twenty distinct references to the Apostolic books."

Clement, who was Bishop of Rome in the year 91 A.D., is constantly referred to by ancient writers as the same Clement whom Paul speaks of, in Phil. iv. 3, as one of his fellow-labourers. He has left an epistle which was sent in the name of the whole church at Rome to the church in Corinth. He quotes many passages of the Scripture with the words, "for the Scripture saith," "by the testimony of Scripture," "the Holy Spirit saith." He exhorts his readers to "look carefully into the Scriptures, which are the true (utterances) of the Holy Spirit." And again, "Ye know, beloved, ye know well the sacred Scriptures, and have looked carefully into the oracles of God." He also speaks of "the spirit of lowliness and awe" with which the Scriptures are to be received and obeyed.

There is another epistle of unquestionably earlier date, and which was ascribed in ancient times to Barnabas, the companion of Paul. We may place it in any case about the year 71 A.D. Passages are quoted from the Old Testament with these phrases: "The Lord saith in the prophet" (Psa. xvii. 45); "The Spirit of the Lord prophesieth" (Psa. xxxiii. 13). He says: "The prophets received their gifts from Christ and spake of Him," and that "Moses spake in the Spirit." He gives the following as one rule of those who walk in " the way of light :" " Thou shalt guard what thou hast received, neither adding nor taking away from it."

The meaning of all this testimony is plain. There is no conflict in it. There is but one view of the Scriptures, both of the Old and of the New Testament—*they are alike the Word of God.* It is within the limits of possibility that this view, entertained by the Christian churches during the three first centuries, may be a mistake. I do not for one moment suppose that any one enamoured of the " New Views " would cast them away merely because they are found to be in conflict with the deepest convictions of " The Fathers." But there can be no shadow of doubt as to the definiteness of their testimony, and as to the sincerity and earnestness with which it was given. And there is one thing more of the utmost importance to our inquiry. *This view has not grown.* It is not a product of Christian evolution. It has been handed down right from the Apostolic times. Were there no other evidence extant as to what the Apostles taught about the Scriptures, I cannot see how the conclusion could be escaped that they must have regarded both the New Testament and the Old as the very Word of God. These disciples of the Apostles would never have spoken so emphatically and so unanimously, unless their masters had been equally emphatic and unanimous. But, fortunately, their own words are still left to us, and I propose now to question these masters themselves.

## CHAPTER III.

WHAT THE SCRIPTURES CLAIM FOR THEMSELVES:

1.—*The Witness of the Old Testament.*

THE testimony, mentioned in the last chapter, has led us back to times close upon those of the Apostles. We discover in that testimony that reverence and love for the Scriptures as the Word of God were then as deep and as full as they have ever been since. The fact is striking; but, striking as it is, it might possibly have an explanation different from that which we are inclined to give it. It is quite conceivable that this opinion about the Bible may not have been the belief of the Apostles themselves. It may, on the contrary, have been an idolatrous departure from their belief. It might be supposed that, coming out of the darkness and superstition of heathenism, it was natural for the first Christians to take something in connection with their new faith that was tangible, and to make an idol of it. And what so tangible as the Bible?

It might well be replied that the Bible was not made an idol of. The early Christians did not set up a copy of the Scriptures in their assemblies, or in their homes, and prostrate themselves before it. They did not turn its words into amulets and charms. No people were ever further from such practices than they. It is *the light* in the Scriptures, the comfort and the direction that they contain, which is rejoiced in as authoritative and Divine. But this matter is easily settled. To know whether the first Christians erred, we have only to go one step further, and to inquire what the Scriptures say of themselves.

We go, first of all, to the Old Testament. I am quite aware of the existence of beliefs about the late origin of the first five books ascribed to Moses, and known from the first among the Jews as "The Law." But these theories need not trouble us at present in any way. Our inquiry is as to how these and other parts of Scripture are regarded in the Scripture itself, and what the Inspiration from which they proceeded was conceived to be.

When we turn to the Law we are met by one striking peculiarity. Every precept in it is taken down from the lips of God Himself. The phrase, "The Lord spake unto Moses, saying," recurs perpetually. The entire book proceeds under the Divine direction. We read, for example, as follows: "These are the words of the covenant, which the Lord commanded Moses to make with the children of Israel in the land of Moab" (Deut. xxix. 1); "And the Lord said unto Moses, Behold thou shalt sleep with thy fathers; and this people will go a whoring after the gods of the strangers of the land, whither they go to be among them, and will forsake Me, and break My covenant which I have made with them. . . . Now, therefore, write ye this song for you, and teach it the children of Israel" (Deut. xxxi. 16-19). Here the covenant is God's covenant; the very words of it are His. The song, which might not unnaturally be supposed to be the spontaneous outpouring of Moses' own soul, is not his. The suggestion of it even did not spring from him. The suggestion and the song were alike of God.

We now open the book of Joshua, and we discover that the writings of Moses are already known under the name of "the Law." Joshua receives his commission from God himself; but Joshua is not to make a law for the people as Moses had done. The revelation given to Moses is complete, authoritative, and, so far as Israel is concerned, final. God takes it up, owns it, and consigns it to Joshua as a full provision for his need—a fountain whence he, the new captain of God's host, will draw Divine wisdom and strength—"The Lord spake unto Joshua: this book of the law shall not depart out of thy mouth; but thou shalt meditate therein day and night, that thou mayest observe to do according to all that is written therein; for then shalt thou make thy way prosperous, and then shalt thou have good success" (Joshua i. 1, 8).

Here the Law is placed by God in Joshua's hands as *His* book. Joshua needs to know, and wants to know, God's mind. He is told that God's mind is revealed here. Let Joshua only read and meditate

## What the Scriptures Claim for Themselves. 35

day and night in this book, and all the inspiration and light that he, as Israel's leader, needs will be given him. It will be confessed that this acknowledgment of the Pentateuch as God's book is as full as words and deeds could make it. It was quite in keeping with the solemn consigning of the Law to Joshua that he, when about to die, should hold it up as the source of direction for Israel. "Be ye therefore," he said, "very courageous to keep and to do all that is written in the book of the law of Moses, that ye turn not aside therefrom to the right hand or to the left" (Joshua xxiii. 6). That book, whose every injunction was to be so scrupulously obeyed, could not have been regarded either by Joshua or by Israel as *man's* book; it must certainly, though acknowledged to have been given *through* Moses, have been looked upon as expressing in its every ordinance the will of God.

That place assigned to the Law at its first introduction is given to it all through the Old Testament history. The reverence is not increased; for it could not be augmented. On the other hand, it is not diminished. When there has been neglect of the Law, the book is never permitted to be set aside. Never once is it imagined that the age is too far advanced for the Law, and that its claims must be quietly ignored. The cause of the book, on the contrary, is the cause of God. Disregard of it is reckoned as high-handed defiance of God Himself; and so Israel is chastised, and brought back into subjection to *the book*. Now, we may make what we will of this fact, but there is no possibility of denying it. Let me cite one instance of the minute compliance with what we might consider slight detail, which was exacted by God. David has resolved to bring up the ark to Jerusalem. Now the Law had given the fullest directions as to how that ark was to be transported from place to place. It had entered into details as to who were to carry it, and as to the way in which it was to be borne by them. The Levites were not even to see it, when it was being covered and made ready for removal (Numbers iv. 17-20). Only the high priest and his sons were to look upon it. It was not to be touched even by them (Num. iv. 15). Staves were prepared, which were to be placed in the rings, and the Levites—the Levites and no others—were to bear it.

These arrangements were minutely explained and strongly insisted upon in the Law. But in the time of David the Law had become a dead letter. It was as little regarded as its worst enemies could desire. When the lords of the Philistines sent back the ark, they had placed it on a new cart and had it drawn by oxen. Irreverent eyes had gazed upon it and even looked into it. Irreverent hands had touched it. Instead of being borne by God's consecrated servants, it is drawn along by "dumb, driven cattle." Now, David, with all his devotion to God, could think of nothing better than to follow, in this matter, the example of the enemies of God's people! There could be no more melancholy indication than is given in this incident, of how fully the Law had been laid aside and forgotten. "They set the ark of God," we read, "upon a new cart" (II. Samuel vi. 3), and oxen drew it along. The climax of lawlessness was reached when Uzzah put forth his hand and laid hold of the ark to steady it. We do not know that Abinadab and Uzzah his son were even Levites; but, though they had been, the Law had solemnly warned Israel that not even the Levites were to touch it—"they shall not touch any holy thing lest they die" (Num. iv. 15).

Uzzah died before the Lord. David was offended, and did not complete his purpose of taking the ark up into Jerusalem. But with time came consideration and repentance. The Law had evidently been meanwhile remembered and searched. A second and greater gathering of Israel was summoned, and there was now neither new cart nor oxen. The heads of the priesthood and of the Levites were called, and were commanded to sanctify themselves and their brethren, that "ye may bring up the ark of the Lord God of Israel into the place that I have prepared for it. For because YE did it not at the first the Lord our God made a breach upon us, for that we sought Him not *after the due order*" (I. Chron. xv. 12, 13).

Nothing could be more eloquent than these events as to how God meant the Law of Moses to be received and obeyed. And they were typical. Israel was judged by the Law, just as Uzzah had been, It was for disregard of it, and disobedience to its injunctions that the Israelites were rooted out of their land. It does not surprise us, therefore, to find that the return from the captivity was not only a return to the land, but was also a return to the Law. Ezra speaks of it as the "Law of Moses which the Lord God of Israel had given" (Ezra vii. 6), and of himself as "a scribe of the words of the commandments of the Lord and of His statutes to Israel" (vii. 11). There is a thrill of awe in this last statement. As Ezra traced the words of the Law upon the skin or the papyrus sheet, or studied them in the ancient copy from which he transcribed, they were not to him like the words of other books which men had written. They belonged to an entirely different category. They were "the words of the commandments of the Lord." We also read in Nehemiah that this book was solemnly brought forth and diligently explained to the returned people. It was treated as the one source of enlightenment in the things of God, and as the one voice which spoke to men with Divine authority. "And all the people gathered themselves together as one man into the street that was before the water-gate, and they spake unto Ezra the scribe to bring the book of the Law of Moses which the Lord had commanded to Israel. "So they read in the book, in the Law of God, distinctly, and gave the sense, and caused them to understand the reading" (Neh. viii. 1, 8).

I glance at two other indications of the place assigned to the Law in the Old Testament. Contempt for it, and even ignorance of its precepts, were treated as high rebellion against God. Isaiah says:

## What the Scriptures Claim for Themselves.

"Therefore as the fire devoureth the stubble, and the flame consumeth the chaff, so their root shall be as rottenness, and their blossom shall go up as dust; because *they have cast away the Law of the Lord of Hosts, and despised the word of the Holy One of Israel*" (Isa. v. 24). Similar passages will be found in the messages sent by other prophets. The Law of Moses was proclaimed as God's Law to every generation of Israel. The other indication to which I refer is the language of the Psalms. No modern words about the Bible exceed in warmth of gratitude or depth of veneration the praises of God's Word contained in those Psalms of Israel which were sung in the Temple, in the synagogue, and in the home. The words spoken to Joshua seem to be the theme of the Psalm which is placed at the threshold of Israel's praise. The man on whom blessing rests is he whose "delight is in the law of the Lord, and who meditates in it day and night" (Psa. i. 2). They sang of it: "The Law of the Lord is perfect, converting the soul; the testimony of the Lord is sure, making wise the simple; the statutes of the Lord are right, rejoicing the heart; the commandment of the Lord is pure, enlightening the eyes; the judgments of the Lord are true and righteous altogether. More to be desired are they than gold, yea than much fine gold; sweeter also than honey and the honeycomb. Moreover, by them is Thy servant warned, and in keeping of them there is great reward" (Psa. xix. 7-11).

By far the longest of the mnemonic Psalms (those

which were specially arranged for being committed to memory) is the 119th. It is divided, as every reader knows, into twenty-two stanzas, according to the number of the letters in the Hebrew alphabet. Each stanza contains eight verses, and the first word in each verse begins with the letter which marks the position of the stanza. Each of the first eight verses begins with the letter A, each of the second eight with the letter B, each of the third eight with the letter G (the third letter in the Hebrew alphabet), and so on. In this way the stanza and the verses belonging to it were easily recalled by the Israelitish children; and the task imposed upon them was thus much lighter than that which has sometimes been performed by the children in a Scotch school, who have frequently committed the Psalm to memory as it stands in our version. What, then, was the object of this elaborate arrangement? What was it that the Psalmist desired so eagerly to fix in the memory and the heart of the young? The Masora has long ago replied to this question by pointing out that, of the 176 verses of Psa. cxix., there is only one which does not mention the Word of God. The Psalm is a prolonged praise of God's Book and an outpouring of the heart's desire to know it better, and to bring the whole life into subjection to its precepts. "I have seen an end of all perfection; but Thy commandment is exceeding broad. O how love I Thy Law! It is my meditation all the day" (Psa. cxix. 96-97).

But we have one more enquiry to make. It is

quite plain that the Law has as high a place in the esteem of the Old Testament writers as the Word of God has ever had in any church and at any time. But what of these writers themselves? Were *they* conscious of any inspiration which placed their own words on the same lofty pedestal? Two testimonies will suffice to set our minds at rest upon that point. David, looking back over his life-work, speaks of the honour which God put upon him. "The Spirit of the Lord," he says, "*spake* by me, *and His word was in my tongue*" (II. Sam. xxiii. 2). Could there possibly be a fuller claim for Verbal Inspiration? It is not enough to say that God spake and uttered His mind through him. Lest any doubt should be left as to what is meant, we are told that the miracle extended to the very selection of the words. The *word* that was on David's tongue, was not David's but God's. We are permitted, in the case of David, to have another glimpse of what is meant by inspiration. He was the architect of the Temple. Solomon was the builder, but he worked according to the plans left by his father. We know that in the erection of the Tabernacle every detail, however minute, was arranged *by God Himself*. Nothing was added, withheld, or altered by Moses. Everything was done "according as the Lord had commanded Moses." Was it the same, then, in regard to the Temple? In following the plans left by his father, was Solomon showing his reverence for the dead, or was he consciously obeying God?

The reply is clear and definite, for we read: "Then

David gave to Solomon his son the pattern of the porch, and of the houses thereof, and of the treasuries thereof, and of the place of the upper chambers thereof, and of the inner parlours thereof, and of the place of the mercy-seat, and the pattern of ALL THAT HE HAD BY THE SPIRIT, of the courts of the house of the Lord" (1. Chron. xxviii. 11, 12). Then after a long and minute enumeration (which has no parallel in Scripture, except in the directions regarding the Tabernacle), "All this, said David, *the Lord made me understand in writing by His hand upon me,* even all the works of this pattern" (verse 19). It is a matter of indifference, so far as our inquiry is concerned, whether David had this plan *direct* from God, or whether Divine light was given him (as some maintain) through study of the directions regarding the Tabernacle. Whatever we may think of that matter cannot alter the explicit statements before us. That which David handed to Solomon he avers *he received from God.* It was not, in any sense, David's. He not only lays no claim to the authorship; he solemnly disavows it. It was *God's* plan without addition, diminution, or mistake. It was given to him by the hand of God upon him, and He made him understand the words of the pattern. He had it—*all of it*—by the Spirit; and the document which David handed to his son was consequently a Divine and faultless document, although it had come from the hands of a fallible man. It permitted no stepping aside to the right hand or to the left. It was God's

## What the Scriptures Claim for Themselves. 43

plan, and in the erection of God's house it was to be the sole guide, and the only authority.

If we are to accept this as an illustration of what Inspiration means—and I am ignorant of any reason why we should not so accept it—then the Scriptures must be as supreme and as faultless as the highest doctrine of Inspiration has ever represented them to be.

The same conclusion is forced upon us by other incidents. At a time of great discouragement, God gave Moses and Israel a sign of how that murmuring people would eventually serve him. The law-giver "gathered seventy men of the elders of the people, and set them round about the tent. And the Lord came down in the cloud, and spake unto him, and took of the Spirit that was upon him, and put it upon the seventy elders; and it came to pass, that when the Spirit rested upon them, they prophesied, but they did so no more" (Numb. xi. 24, 25, Revised Version). God showed that Israel could not wait "round about the tent" without blessing; for He took of the Spirit that was upon Moses and gave unto them. Let us note what followed: "When the Spirit rested upon them, they prophesied," but when the Spirit was withdrawn "they did so no more." Their prophesying was not *of them* but *of the Spirit*. The words which they then spoke were sharply divided from anything they ever spoke before or ever spoke afterwards. Before and after, their words were their own; but the words they now uttered were the words of God. The *Spirit* spake by them.

There are other two incidents which put the matter still more clearly, and with the mention of these I shall close our survey of the Old Testament witness. Jeremiah has been cast into prison. The word of the Lord, which is sharper than any two-edged sword, is somewhat painful to the rulers of the time. They have, therefore, bound the prophet, and cast him into a dungeon, so that they may be no longer troubled by his words. But they are not irreligious men, though they take liberties with inspired authorities! It is a time of peril and of fear. And, though they have imprisoned the prophet, they are quite ready to proclaim "a fast before the Lord to all the people in Jerusalem, and to all the people that came from the cities of Judah unto Jerusalem" (Jer. xxxvi. 9).

Now, if that fast is to avail, people must know why God's anger burns so fiercely against them. Jeremiah lies bound, as I have said, in prison. God might open the prison doors for him, as He afterwards did for Peter and John; but He chooses another way. Jeremiah's book will take the place of his living voice. "And it came to pass . . . that this word came unto Jeremiah from the Lord, saying: Take thee a roll of a book and write therein all the words that I have spoken unto thee against Israel and against Judah, and against all the nations, from the day I spake unto thee, from the days of Josiah, even unto this day" (verses 1, 2).

Jeremiah was bound, but he calls Baruch. "And Baruch wrote from the mouth of Jeremiah all the

## What the Scriptures Claim for Themselves. 45

words of the Lord, which He had spoken unto him, upon a roll of a book. And Jeremiah commanded Baruch, saying, I am shut up; I cannot go into the house of the Lord; therefore go thou, and read in the roll which thou hast written from my mouth, THE WORDS OF THE LORD, in the ears of the people in the Lord's house, upon the fasting day. . . And Baruch, the son of Neriah, did according to all that Jeremiah the prophet commanded him, reading in the book THE WORDS OF THE LORD, in the Lord's house" (verses 4-8).

This passage is of the greatest importance; for it enables us to see the process by which the inspired books have come into existence. The work is done before our own eyes. The great officials of Jerusalem said to Baruch, "Tell us now, how didst thou write all these words at his mouth?" Then Baruch answered them, He pronounced all these words unto me with his mouth, and I wrote them with ink in the book" (Jer. xxxvi. 17, 18). You can picture the scene. In the dim light of the dismal dungeon you see the prophet seated on the rude stone bench with chained limbs. Before him sits Baruch, with the unrolled skin, or papyrus sheet, stretched upon his knees. The reed pen, dipped again and again in the ink-horn, is busily plied. Letter is added to letter, and one by one the words are written down as the prophet speaks them. When that roll is written it is a sacred thing. It is *God's* message to Israel. When Baruch reads the book in the Temple, the prison scene disappears. Neither the process by which the words were transcribed, nor Jeremiah speaking in the dimness, is remembered. What he holds in his hands, and what he reads in the ears of princes, priests and people are "*the words of the Lord.*" The roll is long. It contains every prophecy which Jeremiah has uttered up to that time. But none of the words, many as they are, are given as *his* words. They are, all of them, God's words. "Therefore, go thou," says Jeremiah, "and read in the roll which thou hast written from my mouth, *the words of the Lord.* . . . And Baruch, the son of Neriah, did according to all that Jeremiah the prophet commanded him, reading in the book *the words of the Lord* in the Lord's house."

But this is not all. The incident has something further to say. After Baruch had read the roll to the people he was sent for by the Royal Council and commanded to read it to them. They afterwards brought it to the king; but the monarch had quite enough of it when "three or four leaves" had been read. He asked for the roll, cut it with a penknife, and cast the fragments into the fire. Jeremiah and Baruch were ordered to be taken, and would, no doubt, have been treated with like ferocity; "but the Lord hid them." And now, in their seclusion, another task was set them. "Then the word of the Lord came to Jeremiah, after that the king had burned the roll and the words which Baruch wrote at the mouth of Jeremiah, saying, Take thee again another roll, and write in it all the former words that were in the first roll, which Jehoiakim the king of Judah hath burned . . Then took Jeremiah another roll, and gave it to Baruch the scribe, the son of Neriah, who wrote therein from the mouth of Jeremiah all the words of the book which Jehoiakim king of Judah had burned in the fire, and there were added besides unto them many like words" (verses 27-32).

This incident, it will be seen, is of immense value. It is a more weighty contribution to the discussion of of Inspiration than the most laboured argument. Many, who admit that the Bible is inspired, have rejected the notion that the Inspiration extended to the words. The *thoughts* are God's, they say, in effect, but the *words* are man's. But the words as well as the thoughts are here declared to be God's! The book is repeated *verbatim*. Other words were added, but the body of the second book was, word by word, the same as the first. Here two things are evident : *the very words are cared for*; and Jeremiah receives the Spirit's aid to perform this feat of exact verbal reproduction. Is it not natural to suppose that the words came in the first instance—as they came in the second—from the Spirit of God?

The other incident, to which I refer, is equally clear and conclusive. The Gentile prophet, Balaam, is sent for by the king of Moab. Balak does not dare to confront Israel in battle; but he imagines that he may wither their strength by enchantments. When Balaam comes, erects his altars, and offers his sacrifices, he does not carry to Balak any word that is either originated or moulded by himself. We read that: "*The Lord put a word* in Balaam's mouth, and said, Return unto Balak, and thus shalt thou speak" (Numb. xxviii. 5). Balak expostulates, and Balaam replies, " Must I not take heed to speak that which *the Lord putteth in my mouth?*" (verse 12). When Balaam is sent away in disgrace, because he blesses where he was invited and bribed to curse, he repeats to the king what he before declared to the king's messengers: " If Balak would give me his house full of silver and gold, *I cannot go beyond the word of the Lord, to do either good or bad of mine own mind;* what the Lord saith that will I speak" (xxiv. 13).

Here a *bad* man, with the greatest will and the strongest inducements to *alter* the message, does not do it. The Inspiration which rests upon him determines the form as well as the substance of the communication. It might be supposed that such phrases as "the word of the Lord" and the more emphatic "the words of the Lord," had merely a general signification, and referred to the matter of the message and not to its specific form. But these last illustrations, afforded by Jeremiah and Balaam, show that the Inspiration of the prophet *determined the form and defined the words* of their communications. The Old Testament claims, therefore, the fullest inspiration which has ever been claimed by any school or creed for Scripture. The law comes by Moses, but it is the law *of God*. Like its Author, it bears no human stain. It is perfect. There is no spot, defect, or flaw in it. The word comes to Israel through the prophets, but it is never thought of as being simply *their* word. Their instrumentality is forgotten even by themselves in the awe with which the message is regarded. The words are " the words of the Lord."

## CHAPTER IV.

WHAT THE SCRIPTURES CLAIM FOR THEMSELVES

2.—*The Witness of the New Testament.*

QUESTIONING and attack are at present directed almost exclusively upon the Old Testament Scriptures. The New Testament is popularly believed, and is declared by some of the "critics" to be unassailable. It will be admitted, then, that its testimony regarding the Old Testament is important. Even if we regard its statements, not as the Divine utterance of the Spirit, but merely as the judgment of inspired men, that is much. How do they, who knew the mind of the Spirit, receive, and with what ascription of authority do they hand on to us, the Old Testament? If the apostles were with us now, and, above all, if the Lord were still bodily present with us, how many are there who would hasten to carry all their questionings to them, and who would esteem one word from *their* lips weightier than all that the press has poured forth upon the question! But here we have this very answer. The unquestioned words of the Lord and of His apostles have already decided the matter for all believing men.

When I state that there are about 284 quotations of the Old Testament in the New, and that these quotations are spread over 17 books of the New Testament, it will be felt that there is small chance of our making any mistake as to what opinion of the Old Testament is entertained by New Testament writers. If the Old Testament was believed to have made mistakes and to require correction, then we may expect that in some of these 284 references this will be made plain. If the words quoted are not, to the New Testament writers, inspired words, their estimate will be shown in some degree of hesitation, or reservation, or qualified approval, or indications of dissent. But, on the other hand, if these words are to them the very words of God, this will also be abundantly manifest. The statements will be quoted with a reverence, and accepted with an unquestioning submission, which will speak louder than words.

Let us look, then, at the New Testament evidence. It is gratifying that the quotations are so numerous, and our satisfaction increases when we attempt to classify them. Mr. Turpie* has rendered us invaluable help. The New Testament quotations are taken from twenty-five books of the Old, so that the references cover a wide area. The historical books, the Psalms, the Proverbs, and the Prophets are all referred to and referred to often. How often, and by how many New Testament writers this is done, the following will show:—

*The Witness of the New Testament to the Old* (Hodder and Stoughton).

Genesis is quoted 19 times, and the quotations appear in 9 New Testament books.

Exodus is quoted 24 times, and the quotations appear in 12 New Testament books.

Leviticus is quoted 5 times, and the quotations appear in 8 New Testament books.

Numbers is quoted once, and the quotation appears in 1 New Testament book.

Deuteronomy is quoted 26 times, and the quotations appear in 13 New Testament books.

The Psalms are quoted 59 times, and the quotations appear in 12 New Testament books.

Proverbs is quoted 6 times, and the quotations appear in 6 New Testament books.

Isaiah is quoted 50 times, and the quotations appear in 11 New Testament books, &c., &c.

Here, then, we are not dealing with isolated facts. The quotations and the references are so numerous that there is no chance of our mistaking, or failing to discover, the New Testament estimate of the Old. Let us, then, inquire whether the Old Testament appears to be cited as the one supreme authority, or is quoted as we might now quote "The Pilgrim's Progress" or "Paradise Lost." Is it referred to simply because it is a treasure-house of wisdom and of truths happily expressed, or are its statements adduced as the utterance of the mind and will of God?

This question is answered by what we may call the formula of quotation. Words are again and again cited from the Old Testament and prefaced by

## What the Scriptures Claim for Themselves.  53

the phrase, "it is written." For example, Paul says before the Sanhedrim, " For *it is written*, Thou shalt not speak evil of the ruler of thy people" (Acts xxiii. 5). The meaning plainly is that the fact of these words standing upon the pages of the Old Testament Scriptures (see Exod. xxii. 28) left Paul no choice. He dare not speak against God's high priest. Why? The words might have been written in a thousand books, and yet have put no bridle upon the apostle's lips. How is it, then, that they at once settle the matter and determine the apostle's action simply because they are written in this Book? Is it not that this Book differs from every other in that it is *God's Book*? Do not the words mean that it is also so fully God's Book that whatever command it contains must be received as God's own direction for Paul's life and mine?

I take another instance of the use of this phrase. In Rom. iii. 9, the apostle asks, "What then? Are we better than they? No, in no wise; for we have before proved both Jews and Gentiles, that they are all under sin." He then proceeds, "*As it is written*, There is none righteous, no, not one." These words are quoted from Psa. xiv., and to them he adds other testimonies from other five Psalms and from the book of Proverbs. With the former example before us, we might have said: "Yes, wherever we find a distinct commandment in Scripture, we may conclude that that is the word of God; *the Law* is evidently inspired, and must be received as the expression of God's will." But here are descriptions of human depravity, testimonies to man's fallen condition, contained in what we may call the most human part of the Old Testament—the Psalms and the Proverbs. The former is the outpouring of man's cry to God, the latter the gathering up in human speech of the lessons of man's experience. If there is one part of the Bible which we might have imagined to be of purely human authorship, it is the Psalms and the Proverbs. But here this "It is written" warns us that we are mistaken. These are words that make an end of controversy, for the apostle continues: "Now we know that what things soever the law saith, it saith to them that are under the law; that every mouth may be stopped and all the world may become guilty before God" (verse 19). Here this character of finality is ascribed to every testimony and statement of the Old Testament Scriptures—to "what things soever the law saith." There is no appeal and no escape. The words cannot be corrected; they dare not be argued with. When the Scripture has spoken, there is room only for submission and contrition. "Every mouth must be stopped, and all the world must become guilty before God." Whose words, then, are these? Is there any possibility of escaping the conclusion that, in this view of the Old Testament, everything in it is the declared and recorded mind of God?

If there is a way of escape from that conclusion, I can only say that I do not know it. It is well to notice also that this "It is written" disposes of the distinction that the Bible *contains* the Word of God,

## What the Scriptures Claim for Themselves. 55

but is not itself the Word of God. These things are said not of some impalpable thing that may be in the Bible, but of the written and printed words of the Bible. It is the thing written which we spell out and read—it is *the words* of the Bible—to which this finality is attributed.

This conclusion will appear the more inevitable, the further we consider the matter. The formula "It is written" is used in the New Testament to introduce no fewer than between 80 and 90 quotations from the Old. The mode of quotation has special force. Judges refer in this way to the statute book; and executors naturally use it in interpreting the will or the deed whose terms they are legally bound to execute. *They go by what is written.* They have regard to the very words. Their one aim is to understand and to apply these written or printed words in all their strictness. They themselves interpolate nothing; they allow no one to interpolate anything. There may be different interpretations of a clause or of a word; but they test all the interpretations by what is written. The statute or the deed is supreme; its lightest word is highest law. And there is nothing little, or mean, or irrational, in all this. No man possessed of common sense would dream of making it a reproach to them. He would never think of hurling at them such epithets as "literalists," "worshippers of the letter," "deifiers of a book," &c. He would not counsel them to abandon the literal interpretation; nor would he give to each judge and to each executor power to act according to his own notions. The safety of the State, confidence in contract, and the very existence of world-wide trade and commerce, depend upon absolute loyalty to the letter of that which is written.

Is it, then, such an appeal to the letter, such a reliance upon *the words* of the Old Testament, that is shown in this formula of quotation, "It is written?" Is the Old Testament quoted as authoritative and binding, and that, too, in the very form in which the words stand upon the sacred page? A further example or two will give the answer. We read in John ii. 17: "His disciples remembered that it was written, The zeal of Thine house hath eaten me up." The passage occurs in Psa. lxix. 9— one, be it remarked, of *the imprecatory Psalms*. Jesus had just cleansed the Temple, and so secured, at the very outset of His career, the determined hostility of the rulers. Can we wonder that the disciples were troubled, and that they questioned whether the action was wise? But these words answered their questionings and allayed their apprehensions. They "remembered that it was written, The zeal of Thine house hath eaten me up." They may not have understood at the time that the Psalm was a prophecy of Jesus; but, if it did not apply to their Master in that way, it clearly applied to Him in another. This was the character of the servant whom God approved. The servant of God was one whose zeal no consideration of self-interest or of safety could turn aside or even moderate. "It was

## What the Scriptures Claim for Themselves. 57

written" that God's servant should so regard Him and Him only—written, then, by whom? Who was it that placed *these words* on record, and by them settled for ever the law of service? Does not the phrase plainly mean, and mean only, that these written words are the words of God?

The absolute trust with which the words of the Old Testament were taken as the words of God is illustrated by another incident in the story of the disciples. The Master has passed away. Judas has fallen from the apostleship, and, incomplete in number — eleven men, where before they were twelve—they are waiting for "the promise of the Father." Peter rises and proposes that they seek direction from the Master as to the choice of a twelfth apostle. What leads him to do this? It is a word in Psa. cix. 8—another imprecatory Psalm, but one which, no doubt, the risen Lord had explained as referring to Himself. "For it is written in the book of Psalms," he says, "his bishopric let another take" (Acts i. 20). Here again the phrase, "it is written," is taken as God's direction—as the expression of the Divine will.

Another instance will be found in the First Epistle of Peter. The apostle writes: "As he who has called you is holy, so be ye holy in all manner of conversation; because it is written: Be ye holy, for I am holy" (i. 15, 16). The words occur in Leviticus, and the quotation is plainly based upon the supreme, and unquestioned, and unquestionable authority of the Old Testament. There is no shadow of any distinction between Revelation and "the record of revelation." The fact that these words stand in the record is sufficient. It is enough that "*it is written.*" Nothing could, in this way, be more absolute than the witness of the New Testament to the Inspiration and Divine authority of the Old Testament as it existed in the first century of our era, and as we have it now. It was to this Bible, which we have in our hands to-day, that the apostles turned with reverent submission, and whose words they have handed on as words placed on record by God Himself.

But the truth implied in this oft-repeated phrase finds another, and not less suggestive, expression. Before I deal with this, let me ask the reader to remember that the collection of Old Testament books was absolutely the same in the first century as it is now. Our Hebrew Bible is the Hebrew Bible of the Jew. The copies which we use, and which our translators have rendered into English, are printed from the Jewish manuscripts. The Hebrew Bible, then, of our Lord and of the apostles is the Bible which we have in our hands now, and everything said about it comes direct home to the questioning and the unrest of this year of grace in which we live. Well, then, if we find all these books accepted as a unity and set apart from all other literature, that will be a fact to be reckoned with. That they are so set apart in the New Testament every one is aware. They are sometimes designated "The Law," sometimes "The Law and the Prophets," sometimes more fully "The Law, the Psalms, and the Prophets." But, on the same level with these, no other book, however valued, is even once placed. The traditions of the elders are indignantly set aside. These books are, in the estimation of the New Testament, as separate from all other books as is the Temple from the dwellings of Israel, and as sacred in comparison with all other books as is that dwelling-place of God in comparison with the dwelling-places of His people. Is it possible, then, that this estimate of the Old Testament can be the same as that of the men who now think of it, and deal with it, as Hebrew literature?

But there is a special name by which it is designated and cited. It is called "The Scripture," or "The Scriptures;" that is, "The Writing," or "The Writings." Fifty times is the Old Testament so referred to. This name seems to me to settle much. The Book is accepted, not in the general way, but *in its then form*. It is received not merely in the spirit, but also in the letter. It is received as we have it now, and stamped as authoritative and Divine.

## CHAPTER V.

WHAT THE SCRIPTURES CLAIM FOR THEMSELVES.

3.—*The Witness of the New Testament (Continued).*

WE have noted two facts which are closely connected: (1) the phrase with which quotations are frequently introduced, "It is written;" (2) the names given to the Old Testament in the New—"The Scripture," "The Scriptures," that is "The Writing," "The Writings." In that phrase and in these names everyone, it seems to me, must hear the accent of reverent and grateful submission.

A closer survey of the New Testament will deepen the conviction that it claims for the Old the fullest inspiration with which it is possible to credit it. There is a belief, for example, and one, too, which is frequently expressed, that its predictions "must be fulfilled." The certainty and necessity of their accomplishment are as absolute as that light follows the sun's rising or darkness its setting. Here are a few examples. Speaking of our Lord's entry into Jerusalem after the unusual preparation of sending for a beast of burden, the Evangelist says: "All this was done, that it might be fulfilled which was spoken by the prophet" (Matt. xxi. 4). Again, referring to the price paid to Judas, he says: "Then was fulfilled that which was spoken by Jeremy the prophet," &c. (xxvii. 9). This is not peculiar to Matthew; all the Evangelists contain passages which speak in the same fashion. The unbelief of the Jews is explained in John to be the accomplishment of a prediction by Isaiah: "But though he had done so many miracles before them, yet they believed not on him; that the saying of Esaias the prophet might be fulfilled," &c. (John xii. 37, 38). What seemed to be a disproving of the claims of Jesus was in reality the setting of God's seal to them.

This point of view is, in fact, the point of view of the entire New Testament. I have already referred to the election of a successor to Judas. But Peter's proposal to select one of their number to fill the vacant place, was introduced by the statement that the prediction in the Psalms "must needs have been fulfilled." Now whence sprang this necessity for fulfilment? We frequently put on record our judgment of the results which will flow for good or evil from certain courses of action which we describe, or commend, or dissuade from. But what mortal would ever dream of quoting these forecasts, and saying *of them* that they "must needs be fulfilled," or that events happened that the things we wrote "might be fulfilled?" Would not such a mode of reference to the words of even the wisest and greatest of men pass the bounds of all that is reasonable and endurable, and be condemned as simple blasphemy? It would be ascribing to the words of fallible, short-sighted men the place occupied alone by the words of the all-seeing and infallible God. But, if that be so, we must apply the rule here as well as elsewhere. The New Testament could never have said such things of the Old had its words been regarded as the words of *men*. They must have been looked at, honoured, and revered *as the words of God*.

That this is indeed the witness of the New Testament becomes still plainer when we weigh another of its statements. The attempt has been made by timid friends of the Bible to save it by giving up what, in their judgment, is non-essential. "It is enough," they have said, "if the *doctrine* is left us; we can let the history go." They have maintained, therefore, that, while the doctrinal teaching of Scripture is fully inspired, no inspiration was needed or given for the production of the historical portions. Another distinction, which is somewhat wider, and which has been much in favour with many, is that the Bible was inspired "for the purpose for which it was given." It was given to show the way of salvation, to reveal man's need and God's grace in Christ. All this, then, can be depended upon with absolute confidence. But in history, science, &c., the writers were left to themselves, and we have to accept thankfully any corrections of their statements which fuller knowledge has enabled men to make. These distinctions display the ingenuity of their authors, but would not save the credit of the Scriptures. They owe their existence to the pressure of difficulty, and not to any calm consideration of the contents of the Bible. It was forgotten that doctrine and history are wedded together in such a way that it is simply impossible to separate them; and any serious attempt to make the separation must result in ludicrous failure. Is not the birth, the death, and the resurrection of Jesus history?. If it is a matter of saving faith to believe that God has ever done anything, or, indeed, ever said anything, is not that also history? And, if the history is fallible, how can the doctrine be infallible?

But the statement to which I now ask the reader's attention saves us all further trouble in this matter. The New Testament distinctly ascribes inspiration to the Old Testament history. Reference is made in the Epistle to the Romans to an incident narrated in the Book of Genesis. It occurs in the history of Abraham. We are there told that "he believed in the Lord: and he counted it to him for righteousness" (Gen. xv. 6). In Rom. iv. 23, 24, we read: "Now *it was not written* for his sake alone, that it was imputed to him; but for us also, to whom it shall be imputed, if we believe on him that raised up Jesus our Lord from the dead." Here there is no question whatever about the *truth* of the history. There never is any such question in any part of the New Testament with regard to any statement in the Old. There is no question either about the authorship of the history. The words, as we shall see, take this for granted, and pass on to speak of the real Writer's purpose. The question is, with what intention was the account placed upon the page of Scripture; and the reply is that the fact was placed on record, not only that it might be known that Abraham was justified and how, but also that *we* might know how a man may become just with God!

That is the plain meaning of the Scripture. "It was not written for his sake alone . . . but for us also." Of whom, then, are such things said? Who foresaw our existence, our need, and the provision which God was to make in the latter day? Who laboured to make a plain pathway for the Gentiles who were yet to believe in the Son of God? There can be but one answer. That bit of history in our Hebrew Bible was put there by the hand of God, and it was placed there that *our* hearts might find peace through believing. It is not only there by Inspiration; it is radiant with the glory of the Infinite love that planned our way, and stooped to serve us long ages before we came into this world of sin and need.

It might, perhaps, be said: "Well, that piece of history is so closely and vitally connected with doctrine that we can easily understand *its* full inspiration." But the Scripture will not permit us to accept the reluctant admission. For in the same Epistle we read again: "*Whatsoever things* were written aforetime were written for our learning, that we through patience and comfort of the Scriptures might have hope" (xv. 4). Here the hand of the New Testament witness is laid upon *everything* inscribed upon the pages of the Old Testament. Each and all of the words there are not only from God: they are God's provision *for us*. These things served Israel, but God looked beyond *them*. He foresaw that He would gather a people who would not be supported by national bonds, nor shielded by national bulwarks. They would, frequently, have to break every tie which binds a man to his fellows. They were to be like sheep sent out into the midst of wolves. They would need guidance, consolation, and spiritual support such as men never needed before. And so God made this book for *them*, that through patience and comfort of the Scriptures they might have hope. Yea, He took thought for them and us, both in the making as well as in the recording of the history: "Now these things were our examples, to the intent that we should not lust after evil things, as they also lusted. . . . Now all these things happened unto them for ensamples; and they are written for our admonition, upon whom the ends of the world are come" (1. Cor. x. 6, 11).

The New Testament, therefore, refuses to sustain the contention that the history of Scripture is uninspired and unreliable. On the contrary, *God* had to do both with the making of the history and with the recording of it. And, in short, there is no possibility of *excepting anything* within the compass of the Scriptures from the direct superintendence, intention, and inspiration of God. "WHATSOEVER

THINGS were written aforetime were written for our learning."

It is impossible, therefore, to maintain that the *doctrine* of Scripture is inspired, but not its *history*. There is no part of sacred history that is not covered by the most distinct assurances regarding its inspiration, while many parts of the history, which have specially excited the hostile remarks of the so-called "critics," are made the foundations of the leading doctrines of Christianity. The great Scripture doctrine of human depravity is founded upon the Bible narrative of the fall of Adam: "By one man sin entered into the world, and death by sin;" "By the offence of one judgment came upon all men to condemnation" (Rom. v. 12, 18). The unity of the human race, declared in the history of Genesis, becomes a leading doctrine of Christianity and the watchword of the messengers of the Gospel. God "hath made of one blood all nations of men for to dwell on all the face of the earth" (Acts xvii. 26). Indeed, the doubters of the first century of our era are severely condemned because they set aside the story of the Creation contained in the first chapter of Genesis. "For this," says the Scripture, in a passage which has been marvellously confirmed by recent chemical discoveries, "they willingly are ignorant of, that by the word of God the heavens were of old, and the earth standing out of the water (literally, 'compacted out of water') and in the water" (II. Peter iii. 5).

Another portion of the Creation story is made the

foundation of the duties which pertain to the relationships of marriage (Ephes. v. 22-33). The oath which God "sware to our father Abraham" is confidently appealed to (Luke i. 73). *The very time* at which the promise is said to have been given—namely, *previous* to his circumcision—is shown to be big with important doctrinal consequences (Rom. iv. 11, &c.) The place given to Moses, the priesthood of Aaron, the building and arrangements of the Tabernacle, and the whole Levitical ritual are solemnly recognised as of Divine origin, and are set forth as pictures drawn by God's own finger of the glorious fulness which is stored up for the believer in Christ.

We cannot save the doctrine, then, by sacrificing the history. A man, pursued by wolves, may as soon think of saving his life by cutting off and surrendering his head. No distinction is ever admitted, or apparently ever dreamed of, between the historical and the doctrinal parts of Scripture. Whatever part of the Old Testament the writers of the New touch upon is holy: it is all alike the Word of God.

The clearness of the New Testament witness is also manifest in the way in which it traces the responsibility for what is written to God Himself. Let me cite a few instances. "Now all this was done that it might be fulfilled which was spoken by the Lord through the prophet" (Matt. i. 22, Revised Version). The word came "*through* the prophet," but it "was *spoken by* the Lord." This distinction is repeated again and again. "That it might be fulfilled which was spoken by the Lord through the prophet" (Matt. ii. 15). "Men and brethren, this Scripture must needs have been fulfilled which the Holy Ghost by the mouth of David spake before concerning Judas" (Acts i. 16). "Those things which God before had showed by the mouth of all his prophets" (Acts iii. 18). "Who by the mouth of Thy servant David has said, Why did the heathen rage, and the people imagine vain things?" (Acts iv. 25).

In summing up the testimony of such passages as these, is it unfair to say that their plain meaning is that, while the *voice* is man's, *the words* are God's? Is not that the distinct intention behind the strange but deliberate and definite distinction that *God* spake by the mouth of His prophets? If any doubt could linger around this point it would be swept away by the words in II. Peter i. 21, which tells us that "Prophecy came not at any time (see margin) by the will of man: but holy men of God spake as they were moved by the Holy Ghost." That is, the words which stand upon the page of Scripture *never* originated even in the best of human motives. They are not due to any man's desire to serve God or to help his fellow-men. They *never* came "by the will of man." Their origin, on the contrary, is this: "holy men of God spake, being moved,"—that is, "*because* they were moved," or borne along—"by the Holy Ghost."

In close connection with these words we find a most remarkable statement concerning the Old Testament. The apostle has just spoken of the voice which he and James and John had heard on the mount of the Transfiguration. He speaks of it as "the holy mount." Like the spot surrounding the burning bush, it had been made holy by the revelation of God. It was surely a great matter to be so privileged as to hear from the midst of the Divine glory the testimony of God Himself to Jesus. But the apostle adds that he and we are still more privileged. "We have," he adds, "a surer thing, the prophetic word"—I am translating literally—"to which ye do well, taking heed (to it), as unto a lamp shining in a dark place until the day dawn and the day-star arise in your hearts" (II. Peter i. 19). This passage has startled commentators. What can be more sure than God's own personal testimony? What more convincing than the voice from the Divine glory? But the words cannot be explained away. Many have tried it and all of them have failed. The words still stand there, and they still make the astonishing declaration that we have got in the Scriptures a surer thing than the direct, awe-inspiring, testimony of God heard upon the Mount. We are no losers through not being with the three favoured ones then. We have something still surer—"the prophetic word"— the word given through holy men of God who spa l ( as they were borne along by the Holy Spirit.

That is the statement, and it leaves us no escape from the conclusion that the Scriptures are in the very highest and fullest sense the oracles of God. That *prophetic* word is *His* word. The words communicated to us by God's inspired servants are placed, to say the least, on a complete equality with the words spoken by the lips of God Himself. They are even said to be something that is "surer." I suppose that what is meant is that, being fuller, and more adapted to our need, they carry more conviction with them than the testimony spoken on the Mount conveyed, and they do more for us than that testimony could have achieved. But, I repeat, whether this be the explanation or not, the statement itself is unmistakable: the Scriptures are of God, in the fullest and highest sense in which the words can be understood.

The testimony of 2 Timothy iii. 16, is supposed by many to be considerably weakened by the altered rendering of the Revised Version. I do not believe that the alteration is warranted; but, as doubt has been cast on the rendering of the Authorised Version, let us keep to the revisers' translation. It reads thus: "Every Scripture, inspired of God, is also profitable for teaching, for reproof, for correction, for instruction, which is in righteousness; that the man of God may be complete, furnished completely unto every good work." Now the first thing we have to do is to make sure what Scriptures they are of which these things are said. The phrase, "Every Scripture inspired of God," may appear not only to be indefinite, but actually to suggest doubts. Is the apostle intimating that there are some of the Scriptures which are inspired and some which are not? Turn back to verses 14 and 15, and that notion will vanish: "But abide thou in the things which thou hast learned, and hast been assured of, knowing of whom thou hast learned them; and that from a babe thou hast known the sacred writings which are able to make thee wise unto salvation through faith which is in Christ Jesus."

No one questions that these holy writings are simply the Old Testament Scriptures. Timothy had been nurtured upon them. From a babe he had known them, and all of them are embraced under the common designation, "the holy writings." It cannot, therefore, be with the intention of discriminating between these that he now speaks of "every Scripture inspired of God." He specialises for another purpose. He takes up each of these Old Testament books and demonstrates its inestimable value to the man of God hungering and thirsting after righteousness. The words "inspired of God" are placed upon the sacred page for the simple purpose of reminding us of the high and holy origin and the Divine purpose of the Scripture. "*Every* Scripture"—historical as well as doctrinal, legal as well as prophetic—"being inspired of God," that is "*because* it is inspired of God," is laden with this blessed power. *Theopneustos* (translated "inspired") is literally "God breathed;" God breathed into the Scripture, and hence its surprising qualities. Its spirit is His Spirit.

Now to what does this introduction lead? To the most amazing description which has ever in this world been applied to *a book!* We have had centuries of progress since Paul sent that letter to Timothy.

We have works penned by genius as lofty as the world ever expects to see. But is there a single book, in our own or in any literature, of which any man, who knows the meaning of words, would say that, if read and followed, it would lead him up into the full ideal of God and make him complete—the all-round man God meant him to be, and leave him lacking nothing of the fulness of the stature of the manhood of Jesus? The thought is blasphemy. To say such things of any book would be impious adulation. It would be the most frightful idolatry. It would be ascribing to man the attributes of God. But we have now to ask how all this can be said of every book of the Old Testament? Is it not that each of these books has God for its Author: that its words are God's words; and that each book and word is instinct with His Spirit?

## CHAPTER VI.

### OUR LORD'S ENDORSEMENT OF THE OLD TESTAMENT SCRIPTURES.

WE have listened to what the Old Testament claims for itself, and to the witness which the New Testament bears to it. But, if we should stop here, the chief Witness of all would be unheard. The Son of God, the Lord of glory, has appeared among us. This Bible of the Jew existed in His day. It contained the same books, the same statements, the same words, as it contains now. It was set upon the same high platform, separated from every other book that was ever in the possession of man, and girded with a reverence due, not only to what had come from God, but also to what stood towards men in God's stead. The doctrine of its Inspiration never stood higher than in the days of Jesus. What, then, did *He* say and do in regard to these views? Did He ignore them? Did He condemn them? Did He set them aside as delusive and idolatrous? Or did He accept and enforce them?

These are not vain questions. For Christ-loving

and Christ-fearing men much depends upon the answer which they will find in the things Jesus said and did. We decline to discuss the deductions which some have drawn from a text about His "emptying" Himself (Philippians ii. 7), a text which, under an appearance of learning, is misunderstood and misrepresented. The words are: "Who, being in the form of God, thought it not robbery to be equal with God: but *made Himself of no reputation*, and took upon Him the form of a servant, and was made in the likeness of men," &c. They contend that the words "made himself of no reputation" (*heauton ekenōse*) should be rendered "emptied Himself," that is, of His Divine nature, so that in a matter of this kind He knew nothing more than the men of His day, and that His testimony regarding it is, not the testimony of God, but that of fallible man. In this contention they are *forcing* a sense upon the verb *kenōo* which it will not bear. It is used in the Septuagint, the Greek translation of the Old Testament which was in use in the Apostolic time, and it is used in the sense in which the Authorised Version here takes it. In Jer. xiv. 2, we read: "Judah mourneth, and the gates thereof languish." The word rendered "languish" is in the Septuagint this very word *kenōo*. There is nothing mysterious about the word or its meaning. The gates had only lost their old stateliness; they had not "emptied" themselves, or "been emptied" by anyone, of their nature. They had not ceased to be gates; but their awe-inspiring greatness had gone, and the pomp and power that used to surround them were swept away. And so here the word does not mean that our Redeemer ceased to be God, but that He divested Himself of the Divine glory. Had He ceased to be God, He would have ceased to be Himself. Besides, too, in giving the word a meaning which it does not bear, they have forgotten the context. *We are commanded to imitate the Lord in this matter.* "Let this mind," says the Scripture, "be in you, which was also in Christ Jesus" (verse 5). Now, if the Revisers have translated rightly, and if those are right who hold that the passage teaches that the Redeemer laid aside His Godhead, we must be here commanded to lay aside our manhood, that is, to divest ourselves of our human nature. Will these friends tell us how we are to obey the injunction? And will they inform us what, when we have parted with our humanity, we may expect ourselves to be? Taking the word as translated in the Old Version, we can understand it and obey it. If the way of duty lies through humiliation, we can still press on, rejoicing that we are counted worthy to tread in His pathway, who clung not to the majesty and adoration and service that surround the Godhead; but who "made himself of no reputation," and turned aside from no humiliation through which the pathway ran to serve and to save.

Another statement on which they rest is—that the hour of His second coming was unknown to Christ. How could He be ignorant of that, they ask, unless He had put off His Godhead? Let us turn to the passage (Mark xiii. 32), and we shall find that we have something to ask *them*. The Lord says: "Of that day and that hour knoweth no man, no, not the angels which are in heaven, neither the Son, but the Father only." Here are three grades: "Man," "the Angels," "the Son." It might be supposed that, though man knows it not, the angels may know it; but they do not. Well, then, if the angels are ignorant of it, the Son will surely know. As we pass man to reach the angel-greatness, so we pass the angel-greatness to reach the greatness of the Son. But what is the greatness that rises supreme above that of all the angel host, if not the greatness of the Deity? If the Redeemer had emptied Himself of His Godhead, and had become nothing more than we are, how could He be the possessor of a super-angelic nature?

The words find their explanation in those of the Risen Master. Repeating the statement, He said: "It is not for you to know the times or the seasons, which *the Father hath put in His own power*" (Acts i. 7). It is the Father's *to determine* when the era of mercy shall cease and when the dread era of judgment shall begin. The decree waits, and the Son—in all the greatness and in all the consciousness of Godhead—leaves that decision with the Father. But neither this nor any other misunderstood passage of Scripture can blot out the direct testimony that Jesus was God manifest in the flesh; that in Him "dwelt all the fulness of the Godhead bodily;" that they who had seen Him had seen the Father, and that the interpenetration of the Divine Persons was as true of Jesus in the days of His flesh as it is now. "Believest thou not," He asks Philip, "that I am in the Father and the Father in Me?" (John xiv. 10). The consciousness of Christ embraced every thought of God, and the consciousness of God embraced every thought of Christ.

The Lord further tells us in the same passage that His words and His works are not His only, but the Father's also. "The words that I speak unto you I speak not of myself, but the Father that dwelleth in Me, He doeth the works" (John xiv. 10). That statement has a most momentous bearing upon the question now before us. The testimony of Jesus regarding the Scriptures is the direct testimony of the Father. What, then, we ask, is this testimony? for surely, having it fully and clearly, we have reached the end of controversy on this matter. Who is the man that, puffed up with the pride of supposed discoveries, will set his mouth against the heavens— his judgment against the decree of God?

Mention has already been made of the sacrifice which some propose to make of the Old Testament history. "Let the history go," they say; "what need we care, while the doctrine remains?" But if the history go, the reliableness of the testimony of Jesus goes with it. We are simply amazed when we consider how the words of Jesus have grasped almost the entire range of the Old Testament history and have embedded it in the New. When the Pharisees came tempting Him with the question, "Is it lawful  for a man to put away his wife for every cause," He answered and said unto them: "Have ye not read that He who made them at the beginning, made them male and female, and said, For this cause shall a man leave father and mother and shall cleave to his wife; and they twain shall be one flesh?" (Matt. xix. 4, 5). What did the question mean? Was there not an accent of blame in it for not having duly marked an authoritative statement which really made an end of all question regarding this matter? But our Lord has left no room for doubt as to His meaning, for He founded His decision upon the words. "Wherefore," said He, "they are no more twain, but one flesh. What, therefore, God hath joined together, let no man put asunder" (verse 6). Our Lord's argument has force in it only upon one supposition—that those words, taken from the first and second chapters of Genesis, are the words of God. But it is plain that our Lord believed the quotation not only to have force in it, but also to be absolutely conclusive. The words are, therefore, quoted as the words of God Himself.

In the same way Jesus turns again and again to the Old Testament history as to a storehouse of unquestioned and unquestionable facts. Can anyone read the words, "But as the days of Noe were, so also shall the coming of the Son of Man be. For as in the days that were before the flood they were eating and drinking, marrying and giving in marriage, until the day that Noe entered into the ark, and knew not until the flood came, and took them all away" (Matt. xxiv. 37-39)—can anyone read these words without the conviction that to Jesus all this was fact? Quite in the same way He cites the institution of circumcision, the feeding of the Israelites with manna in the desert, the lifting up of the brazen serpent, the overthrow of Sodom and Gomorrah, and the judgment which fell upon Lot's wife. Questioned on one occasion by the Sadducees regarding the resurrection, He replied by an argument at once so novel and so crushingly conclusive that from that hour His enemies ceased from what was now recognised as a vain attempt to entrap Him by their subtleties. What was the argument? It was founded upon a name which the *history* of the Book of Exodus tells us was applied to God by Himself. He announced Himself to Moses and through Moses to Israel (Exodus iii. 6, 15), as "the God of Abraham, the God of Isaac, and the God of Jacob." Standing upon that record as upon absolute truth—taking it as word for word the declaration of God Himself—Jesus added: "He is not a God of the dead, but of the living" (Luke xx. 38). Incidents in the histories of Elijah and Elisha are referred to in the Synagogue at Nazareth. When attacked on account of His supposed breaking of the Sabbath, Jesus reminds His questioners of David's eating of the shewbread. When He was urged to give a sign to certify His claims, He intimated that it would come in a way they little expected. They would receive the sign of the prophet Jonas; "for as Jonas was three days and three nights in the whale's belly, so shall the Son of Man be three days and three nights in the heart of the earth" (Matt. xii. 40). The slaughter of Jesus would be the end neither of His life nor of His service, and as men saw in the deliverance and the after ministry of Jonah the seal of God, so should it be with the Son of Man. His enemies would receive the sign of the prophet Jonas. On the same occasion the repentance of the men of Nineveh and the Queen of Sheba's answer to the fame of the wisdom of Solomon are both referred to with the same full and untroubled acceptance of them as unquestionable facts. If the Lord's claim to speak the words of the Father is to be regarded, this testimony settles the matter. Wherever it may be that we meet open denial of the accuracy and inspiration of the history of Scripture, there is not a shadow of it to be found with Jesus. There is no atmosphere of doubt here. The lowly disciple of this Master, who will accept as decisive the testimony of Jesus, will leave behind him every remnant of doubt and questioning, and come into the pure, bright joy of trust.

The reader of the Gospels is struck by another feature—our Lord's *reverence* for the Scriptures. So marked is this that no one, in enumerating the characteristics of the Lord Jesus, could omit it without afterwards confessing that he had been guilty of a great oversight. The Scriptures are the theme of His ministry. They are with Him in His solitary conflicts. They seem to be ever in His thoughts. There is One who holds a like place in the reverence of Jesus—it is the Father. How did it happen that these Old Testament books rested, in the Lord's judgment, on that high level? There is no one whom Jesus so regarded save God. The authority of man in the past, or in the then present, was lightly esteemed. I do not see how the conclusion can be escaped that Jesus so reverenced the Scriptures for the sole reason that they are of God in the highest sense in which those words have ever been understood. The Old Testament was to Jesus God's Book—the Father's expressed mind and will.

A nearer view of our Lord's testimony confirms this conclusion. We are permitted to follow Him into the wilderness and to witness His temptation. The Lord is tempted in like manner as we are. He is attacked by the same specious arguments. Satan comes arrayed as an angel of light. But Jesus does not reason out the matter. Like a child He casts Himself upon the Scripture. He replies "It is written." There was no call for *Him* to decide: all was already decided. He did not require to reason as to which path He should take. It had all been settled long before, and the word of command had been given and recorded upon the page of Scripture. Who recorded it? Who decided it? Who arranged that perfect way for Christ's feet and for ours, so that not even He had to take any further thought for the matter than simply to mark what was written? Can anyone mistake the answer? Is there any answer but one—that these words were God's words—and therefore, being God's words, are errorless and absolutely reliable?

Our Lord, in one of His parables, assigns to "Moses and the prophets" a place which it seems impossible to explain except in the same way. The rich man pleads in his torment that Lazarus may be sent to warn his brethren. Abraham replies that they have Moses and the prophets, and adds, "Let them hear them" (Luke xvi. 29). The once rich man still pleads: "Nay, Father Abraham, but if one went unto them from the dead, they will repent. And he said unto him, If they hear not Moses and the prophets, neither will they be persuaded though one rose from the dead" (verses 30, 31). Put the pleader's words in another form, and they amount to this: "A miracle will move these careless men. Let them only be brought into sharp contact with some messenger from the Unseen, and they will repent." Put the answer in another form, and is it not this: "There is no need to send Lazarus; the work is already done; the miracle has been performed; the messengers from the Unseen are already with them; the message of God is already sounding in their ears"? "Moses and the prophets," that is, the Old Testament which we now possess, is, in itself, more strikingly miraculous than one sent from the dead with a special individual message from God to us could be! If the presence of this Book does not speak to us and rouse us, then a message from the dead would avail us nothing. In what, then, does this supreme miraculousness of the Old Testament consist? What gives it this character? It appears to me that, if we are to interpret this with perfect honesty, only one reply is available. This Book is more startling and more convincing than a visit from the dead, solely because it has come direct from God and bears upon its every page God's image and superscription. It is the word, not of a messenger, but of the Master. He that returned from the dead would, after all, be only a creature; but He that speaks here is the Creator. Hence, if God has failed, what can be hoped for even from one returning from the dead? It seems to me, I repeat, that behind these words of Jesus there stands the knowledge that the Bible is the direct speech of God.

The Sermon on the Mount has been appealed to by some as proof of how lightly the Old Testament was esteemed by our Lord. We are told that its commandments were revoked, and that it was generally set aside as an antiquated thing. The Lord's words were no doubt open to that misconstruction; for He has specially guarded against it. "Think not," He said, "that I am come to destroy the Law or the Prophets; I am not come to destroy, but to fulfil. For verily I say unto you, Till heaven and earth pass, one jot or one tittle shall in no wise pass from the law, till all be fulfilled" (Matt. v. 17, 18). The demand of Jesus is one for a fuller righteousness than that of the Law. To the *justice* of the Old dispensation the *mercy* of the New has to be added. It is here that the misconception about our Lord's abrogating the Law has come in. The justice of the Law is not cast away; for how shall the Lord judge the world, save on the very principle, "an eye for an eye, and a tooth for a tooth?" But in view of that judgment, now hastening onward, believers must inscribe upon their banners, and must proclaim in all they do and in all they suffer, that now there is mercy if men will only turn and flee. They put aside every offence; they forgive even unto and beyond seventy times seven; they are defrauded and oppressed, and take it lightly; they go to prison and to death, patiently bearing the weight of enormous wrongs; they fill up what is behind of the sufferings of Christ, that men may look and recognise Him that waits to be gracious. That is no more an abrogating of the Old Testament than a man's yielding his rights is an abrogating of the laws of England. The law still stands, but this is the burden of those who, in this Gospel era, serve the Saviour of men, and who therefore take up their cross and follow Him.

This superadded law of mercy and of patient endurance of wrong is, therefore, by no means an abrogation of that justice which is eternal. Let us now turn back to the Lord's words: "Think not that I am come," He says, "to destroy the Law or the Prophets. I am not come to destroy, but to fulfil" (Matt. v. 17). To fulfil! What, then, is *that*, the fulfilling of which sums up the mission of Jesus? Can it be a thing of error and mistake and human shortsightedness—a book marred by historical, moral, and scientific blunders? Jesus, we may safely say, never left heaven to fulfil the word of man. We have only to imagine such a thing to see how utterly incongruous and blasphemous the supposition would

## Our Lord's Endorsement of the Old Testament. 85

be, Could we put, for example, the Republic of Plato in the place of "the Law and the Prophets," and imagine our Lord saying that He came to fulfil *that*? What production of man could have even outlined the work of Jesus, not to speak of filling up its details and determining the path He was to pursue and the things He was to do and to suffer? That to which our Lord makes Himself servant, is not of man but of God.

This testimony is full enough; but let us take also the words which follow: "Verily I say unto you, Till heaven and earth pass, one jot or one tittle shall in no wise pass from the law till all be fulfilled" (verse 18). Here, unless we are to set down this solemn testimony as reckless exaggeration, inspiration is claimed for the very letters of the Hebrew words. Not the smallest letter (the yod or jot) found on the page of the Hebrew Bible, nor even a tittle (a point which distinguishes one letter from another), shall in any wise pass from the law till all be fulfilled. Heaven and earth shall pass away, but these *words*, traced by inspiration of the Spirit of God, shall not pass away. The words of the Old Testament are more sacred to God than the most stupendous of His works. Every jot and every tittle was placed upon the page under His direct control, and God has thereby pledged Himself to each. That is the Lord's statement. Believing in an inspiration which had to do with *everything* in the original document, not only with the thought, and not only with the words, but also with the very characters traced upon it—believing in Inspiration of that kind, we can understand this statement of Jesus. It is intelligible and luminous. It is satisfying. It gives us a Bible as free from shortcoming and mistake, as inerrant and perfect and Divine, as its Giver.

I conclude this brief review of our Lord's testimony with a statement which is equally strong. The context in which the words stand (John x. 30-36) need not detain us. Meeting an accusation of blasphemy, our Lord quotes a statement from the 82nd Psalm, with the remark that "the Scripture cannot be broken." That is, it cannot be loosed (*luthēnai*), or dissolved. If it has tied a bond, we cannot undo it and let that which was bound go free: if it has flowed into a certain mould and taken a certain shape, it cannot be melted again and made to wear another shape. The thing it has done abides; the form that it has taken it wears for ever.

That is our Lord's statement in introducing this quotation from the Psalm. Will the reader mark its position? The statement forms the major premise in a syllogism. Put in logical form, the argument stands thus:

Major Premise—No Scripture can be broken.

Minor Premise—This (Psalm lxxxii. 6) is Scripture.

Conclusion—Therefore the words, "I have said ye are gods" cannot be broken. They remain unalterable. They are eternally true.

The significance of this testimony of Jesus will now be apparent. He, in effect, places His hand upon the entire Scripture, and declares it absolutely inerrant. It is sometimes said that the doctrine of Verbal Inspiration recklessly imperils our faith. But does not our belief in the theory of gravitation do the same? You have only to show that one speck of dust, hovering in the air, does not obey the alleged "law," and you demolish the law utterly. If it fails to affect the dust, it cannot control the universe. Every principle carries its consequences, and if we believe that God gave the Scripture we dare not throw away our faith before the little things any more than we can throw it away before the great things. It is this position which is taken by our Lord. Show but one mistake in the Bible as originally given, and it is no longer true that *all* Scripture is eternally changeless. Prove that there is one exception to this law, and our Lord's argument falls to the ground. For it could then be no longer said that the Scripture could not be broken, and that *therefore* Psalm lxxxii. 6, and every other text in the Bible must be accepted as fully and everlastingly true.

That this is the conviction of every writer of Scripture, and the testimony of every book which it contains, is admitted fully by the rationalists themselves. Reuss says, in his *"History of Christian Theology in the Apostolic Age* : "The Apostles adopted, without alteration, the dogmatic theories applied by the Jews to this canonical collection. The doctrine of the inspiration of the prophets, and of the sacred writers generally, had received in the schools *the fullest development of which it was capable.* That inspiration was regarded as something altogether exceptional, as the peculiar privilege of a small number of individuals chosen by Providence, or as bestowed only to meet special and solemn emergencies.† The communications made to Israel by the prophets were so emphatically the word of the Lord and of His Spirit, and not the counsel of the speaker's own wisdom, that the significance of what they said was often not perceived by themselves until the fulfilment of the prophecy made it plain. It was not needful, therefore, to cite the names of the various sacred writers, in order to give weight to their testimony to religious or prophetic truth; though custom allowed this to be done. It was enough to appeal to Scripture in a general and abstract manner; or rather it was a natural consequence of the dogmatic principle laid down, to speak of Scripture as a single, continuous, organic and personal authority, itself speaking, and which, having prevision of the future before uttering its prophecies, in a manner fulfilled its own predictions, since by the light of those predictions alone the fulfilment was recognized. This character of absolute authority, moreover, belongs to it, not only as a whole, but is possessed in the same degree by every subordinate part, so that all are spoken of as *the Scriptures* ‡—that is, special and indubitable manifestations of the will of God."

It is plain, therefore, that, if our Master is to be Judge in this matter, or if we are to give heed to the

---

† *Acts* i. 16; ii. 30; *Heb.* iii. 7; ix. 8; x. 15; 1. *Peter* i. ii; comp. 11. *Peter* i. 21, &c.
‡ See *Acts* i. 16; viii. 35; *James* ii. 8, 23; *John* xix. 37; *Luke* xxiv. 27, etc; comp. *John* x. 35.

## Our Lord's Endorsement of the Old Testament. 89

testimony of His Apostles and of the Scriptures, our question is fully answered. Doubt is no longer possible as to the reality or the extent of the Inspiration of the Bible. The Book has God for its Author. Its every utterance and its every word are His. But this testimony is openly set aside or silently ignored by those who claim to be heard as authorities in the Christian Church.. The so-called Higher Criticism sits unchallenged in our Divinity Halls, our Colleges, and our Universities. It is moulding the future ministry of every denomination in the land. It is issuing text-books, commentaries, treatises, and magazine articles, in which the public is informed that the former teaching regarding the Bible can no longer be maintained. Before we consider the statements made by these "authorities," who so imperiously set aside the authority of Christ, it may be well to ask who and whence they are. It may help us to account for much if we are acquainted with their history, and I now ask the reader's attention to a brief account of the Genesis of Rationalism.

# BOOK II.

# THE GENESIS OF RATIONALISM.

# THE GENESIS OF RATIONALISM.

## CHAPTER I.

### THE PRE-REFORMATION PERIOD.

WE have listened to the claims which the Old Testament makes for itself and to the witness borne to it by the New Testament and by our Lord. The claim and the testimonies are in absolute agreement. In neither is there any exception or any hesitancy. By each and all, the Old Testament Scriptures are handed to us in their entirety as the oracles of God, and their very words are guaranteed as the utterances of the Divine lips.

This is not the opinion, as we have already said, of many who are now recognised as Christians and as Christian teachers. The Old Testament (they tell us) cannot be regarded as the Word of God in the sense which we have hitherto attached to that phrase. They explain clearly what they mean. God is not (they say) the author of the Bible in the same sense that John Milton is the author of Paradise Lost. There are low moral conceptions in it (they further allege) which could not have proceeded from God.

There are inaccuracies and mistakes (they say) of which God could not have been the perpetrator. The writers of the Bible may have imagined that they were giving us history; but they have only, in many instances, handed down to posterity myths, legends, and Jewish folk-lore. The way to truth and to God does not lie, therefore (some earnestly assure us), along the childlike acceptance of these parts of the Bible. They misrepresent God; they misinform us in regard to much besides; and if real progress is to be made, the old views about the Bible must be seriously modified, if not utterly abandoned.

That such things should be said by opponents of the Christian faith need not surprise anyone. The world rejected and crucified the Incarnate Word, and it is only in keeping with the spirit that is in it that it should reject and vilify the written Word. But that these things should be said by the custodians and expounders of the Bible—that the assault upon the Scriptures should now be carried on by men within the very citadel of Christianity—that this assault should be made by the officers and chief captains of the defending host, and that they should call upon the rank and file to rend what they have hitherto revered—this is the marvel of nineteenth century Christianity. What has led to this startling revolution, and what can explain a change of front, the most astonishing in the whole of the Church's chequered history?

The best answer to the question will be a brief sketch of the Church's history, and the reader will kindly bear with me while together we rapidly survey the Christian ages. There is one lesson written across those eighteen centuries, which is highest wisdom for the present hour. *Whenever the Church ceases to be the faithful interpreter of Scripture teaching, we shall find that in the very same measure it presents the features of the age by which it is surrounded.* This may be taken as the simple law of all ecclesiastical aberrations. Whatever darkness we note in any age of the Church's thought, it is merely the shadow cast by that which stands at the Church's side. On the other hand, we can always conclude from these aberrations what were the characteristics of the age in which they occurred. Cut out what page of the story of Christian thought we may, we can analyse it in this simple fashion; and, when we have put what is purely Scriptural on one side, we shall find in the remainder the mud and the various ingredients which enable us to say what was the soil through which the pure stream of truth was then running. There is no more telling proof of the high and all-pervading inspiration of the Bible than that which this fact supplies. Here alone the ages have left nothing of their darkness or of their stain. Every one of these books was in the world; but in no single respect is it of the world. There is no literature of any—even the purest—Christian age which could be separated, and be made the example and guide of all after time. Age errors, misconceptions, falsities, injustices, and immoralities would be bound upon posterity as well as righteousness and everlasting truth. There is only one literature of all that has ever sprung from humanity that can be put in the place of guide and law for all generations, and this one literature is that which is embraced in the Old and New Testaments. Whence has it this high and holy quality? How is it that it so resembles Him whom it reveals, and, though coming by man, is nevertheless "holy, harmless, undefiled, and separate from sinners?"

No student of human history can ignore the blessing which has attended the introduction of Christianity. In an age of deism, Gibbon was compelled to speak of it as "a pure and humble religion," and to describe the darkness which so soon obscured it as "the inevitable mixture of error and corruption, which she contracted in a long residence upon earth, among a weak and degenerate race of beings."\* The noblest fruits of the Christian religion naturally escape the analysis of a writer like Lecky; but enough remains to be fashioned into praises that can form a crown for nothing else that is earthly. "Imperfect and inadequate," he says, "as is the sketch I have drawn, it will be sufficient to show how great and multiform have been the influences of Christian philanthropy. The shadows that rest upon the picture I have not concealed; but when all due allowance has been made for them, enough will remain to claim our deepest admiration. The high conception that has been formed of the sanctity of human life, the protection of infancy, the

---

\* *The Decline and Fall, &c.*—Chap. xv.

elevation and final emancipation of the slave classes, the suppression of barbarous games, the creation of a vast and multifarious organisation of charity, and the education of the imagination by the Christian type, constitute together a movement of philanthropy which has never been paralleled or approached in the Pagan world."*

He notes that Tertullian, in the second century, "contrasts the Christians of his day with the gymnosophists or hermits of India—declaring that, unlike these, the Christians did not fly from the world but mixed with the Pagans in the forum, in the market-places, in the public baths, in the ordinary business of life." The current of Christian thought still ran strong and pure. There was a repellent force in it that preserved it from intermixture with the turbid waters which surged around it. But Paganism, with its foulness and superstition, and misconception of God, was unchanged; and, as more heed was given to it and less to the Scriptures, the worldly admixture was manifested. The thought of the ascetic, that God had to be appeased by the soul trampling upon every enjoyment and inflicting upon itself every possible burden and torment, became by degrees, the ruling thought of the so-called Christian Church. Religious earnestness took that direction with ever-increasing force. Men and tender women fled from city and fertile field to barren waste and still wilder mountain. "St. Jerome declares," says Lecky, "with a thrill of admiration, how he had seen

---
* *History of European Morals.* Vol. ii., Chap. iv.

a monk, who for thirty years had lived exclusively on a small portion of barley bread and of muddy water. . . . For six months, it is said, St. Macarius of Alexandria, slept in a marsh, and exposed his body naked to the stings of venomous flies. He was accustomed to carry about with him eighty pounds of iron. His disciple, St. Eusebius, carried one hundred and fifty pounds of iron, and lived three years in a dried-up well. St. Sabinus would only eat corn that had become rotten by remaining for a month in water. St. Bessarion spent forty days and nights in the middle of thorn bushes, and for forty years never lay down while he slept. . . .

"But of all the evidences of the loathsome excesses to which this spirit was carried, the life of St. Simeon Stylites is probably the most remarkable. It would be difficult to conceive a more horrible or disgusting picture than is given of the penances by which that saint commenced his ascetic career. He had bound a rope around him so that it became embedded in his flesh, which putrefied around it. 'A horrible stench, intolerable to the bystanders, exhaled from his body and worms dropped from him whenever he moved, and they filled his bed.' Sometimes he left the monastery and slept in a dry well, inhabited, it is said, by demons. He built successively three pillars, the last being sixty feet high, and scarcely two cubits in circumference, and on this pillar, during thirty years, he remained exposed to every change of climate, ceaselessly and rapidly bending his body in prayer almost to the level of his feet. A spectator attempted to number these rapid motions, but desisted from weariness, when he had counted 1,224."*

This was simply the invasion of the deep-rooted beliefs of surrounding heathenism. Men received the illumination of the Bible regarding sin and the holiness of God, and bound this up with their own dark conceptions as to the implacableness of the Divine vengeance. The Gospel message was forgotten, the praises of the redeemed were exchanged for the terror-stricken cries and the frantic efforts of men fleeing from damnation. The darkness swept in from other sides as well. The ordinances of baptism and of the Lord's supper became magic rites. The services of the Church were more and more assimilated to the ceremonies of heathen worship. The Christian minister took the place of the heathen priest. God, Christ, the Virgin Mary, angels, saints, and martyrs were put in the places of the fallen gods in the heathen pantheon. The holy places of Palestine, the spots where martyrs suffered, their bones, their clothing, and their finger-nails were substituted for the heathen shrines and charms. There were protests from Vigilantius and others, but these were rudely and savagely hushed. The darkness had well-nigh triumphed by the beginning of the fifth century, and the victory of evil was helped and hastened by saintly men like Augustine. "Augustine, the hope —the *last* hope of his times," writes Isaac Taylor, "joined hands with the besotted bigots around him

---
* *Ibid.*

who would listen to no reproofs:—he raised his voice among the most intemperate to drown remonstrance. Superstition and spiritual despotism, illusion, knavery, and abject formalism, received a new warrant from the high seat of influence which he occupied: the Church drove its chariot with mad haste down the steep, and thenceforward nothing marks its history but blasphemy, idolatry, and blood. The popery which even now is gathering over our heavens from all quarters, is little else than the digested superstition which the good Augustine set forward in his day."*

Augustine was the victim of the optimism by which so many really great and good men are fatally misled at such times. He *knew* that God must triumph, and he therefore refused to read in the fast multiplying signs the advent of darkness. It was only a passing cloud, if even so much as that, and the Sun of Righteousness would burst forth again in brighter splendour than ever! Such men forget that, though God will triumph, multitudes of men and of churches will fail. Salvianus read the signs of the times more truly. To him it seemed that those lands had had their chance and had lost it. God was forsaking them and handing them over for judgment. "The church," he said, which ought everywhere to propitiate God, what does she, but provoke Him to anger? How many may one meet, even in the church, who are not still drunkards, or debauchees, or adulterers, or fornicators, or robbers, or murderers,

---

*Ancient Christianity, Vol i., p. 445.

or the like, or all of these at once without end? It is even a sort of holiness among Christian people to be less vicious. From the public worship of God," he continues, "and almost during it, they pass to deeds of shame. Scarce a rich man, but would commit murder or fornication. We have lost the whole power of Christianity, and offend God the more that we sin as Christians. We are worse than the barbarians and the heathen."\*

It was the triumph of heathen darkness. The errors of the time, long fought against, began slowly and at first imperceptibly to affect Christian belief and practice. Then came the open manifestation of the enemy in the camp; and, last of all, the subjugation of the Christian Church *by betrayal*. The best and most trusted Christian teachers of the time gave way to a movement which they ought to have resisted. They encouraged the foe and assured his victory, while they maligned and persecuted the men who tried to resist him. The churches of the east and west went down *and have never been restored*. The lands were given over to judgment. The light itself seemed to perish. In one quarter alone did the scattered ashes grow bright under the Spirit's breath and break forth into flame. Paul had spent his strength in planting and watching over the churches in Asia Minor. His toil was neither fruitless nor forgotten. Paul-like men, who were hailed as such by their contemporaries and named *Paulikoi*, were stirred amid the growing need to imitate the Apostle

---

\**Schaff's History of the Church* (T. & T. Clarke), Vol. i., p.p. 88, 89.

to the Gentiles in his zeal and self-sacrifice for threatened truth and endangered souls. They wrote out and multiplied copies of the Scripture, specially of the Pauline epistles. They spoke to loiterers in the market-place, to travellers by the way, to all men wherever and whenever they had an opportunity. The people listened, were converted, and swept back the invading darkness. They returned to the sweet, glad, holy light of New Testament belief, and to the simplicity of New Testament worship.

The movement swept over the cities and or the provinces, and alarmed the ecclesiastics and the statesmen even of distant Constantinople. It speedily received a name. The followers of these *Paulikoi* were called *Paulikianoi;* and the "*Paulicians*" have taken their place in history written by their ecclesiastical enemies and traducers. Armies were sent against them; and where the arguments of a heathenised Christianity were powerless to convince, the sword tried to terrify. But the fleshly arm could not slay the truth. The harassed believers were refreshed by tokens that God was with them. One general, for instance, who knew nothing of the people or their beliefs till he was charged by the Emperor with their suppression, found, when he returned to Constantinople, that he had no rest till he laid down his appointments, forsook everything, and joined the people whom he had been sent to persecute. The Paulicians were unconquerable till, goaded by ages of injustice, they betook themselves to the sword. From that day their strength decayed until they were

## The Pre-Reformation Period. 103

finally overpowered. They were banished from Asia Minor, and, leaving their fatherland for ever, passed over into Europe. They travelled along the rivers and valleys of their new world, and settled in quietness here and there, taking with them, as their choicest treasure, the Word of God and the simplicity of worship for which their fathers died. The historian meets them again in communities and peoples that live apart, and which Rome stamps out one after another. But the truth they preserved lives on, and bursts forth at last in the splendours of the Reformation.

## CHAPTER II.

### THE PRE-REFORMATION PERIOD *(Continued)*.

WE have now to glance at the Church in the Western Empire; for there alone was there to be any permanent revival. The corruption of the old eastern civilisations poured their vileness into that worthy receptacle of the Grecian Empire, and every Christ-like and every manly virtue in Church and people rotted away, till the Mahomedan scimitar dealt out the long delayed vengeance. The Roman Empire in the west was more speedily judged, and Europe was covered with barbarian hordes who brought with them a rough sincerity, a whole-hearted earnestness, and a manly freedom that formed a better soil for the Gospel seed had there been hands fit to sow it. Christianity had gone down in the east; but there was still a chance for it in the west.

The Church of the west had entered very largely into political relationships before the fall of the Empire. The Bishop, as head of the Church in a city, was naturally, when Christianity became the religion of the Empire, a personage of very considerable importance. As the hold of the Empire upon its provinces grew weaker, more was referred to the Ecclesiastical Dignitaries, till they were as much engrossed with the temporal concerns of the district as the civil functionaries themselves. We read, for example, in the code of Justinian: "With respect to the yearly affairs of cities, whether they concern the ordinary revenues of the city . . . whether public works, or depôts of provision, or aqueducts, or the maintenance of baths, or ports, or the construction of walls or towers, or the repairing of bridges or roads, or trials in which the city may be engaged in reference to public or private interests, we ordain as follows:—The very pious bishop, and three notables from among the first men of the city, shall meet together; they shall, each year, examine the works done; they shall take care that those who conduct them . . . shall regulate them with precision, render their accounts," &c.\*

Other edicts conferred other privileges and imposed other obligations, till the Bishops were as supreme in civil as they were in ecclesiastical matters. "The preponderance," says Guizot, "of the clergy in the affairs of the city succeeded that of the ancient municipal magistrates, and preceded the organization of the modern municipal institutions."

The foundation was laid in this way of the temporal power and of the long-continued struggle between the Church and the sovereignties of Europe for

---

\* *Guizot's History of Civilisation.*

supremacy. The spirit of the world had thus become the spirit of the Church. This was also shown on another side. The great Roman nobles and officials of the fourth and fifth centuries gave evidence everywhere of the decay which had fallen upon the Empire. Even the most virtuous lived merely for pleasure. Learning developed into literary trifling. This spirit passed from the nobles to the bishops. A few gave themselves to asceticism and to prayer; but they were regarded with an astonishment and veneration which show how rare in those ages was the zeal they displayed. The following extracts from a letter of Sidonius to a fellow bishop will enable us to look into the life of the time. Eriphius, the recipient of the letter, wishes to know the circumstances which led to the composition of some trivial impromptu verses by Sidonius. "We were met," he writes, "at the sepulchre of St. Just, illness preventing you from joining us. Before day, the annual procession was made, amidst an immense populace of both sexes, that could not be contained in the church and the crypt, although surrounded by immense porticoes . . . The narrow dimensions of the place, the crowd which pressed around us, and the large quantity of lights, had choked us; the oppressive vapour of a night still bordering upon summer, although cooled by the first freshness of an autumnal dawn, made this enclosure still warmer. While the various classes of society dispersed on all sides, the chief citizens assembled around the tomb of the consul Syagrius, which was not at the distance of an arrow-shot.

"Some were seated under the shade of an arbour formed of stakes covered with the branches of the vine; we were stretched upon the green turf embalmed with the perfume of flowers. The conversation was sweet, cheerful, pleasant; moreover (and this was far more agreeable), there was no question either of powers or tributes; no word which could compromise, nor person who could be compromised. Whosoever could, in good terms, relate an interesting history, was sure to be listened to with earnestness. Nevertheless, no continuous narration was made, because gaiety frequently interrupted the discourse. Tired at length of this long repose, we desired to do something else. We soon separated into two bands, according to ages. One party loudly demanded the game of tennis; the other, a table and dice. For myself, I was the first to give the signal for tennis, because I love it, as you know, as much as books. On the other side, my brother Dominicius, a man full of kindness and cheerfulness, seized the dice, shook them, and struck with his dice-box, as if he had sounded a trumpet, to call players to him. As to us, we played a good deal with the crowd of scholars. . . . The illustrious Philimathius himself . . . constantly mixed with the players at tennis. He succeeded very well at it when he was younger, but now, as he was often driven from the middle, where people were standing, by the shock of some running player; as at other times, if he entered the arena, he could neither make way nor avoid the ball, and as, frequently overthrown, he only raised himself with pain from the unlucky fall, he was the first to leave the scene of the game—heaving sighs and very much heated," &c., &c. All this elaborate description is nothing more than a preface to the statement that the verses were composed at the urgent request of Philimathius as an address to the towel which had served the useful purpose of drying the water with which he bathed his heated face!

Here, again, the Church reflected the age. Instead of guiding and controlling the spirit of the time, it was conquered and led captive by it. Had the Church drunk in the spirit of the unchanging Redeemer, it would have raised and saved the age. But heart and eye were turned away from Christ. The Church became like the world and shared its judgment. The story need not be retold of that avalanche of bloodshed and ruin that swept in from the savage north, and of the chaos which Europe afterwards presented for many a day. Nor do we require to enter into the struggles of the Church to reimpose its yoke upon the people. There were movements—such as the attempt of Charlemagne to enlighten the barbarian darkness which rested upon the peoples under his sway —over which we might linger. One feature of these has indeed a special attraction for us. Those benefactors of humanity often laboured to make the people acquainted with the Scripture. Councils and assemblies of bishops and clergy urged the importance of preaching, which was falling more and more into disuse, the priests contenting themselves with going through the ritual. But these movements bore no fruit. The spirit of slumber fell more and more heavily upon the clergy, till bishops and ecclesiastical gatherings ceased to urge the duty of preaching, and when here and there attempts were made to revive an interest in the Scriptures, they smelled so rankly of heresy that they were swiftly suppressed.

We have to note rather a two-fold movement in which the awakening spirit of the Western Church began to manifest itself. The first of these was the great scholastic movement which laid the foundation of the Universities and the educational institutions which have done so much for our own and previous times. It carried education outside the Church and opened a sphere where men, who were not necessarily ecclesiastics, might concern themselves with the study even of Theology. The scholastics have been decried, not altogether without cause, as we shall immediately see; but it ought ever to be remembered to their praise that they laid the foundations of some of our dearest institutions, and that they aroused the slumbering and besotted intellect of Europe to ponder the deepest questions that concern humanity. Victor Cousin* has said that, from the efforts of the scholasticism of the middle ages, "little by little, arose a more methodic and more regular system of instruction in the cloisters; then the universities; finally, a thousand systems;" and adds that if we were to examine the scholastic philosophy it is probable that "we should be so sur-

* *Lectures on the History of Modern Philosophy* (T. & T. Clarke), Vol. i., p. 38.

prised to comprehend it and to find it very ingenious that we should pass at once to admiration."

The name originated in the schools, or *scolae*, instituted by Charlemagne; and the movement endured for nine centuries, from the eighth to the seventeenth. It passed through three distinct phases. There was first of all absolute subordination of philosophy to theology. "The masters of scholasticism did little else than comment on that beautiful expression of one of them: 'There are not two studies, one of philosophy and the other of religion; true philosophy is true religion, and true religion is true philosophy.'"*

The second period began with the opening of the 13th century. Till then European scholars had possessed only the *Organum* of Aristotle. But the Arabs, who in the seventh century swept over the Grecian Empire, sat by and bye at the feet of those whom they had conquered, and drank in the famed learning of the Greeks. The works of Aristotle were translated into Arabic and were carried over into Spain, one of the European conquests of the Mahommedans. Christians occasionally studied in the Arabic schools of Spain, but the communication to the scholars of Europe of a wider knowledge of the works of the old Greek philosopher was due most of all to the Jews. They translated the works of the Arabic philosopher into Hebrew. These translations were again rendered into Latin. The new thought was deeply impregnated with doubt that was equally

* *Ibid*, Vol. ii., pp. 13, 14.

new. This led to the second phase of scholasticism, which was distinguished by the labours of such men as Thomas Aquinas and Duns Scotus. This second stage was an alliance between Scholasticism and Theology. The philosophers come to the aid of the threatened beliefs; scholasticism was now the advocate and defender of theology.

The third period witnessed the separation of the two sciences. The scholastic theology appealed to the Fathers and the Scriptures. The scholastic *philosophy*, on the other hand, in its attempt to prove the doctrines true, rested more and more on "reason." The camps, though allied, became increasingly distinct. The only thing that was now needed to form a separation was for philosophy to interest itself less in theology and more in the investigation of nature and of mind. The latter studies grew more absorbing and, as the ages rolled on, the two sciences —like men, who when children, roamed and played together and who, in boyhood, were still friends that looked forward to an eternal union—were sundered more and more widely, till the old ties were utterly broken and the old relationship was completely forgotten.

The second period, that of the defence of theology, was ushered in by the necessities of the time. The Arabic philosophy might have been comparatively powerless in itself; but the crusades had given a sudden and startling enlargement to the thought of Europe. Men of every nationality came into contact with people of other creeds, and discovered that these were not the incarnate demons which they had imagined them to be. The very fact that Christianity was then broadly challenged by multitudes who held another faith, shook the confidence of that ignorant and unthinking superstition which went under the name of Christian belief. As usual, the unbelief of the time found some advocates in the ranks of "Christian" learning. The University of Paris became the stronghold of the new unbelief. About the year 1200, Simon of Tournay went so far as to bracket Moses, Christ, and Mahomet as "the three Impostors" who had deceived the Jews, the Christians, and the Mahommedans. The contest was long maintained. Seventy years afterwards we find the Archbishop of Paris proceeding against the University because, among other opinions, the following were taught: "God is not triune; God cannot beget one similar to himself; a future resurrection is not to be admitted; there is only one intellect numerically; the world is eternal; there are fables and false statements in the Christian religion, just as in other religions."* The attempt was made to justify the holding and even the teaching of these views by a plea, the ingenuity of which was worthy of the schoolmen. They were said to be theologically false, but at the same time philosophically true; so that, as a philosopher, a man could be a deist, a pantheist, or an atheist, and at the same time be, in his capacity as a theologian, an orthodox believer! Fortunately, the distinction could not impose upon

* *History of the Christian Philosophy of Religion*, Pünger, 40. 41.

## The Pre-Reformation Period.

those who were concerned for the maintenance of Christian belief. Both the scholastics and the Church fought these errors till they were suppressed, and the nations were saved from having the blackness of atheism added to the darkness of the middle ages.

Another, and nobler, feature of the middle ages is its mysticism. The heart played its part as well as the intellect in the thought and life of the time. There were men who turned away wearily from the schools and from the writings of "the irrefragable," "the seraphical," "the angelical," and the other doctors. They could not feed on the husks of metaphysical abstractions, nor find delight in a wilderness of dry definitions and endless distinctions. Those clattering logic mills ground nothing which they could fashion into bread for men's souls. But they, in their turn, fled to that which cannot save. The schoolmen trusted in logic, and imagined that, by laying down a pathway of correct definitions and well-tested conclusions, they would at last come out into the heavenly light. The mystics believed, in their turn, that, by entering into themselves, they could pass out by the door of an inner quietness, right into the fulness of the life of God. In both systems it was unknown, or forgotten, that God Himself has opened up a way, and that, besides it, there is no other. It is only where we find the mystics beholding Christ and walking in the light of the Scripture, that we are instructed and helped.

There can be no doubt, however, that by their testimony to the fact that neither the schools nor the

Church of the time could satisfy man's need, the mystics prepared the way for the Reformation. This is seen, for example, in Richard, of St. Victor, in the twelfth century. "Loud and indignant are his rebukes of the empty disputation of the mere schoolman—of the avarice and ambition of the prelate. His soul is grieved that there should be men who blush more for a false quantity than for a sin, and stand more in awe of Priscian than of Christ. Alas! he exclaims, how many come to the cloister to seek Christ, and find, lying in that sepulchre, only the linen clothes of your formalism! How many mask their cowardice under the name of love, and let every abuse run riot on the plea of peace! How many call their hatred of individuals hatred of iniquity, and think to be righteous chiefly by mere outcry against other men's sins!"\*

These are words which bring us to this man's feet. But when he ceases to condemn and would lead us away from it all into the sinless life, we lose our guide in a mist of words. Take the following: "The ark of the covenant represents the grace of contemplation. The kinds of contemplation are six, each distinct from the rest. Two of them are exercised with regard to visible creatures, two are occupied with invisible; the two last with what is divine. The first four are represented in the ark, the two others are set forth in the figures of the cherubim. . . . In the consideration of *form* and *matter*, our knowledge avails a full cubit. (It is equivalent to a cubit when

---

\* Vaughan's *Hours with the Mystics*, Vol. i., 163.

complete). But our knowledge of the *nature* of things is only partial. For this part, therefore, we reckon only half a cubit. Accordingly, the length of the ark is two cubits and a half." According to him there are "three heavens within the mind." In the first are contained the images of all things visible; in the second lie the definitions and principles of things seen, the investigations made concerning things unseen; in the third are contemplations of things divine, beheld as they truly are—a sun that knows no going down—and there, and there alone, the kingdom of God within us in its glory." *

There were occasionally moral as well as mental aberrations bound up with mysticism. The long laboured and fruitless attempts, both within and without Christianity, to find a way to God, sometimes by the reason and sometimes by the soul, have written this truth along the ages in sighs, and tears, and groanings which cannot be uttered, that, if we are ever to find a way to God, *God* must make it by coming to us. The Church had allowed that way, the path of revelation, the teaching of the Word, to be overrun with grass and weeds, and thorns and briars, till it was hidden from men's sight. There will be no hope for the ages till, in the full acceptance and understanding of the Scriptures, men see Him who alone is the Way, the Truth, and the Life, and behold Him in that mirror of the Scriptures from which alone, of all things earthly, the radiance of His glory streams.

* *Ibid*, Vol. i., 373, 374.

## CHAPTER III.

### THE REFORMATION.

SCHOLASTICISM was an attempt to climb into heaven by laborious intellectual effort. Tier upon tier of this new Tower of Babel was reared by the giants of the middle ages—with the old result. Heaven was not entered, and men were sundered. Mysticism, on the other hand, tried to make, or find, heaven in the heart. It is true that the kingdom of heaven is "within" us; but it is so only when God is there revealed. There must be light first before there is peace, and only in *His* light can we see light.

To enter heaven's gate, men needed the key at whose touch the bolts would fly, the solid leaves roll back, and the seekers after salvation pass from the thick darkness into the glad, inspiring light of God. Some found it early. They made others sharers in their joy; and then came the time when the kingdom of heaven once more rushed in violently and the violent possessed themselves of it. This is indeed *the* lesson of the Reformation, and one which ought to be well pondered by the present time. The Bible, and the Bible alone, delivered the nations, led out the Church, gave it light, freedom, spiritual beauty, manly strength, and temporal prosperity. Dorner, in his *History of Protestant Theology*, has seen this clearly, though he did not then fully note, as he might have done, and as he afterwards did, its teaching for the present hour. "Temperate natures," he says, "of a practical and empiric turn, far removed from all speculation and religious originality, but honest, simple, and candid, were selected to be the first to re-establish the connection with historical primitive Christianity, and to diffuse the taste for it. The first in this rank are the *Waldensians*, so well-informed in the Bible, that their simple teachers had large portions of the Holy Scriptures verbally committed to memory. Their services of worship were a kind of Bible lecture (with short devotional exercises), aided by translations into the native dialect; and whoever was informed in the Bible considered himself entitled to preach. The laity went forth, as of old the Christians in the Apostolic age, to preach the Word of God in the popular tongue."* They had learned the secret, "The entrance of thy words giveth light." Had that Word been to them the human, blurred, inaccurate, and misleading thing men seem now to think it—had it been to them less than the very Word of God to be received in its every particular with adoring and grateful joy, their work had never been done, and the darkness would still rest on the nations and gross darkness still cover the people.

---

* Vol. i., pp. 63, 64.

The Waldenses were true to their mission. "Wherever they went," says Dr. George P. Fisher, "they kindled among the people the desire to read the Bible."* They overran the south of France and north of Italy. Before the end of the twelfth century they had also established themselves in Holland. There are traces, too, of a Waldensian settlement in Kent towards the end of the century, which paid rent to the see of Canterbury. There were also "Waldensian preachers and followers in England as early as the middle of the twelfth century."† The same prominence was given to the Scriptures in the work of Wiclif, to which we in England owe so much. "Before everything else," writes Lechler, "Wiclif holds up the truth that the preaching of the Word of God is that function which subserves, in a degree quite peculiar to itself, the edification of the Church; and this is so, because the Word of God is a seed (Luke viii. 11). 'The seed is the Word of God.' In reflecting upon this truth, he is filled with wonder and exclaims, 'O marvellous power of the Divine Seed! which overpowers strong men in arms, softens hard hearts, and renews and changes into divine men, men who have been brutalized by sin, and departed infinitely from God. Obviously such a high morality could never be worked by the word of a priest, if the Spirit of Life and the Eternal Word did not above all things else work with it.'"‡

---

\* *The Reformation*, p. 57.   † *History of Protestant Theology*—Dorner, i. 437.
‡ *John Wiclif and his English Precursors*, Vol. i., 285.

## The Reformation. 119

So large a place did this testimony to the Bible occupy in Wiclif's work, that Lechler recurs to it more than once. "God's Word," he says, summing up the Reformer's teaching, " should be preached, for God's Word is the bread of souls, the indispensable, wholesome bread; and therefore, he thinks, to feed the flock, in a spiritual sense, without Bible truth, is the same thing as if one were to prepare for another a bodily meal without bread. . . . . If the prophets of the Old Testament preface their prophecies with "Thus saith the Lord," and if the Apostles proclaim the Word of the Lord, so must we too preach God's Word and proclaim the Gospel according to the Scriptures."* It was not enough for Wiclif to follow personally his own counsel and to preach the Word of God. He could not be everywhere; and yet, in every place, as well as in Oxford and at Lutterworth, men needed this ministry. He therefore multiplied himself, so to say, by instructing and sending forth men taught in the Word to sow it broadcast over the land. The towns of Oxford and of Leicester were the two centres of this new and (for the times) strange movement. "One of the first who appeared as an itinerant preacher was John of Aston. He was followed, also in Wiclif's lifetime, by William Thorpe . . . and others. These men went forth in long garments of coarse red woollen cloth, bare-foot and staff in hand, in order to represent themselves as pilgrims, and their wayfaring as a kind of pilgrimage; their coarse

---
\* *Ibid*, Vol. i., 291.

woollen dress being a symbol of their poverty and toil ('poor priests'). Thus they wandered from village to village, from town to town, and from county to county, without stop or rest, preaching, teaching, warning, wherever they could find willing hearers; sometimes in church or chapel, wherever any such stood open for prayer and quiet devotion; sometimes in the churchyard when they found the church itself closed; and sometimes in the public street or market place."*

Their work was like their Master's. "Their sermons were, before everything else, full of Bible truth . . . They had learned to regard as their chief duty 'the faithful scattering of the seed of God's Word.'"† To have lifted his own testimony and to have multiplied it in the work of these like-minded men was much, but Wiclif saw that more might and must be done. Men must be put in possession of the Bible itself. He therefore set himself to the work of translation; and he laid the foundation of the England that was to be, in the first complete version of the Bible ever written in the English tongue. The enemies of the Gospel were alarmed and appalled by this last effort. Knighton, a chronicler, writing before the year 1400, complains heavily that, while "Christ gave the Gospel, not to the Church, but only to the clergy and doctors of the Church, to be, by them, communicated to the weaker sort and the laity, at need, Wiclif has rendered the Gospel from the Latin into English, and through him it has

---

\* *Ibid*, Vol. i., 310.   † *Ibid*.

become the affair of the common people, and more accessible to the laity, including even the women who are able to read, than it used to be to the well-educated clergy. The pearl is now thrown 'before swine and trodden under foot,'"* The Archbishop of Canterbury and his bishops petitioned the Pope in 1412 to condemn Wiclif, and instanced, as the crowning effort of his "malice," his "having devised the plan of a translation of the Holy Scriptures into the mother tongue."† The chronicler and the Archbishop were not mistaken. The giving of the Bible to the people was the writing on the palace wall. The days of Popery in England were numbered. From the pages of that opened Bible light has sprung which has swept away the darkness that no other agency could dispel.

The same feature marked the movement of John Huss and his followers in Bohemia. Though overpowered for a time, the movement, fed by increasing knowledge of the Word of God, lived on. The Hussites were brought by this Scriptural bond into fellowship with the Bohemian Waldenses, and in 1457 were known as "The Brethren of the law of Christ," better known to us as "The Moravian Brethren." "The Holy Scripture continued always," says Dorner, "to be their ultimate authority; there they strengthened their reformatory power, which had already manifested itself even in the matter of organisation, in the regulation of congregations under elders, and in the connection of the congrega-

---

* *Ibid*, Vol. i., p. 332. † p. 333.

tions by bishops. This Biblical movement—which spread, especially during the fourteenth and fifteenth centuries, from the south of France and Piedmont, through Switzerland, along the Rhine, to the Netherlands and England, and in its eastern current over Bohemia, Poland, and Moravia—contributed mightily to the diffusion throughout Christendom of the principle—as an incontrovertible and operative axiom—that the Church must submit to be tested by the Holy Scriptures."* In other words, the growing knowledge of the Bible was the impelling motive as it was the purifying force and recreating energy of the Reformation.

This unique power of the Bible was universally recognised by "the Reformers before the Reformation." We find them everywhere labouring to make the people acquainted with the Scriptures, and those who have investigated the matter have been astonished at the proofs of their activity. Their "translations were much more numerous than is generally supposed. Turning first to Germany, we find that in the beginning of the fifteenth century there certainly existed a complete translation of the Bible into German, and that within the last half of the fifteenth century and the early years of the sixteenth, previously to Luther, there were no fewer than at least fourteen different editions of the complete Bible published in High German, and four in Low German. In France there appeared within the latter half of the fifteenth century two editions of the

---

* *History of Protestant Theology*, Vol. i., 68.

New Testament (Lyons, 1477), and then a complete Bible (that of De Rely, published in Paris), which went through at least twelve editions. In England, Wiclif's translation had appeared in the end of the fourteenth century, but had of course been circulated only in manuscript copies. In Italy again, two translations were published in the period referred to, the one known only by its title, the other that of Di Malherbi (1471), who in his introduction speaks of older translations. Vernacular translations of the Bible appeared also, within the same time, in Bohemia, Poland, and Holland. But to have a just conception of the extent and influence of this movement, it must still further be remembered that, in addition to these translations of the complete Bible, there were in all the countries that have been named, and also in Spain and Denmark, even more numerous translations into the vernacular of larger or smaller portions of the Scripture."\*

Two inventions came to swell this growing tide of Bible light. Paper had been invented by the Chinese before the close of the first century of our era; but it was many centuries before the invention crept along to the lands of the West. It was introduced at Samarcand about the year 649. Fifty-six years afterward, that city was conquered by the Arabs, and the invention was then carried by one Joseph Amrou to Mecca, his native city. Cotton was used in the manufacture, and the first paper of Arabian manufacture was produced by him in 706. It was

---

\**Ibid*, note F., Vol. i., 441.

then the heyday of Arab literary activity, and the invention spread swiftly through their rapidly increasing territory, and specially in Spain. But although the invention was brought so near, it did not penetrate into Christendom till the end of the thirteenth century, when paper mills were established in the Christian states of Spain by Alfonso X., King of Castile. In the fourteenth century it passed into Italy.

These halting steps seem as if the discovery were loitering to meet another which was to stir up European society to its lowest depths, and to change the face of the world. Printing from blocks was in use in the beginning of the fifteenth century. But modern printing only really began when Gutenberg invented cut metal types in 1444. A further advance was made by Schoeffer's invention, in 1452, of types cast from cut matrices. The Book of Psalms was printed by Faust and Schoeffer in 1457, and by 1471 Caxton's press was at work at Westminster. Everything was now prepared for that harvest of effort and prayer and testimony and suffering which we call the Reformation. Luther reaped most largely in the great harvest field, and he was prepared for successful toil in the same way as those who had ploughed and sowed in pain and tears. The Word of God laid hold of him. Its teaching was the thread which led him out of the labyrinth of Romish superstition and idolatry. In the early days, when he had no suspicion of what lay before him, he was a diligent student and expounder of the Scripture.

## The Reformation.

The joy and power which he himself experienced pointed the way for others. He "recommended everywhere the reading of the Bible, and pointed back from the schoolmen, with their human precepts, to the original Gospel."\*
When he came out into the light, there was nothing earthly in which he so rested or in which he so rejoiced as in the Bible. All that is now urged against the Bible was urged then, and objections were added of which we hear little to-day. In the face of these Luther answered with that impatient fervour so characteristic of him. He used expressions which sometimes seem as if he admitted the contradictions and inaccuracies that were urged by his opponents. But his true position is shown in the following. "If anyone," he says, "should press thee with expressions which speak of works, and which thou canst not bring into concord with the others, thou ought'st to say, since Christ Himself is the treasure whereby I am bought and redeemed, I care not the slightest jot for all the expressions of Scripture, to set up by them the righteousness of works and to lay down the righteousness of faith. For I have on my side the Master and the Lord of Scripture, to whom I will keep, and I know He will not lie nor deceive me,—and let them go on in their hostile cry, that the Scriptures contradict themselves! *At the same time it is impossible that the Scriptures should contradict themselves, save only that the unintelligent, coarse, and hardened hypocrites imagine it.*"†

---

\* *Dorner*, Vol. i., p. 86.    † *Ibid*, Vol. i., pp. 244, 245.

That declaration is definite enough, and ought to set at rest all questioning as to Luther's belief regarding Inspiration and the Bible: "It is *impossible* that the Scriptures should contradict themselves" is a confession of faith about which there is no ambiguity. Any other judgment regarding the Bible would be not only a contradiction of the Reformer's entire belief and work, but also an unsaying of some of the most explicit testimonies ever penned or uttered. In discussing the Christian's freedom he is careful to say that he is not free *from* the Word, but free *in* the Word. "There is nothing else," he says, "in heaven or in earth, wherein the soul is pious and free, than the holy Gospel, *the Word of God* concerning Christ. The soul can want everything but the Word of God; without this nothing else will help it; in the Word it has enough food, joy, peace, light, skill, righteousness, wisdom, freedom, and everything good." Again, "In the Word thou shouldest hear nothing else than thy God speaking to thee."\*

Turn where we may during the Reformation period, we find the Scriptures doing the same work and evoking the same testimony. Not only is the Bible, and the Bible alone, the religion of Protestants: it is also the cause of their existence. Apart from the Bible there might have been revolt against a heathenised Christianity, but it would have been the revolt of the flesh. It was through the Bible alone that men got back into the light and freedom of the Apostolic times. It was the Bible which led

---

\* *Ibid*, Vol. i., p. 107.

Zwingle into rest; and "hence," says Dorner, "he assigns to the Scriptures a unique position." "The Scriptures," writes the Swiss Reformer, "come from God, not from man; and even that God who enlightens will give thee to understand that the speech comes from God. The Word of God is to be held in the highest honour, and to no word is such faith to be accorded as to it. It cannot fail, it is bright, it teaches itself, it discloses itself, and illumines the soul with all salvation and grace, comforts it in God, humbles it, so that it loses and even forfeits itself and embraces God into itself."\*

Calvin was about to enter into the Romish priesthood, when he was led to study the Bible, through the influence of a relative, "Peter Robert Olivet, the person," says Beza (in his brief life of Calvin), "to whom the Churches of France owe that translation of the Old Testament from the Hebrew which was printed at Neufchatel." The light he received not only led him to give up the idea of taking orders, but also to cease attendance upon the public services of the Church. His testimony regarding the Bible is unmarred by a single hasty utterance. In a letter to Cardinal Sadolet he reminds him of the transformation which the study of the Scriptures had even then effected. He says, "I would have you again and again consider with what reason you can charge it upon our people, as a fault, that they have studied to explain the Scriptures. For you are aware that by this study they have thrown such light upon the

---

\* *Ibid*, Vol. i., p. 287.

Word of God that, in this respect, even envy herself is ashamed to defraud them of all praise."

"You are just as uncandid when you aver that we have seduced the people by thorny and subtle questions, and so enticed them by that philosophy of which Paul bids Christians beware. What? Do you remember what kind of time it was when our Reformers appeared, and what kind of doctrine candidates for the ministry learned in the schools? You yourself know that it was mere sophistry, and sophistry so twisted, involved, tortuous, puzzling, that scholastic theology might well be described as a species of secret magic. The denser the darkness in which anyone shrouded a subject, the more he puzzled himself and others with preposterous riddles, the greater his fame for acumen and learning. When those who had been formed in that forge wished to carry the fruit of their learning to the people, with what skill, I ask, did they edify the Church?

"Not to go over every point, what sermons in Europe then exhibited that simplicity with which Paul wishes a Christian people to be always occupied? Nay, what one sermon was there from which old wives might not carry off more whimsies than they could devise at their own fireside in a month? For, as sermons were then usually divided, the first half was devoted to those misty questions of the schools which might astonish the rude populace, while the second contained sweet stories, or not unamusing speculations, by which the hearers might be kept on the alert. Only a few expressions were thrown in from the Word of God, that by their majesty they might procure credit for these frivolities. But as soon as our Reformers raised the standard, all these absurdities, in one moment, disappeared from amongst us."*

Calvin's appreciation of the Scriptures is in conformity with his estimate of the startling change which the revived knowledge of them had made even in the preaching of the Romish Church. In a confession of faith drawn up by him for the Reformed Churches of France, he speaks of the Bible as that "on which alone our faith should be founded, as there is no other witness proper and competent to decide what the majesty of God is, but God Himself."† In another "Brief Confession of Faith" he similarly speaks of "the sacred Scriptures, to which nothing can, without criminality, be added, from which nothing can be taken away."‡ What could be more explicit, and what doctrine of Inspiration ever rose higher than the following, taken from this Reformer's comment on 2 Timothy iii. 16? "This is a principle which distinguishes our religion from all others, that we know that God hath spoken to us, and are fully convinced that the prophets did not speak at their own suggestion, but that, being organs of the Holy Spirit, they only uttered what they had been commissioned from heaven to declare. Whoever, then, wishes to profit in the Scriptures, let him, first of all, lay this down as a settled point, that

---

\* *Calvin's Tracts* (Calvin Translation Society), Vol. i., pp. 39, 40.
† Vol. ii., p. 141.   ‡ p. 133.

the Law and the Prophets are not a doctrine delivered according to the will and pleasure of men, but dictated by the Holy Spirit. . . . This is the first clause (of the text) that *we owe to the Scripture the same reverence which we owe to God; because it has proceeded from Him alone, and has nothing belonging to man mixed with it.*"

Wherever we look over the wide field of Reforming activity we find the same overpowering conviction of the miraculousness of Scripture, the same rejoicing in its teaching, and the same zealous haste to make the people acquainted with it. William Tyndale, to whom we owe our English Bible, said to a priestly opponent: "If God spare my life I will cause a boy that driveth the plough shall know more of the Scripture than thou dost." And God granted him his heart's desire; his life was sacred till that work was done. Poor artisans went before priest, and judge, and king, armed with no other weapon, and came out of the conflict more assured than ever that there was none like unto it. The Church of the Reformation sprang from the Scripture, and was wise enough to know, and loyal enough to acknowledge that, in the fullest acceptance of it as the Word, not of man, but of God, lay its strength and its life.

## CHAPTER IV.

### Decay and Doubt.

THE thirty years of peace which succeeded the Peace of Utrecht (1714), was the most prosperous season that England had ever experienced, and the progression, though slow, being uniform, the reign of George II. might not disadvantageously be compared for the real happiness of the community with that more brilliant, but uncertain and oscillatory condition which has ensued. A labourer's wages have never for many ages commanded so large a portion of subsistence as in this part of the 18th century.' (Hallam, *Constitutional History*, ii. 4-64),

"This is the aspect which that period of history wears to the political philosopher. The historian of moral and religious progress, on the other hand, is under the necessity of depicting the same period one of decay of religion, licentiousness of morals, public corruption, profaneness of language—a day of 'rebuke and blasphemy.' Even those who look with suspicion on the contemporary complaints from the Jacobite clergy of 'decay of religion' will not hesitate to say that it was an age destitute of depth or earnestness; an age whose poetry was without romance, whose philosophy was without insight, and whose public men were without character; an age of 'light without love,' whose 'very merits were of the earth, earthy.' In this estimate, the followers of Mill and Carlyle will agree with those of Dr. Newman."

With these words Mr. Mark Pattison begins his paper on *Tendencies of Religious Thought in England, 1868-1750*, published in *Essays and Reviews*. We shall, by-and-bye, have painful evidence of their truth; but they have a bearing which Mr. Pattison did not sufficiently consider. They explain what seems otherwise so mysterious in these invasions of unbelief, and show especially from what source "the Higher Criticism" has sprung. We, in England, are only reaping what we ourselves have sown. We cast our scepticism into the thought of Germany, and Germany now repays the service by scattering the seeds of her unbelief over the wide field of English-speaking Christendom.

The Revival of learning in Italy sprang up and strengthened entirely apart from Christianity. The classics, in the perusal of which the "Humanists," as they were called, revelled, led them into practical heathenism. The effects of this culture were painfully evident in the Reformation era. Roman priests, it is said, made a jest of the mass and blasphemed at the altar. The Pope, Leo X., boasted of a learning and culture in which there was nothing that could be called specifically Christian. His secretary, Cardinal Bembo, is said to have advised one friend "not to read St. Paul's Epistles for fear of spoiling his style;" and to have said to another, who had written a commentary on the Epistle to the Romans: "Let those fooleries alone; they don't become a grave man."\* A curious illustration of how this unbelief had percolated down into the lower strata of society, is afforded by the trouble and dismay caused by certain midwives who, in daring blasphemy, had baptized children in the name of the devil.

The same evil threatened at one time to lay its defiling touch upon the Reformation. It seems to have been hard for Italian Protestants to dissociate themselves entirely from the free-thinking so intimately bound up with the learning of their country. The Churches of the Reformers, on the border lands of Italy and Switzerland, had more than one unpleasant struggle with Italian scepticism; but the faith of the Reformation was too Scriptural to be entangled with unbelief, and too full of whole-hearted devotion to endure its presence. The tempter was before his time.

Much had to be done before his opportunity came. While it was broad day-light, and while men were about, and were anxiously watching, the tares could not be sown among the wheat. I have already spoken of the law which rules in all changes of church life and doctrine. They are the reproduction

---

\* *Bayle's Dictionary*—article "Bembus."

in the Church of life and opinion in the world around it. The Church must be first subjected to a long protracted siege, before there is any hope of its capture. But even then the hopes that are apparently best founded will be disappointed, unless one thing is done. While the Church's own life is full, there is a repellent power about it which dams back the mightiest tides of worldly influence. So long as the Church is filled with God, the world can find no place in it. It is only when the Church's own life is low, that the world-life has its opportunity. Then the repellent power dies down, the surrounding tide flows in, and the truth is mixed with error, and may even be finally displaced by it.

The light had first, therefore, to be darkened, and the vigilance to be dulled, before the triumph of evil could be secured. This preliminary work was skilfully done. In every spot where the Reformation sprang up, the politician either selfishly marked his opportunity, or mistakenly imagined that his services were wanted. In England the new movement fell in with the requirements of Henry VIII. So much of the force of the English Reformation was utilized as was needed to turn his mill; the rest was imperiously swept aside. Elizabeth's worldly common-sense, and her sage councillors' caution, sat upon the movement and sternly frowned down whatever refused to square itself with the imagined necessities of Church and State. But the movement lived on among the people; and, in a subsequent age, forgetting that its weapons were not carnal, swept

Laud and his master aside, and burst forth in rebellion and blood.  It was a swift and brilliant, but dearly purchased, triumph.  The Ironsides, whom we admire as soldiers, would have inspired and hallowed us as martyrs.

The self-inflicted defeat of those wondrous victories was soon apparent.  There were division and alienation in the camp of the victors.  Roots of bitterness, springing up, troubled them, and thereby many were defiled.  The house divided against itself had an end.  The Rebellion was followed by the Restoration, when our nobility and their followers, reeking with the abominations that clung to them from their bath in French filthiness, filled society and literature with a viciousness that gloried in its shame.  The re-instated Church trampled under foot the sects by which it had been temporarily displaced, and put under a ban godly men whose teaching and life would have sown the seed of a purer and mightier Church than England had yet seen.  The Established Church was also distressed by fears which repressed her own vitality.  "The majority of the clergy," writes Abbey and Overton, "shrank, not unnaturally, from anything which might seem in any degree to assimilate them either to Romanism or Puritanism.  Recent experience had shown the danger of both.  The violent reaction against the reign of the Saints continued, with more or less force, almost to the end of the eighteenth century, . . . fervency and vigour in preaching were regarded with suspicion, as bordering too nearly upon the habits of the hated

Puritans of the Commonwealth, and a dry, dull, moralising style of sermon was the result."\*

Matters were not improved by the Revolution of 1688. One eloquent indication of the decay of religious sensibility, and even of ordinary conscientiousness, is the heaping together of various Church appointments to enrich a few favoured individuals. The majority of Churchmen had apparently ceased to think of the duties connected with their sacred calling, and could see nothing in it but a good chance of attaining distinction and amassing wealth. When Bishop Newton, the author of the *Dissertation on the Prophecies*, was promoted to the Bishopric of Bristol, he plaintively remarks that "he was obliged to give up the prebend of Westminster, the precentorship of York, the lecturership of St. George's, Hanover Square, and the genteel office of sub-almoner." Bishop "Hoadly held the see of Bangor for six years, apparently without ever seeing the diocese in his life. . . . Bishop Watson of Llandaff gives a most heartless account of his non-residence. 'Having,' he tells us, 'no place of residence in my diocese, I turned my attention to the improvement of land. I thought the improvement of a man's fortune by cultivating the earth was the most useful and honourable way of providing for a family. I have now been several years occupied as an improver of land and planter of trees." The same Bishop gives us a most extraordinary description of the sources from whence his

---

\* *The English Church in the Eighteenth Century*, Vol. ii., p. 5, 6.

clerical income was derived. "The provision of £2,000 a year," he says, "which I possess from the Church, arises from the tithes of two churches in Shropshire, two in Leicestershire, two in my diocese, three in Huntingdonshire, in all of which I have resident curates, of five more appropriations to the Bishopric, and two more in the Isle of Ely as appropriations to the archdeaconry of Ely."\*

Appointments were made with the most reckless disregard of fitness. Bishop Watson "was appointed to two professorships at Cambridge when, by his own confession, he was totally unqualified for performing the duties of either. In 1764, when he was only twenty-seven years of age, he 'was unanimously elected by the Senate, assembled in full congregation, Professor of Chemistry.' 'At the time this honour was conferred upon me,' he tells us with charming frankness, 'I knew nothing at all of Chemistry, had never read a syllable on the subject, nor seen a single experiment in it.'"† It is almost impossible to imagine that men could go further in their contempt of evident duty. The favouritism of "the Senate assembled in full congregation" was equalled by the scramble of the bishops and other dignitaries for court favour and court gifts. It mattered nothing to these successors of the apostles that a Lord Chancellor was living in open sin. His house was frequented by bishops and "by ecclesiastics of all degrees who celebrated the orthodoxy of the head of the law, and his love of the Established Church."

---
\* *Ibid.* Vol. ii., pp. 11, 12.   † *Ibid.* p. 37

The religious teaching could not possibly be higher than the life. Sir William Blackstone, the famous lawyer, had the curiosity, early in the reign of George III., to go from church to church, and hear every clergyman of note in London. He says that he did not hear a single discourse which had more of Christianity in it than the writings of Cicero, and that it would have been impossible for him to discover, from what he heard, whether the preacher were a follower of Confucius, of Mahomet, or of Christ."* Deep poverty was the lot of a large section of the clergy, and this, combined with the absence of vital Christianity, led to immorality and to startling scandals.

It had fared no better with the Nonconformists than with the Established Church. "We might naturally have expected," say the authors I have already largely quoted, "to find the zeal which was lacking in the National Church showing itself in other Christian bodies. But we find nothing of the sort. The torpor which had overtaken our Church, extended itself to all forms of Christianity. Edward Calamy, a Nonconformist, lamented in 1730 that 'a real decay of serious religion, both in the Church *and out of it*, was very visible.' Dr. Watts declares that in his day 'there was a *general* decay of vital religion in the hearts and lives of men'... In 1712, Defoe considered 'Dissenters' interests to be in a declining state, not so much as regarded their wealth and numbers, as the qualifications of their ministers,

---
* *Ibid*, p. 37.

the decay of piety, and the abandonment of their political friends.' . . It is a fact patent to all students of the period, that the moral and religious stagnation of the times extended to all religious bodies outside as well as inside the National Church. The most intellectually active part of Dissent was drifting gradually into Socinianism and Unitarianism."*

To this I may add the following Nonconformist testimony. Herbert Skeats, in his *History of the Free Churches of England*, says: "If, as was undoubtedly the case, breadth of thought and charity of sentiment increased, and, to some extent, settled into a mental habit of the nation, religious activity did not increase. *The Churches were characterised by a cold indifferentism.* The zeal of Puritanism was almost as unknown as it was unimitated."† It was the "Sardis" period, not only at home, but also (as we shall see) abroad. The Churches of the Reformation had a name that they "lived," and were dead. They boasted of their life, even where there was not enough of it either to lay hold upon God or to work for God. There were, indeed, "a few names even in Sardis which" had "not defiled their garments." There were men like Watts and Doddridge in the Dissenting Communions, and Newton, Venn, Cecil, and Romaine in the Established Church. In Church and in Dissent there were those who knew and who preached the truth that saves. But the darkness over the land was dense. It took John Wesley years, even with the intensest earnestness, to get into the

---

* *Ibid*, p. 51.  † (Edition, 1891), p. 250.

light, and to know and preach that Gospel of Christ which is the power of God unto salvation to every one that believeth.

This was the time, therefore, when the life of the age might find entrance into the life of the Church. The fulness of spiritual life and its repellent power were gone. It was an age of shallow philosophy and of proud, self-conscious science. Its literature was marked by a self-conceited simper, as with Addison; or by an enjoyment of sonorous sound and finely balanced antithesis, as with Johnson. Literary men were artists, not thinkers. Sir Isaac Newton was as much an astonishment for his unexampled modesty as for his marvellous discoveries. Such an age felt itself seated on the pinnacle of knowledge, and saw all antiquity ranged beneath it and covered with deepening darkness. It was a time, consequently, for the re-opening of all questions, and for the re-adjustment, in the then "fuller light," of all past beliefs! The early English Deists, Lord Herbert and Hobbes, felt themselves on dangerous ground, and their work was marked by a corresponding timidity. Their successors of the eighteenth century were bolder; for they felt that the Church of the time was better prepared.

The attack commenced with John Toland, whose career began in 1670 and ended in 1722. The Israelites, according to him, were Egyptians, and Moses was an Egyptian priest or king. The pillar of cloud and fire was an ordinary watch-fire raised upon a pole. He was followed by Anthony Collins,

## Decay and Doubt. 141

an Essex squire, and a friend of John Locke. He may be said to be the father of the so-called "Freethinkers." His work was mainly an attack upon Prophecy, and was distinguished by a denial of the Book of Daniel, and an assignment of it to the times of the Maccabees. Thomas Woolston, a fellow of Sidney College, Cambridge, entered the field about the same time, and directed *his* attack against the miracles of our Lord. They were denounced as incredible and absurd. Matthew Tindal, a fellow of All-Souls, Oxford, attempted to sweep away the entire structure of revealed religion. A revelation, according to him, was impossible, and any attempted proof of it was an absurdity. The light of nature was quite sufficient, and nothing could either exceed it or correct it. Thomas Chubb, a self-taught glove-maker of Salisbury, attacked the morality of the New Testament. In his last works, published after his death, he expresses his disbelief in prayer and in the immortality of the soul.

The attack was reinforced by the scepticism of Hume and Gibbon; but I must now draw attention to one who is only a name to-day but whose transmitted influence is touching us at this very hour. Henry St. John, better known as Lord Bolingbroke, was one of the most richly endowed of mortals. "Lord Bolingbroke," says Aaron Hill, "was the finest gentleman I ever saw." To a tall, commanding figure, and to a face of classic beauty, he added a grace and dignity that made the phrase "to make St. John more polite" a temporary substitute for

Shakespeare's "to gild the most refinèd gold." He had a clear judgment, a vivid imagination, and a power of intense application. Chesterfield said: "He joined all the politeness, the manners, and the graces of a courtier, to the solidity of a statesman and the learning of a pedant." He excelled as an orator. "I would rather," said Pitt, "have a speech of Bolingbroke's than any of the lost treasures of antiquity."

But, with all these endowments, he made shipwreck of things temporal, and it need not astonish us if he succeeded no better in regard to things eternal. "The virtues which balance and control," says a biographer, "sobriety, moderation, consistency, had no part in his composition. His impetuosity and intemperance amounted to disease. To the end of his long life he was the slave not merely of every passion, but of every impulse; and what the capricious tyranny of emotion dictated, had the power of completely transforming him. He exhibited, by turns, the traits peculiar to the most exalted and to the most debased of our species." His attack on the Scripture partook of the inconsistency of his character. He contended, at one time, that man has no need of a revelation, and that none has ever been given. At another time, he maintained that a revelation had been given, and that it was to be found in the Gospels.

Bolingbroke, however, was one of the most mighty social forces of his time, and it is this circumstance that has perpetuated his influence.

Voltaire had made his acquaintance in Tourraine, where Bolingbroke had estates, and where the latter nursed Voltaire through an attack of small-pox in 1722. The result was a close friendship, which was deepened during the poet's visit to this country.* Voltaire was in his thirty-second year when he arrived in England, and was introduced to the society and the deistical literature of the time. Till then he had been only a poet and a satirist; but his English sojourn marked the beginning of a new era in his life and work. "In his own opinion," says Collins, "it was the turning point in his career. In the opinion of Condorcet, it was fraught with consequences of momentous importance to Europe and to humanity. . . . It penetrated his life. 'From that moment,' says Condorcet, 'Voltaire felt himself called to destroy all the prejudices which enslaved his country.'"† When he arrived in England, the deistical controversy was at its height, and was the theme of discussion with Bolingbroke and the society in which he moved. "Upwards of two years had passed since Anthony Collins had published his 'Discourse on the Grounds and Reasons of the Christian Religion.' No work of that kind had made so deep an impression on the public mind. It had been denounced from the pulpit; it had elicited numerous replies from the press. Other works of a similar kind succeeded, each in its turn aggravating the controversy. In 1727 appeared,

---

* Collins' *Bolingbroke, a Historical Study;* and *Voltaire in England* (Murray, 1886) pp. 7-9.  † *Ibid*, p. 227.

dedicated to the Bishop of London, the first of Woolston's 'Six Discourses on the Miracles of Christ,' a work which brought into the field the most distinguished ecclesiastics then living. We believe that Voltaire owed infinitely more to Bolingbroke than to all the other English deists put together, but how carefully he had followed the course of this controversy is obvious from the innumerable passages in his subsequent writings. Of Woolston, in particular, he always speaks with great respect."*

Voltaire's biographers are compelled to make the English sojourn the dividing line in his career. He left France a poet, litterateur, and wit; he returned the declared and determined foe of Christianity. From that time onward he was a man with a mission. "I am tired," he said, "of hearing them repeat that twelve men sufficed to establish Christianity: and I long to prove to them that it requires only one man to destroy it." His literary power never served him better than in this terrible attack upon Divine truth. He stimulated the infidelity of the French Encyclopædists, and carried the war into Germany. What he effected there, and how the seed he sowed sprang up into a harvest—seed from which is now being blown back upon our own soil—we shall see when we have taken one more glance at the fruits of Christian Decay in England.

---

* *Ibid.* pp. 261, 262.

## CHAPTER V.

### THE BEGINNINGS OF ENGLISH RATIONALISM.

BEFORE we leave our own country, to mark the fortunes of that battle between truth and error which was waged upon the Continent, we have to note some further effects of lowered Christian life on Christian thought in England. Error within the Church made answer to the error that was without. Arianism lifted its head in the Established Church, but was sharply dealt with, and was soon dislodged. William Whiston, Professor of Mathematics at Cambridge, was expelled from the University; and both he and Samuel Clarke were censured by Convocation. The Presbyterians of Ireland were equally alert. A minister, Thomas Emlyn, went from England to take the pastoral charge of an important Church in Dublin. His views regarding the Trinity were discovered by a member of the Church. The ministers of Dublin immediately met and forbade his preaching either in Ireland or in England. He became an avowed Unitarian.

But all the Nonconformists were not prepared to take the same uncompromising stand. James Pierce, minister of one of the four Presbyterian churches of Exeter, was suspected of holding Anti-Trinitarian views. The matter was carried from one conference of ministers to another, till it became the burning question of the day. An important meeting of the London Nonconformist Ministers was called to consider the matter. Calamy, Watts, and Neal declined to attend. This was enough to show that the firm front presented by the Dublin ministers was not to be expected from their London brethren. More than one hundred and fifty attended; but a proposal, that every minister present should subscribe the Article of the Church of England regarding the Trinity, was rejected by seventy-three to sixty-nine. The minority, which embraced nearly the whole of the Congregationalists and about half of the Baptists, seceded and met as a separate assembly. The majority excused their refusal to subscribe the required test, partly on the ground that by doing so they would have been taking a side against one of the Exeter parties! "From this time," says Skeats, "Unitarianism spread with unexampled rapidity. . . . Nearly every Nonconformist Church in Exeter, and some of the principal Churches in Devonshire and Somersetshire" lapsed "from the orthodox standard. The Presbyterian Churches of London, Lancashire, and Cheshire became similarly infected. In less than half-a-century the doctrines of the great founders of Presbyterianism could scarcely be heard from any Presbyterian pulpit in England. The denomination vanished as suddenly as it had arisen;

and, except in literature, (it) has left little visible trace of the greatness of its power."* Presbyterianism has been replanted in England by shoots from another and sturdier vine. The representatives of Presbyterian and Baptist and other Unitarianism are still with us; and if any man wishes to know what doctrinal error, or rather schism between a Church and the Scriptures, will eventually mean, he has only to look at these. Their barrenness and decrepitude will preach better than a score of treatises on the death that is wrapped up in the seed of rationalism.

But the decay of vital Christianity brought with it other results. Deism was met by a vigorous opposition, and it is customary to look upon this as the golden age of Christian apologetics. But the defence was cold, halting, half-hearted. There is little of the deep fervour, the glowing love, the impassioned loyalty, and the whole-hearted faith of the earlier time. To pass from Luther to Lardner or even from Baxter to Paley, is to exchange the warmth and luxuriance of the tropics for the cold and barren splendours of the Arctic regions. Enthusiasm and even warmth of feeling were frowned upon as fanatical, and a chilling judicialism was regarded as the only proper attitude. The attacks of Deism and Unitarianism revealed the decay of orthodoxy. The age of vital faith had gone, and that of English Rationalism had begun.

When Brian Walton published his *Biblia Poly-*

---

* *History of the Free Churches*, pp. 247, 248.

*glotta*—in which, by a patient comparison of existing manuscripts, he had endeavoured to present the original text of the Scriptures—John Owen attacked him on the ground that he had unsettled men's minds as to what was the Word of God, and added that "men take upon them to correct the Scriptures, which are *the Word of God*." Here there was no uncertain sound as to the complete and all-pervading inspiration of the Bible. He who corrected that, stretched out his hand to touch "the Word of God." It might be imagined that Walton placed the Scriptures upon a lower level than Owen did. But there was no divergence whatever between them in that matter. "Walton," says Hunt, "was as much a Scripturalist as Owen. He maintained that the original texts had not been corrupted either by Jews, Christians, or heretics. He said that their authority was supreme in all matters of doctrine, and that they were the rule by which translations were to be tried. The copies which we now have are the true transcripts of the first autographs. The special providence of God, Walton said, had watched over these writings to preserve them pure and uncorrupt, and they will be so preserved to the end of the world, in spite of all sectaries and heretics. The various readings are all such as may be rectified and emended by collation of other copies. To correct an error crept into the original is not, Walton said, to correct the original, *for no error can be a part of the original text*." \*

---

\* *Religious Thought in England*, by Rev. John Hunt, M.A., Vol. iii., pp. 305, 306.

That was the undisturbed conviction of the Churches in England at the Restoration. But the life of all of them became rapidly enfeebled. Instead of moulding the thought of the age, Christian conviction was moulded more and more by the age. It was an age of unbelief. Scepticism was the prevailing, we might say the universal, tone of fashionable society. From the higher classes it spread over the whole land. Bishop Parker said that even the common people set up for sceptics, and defended their sins as harmless actions. The Bishop may be regarded as an unprejudiced witness. Bishop Burnet describes him as "a man of little virtue, and, as to religion, rather impious," and adds that James II. made him a bishop to help on the ruin of the Church. Unbelief fell on England like a blight. The sudden expansion of thought, caused by the discovery of America, as well as by the marvellous advances made in astronomy and in science generally, cracked and shattered many traditional beliefs. Men found that former ages had been mistaken in regard to so much, that they seemed to conclude that mistake had been universal. Everything had to be re-examined, if it had not to be re-constructed. Men were intoxicated by the first draughts of the strong drink of knowledge. They spoke of their own time as "the age of reason," "of common sense," "of experience," and "of inquiry."

Even where the unbelief of the time was resisted, the spirit of the age impressed itself and modified the defence of faith. "The apologists of Christianity," says Skeats, "built up, with masterly ability and acknowledged success, the external defences of their faith; they proved beyond cavil the superiority of Christianity as a moral agent; but they did little more than this. . . . They fell into a habit of treating Christianity as an intellectual creed, a system of morals, and a means of virtue. . . . Preaching, if accurate and polished, was cold and heartless. Foster's sermons are the best illustrations of the most popular Christian oratory of the Deistic period. He was an Addison in the pulpit, but he expressed even less of Christian affectionateness than the moral essayist. Amongst, however, the most eminent of preachers and writers, Watts was one who carefully guarded himself against this danger. In three sermons on the Inward Witness of Christianity, or an evidence of the Truth of the Gospel from its Divine Effects, Watts proclaimed the superior character of the testimony derived from the conscience and experience of man to that of any external evidence. He warned the Christian world against a religion which consisted in merely correct morals and a correct theology, 'while devotion freezes at the heart,' and he vindicated zeal in the ministry of the Word from the ridicule of an age which pretended to 'nothing but calm reasoning.' But even Watts was careful to abjure the charge of 'enthusiasm,' and appealed to 'common sense and reason' in defence of preaching characterized by 'the movements of a sacred passion,' and by a living fire."\*

* *History of the Free Churches*, pp. 265, 266.

Any one who has looked into the sermons of the period has had ample proof of this prevailing tendency. It required a bold man to preach the old doctrines, and the result was a silent surrender to the spirit of the time. Moderation was the watchword of the hour. Referring to such doctrines as The Trinity, Christ's Sacrifice, and Sanctification by the Spirit, Archbishop Secker said: "The truth, I fear, is that many of us have dwelt too little on these doctrines in our sermons; by no means, I believe, as disbelieving or slighting them, but partly from knowing that formerly they had been inculcated beyond their proportion, and even to the disparagement of Christian obedience . . . . But, whatever the cause, the effect hath been lamentable. Our people have grown less and less mindful (1) of the distinguishing articles of their creed; (2) as will always be the case, of that one which they hold in common with the heathens; they have forgotten, in effect, their Creator, as well as their Redeemer and Sanctifier; seldom or never worshipping Him, or thinking of the state of their souls in relation to Him; but flattering themselves that what they are pleased to call a moral and harmless life, though far from being either, is the one thing needful." Paley spoke in the same strain, though himself exemplifying not a little conformity to the world in which he moved. "We are setting up," he said, in one of his charges, "a kind of philosophical morality, detached from religion and independent of its influence, which may be cultivated, it is said, without Christianity as well as with it, and which, if cultivated, renders religion and religious institutions superfluous. We are in such haste to fly from enthusiasm and superstition that we are approaching to an insensibility to all religious influence. I do not mean to advise you to bring men back to enthusiasm, but to retard, if you can, the progress towards an opposite and worse extreme."

Such were the complaints made again and again by men who were themselves caught in the strong current of the era of "common-sense," and "reason." They had perception enough left to mark whither the churches were being borne. But many were prepared to make further sacrifices in deference to the unbelief by which they were hemmed in. Silence about the distinctive doctrines, and the giving up of any troublesome importunity in pressing home the demands of God or the offer of salvation were not enough. There must be added surrender to some extent of the doctrines themselves. The miraculous was stoutly denied, and it must therefore be given up wherever possible. It was this desire which paved the way for so many ministers and churches into Unitarianism. Mystery was something which was not to be endured. What could not be understood, must be denied or explained away. Dr. Lardner removed the difficulty as to the demoniacs of Scripture, by attempting to show that they suffered from lunacy, and were not literally possessed by evil spirits. Archbishop Tillotson's defence of Christianity gives us another and more

## The Beginnings of English Rationalism. 153

painful instance of compromise. "If men," he says, "would be contented to speak justly of things, and pretend to no greater assurance than they can bring evidence for, considerate men would be more apt to believe them." He, therefore, tries to meet those "considerate men." He admits that the evidence for the truth of Christianity does not amount to absolute certainty. There is moral certainty, but not "absolute certainty." The doctrines of Christianity can be proved by miracles, he maintained, only in so far as they do not contradict natural notions. They must be credible and possible. In other words, reason is the judge of revelation; and there must be nothing in revelation which is above reason, and certainly nothing which shocks reason! Judged by that standard, our Lord's teaching would have been condemned daily, and both Nicodemus and the men of Capernaum would have been amply justified in rejecting what was communicated to them by the lips of the Son of God.

Tillotson was equally accommodating in other debated matters. Natural religion was more certain, in his estimation, than revealed. The duty of mothers to nurse their own children, for instance, is "of a more necessary and indispensable obligation," he says, "than any positive precept of revealed religion." It need not surprise anyone to learn, after this, that he rejected "Verbal Inspiration," and adduced the variations in the Gospels as fully justifying his position. "The Evangelists, in relating the discourses of Christ, are very far from agreeing in the particular expressions and words, though they do agree in the substance of the discourses; but if the words had been dictated by the Spirit of God, they must have agreed in them. For when St. Luke differs from St. Matthew, in relating what our Saviour said, it is impossible that they should both relate it right as to his very words and forms of expression, but they both relate the substance of what he said. And if it had been of concernment, that everything that they wrote should be dictated *ad apicem*, to a tittle, by the Spirit of God, it is of the same concernment still, that the Providence of God should have secured the Scriptures since to a tittle from the least alteration" (Collected Works, Vol. xii., 134). Now it has been the astonishment of every textual critic and student that the Providence of God *has* so watched over the Scriptures that with the most trifling exceptions we can be absolutely certain, not only as to the very words of the original autographs, but also as to *the very order* in which the words were originally penned. The Archbishop was equally at fault in his argument from the variations of the Gospels. If each Gospel has a distinct purpose, and if these variations, in every case, serve to fulfil that purpose, then surely the variations could not have been a matter of indifference to the Spirit of God, whose purpose these very differences were carrying out. They would each, in that case, reveal the moulding touch of the Spirit's hand, and thus prove that there has been a Divine superintendence of the very words of the Bible, and so uphold the doctrine which they were supposed to overthrow.

Dr. Thomas Burnet, master of the Charterhouse, rejected the literal interpretation of the Scripture accounts of the Fall and of the Creation. Dr. Conyers Middleton regarded them only as allegories, and justified Tindal, the Deistical writer, in his rejection of them. He also maintained that it was necessary to admit the contention of the Deists that the Scriptures were not infallibly inspired. Bishop Marsh's work on the Gospels, in the beginning of the present century, indicated how easily we might have had full-blown rationalism in our midst long before the present invasion. But that revival of vital religion, with which God was pleased to visit this country, killed English rationalism while yet in the bud. The ever-vigilant foe of faith had to wait for another opportunity, when belief had once more lost its fervour, and the Church of Christ in these lands was again conforming itself to the world which it had been commissioned to change and to save.

## CHAPTER VI.

### CONTINENTAL PREPARATIONS FOR THE RATIONALISTIC HARVEST.

THE changing scenes in this tragedy of unbelief now remove us to Germany. The Churches in that land must first be overcome before our own can be seriously invaded. The history of German Protestantism forms sad reading. The spirituality of the early Reformers was not shared by their successors. Luther, Melancthon, and many another fought to preserve access for themselves and the world to the fountain of everlasting life; the men that followed seem to have been devoured by a blind rage for conflict. Melancthon survived Luther fourteen years, and felt the chill of the ice-age that was about to settle upon his country. Just before he died he noted down some thoughts upon a piece of paper. It was found on a table by his bedside after his death. The writing was in two columns. On the right side were the words: "Thou shalt come into the light; thou shalt see the Son of God; thou shalt learn to know what thou hast not been able to comprehend in this life." On the left side were these words: "Thou shalt renounce sin; thou shalt be delivered from all troubles and *a rabie theologorum*" —*from the mad rage of theologians*!

"Certainly," says Amand Saintes, "they remained faithful to the fundamental principles of Protestantism, of which the ancient ideas of inspiration and revelation were the essential elements, but they entered into refinements on the connection of grace with the free-will of man; on the nature of election and predestination, and the restrictions to be imposed on that doctrine; on the ubiquity in the Lord's Supper, and the infidelity of the Reformed party (the followers of Calvin) in denying it. On these questions did the theologians of the sixteenth and seventeenth centuries spend all their talents and intelligence."\*

The sermons of the period will give us a glimpse of how this spirit worked. Joseph Andreä was one of the leading men of the time, and his discourses were published at the close of the sixteenth century. One sermon has four divisions. The first head deals with the difference between Lutheranism and Popery; the second, with the difference between the Church of Christ and the Zwinglians; "the third is devoted to a disputation with the Schwenkfeldians; and the fourth is directed against the Anabaptists."†
"Artomedes, another Lutheran preacher, commences in the following manner a sermon on the Lord's

---

\* *A Critical History of Rationalism in Germany* (English Translation, Simpkin, Marshall), p. 35.   † *Ibid.*

Supper: 'There are two furious armies of devils incarnate, disputing about the Lord's Supper; on one side the Papists, on the other the haughty and captious Calvinists. Our miserable pagan, Ovid, is a better theologian than any of these Calvinists,' etc. And still more offensive expressions follow, in a style truly disgusting. The introductions to these sermons generally consisted of a grammatical explanation of the text, followed by a noisy discussion, which they had the hardihood to term a practical application. I shall quote only one other example. It is a discourse of the preacher Hermann, a Silesian by birth, of which Zacchaeus is the subject. The text is 'Zacchaeus was a little man,' a subject, we see, of immense interest, which he divides thus: 'We consider, first, the word *he*, which acquaints us with the nature of the person; secondly, the word *was*, which will teach us the frailty of life; thirdly, the word *little*, which tells us of the personal appearance of Zacchaeus.' Now, let us see the practical application to his audience made by the preacher. 'Zacchaeus,' says he, 'ought to teach us in the first place what great variety there is in the works of God, since he takes care of the little, whose comforter he is... Finally, the history of Zacchaeus should teach us the necessity of compensating for our personal defects by our virtues.'"*

It would accomplish little good to bring up from the dead any specimens of the rancour and hate into which Christian controversy descended. The

---

* *Ibid*, 36.

extremes to which learned men allowed themselves to go are almost incredible. Calixtus, for example, was pained by the bitter animosity which split up the Reformed Churches. He strove by his personal exertions and by his writings to infuse a different spirit and to heal divisions. He contended that, while insisting upon terms of communion, a distinction should be made between what is essential and what is not essential to salvation. We must love all men, he urged, even idolaters, in order to save them. "The Jews and Mohammedans," he reminded the fierce disputants of his time, "stand nearer to us" than idolaters, "and we should cherish affection also for them. Those who are the most closely united to us are all who believe that they can be saved only by the merits of Christ. All who thus recognize the saving power of Christ are members of His body, brothers and sisters with Him. We should live, therefore, as members of one family, though adhering to different sects. We must not, however, be neutral. Everyone should join the Church to which his own conscientious convictions would lead him. Yet when we do this, we must love all who think differently. The outpouring of the Spirit would be meagre indeed if the Church existed for the stringent Lutherans alone."

These sentiments drew down upon Calixtus the concentrated fury of the unspiritual dogmatists who then dominated the Lutheran Church. He was vilified in the most shameless fashion. A man of stainless life, he was, nevertheless, said to have derived his ideas of conciliation from the taverns and vicious resorts which he had frequented in France and in Italy! It was added that it was nothing for him to be a heretic, for he had fallen lower than the devil! His calumniators were men of position, and were backed by the influence of the three Lutheran Universities of Leipzig, Wittemberg, and Jena. His friends were declared to be "bloodhounds and perjurers," and one man, who ventured to say that Calixtus was "a good and venerable theologian," was subjected to a heavy fine!

Such a spirit boded ill for Germany, and God visited it with heavy chastisement. The Thirty Years' War, with its slaughter, devastation, and unutterable horrors, burst upon the land. Protestantism had to fight for its existence, and was baptized in blood. The spirit that ruled in the Inquisition was displayed in the breaking of treaties, on the battle-field, and in the sack of captured cities. The spirit of the times had corrupted the rulers, and seldom or never have the princes of any country presented such a spectacle of weakness, selfishness, and treachery as was then displayed by the nobles of Protestant Germany. Protestantism was suppressed in Bohemia, and was left in Germany, a maimed, charred, and almost unrecognisable thing. At first, danger, and even calamity, drove the people to God. Frivolity was exchanged for a new seriousness. They encouraged each other to put their trust in God. But as the scourge fell more heavily and was drenched more deeply in blood, their hope failed.

## Continental Preparations.  161

When Tilly took Magdeburg, his soldiers "spared," says Menzell, "neither age nor sex. Some of his officers, who entreated Tilly to put a stop to the massacre, were told to return to him on the expiration of an hour. The most horrid scenes were meanwhile enacted. Every man in the city was killed, numbers of women cast themselves headlong into the Elbe, and into the flames of the burning houses, in order to escape the brutality of the soldiery; fifty-three women were beheaded by the Croatians whilst kneeling in the church of St. Catherine. One Croat boasted of having stuck twenty babes on his pike. One hundred and thirty-seven houses and the fire-proof cathedral, in which four thousand men took refuge, were all that remained of the proud city. The rest of the inhabitants had fallen victims to the sword or to the flames. The slaughter continued until the 22nd, when Tilly appeared and restored discipline and order. The refugees in the cathedral were pardoned, and for the first time for three days received food. Tilly, a tall haggard-looking man, dressed in a short slashed green satin jacket, with a long red feather in his high-crowned hat, with large bright eyes peering from beneath his deeply-furrowed brow, a stiff moustache under his pointed nose, ghastly, hollow-cheeked, and with a seeming affectation of wildness in his whole appearance, sat, mounted on a bony charger, on the ruins of Magdeburg, proudly looking upon the thirty thousand bodies of the brave citizens now stiffening in death, which, at his command, were cast into the Elbe. The river was choked up by the mass near the Neustadt."\*

Beneath these fearful and repeated strokes the slenderly-rooted faith died out. The outward desolation was terrible. In Saxony, 900,000 men had fallen in two years. The city of Augsburg had 18,000 instead of her 80,000 inhabitants. Every town and district had suffered similarly. The working classes had almost wholly disappeared. Immense provinces were left without an inhabitant, and had to be repeopled by importing foreigners into the country. The outer desolation was only a picture of the inner. The end of the war is declared by Kahnis to have been the beginning of German Secularism. "Up to the period of the Thirty Years' War," he says, "religion was the chief moving power of the time. The question regarding the Confession prevailed over everything, and even secular questions, that they might excite interest and be carried, were compelled to clothe themselves in the garb of religion. But the result of the Thirty Years' War was indifference not only to the Confession, but to religion in general. Ever since that period, secular interests decidedly occupy the foreground, and the leading power in Europe is France."

The evil was aggravated by the repression of individual effort. The German Reformation was from the first subordinated to the Princes in whose territories it was protected. The result was a state supervision which left little freedom. The Christian

\* Menzel, *History of Germany.*

ministry became a kind of state police, and men would as soon have thought of interfering with the work of the magistracy as of busying themselves in the ministry of the Word. Lay effort, and even meetings for edification or prayer, were utterly unknown. The exposition of Scripture was neglected alike in the pulpit, in the Universities, and in theological literature. There were many who did not defile their garments, but the general declension was frightful. "The scenes of clerical immorality," says Hurst, "are enough to chill one's blood even at the distance of more than two centuries."\* Charges of the grossest immorality were treated with indifference, and repelled by pastors with the cool observation that "others do the same thing." The example set by the authorities in the Universities was no better. "One professor was so deeply in debt that he could not pay his creditors 'if every hair on his head was a ducat.' Another was 'in bed with seven wounds received in a fall when he was coming home drunk.' Some read their newspapers at church service. Nor did the wives and daughters of the professors lead any better life. They were guilty of deeds of the grossest immorality."†

The upper classes showed the same laxity, and the corruption and infidelity which made the courts of Germany a byword in later times began to manifest themselves. A court-chaplain wrote as follows in 1637: "I would much rather be silent concerning my sore misfortune which I am here undergoing, than,

---

\* *History of Rationalism*, p. 57.   † *Ibid*, p. 58

by speaking, to make the wounds of my heart break out afresh. These infernal courtiers, among whom I am compelled to live against my will, doubt those truths which even the heathen have learned to believe." Similar testimony is borne by an author who wrote in 1630. He distinguishes three classes of sceptics among the nobility of Hamburg. There are (1) those who believe that religion is a pious device, invented to keep the lower classes in restraint; (2) those who think that all religions have some truth in them, and that no one of them is superior to the rest; and (3) those who believe that there is one true religion, but, being unable to decide which is the true, believe in none!"† The unbelief and immorality of the higher classes naturally set the fashion for all. The outlook was drear and terrible. It needed only one or two generations more of deepening darkness, and Germany would be morally and spiritually in a worse condition than it was before the light of the Gospel had brightened the land under the preaching of Luther.

---

† Hurst, 60.

## CHAPTER VII.

### Rally and Defeat.

AT the close of the Thirty Years' War there was a wide-spread consciousness that German Protestantism had left her first love. Signs were not wanting of a coming revival, and it seemed quite within the limits of what was probable that German Christianity might yet expel, by the very force of reviving spiritual life, the chill of death and the poison of error. Every movement of the kind seems to require the service of some one gifted man, who may be the Moses of his time. And, if the German Revival failed, it was not for lack of such a leader. God had prepared him, and he was manifested in due season.

Philip Jacob Spener (1635-1705) was thirteen years old at the close of the war. He possessed every facility for acquiring all the equipment which the learning of the day could give him. He was an apt scholar; and, · after finishing his theological studies at Strassburg, he spent three years in visiting the Universities of Basle, Tübingen, Freiburg, Geneva, and Lyons. On his return, he entered upon his work as a preacher; and, after a short stay at Strassburg, settled at Frankfort-on-the-Main. He saw the necessity for devoting greater attention to the instruction of the young, and the success which attended his work in that department revolutionised the system of catechetical instruction in many parts of Germany. He also observed that, in the customary style of sermon, the preachers soared far above the heads of their hearers. Not content with speaking to his parishioners in a style which enabled them to follow and to understand him, he started weekly meetings in which the Sunday sermons were discussed, questions were asked and answered, and difficulties were explained. These meetings were designated by a name which testifies to the scholasticism of the time; they were called *collegia pietatis*, "Schools of Devotion." The name was avenged in the nicknames of "Pietists" and "Pietism," by which the system and the men are now known to history.

The scholasticism, fortunately, stopped at the name; everything else was natural, earnest, and free. The meetings, at first poorly attended, rapidly grew in interest. The attendance increased, till Spener's drawing-room had to be abandoned for the church, and that, too, was soon filled to its utmost capacity. The usual results followed. There was a recognition of the brotherhood of all believers, and of their fellowship in labour as well as in faith and love. "The Christian laity possess," Spener taught, "not only the right of offering to God the sacrifice of prayer, both for themselves and others; they may also exercise their priestly office, whether at home or among friends, may help to edify the church in their house, have the right mutually to edify each other—especially under the direction of their minister—from the Word of God, and to open their mouths both in question and answer in devotional meetings."\* Out of these gatherings grew a kind of Pastor's College. Spener gathered round him a band of young men whom he entertained and prepared for the ministry. These took part in the devotional meetings, and were trained to meet the needs of the people.

Spener's views and methods were made known in his great work *Pia Desideria*, which he published in 1675. "Here," says Hurst, "he laid down his platform: That the Word of God should be brought home to the popular heart: that laymen, when capable and pious, should act as preachers, thus becoming a valuable ally to the ministry; that deep love and practical piety are a necessity to every preacher; that kindness, moderation, and an effort to convince should be observed toward theological opponents; that great efforts should be made to have worthy and divinely-called young men properly instructed for the ministry; and that all preachers should urge upon the people the importance of faith and its fruits."† Spener was ever mindful of the

---

\* Dorner, *History of Protestant Theology*, Vol. ii., pp. 209, 210.
† *History of Rationalism*, p. 70.

injunction of Scripture: "This is a faithful saying, and these things I will that thou affirm constantly, that they who have believed in God might be careful to maintain good works." Strange as it may sound, it is nevertheless true that this doctrine was one of the most novel features of the Pietistic revival. It had been no novelty in the Reformation teaching; but the dead orthodoxy which followed the Reformation, looked upon Christianity as a matter of intellectual beliefs, supplemented or expressed by external forms of worship. It had the form of godliness while denying the power. Spener's teaching on this point was, in the then state of practice and belief, simply revolutionary. It summoned men from quietude to zeal, from the natural to the supernatural, from sleep to action, from death to life. Man, he taught, is not passive in this work of God. Desire and will must be aroused from the outset. There must be contrition and thirsting after righteousness, even from the beginning. And all along the Christian course there must be separation from sin, crucifixion of the flesh, growth in knowledge, holiness, and love. But while man was in this way made more of than orthodoxy then reckoned, there was, on the other hand, a bigger place given to God. The gift of the Spirit was a reality. Men were still in the age of miracles, and the Divine love embraced, and the Divine power rested upon, the believer. Spener "represents," says Dorner, "direct communion with God, a participation in the Divine life, and the reception of the Divine Spirit as not only a possible favour, but as that which it is the first and universal duty of every Christian to seek. Spener knows a living God, not a God who has betaken Himself to rest behind those means of grace which are to work as His substitutes, but which, instead of being able to supply the place of personal communion with Himself, are but designed to lead to it."*

All these things were daring novelties to the dead Protestantism of the seventeenth century. The theologians were indignant. If *that* was Christianity, then, *what* were they, and what was their system? The picture was an accusation; and the offence which it gave was deadly. Spener, the meekest and most conciliatory of men, was assailed by a storm which raged around him till his dying day. He was assailed by pamphlets, treatises, misrepresentations, calumnies, intrigues, persecutions. Spener dealt constantly with the Scripture, and sparingly with the Confession. The Divines of Wittenberg published a work in which he and the German public were informed, in effect, that the Confessions and Catechisms are a more exact standard than the Bible, and that whatever is not embraced in them is not to be listened to, however much it may seem to be the teaching of Scripture. It was utterly wrong, his opponents maintained, to talk of reforming the Church. The Church—not the Church "invisible," be it remarked, but the Lutheran Church as it then existed—*could not be reformed!* That Church

---

* *Ibid.* pp. 214, 215.

was perfect, and in her most flourishing condition, because, forsooth, *she possessed "correct doctrine!"* Once more we recognise the features of Sardis: "Thou hast a name that thou livest, and art dead;" and it is no wonder that the cry came as an unbearable rebuke: "Be watchful and strengthen the things which remain, that are ready to die: for I have not found thy works perfect before God" (Rev. iii. 2).

The controversy revealed, in its progress, one depth of degradation after another. The Creeds and Confessions were regarded as if inspired. A kind of inspiration was supposed to attach itself in like manner to the ministerial office. Spener was told that his demand, that students for the ministry should seek the illumination and regeneration of the Spirit of God, was superfluous. They "had been regenerated in baptism, and had received the gift of the Holy Ghost once for all." Spener removed from Frankfort to Dresden, whither he had been invited as court preacher. But his straight preaching was not courtly, and was anything but agreeable to men who, if they wanted anything beyond ordinary forms, desired consolation and not counsel. His zeal also to instruct the people, and the response manifested in the crowds that attended the services, were not suited to the serenity and dignity of a court, and were, therefore, an additional offence. An invitation came from Berlin, of which Spener gladly availed himself. He spent there the last few years of his laborious life. The storm still raged over his grave. They tried to hinder the influence of the writings which he left behind him by assailing his memory and maligning his moral character. His enemies even went so far as to deny to those who loved him the hope of meeting him in heaven. Professor Teck, of Rostock, in a work which he published on *The Happiness of those who die in the Lord*, declared "that heaven will open its gates sometimes to the extremely impious who die without any external mark of repentance, and also to those who die in gross sin; *but not to such a man as Spener!*"

Spener had much to console him, however, during his stormy career. Students trained in the *collegia pietatis* became useful ministers, and multiplied his teaching and influence. Worthy colleagues also gathered round him, and helped manfully in the labour of replanting a vital Christianity in the Lutheran Churches. One of the most ardent of these was J. A. Francke (1663-1727). Like many another in the ministry of all the Protestant Churches of the time, he was a preacher although he was not a Christian. He himself has told the story of his conversion. He was about to preach from the words: "But these are written that ye might believe that Jesus is the Christ, the Son of God, and that, believing, ye might have life through his name." "My whole former life," he says, "came before my eyes, just as one sees a whole city from a lofty spire. At first it seemed as if I could number all my sins; but soon there opened the great fountain of them—my own blind unbelief, which had so long deceived me; I was terrified with my lost condition, and wondered if God were merciful enough to bless me. I kneeled down and prayed. All doubt vanished; I was assured in my own heart of the grace of God in Christ. Now I knew Him, not alone as my God, but as my Father! All melancholy and unrest vanished, and I was so full of joy, that from the fulness of my heart I could praise my Saviour. With great sorrow I had kneeled, but with wonderful ecstacy I had risen up. It seemed to me as if my whole previous life had been a deep sleep, as if I had only been dreaming, and now for the first time I had waked up. I was convinced that the whole world, with all its temporal joy, could not kindle such pleasure in my breast."

Several of these friends rallied round Spener in Berlin, and a new University was founded at Halle for the purpose of promoting personal piety, Scriptural knowledge, and practical preaching throughout the land. Francke was one of the Professors. Crowds of students flocked to the new teaching, and it seemed for a time as if the widespread revival for which Spener had prayed and toiled was to be realized. The new life began to show itself in new deeds. Francke's Orphan House at Halle was a surprise and an inspiration to Christendom. Besides being a Professor at the University, Francke was also Pastor of one of the Halle churches. It might be supposed, therefore, that, whoever had leisure for further work, Francke, at least, had none. But where love is, capacity and ability seem to be endowed with love's own expansive power. The poor of the town used to assemble weekly to receive their share of what had been contributed for their support. It occurred to Francke that those who came for alms might also have the bread of everlasting life. He therefore made use of the opportunity for religious teaching. But thought of these led to thought of their children. The parents, ignorant and poor, could do nothing for their children's education. His first idea was to get some money together and to distribute it to the parents for the education of their children. That arrangement was not satisfactory. Francke then saw that more personal supervision was needed. He placed a box in his own house that his friends might contribute. The small beginning led, through varying phases—often most disappointing in themselves—to the establishment of an Orphan Home, out of which, in the same gradual fashion, other institutions sprang, till the work, by its magnitude, as well as by its exhibition of Christian beneficence, challenged the attention of Europe.

The fruits of the new life were not confined to these charitable institutions. Thomasius, the Principal of the University of Halle, introduced, or at least advocated, some of the greatest reforms of the time. Till then the Latin language was the medium of all learned communications, and the tongue in which all academical instruction was delivered. He warmly urged the substitution of French, and subsequently of German. While still a teacher at Leipzig, he announced a series of German lectures. Notwithstanding the outcry that was raised, the lectures were delivered, and all his after instructions were conveyed in his mother tongue. This daring innovation marked an era in the transition from the old time to the new. He was the first, also, to denounce prosecutions for witchcraft and the employment of torture to obtain evidence in criminal trials. It was quite as startling, and a still more fruitful innovation, to inaugurate missions to the Mohammedans and the Jews. The Church had forgotten the Saviour's great command to preach the Gospel to every creature; and to the Pietists of Germany the Christian world owes the re-awakening of missionary effort. The happy contagion spread on every side, notwithstanding the opposition of the Theologians. The more important cities of Germany, and even the Universities that were most bitterly opposed to Spener, began to show signs of awakening faith. Switzerland gave a marked response to the new teaching. Denmark, Norway, Sweden, England, and the Protestants of France were all touched and quickened; while the crowds of students who flocked to Halle and passed out to fill the pulpits of the land gave promise of still larger influence in days to come. "The Protestant Church of Germany," says Tholuck, "never possessed so many zealous Christian ministers and laymen as in the first forty years of the eighteenth century."

Had this new faith and zeal filled the Churches, the unbelief, maintaining its siege around it, would have been conquered or scattered. But the decay of the new movement was as sudden and surprising as its rise. The Professors at Halle were succeeded by men who lacked the insight and the spiritual fervour of their predecessors. Elsewhere Pietism developed into mysticism and superstition, or fell back into a pretentious formalism. The attempt to revive the German Church had been made in vain, and now came the time of its visitation. The surrounding unbelief had, meanwhile, been deepening. The writings of the English deists were being studied in Germany. Bayle's Dictionary had long been favourite reading with the German nobles. The learning of the French Encylopædists, and the glittering raillery of Voltaire, were to complete the victory of evil and to sweep the field. Berlin, which had welcomed Spener and his fellow-labourers, was to become, under Frederic the Great, the centre of scoffing atheism; and the University of Halle, which had been founded to flood Germany with the new life of faith, was soon to be known as a welling fountain of blighting Rationalism.

## CHAPTER VIII.

### THE RISE OF GERMAN RATIONALISM.

ENGLISH Deism had been greedily absorbed by France. Unbelief it had long known, but not such unbelief as this. The Deism of England was high-souled, a feature which it owed to the earnest and enlightened faith which it rejected. It posed as a philosophy more clear-eyed, more complete, and harmonious—in one word, more reasonable—than Christianity. To the scepticism of France, therefore, the Deism of England came as a justification and as a fresh inspiration. Voltaire returned from his English sojourn, not only charmed with the new light, but imbued with the devotion of an apostle. This happened at a period which Germans now recall with shame. Their leaders in literature looked to France as the land of all enlightenment and the standard of taste. No man was considered educated, or fit for courtly society, who had not worshipped at this shrine.

In this way the flood of French Scepticism poured

over Germany. In due time there came a revolt against French influence, but none against French infidelity. The new literature, created by lovers of Germany, weary of French supremacy and blushing for the dishonour cast upon their native writers and their native tongue, was nevertheless steeped in the French unbelief. It is true that with German thoroughness they went to the sources from which their French masters had helped themselves. All the English Deists were honoured by German translations of their works, and some of them had many translators. Toland was received and honoured at Berlin by Frederick William I. But it was Voltaire, whom we had baptised in English Deism, that was, after all, the hero in this onslaught of darkness. Laukhard, a German freethinker of the period, has left behind him the following confession: "I learned from Voltaire," says he, "only how to scoff; for other works, and particularly those of the English Tindal, had already brought me into a proper state of mind to form a just judgment on the doctrines of the Church. It is true that I have derived infinite enjoyment from reading the French poet, who, with his pleasantries, at once gross and delicate, has done more to injure the religion of the priests than have all the works of the other French and English Deists. While in England and Germany an author sets out from some declared principle, and seeks to convince the reader by philosophical arguments, Voltaire negligently throws out some futile reasonings, glances over the question as over a law suit, afterwards rails at the whole as if he had completely demonstrated what he has advanced. This does not convince, but his numerous readers consider themselves convinced, and honour the philosopher with all their suffrages. It is thus that Voltaire has been able to make so many proselytes to unbelief. He did not write for the learned; they, he thought, might seek elsewhere for the means of rectifying their ideas. He wrote for the unlearned; for ladies, princes, and merchants; to them he addressed himself to make the scales fall from their eyes, and it must be confessed that he took the right way to do so. All the attacks of his adversaries, from Nonnote to Less, have been unable to weaken his credit. No one now reads Nonnote, and Less finds readers only among a small number of ecclesiastics. The works of Voltaire, on the contrary, are in all hands, and are translated into all languages. They will be read with pleasure when the very existence of such adversaries shall have been long forgotten." *

The effect of this infidelity upon the public mind of Germany may be imagined. Its influence was all pervading, and long continued. Albert Thaer, who was born in 1752, tells how Ferry, his bosom friend, who was also his instructor in languages, gave him his first lessons in infidelity. "To read the works of Voltaire," says he, "was my only recreation when I was tired of my amours. Ferry made me read, besides Voltaire, nearly all the other French writers; and when I had, at a later period, learned their

---
*Amand Saintes, *History of Rationalism*, p. 75.

language, I read the works of all the English free-thinkers." It was thus, he adds, that he prepared for his first communion, already fully convinced that Christianity was folly. He afterwards tells us that at Göttingen he became associated with a party of friends, "a band of scoffers at all religion, theoretical and practical."* He claims to have been practically the author of Lessing's book, *The Education of the Human Race*. This desolating work was carried on by native as well as by foreign authors. The central figure in the propaganda was Frederic the Great, whose military successes and growing power fixed upon him the gaze of Europe. Berlin, which, in his father's time, had been the rallying point of the pietists, now became the Jerusalem of German Infidelity. He gathered round him the Infidel wits and litterateurs of France, and inoculated German society with the light raillery and scoffing scepticism of Paris. "He hesitated not," says Hurst, "to supplant evangelical professors and pastors by Free-thinkers, and at any time to bring ridicule on any religious fact or custom. That thin-visaged man in top-boots and cocked hat, surrounded by his infidels and his dogs at Sans Souci, dictated faith to Berlin and to Europe . . . But Frederic lived to see the day when insubordination sprang up in his army, and in many departments of public life. It came from the abnegation of the evangelical faith. And it is no wonder that, when the old king saw the disastrous effects of his own theories upon his subjects, he said

---

* *Ibid*, 85.

he would willingly give his best battle to place his people where he found them at his father's death." *

Another influence which told powerfully upon many of the studious was that of the Dutch Jew Spinosa (1632-1677). He is the prince of pantheists; and he has made good his claim to that dignity, not only by the charm which his writings possess for all who, while they believe in God, desire to rob Him of His vitality, but also by the fact that he has anticipated, if he has not suggested, every attack which has been made upon the Scriptures, or upon the possibility of revelation. This desolating unbelief was deplored by many, and an attempt was now made to meet it, which only added a fresh disaster. Wolff (1679-1754), Professor of Metaphysics at Halle, Spener's University founded for the purpose of propagating evangelical belief, was actuated by the best intentions. He spent his earlier years, he tells us, at Breslau, his native town. There he lived among Catholics, and was a constant witness of the disputes between them and the Protestants. Could no way be discovered of so proving the truth that the demonstration would be final, and that all discussion should cease? That was the question which the times forced upon him. It seemed to him that a way might be found, and it became his one ambition to discover it. He heard that the demonstrations in mathematics were so absolutely certain that not a single step could be shaken, nor a single conclusion be escaped. He studied that science that he might

---

* *History of Rationalism*, p. 107.

acquaint himself with the method which mathematicians followed with such signal success. He saw that they started from principles, the truth of which could not be denied. On these truths, as on a solid bed of rock rising up amid a surrounding sea of uncertainty and perpetual change, they built one truth after another, till the fair edifice of their science stood erect in a beauty and a majesty that bade defiance alike to doubt and to time. What they had done for Mathematics, could not he accomplish for Theology?

He laid hold of the principles laid down by Descartes and Leibnitz. One of his proofs of the existence of God was as follows: We exist. Our existence, therefore, has to be explained. It is an effect, and it must have had an efficient cause. That cause, to be a full and sufficing explanation, must not be one that owes its existence to another being; and so on the reasoning pursues its way, till we find that the fact of our existence involves the existence of an eternal and omnipotent God. The reality and the attributes of the God of the Bible were also demonstrated, in the same way, apart from the Bible. The like method was followed in proving that a Revelation is possible. Only there were limitations here in which an acute observer might have caught a glimpse of coming perplexity. A Revelation, in order to be necessary, must contain things which it is essential for man to know, and which he cannot learn in any other way. Wolff then proceeds to determine the *kind* of revelation which alone is possible. It must be in harmony with God's attributes, with itself, with the principles of reason, and with the facts of experience. Here reason, summoned to be an ally of Revelation, ends by becoming the judge of Revelation. "Thus," says Pfleiderer, "though Wolff did not intend to question the occurrence of Revelation, nor to cast doubt upon it, yet, as a matter of fact, he made it impossible to allow that such a thing had taken place. He made it depend on conditions which are nowhere fulfilled in the sacred history, and which could never be fulfilled."* Reason might well have taken the place of judge of the necessities which led God to make known Himself and His will, *had it known everything that God knew.* But, limited, and blind, and foolish, how could it judge God or presume to say when and what He should speak to men? And, further, if the reason of all men already knew all this, what need was there for any Revelation? The demonstration refuted itself.

We can easily imagine, however, the eagerness with which a proof, at once so simple and apparently so complete, was taken up by almost every one who desired to see religion triumph over its adversaries. Wolff himself popularised his system so as to bring it within the range of the unlearned. It immediately attained a wide popularity. It was embraced even by Roman Catholics, and his books were used as text-books in several of their universities. But reason was a poor exchange for Scripture, and the result was

---

* *The Philosophy of Religion,* Vol. i., p. 102.

barrenness and pedantic stupidity. The students who now went out from Halle to occupy the pulpits of the land, instead of taking with them, as their predecessors had done, "the finest of the wheat," carried, as a priceless treasure, this "beaten-chaff well-meant for grain." Instead of the assurances of the Gospel, or instruction in righteousness, they supplied their hearers with mathematical phrases, with definitions, and arguments drawn out according to the strictest rules of logic. The definitions frequently defined things that needed no defining, and teaching became empty, cold, and formal. In commenting upon the Sermon on the Mount, one preacher thought it necessary to define a mountain as "a very elevated place;" and, in speaking of Jesus stretching forth his hand to heal the leper, to tell his hearers that "the hand is one of the members of the body." The same childish pedantry displayed itself in new words and names which bore a like stamp of sheer stupidity. The Israelites were called "Israels," the Moabites "Moabs." Peter the Apostle must thenceforth be spoken of as "Peter the Ambassador," and the Old Testament as "The Divine Writings before the time of Jesus, the Messiah!" Pietism, already declining, was buried under this daily accumulating mass of wood, hay, and stubble.

The field was now cleared for the development of unbelief. We have already seen that two things are needed for the overthrow of faith. There must be lessened vitality in the Church, and a circumference of pronounced and aggressive infidelity. Germany now presented both these conditions, and the time had come when infidelity might have a place within, as well as without, the Church. But it had to change its form; Satan had to array himself as an angel of light. There is, consequently, one error against which the reader must guard himself. *Rationalism is not Infidelity.* Rationalism may lead to Deism, and even to Atheism; but it is not Atheism, nor even Deism, *to begin with.* Its attitude and motive are entirely different from theirs. They are antagonistic to the Scriptures, and it is friendly; they seek to destroy, and it comes to save. It is *in the method by which it seeks to save* that its deadly error lies. It imagines that the ordinary defenders of the Bible are utterly wrong. In its judgment, they are wasting their strength in the defence of an untenable position, and perilling everything by an obstinate refusal to admit facts. The Rationalists are the party of panic. When Science began to lift its head, they immediately surrendered the Scriptures, and prepared themselves and others for a coming avalanche of discrepancies and errors, by loudly proclaiming that "the Bible was never meant to teach science." When Geology appeared to contradict Genesis, they at once gave up the stories of the Creation and of the Flood. These were mere poetic representations, the purpose of which was less to instruct than to impress a nation of escaped slaves. The Christian Church had consequently been deluded in treating them as narratives of actual fact. It was, strangely enough, forgotten that the Apostle Peter and our Lord Himself had so treated them; and it need not be added that Science itself is now astonished to discover that the Bible was right after all!

Rationalism is panic and surrender; and as anything can be extorted from fear, there is nothing that Infidelity demands that Rationalism will not eventually yield. Time and continued pressure alone are needed. The Rationalists tried to save the Bible by distinctions between Revelation and Inspiration; between Revelation and a Record of Revelation; between the Word of God and a Book containing the Word of God. They retreated still further. It was enough for them if what pertained to faith and practice was left intact; the history and everything else could go. Now, they find that nothing can save the Bible! Inspiration is a myth, or something, at least, to which no definite notion can be attached. The Scriptures are only Hebrew Literature, and are, in many parts, even on a lower level still! They are largely a bundle of pious frauds and interpolations and editorial patchings, such as never disgraced any other literature in all the world's history!!

No infidelity ever dreamed of making worse havoc with "the Oracles of God" than these defenders of them have at last worked with their own hands. But, to be just to these men and to understand their work, we have to remember that they have always been, and are even now, the party of mediation.

They value the Bible, they say; but they must save it from those who love it not wisely but too well! Science is thundering at the gates; and its terms must be ascertained and accepted at once. The Bible, committed by God to us as a sacred trust for men, must be surrendered to the misunderstandings and vagaries of those whom it was meant to enlighten and to guide! It need not surprise us that the Rationalists, or men who boast of their following and yielding to reason, are found within the Christian Church. In their own judgment, they have the best right to be there. But they are mutineers, who have lost faith in the cause which they originally swore to defend, and who are now ready to murder their officers and to surrender the citadel to the foe. "When I have recorded their labours," says Amand Saintes, the chief historian of Rationalism, referring to the Rationalistic leaders, "I think it will be evident that the Church of Christ contains in its own bosom an adversary the more to be dreaded, from the fact that, like a child who has been substituted for the real heir of a family, it believes itself to be true Christianity, and, as such, claims all its rights."[*]

Semler, who was born in 1684 and died in 1766, is universally regarded as the father of German Rationalism. He was educated in Francke's Orphan Schools, and obtained a Professor's chair in Halle University. The piety of his youth seems to have clung to him through life, and no charge could be brought against him personally. This peculiarity has

---

[*] *History of Rationalism*, p. 3.

been most marked throughout this long revolt against the Word of God. Those who have laboured most earnestly in the work of destruction have frequently been men of most estimable private character. But, while their virtues have contributed to their influence and have calmed the apprehensions of many, it has been forgotten that the virtues were the fruit, not of *their* views, but of the very beliefs which they were overthrowing. Their excellencies and their piety have been used as a shield to frustrate the efforts of those who would expose their errors. How can such good men, it is asked, be the enemies of God? But the argument really tells the other way. If such fruits as these have followed the opinions which these men are using their talents and their influence to overthrow, how could these opinions have sprung from mistake and falsehood? The virtues of Semler could not logically be used to stop the mouth of his opponents; they ought to have stopped his own.

Semler found two armies in hostile array. The Philistines of Deism and Pantheism and Atheism had invaded the land; and the armies of Israel, with their soulless orthodoxy and effete Pietism, were certainly no reassuring spectacle to Semler. Changes must be made, and rusty armour must be thrown away. Ground that, in his estimation, could no longer be defended, must be abandoned, and the enemy's attack must be foiled by the orthodox themselves blowing up the fortifications which infidelity was besieging! In this way, he imagined the conflict would be brought to an end, and infidelity would acknowledge that those things which remained were things that could not be shaken. He did the work which he judged to be needful, with unflagging zeal and unquivering nerve. He had to destroy what he imagined to be worship of the Bible. The Canon of the Old Testament was involved, he contended, in uncertainty, and each man must judge by his own sanctified common sense what books had a right to be counted inspired and what books had no such claim. He rejected The Song of Solomon, Ruth, Ezra, Nehemiah, Esther, and the Chronicles. Joshua, Judges, Samuel, Kings, and Daniel were doubtful. Ecclesiastes was probably the work of several writers. Astruc had published his theory of Genesis, and suggested the now famous distinctions of Jehovistic and Elohistic writers. Semler willingly surrendered Genesis and the Pentateuch to him. He was equally liberal with the New Testament. There was no such thing as demoniac possession. Those out of whom our Lord appeared to cast forth devils were only mad people, and Jesus, in pretending to hold conversations with demons and to command them to come out, was merely accommodating Himself to prejudices which He judged it unwise to combat.

This doctrine of accommodation to the errors and prejudices of the time was carried to still greater lengths. "Men may be accused," says Amand Saintes, "of dissimulation when they pass over in silence that which they dare not openly condemn; or of hypocrisy or actual deception when by their

## The Rise of German Rationalism. 189

words they give us to understand that they consider as true that which they know to be only the offspring of error or superstition. And undoubtedly Semler, and the Rationalists after him, accuse Jesus of these sins, when they say that—speaking of angels, of the expectation of the Messiah, of the last judgment, of demons, of the resurrection of the dead, and, finally, of the inspiration of the sacred scriptures—He did so only to accommodate Himself to the notions of His day, in order that by not contradicting them He might the more easily succeed in overturning the Mosaic religion."* But Semler's whole conception of Christ's work was of a piece with this. The following was his pet theory, and one which he often and lovingly dwelt upon. It explained everything, he believed, in the work of the Redeemer of men. There were two parties in the Jewish Church. One wished to unite philosophical thought with Jewish ceremonialism; the other asserted the entire independence of reason. "Christ appeared to conciliate them. Thus we see, that when He spoke with the Jewish party, He was eager to do homage to Moses; and when, on the contrary, He addressed Himself to the gnostic party, He spoke strongly against the prejudices of His nation. After the death of Jesus, His disciple Peter placed himself at the head of the Jewish party, and for this reason he confined the sphere of his activity to Judea. Paul declared himself for the gnostic party, and therefore are *his* views so liberal and *his* ideas more applicable to human kind. It

---
*Ibid. p. 103.

was an inevitable consequence, after the death of the Apostles, that these two parties should be divided into an infinity of smaller ones. The Christian churches felt the inconveniences of this, and the project of a universal or Catholic Church was formed. The bishops, therefore, met in council, and united the views of Peter and of Paul!"*

Everything was brought down to the pitifully low level of these views. With such admissions there was nothing left for infidelity to attack. Christianity had abandoned the Word of God, and had denied its Lord; and what could the enemies of either now accuse it of? Christianity—the Christianity of the New Testament, of the early Church, and of the Reformation—had turned its sword against itself and committed suicide. Its enemies could well afford to leave the poor, corrupting carcass undisturbed.

* *Ibid.* p. 107.

## CHAPTER IX.

### BLIGHTED HOPES.

SEMLER and his sympathisers were animated by the hope of saving Christianity. To effect this nothing had, in their judgment, any chance of success but a surgical operation. Limbs were freely sacrificed so that the vital parts might be spared. The Theologians were not alone in this endeavour. The necessities of the times appealed quite as strongly to the Metaphysicians to stem the tide of unbelief. Kant (1724-1804) laboured at Koenigsberg to build up a system of assured knowledge which would form a new basis for religion. A place was found for a Kantian Trinity and for other Christian beliefs, which were explained in his own fashion; but the Atonement was not needed, nor the operations of the Spirit, nor prayer. The result was a soulless, passionless, religion, which was devoid of life, of reality, and of influence. Fichte (1767-1814) attacked the problem on another side, and built up a system of idealism in which God was reduced to a form of thought. Those who missed vital religion in Kant, found that even the conviction of the reality of the Divine existence failed them in Fichte. Hegel (1770-1831) came anew to the rescue, and failed worse than either. He called his system "the final expression of the human intellect." It bears the mark, indeed, of highest metaphysical genius; but it is simply the fullest demonstration which man ever gave that reason is utterly powerless to supply the place of revelation. His "works," says Amand Saintes, "entitle their author to a place among the oracles who will be frequently consulted in philosophical science; but they cannot exculpate Hegel from the charge of having perverted all the ancient Christian opinions which he attempted to restore." Hegel, while professing to establish the great Christian verities, really explains them away; and the believer, in this highest attempt of mental science to endow him with the fullest knowledge of all things, has reason to remember the Spirit's warning to beware lest he be spoiled by philosophy and vain deceit.

Philosophic Rationalism thus failed utterly to raise a bulwark against Infidelity; Theological Rationalism failed as completely. Semler had painful proof of this in one of his own Rationalistic children. Charles Frederic Bahrdt (1741-1792) threw himself with ardour into theological studies, and while yet a young man became Professor of Biblical Theology at Leipzig. Here, when only twenty-six, he gave promise of the future by publishing his *Wishes of a Dumb Patriot*. Shortly afterwards an affair, in which his moral character was compromised, compelled him to give up his professorship and to leave Leipzig. From that time his faith rapidly decayed, and his boldness and scurrilous witticisms increased, until he became a kind of German Voltaire. His abilities and his rationalism obtained for him many warm friends, who procured him one position after another, sometimes in important ecclesiastical offices, sometimes as head of educational institutions. But nothing could prevent or retard his downward progress. In his autobiography, he lets us see how the foundations of a dead orthodoxy began to crumble away till the whole structure fell with a crash. "I came," he says, "to Giessen" (after leaving Leipzig) "as yet very orthodox. My belief in the divinity of the Scriptures, in the direct mission of Jesus, in His miraculous history, in the Trinity, in the gifts of grace, in natural corruption, in justification of the sinner by laying hold of the merits of Christ, and especially in the whole theory of satisfaction, seemed to be immovable. It was only the manner in which three persons were to be in one God, which had engaged my reason. I had only explained to myself a little better the work of the Holy Spirit, so as not to exclude man's activity. I had limited a little the idea of original sin, and in the doctrine of the Atonement and of justification I had endeavoured to uphold the value of virtue, and had cleared myself from the error that God, in his grace, should not pay any regard at all to human virtuous zeal."

The reader can measure his fall by bearing in mind the above confession and noting those beliefs which, he says, he still retained when at Giessen. Everything went. The notions of virtue, for which he had contended, went also. He became a man of most abandoned life. After wandering about through Germany and even to England, he settled at Halle. Here he was repulsed by Semler and his colleagues. He revenged himself by taking a mountain inn near to the town, where his followers crowded about him, and where he died a victim to his licentiousness. He poured out his hatred and mockery of Christianity in a series of works written for the masses, but which obtained an immense popularity among all sections of German society. "His writings were perused alike in palace and in cottage." *

But Semler was fated to have a still clearer demonstration that the concessions of Rationalism had strengthened Infidelity instead of disarming it. Three men who were destined to give a powerful impetus to their age were friends in their youth. Nicoläi (1733-1811) was the son of a Berlin bookseller. He employed his leisure moments in studying languages, philosophy, and the history of mathematics. When he was twenty-two he intervened in a controversy between two well-known literary men and published a pamphlet which, by its ability and impartiality, attracted the attention of Lessing (1729-1781), the prince of German prose-writers, and, in a sense, the creator of modern German literature. Lessing was

---

' Hurst, *History of Rationalism*, p. 120.

four years older than Nicoläi. His history is significant of the unrest of the time. The son of a pastor, he was destined for the Church, and was sent to Leipzig to study theology. He exchanged theology for medicine; and this he afterwards abandoned for literature and philosophy. There were other changes quite as significant. He frequented the society of the actors of the Berlin theatre, and had as his closest friends literary men of "advanced" views, who exercised a powerful and permanent influence upon his own opinions. At the time of Nicoläi's publication, Lessing was engaged in literary work in Berlin. Impressed by the work of Nicoläi, Lessing sought out the writer and introduced to him Moses Mendelssohn (1729-1786), a young Jew of Lessing's own age. Mendelssohn left behind him a great reputation as a metaphysical writer, but the name is now better known through the fame of his grandson, Felix Mendelssohn, the musical composer.

Conscious of their powers, the three friends often spoke of making a united effort to deliver Germany from the yoke of pedantry. Their dreams were prophetic; Nicoläi became a publisher, and his two companions united with him in the establishment of literary magazines and in the publication of a "Universal German Library," which revolutionised German taste and gave an impetus to the literature of their country, the effect of which it feels at the present hour. The convictions of these regenerators of German literature were like a strong undercurrent which carried with it the thought of the time. They did not engage in open warfare against Christianity; but Christian beliefs were distinctly ignored, and the Berlin publications became the most potent allies of infidelity.

This negative attitude was eventually exchanged by Lessing for declared war. A mystery long hung over the famous *Wolfenbüttel Fragments*, and has only in recent times been cleared away. There resided at Hamburg a certain Samuel Reimarus, a professor of philosophy and author of various works. He died in 1765, and left behind him a work which, for reasons that will soon appear, he had not had the courage to publish. His widow showed it to Lessing, who seems to have immediately conceived the desire to give it to the public. He was at that time Librarian to the Duke of Brunswick at Wolfenbüttel, and had the privilege of printing without submittting the work to the ordinary press-censorship. He procured a copy of Reimarus's work, which bore the title: "An Apology for the Rational Worshippers of God."

It was too strong meat even for that rationalistic age, and Lessing resolved to publish it in parts, beginning with the least offensive portion. In his "Documents for History and Literature," he published in 1774 a first selection under the title "Fragments by an Unknown Man." This merely pleaded for the toleration of the Deists. Another Fragment, published three years afterwards, found fault with Revelation in general, and then with the Old Testament. It was only in the last Fragment that the full attack upon the Christian Faith and the

Saviour of men was delivered. "Not content," says Vigouroux, "with having treated Moses as an impostor, 'The Unknown,' whom most people believed to be Lessing himself, did not blush to bring the same accusation against our Lord Jesus Christ. The writer strongly maintained, as the majority of German Rationalists have since done, that he had not ceased to be a Christian. To listen to him, he alone was the true Christian! It is not for Rationalists to leave the Church; it is for the members of the Church to become Rationalists! At the very moment when he thus proclaims himself the votary of Christ, he reduces his Master to the proportions of a patriot, who had not recoiled from knavery in order to reach his ends. The *intention* of Jesus was noble and generous! He desired to animate the Jewish people with a new life, and to restore to the old theocracy its ancient splendour. In order to succeed, all means seem to Him good. He had an understanding with John the Baptist, who became His accomplice. They mutually agreed to commend each other, and thus to double, while they enjoyed in common, their popularity and their influence upon the masses. The moment fixed for giving effect to the plan of Jesus was the feast of the Passover. On the day, which we call Palm Sunday, the Reformer, by his revolutionary entry into the capital of Judea, excited the multitude against the chief priests and the leaders of the people. Then, by an act of unheard-of temerity and hardihood, He violated the majesty of the Temple. It was too much to attempt all at once. His ardour had carried Him beyond bounds. He was arrested, condemned, executed. All those magnificent projects for the social regeneration of the Jewish people thus dashed themselves against an obstacle which He had not foreseen—the cross. He then repented of His enterprise, and expired complaining that He was forsaken by God. The apostles extricated themselves from the critical situation into which His punishment had thrown them, only by inventing the story of the Resurrection, and by spiritualising His doctrine of the Kingdom of God."\*

The horror with which the avowal of these sentiments filled the dead orthodoxy of Germany, may be imagined. The horror was succeeded by a perfect storm of indignation, in which even Rationalists played their part. Semler said that Lessing ought to be shut up in a madhouse! But the indignation of neither the Rationalists nor the Orthodox could stop the progress of corruption. In the preface to a refutation of the Fragments, Semler deplored the havoc wrought by the unbelief which he himself had let loose. He had imagined that by making a channel for a streamlet, he could prevent the fatal rush of a torrent. But the streamlet had only prepared the way, and the torrent followed. "More than one young man," he wrote, "received with enthusiasm the railleries directed against Revelation, accentuated them, and propagated them even among the common people, and among a class

---

\* *La Bible et les Decouvertes Modernes.*—Vol. i., pp. 22, 23.

## Blighted Hopes. 199

of followers of which the author had certainly never dreamed. More than one young man of serious inclinations, who had devoted himself to the sacred ministry, saw his convictions overthrown and found himself plunged in difficulty; more than one even chose another career rather than strive any longer with growing uncertainty."

What other fruits could be looked for? Semler had sowed the seed; Reimarus came and reaped the harvest. Blank Infidelity was simply the interpretation of what Rationalism meant. Believers in "a happy medium" substitute imagination for fact, and find by-and-bye that a stern necessity compels them to be either one thing or the other. The supposed "happy medium" is merely a "fool's paradise." Lessing appears to have seen that he had gone too far, and assumed the part of a defender of Revelation! But his defence of it was neither a disavowal nor a refutation of the opinions which he had published. He replied to his opponents that, even if the Fragmentist was right, Christianity remained intact! It was only the *letter* of the Scripture that was set aside; and, somehow, this could be done, and yet the *spirit* of the Scriptures be all the better for the change! The Rationalists understood the Bible better than the Bible understood itself, and they kindly removed the encumbering statements in which it had been trying to explain itself, and left to the spirit of the Bible that glorious freedom in which religion is associated with no definite statement or fact, and which enables every one to make it suit himself! The truths of religion, he said, *have nothing to do* with the facts of history! People could still be Christians though Jesus never died for our sins nor rose again for our justification!

Indefiniteness was the very essence of Lessing's idea of religious liberty. It was not the liberty to which possessors of revealed truth are raised, but a liberty to engage in an unending search for truth. It was the pleasure of seeking, not the delight of finding, that he desired. "If God," said he, "should hold in His right hand all truth, and in His left the ever-active impulse and love of search after truth, although accompanied with the condition that I should ever err, and should say 'choose,' I would choose the left with humility, and say, 'Give, Father! Pure truth belongs to Thee alone!'" The man who could speak in this way had lost all belief in the attainment of certainty; and in his poem of *Nathan the Wise*, he clearly intimates that for him all religions are equally true—and equally false! Nathan, a Jew of Jerusalem, seeks out Saladin to warn him that unbelief is dangerous to the State. Saladin says:—

Seeing thou art so wise, tell me what faith, what religion, seems to you the best.

NATHAN—Sultan, I am a Jew.

SALADIN—And, for my part, I am a Mussulman. Between us is the Christian. Of these three religions one alone can be true. A man like you does not remain where the chances of birth has placed him; or, if he does remain there, it is from reflection, from reason, from choice. In short, let me know your opinion.

NATHAN—Sultan, before I reply to you with all confidence, permit me to tell you a story. . . . Long ago there lived in the East a man who possessed a ring of inestimable value, and which came to him from a hand that was very dear. The stone was an opal, from which a thousand beautiful colours were reflected, and which possessed the mysterious power of rendering him who carried it with confidence acceptable to God and man. .... (The possessor) bequeathed the ring to the best beloved among his children, and he decreed that it should pass from hand to hand to the most deserving of the family, who should thus become, without regard to birth, and in virtue of the possession of the ring, the chief and the prince of the family . . . The ring passed thus from son to son, till it came to a father who had three sons, all of them equally obedient, equally lovable, and consequently equally beloved. . . When the moment of death drew near, the good father was in great perplexity. How could he deprive of the ring two of his sons who deserved it ? What was he to do ? He caused a workman to be brought to him secretly, and ordered him to make two other rings resembling it in every particular. Neither expense nor pains were spared to make the resemblance perfect. The jeweller succeeded so well that, when he brought the rings, the father himself was not able to distinguish that which had been used as the model for the two others. Pleased and satisfied, he called his three sons separately, gave to each of them his blessing and his ring, and died. He had hardly breathed his last sigh, when each of the sons came with his ring and desired to become the chief of the family. They examine, they quarrel, they complain. All is of no avail. The true ring cannot be recovered—(he pauses, awaiting a reply from the Sultan, then proceeds)—it is equally impossible to recover now for ourselves the true religion.

Lessing has himself pointed out the significance of these words. "The opinions of Nathan," he says, "on all the positive religions has for a long time been my own." In Lessing's view, all religions were, therefore, equally true, and all of them equally false. It can easily be imagined what kind of help was obtained by his defence of Christianity at the expense of the Bible. It was a Christianity without doctrine and without facts; a religion without power for the present, and without hope or blessing for the future. But "The Fragments" was not the only publication which led the Rationalistic Exodus to the frightful wilderness of unbelief. I have spoken of Lessing's friend and co-worker, Nicoläi, the Berlin Publisher. He employed a staff of literary helpers who moulded, by a lively periodic literature, the thinking of the age. Every touch of the fingers of these one hundred and thirty-three authors swept away what they called "superstition," or sharpened some anti-Christian sentiment or conviction. Nicoläi himself published at this very time a novel entitled "The Life and Opinions of Mr. Sebaldus Nothanker." Its object was to throw ridicule upon the ministers who still remained faithful to the old beliefs and to the teaching of Scripture. On the other hand, the hero is presented for the reader's admiration, and possibly for his imitation. He is a preacher, but a preacher of the new and better order. He uses texts from the Bible as "a somewhat dangerous medium for inculcating useful truths." Temporal happiness is set forth as the supreme end of life. His sermons deal with health and with the art of prolonging one's life. There is a good deal of useful information about diet, early rising, and kindred themes. His hearers are told how to care for their cattle, and how to cultivate their fields, so that they make money. That was the rationalistic creed, catechism, and summary of "the things most surely believed among us." Christianity was reduced, as Vigouroux has said, to "*la morale du pot-au-feu*"; or, in other words, Revelation was given to show us how "to make the pot boil"!

But there were other fruits besides Lessing's writings and the literature poured forth from Nicoläi's printing presses. The spirit of doubt, let loose within the Church, desolated everything. A host of writers for the young sprang up, whose books poured unbelief into the school and the home. "Epitomes of the Scriptures on a philosophical plan," says Hurst, "were introduced." Ammon, in one of his works, tells the young people that the books of the Old Testament have no divine worth or character for us, except so far as they agree with the spirit of the Gospel. As to the New Testament, much must be figuratively understood, since many things have no immediate relation to our times. Christ is a mere man. Dinter was a voluminous writer on theological subjects, and in his books he tells the children that the Scriptures are marked by wrong teaching regarding God, angels, and miracles. He gives teachers directions how to teach the new views and yet avoid the censure of the Orthodox. He recommends two plans of catechising. In catechising about Jonah, for example, he suggests one style before an audience not sufficiently enlightened, and where all remains in its old state; and quite another for places which have more light. We know something of such Jesuitry even now; Rationalism has certainly the crookedness, if not the wisdom, of the serpent. In the prophecies concerning the Messiah a double explanation is given for the same reason. One is the old orthodox way, the other a more probable, neological plan. A clever teacher is to choose for himself; a dull one may ask the Parish Clergyman how far he may go!" *

---

\* *History of Rationalism*, pp. 156, 157.

Becker published a "Universal History for the Young." He explains the rise of Christianity as follows: "Jesus probably got the first notion of His undertaking from being a friend of John, and going often to his father's, who was a priest; and from the Gospel it appears that the sight of feasts and of the crowd of worshippers had a great effect on Him. . . The indications of the Messiah in the Old Testament had produced a great effect on Jesus and John, who were both hot-heads, such as destiny raises up for some great purpose." It is painful to reproduce these blasphemies; but it is well to know what rationalism is prepared to teach children in order to save them from infidelity! He speaks of the Evangelists as "wretched biographers." This food for babes was still further poisoned. There was no truth in the story of Christ's death on the cross, and none in that of the resurrection. The seeming death was only a prolonged faint, of which He took advantage to make his disciples believe that he had conquered death and was alive for evermore!

The sanctuary was invaded as well as the school and the home. We are not unacquainted with the painful manipulation of hymns for Christian worship by rationalistic hands. Our home rationalists are only imitating the work of their foreign predecessors. The congregations could not be permitted to sing beliefs which the preachers had either quietly discarded, or were openly denouncing as superstition. "New hymn books were introduced into many of the churches, and the people sang rationalism. General

Superintendents, Consistorial Counsellors, and court preachers, rivalled each other in preparing a new volume of religious songs for the territory under their charge."* This was a deadly blow to German Christianity. Music and song are dear to the German heart, and so long as the old hymns and chorals were left alone, Christianity had still a hold upon the people. But the rationalists were quite aware of this, and steps were taken not only to alter the hymns, but to introduce music from the beer-garden and the opera, in which the people could not join. From that time sacred song began to lose its ancient power to comfort the weary and the heavy-laden, to inspire trust, and to lead back wandering feet to God.

* *Ibid.* p. 160.

## CHAPTER X.

DEEPENING DECAY.—THE RISE OF THE HIGHER CRITICISM: EICHHORN AND PAULUS.

WE might have expected that the attack of Reimarus upon the Scripture would have warned the Rationalists that there were breakers ahead, and that they would have turned while there was yet time. Hopes of this kind have often been held out in the midst of similar declensions. They are deluding many to-day. The extravagancies of some, we are assured, will lead to a conservative attitude in others. It is true that there is a pause, and, perhaps, for the moment, grief and consternation. But there are forces behind as well as terrors before. Those on board a fated ship may see the breakers raging in front of them, but they cannot turn and flee from destruction. Wind and tide forbid—the same wind and tide that drove them toward the shore. More easily driven, or less able to resist, Reimarus is only the first of a doomed fleet to reach the rocks. They have all of them abandoned beliefs which once kept them securely anchored, and their staying power is gone. They have adopted other convictions which must reveal themselves, and which will relentlessly draw those who have embraced them to the unbelief and despair from which they sprang.

The publication of the views of Reimarus had indeed raised a storm in Protestant Germany, but neither storm nor dread drove men back to the old faith in the Bible. They only produced a further advance into unbelief and a deeper degrading of the Scriptures. It is at this point that we mark the rise of "The Higher Criticism." The name as well as the thing is due to Eichhorn (1752-1827), who became the leader in this new advance. He studied at Göttingen under J. D. Michaelis. When 23 years of age he became professor of Oriental Languages at Jena, and 13 years afterwards removed to Göttingen, where he held a similar position. He was a man of vast erudition, but, even in the judgment of leaders of the critical school which he founded, he was lacking in that most essential quality for a writer on Scripture—spiritual insight. Ewald says that, as far as the religious view-point was concerned, the Bible was to Eichhorn, from first to last, a sealed book. This fact will explain much that follows.

In the preface to his "Introduction to the Old Testament" he named the new science, which he thought it necessary to found, "The Higher Criticism." He recurs to the name again in the preface to his "Introduction to the New Testament." The Lower Criticism, *die niedere Kritik*, is that which concerns itself with the text of the Scriptures and with kindred matters. But it was now necessary, he imagined, to take a higher flight. It was not enough to ascertain whether the manuscripts which we now possess accurately represent the original autographs. Even though we had the autographs themselves, and though the Lower Criticism was rendered unnecessary, questionings and inquiries would remain; and to these the Higher Criticism addresses itself. What has been the origin of the Books? How are we to judge of their contents? In what way are their statements to be understood? Though the eighteenth century of the Christian era had well-nigh run its course, it seemed to Eichhorn that this great field of investigation had not been so much as entered upon. In the New Testament, he said, while the Lower Criticism had done much, the Higher Criticism had as yet hardly tried its powers. In regard to the Old Testament, on which his strength was spent, he felt himself to be like an adventurous discoverer surveying an unknown territory.

What led him, then, to these new investigations? He has told us that "The Fragments" of Reimarus made a deep impression upon him. He thought that Reimarus "went too far." The phrase is deplorably familiar. It is the invariable introduction used by those who are prepared to hand over the Bible to the tender mercies of its foes. Like the foolish Eli, whose weak remonstrance only added zest to his children's sin, they shake the head and express, with studied courteousness, that they are really of opinion that things are being carried "too far." Eichhorn, instead of meeting Reimarus's infidelity with unyielding front and vigorous repudiation, attempted to gain over his school by conciliation. He himself could not admit that the Old Testament owed its origin to imposture. But there was one fundamental position, as to which he and Reimarus were quite agreed—*there had been no supernatural intervention*. God is certainly said to have appeared, to have spoken, to have sent one messenger after another, and to have worked miracles. All this was incredible. But was not the denial of the miraculous equivalent to the endorsement of the position of Reimarus that the Bible was an imposture? By no means, replied Eichhorn. The credit of the Bible could still be saved, though the miraculous was denied. To accomplish this was the task of the Higher Criticism; and in this way the new science, like all its rationalistic predecessors, came to the help of the Bible! It was the friend and ally, and by no means the enemy, of Revelation! Like the rash surgeon, who, eager to exercise his art, notes what he hastily concludes to be alarming symptoms, makes deadly incisions, or severs one limb after another, and leaves to those whose fears he came to allay a hideously maimed carcase, so the Higher Criticism rushed in to save Christianity by the free application of its surgical instruments to the books of Revelation. Or, to follow a truer figure, Satan once more appeared as an angel of light. He had helped the fearful friends of Revelation before: he was equally ready to assist them again, and to lead to new developments.

In order to save the Bible, while rejecting the miraculous, he laid down three principles. The first is that all ancient peoples, the Greeks as well as the Orientals, attributed to the direct action of God everything which impressed them by its grandeur or which surpassed their powers of understanding. We have to take this into account in dealing with all ancient literature. Hitherto an exception had been made in the case of the Bible; but, from this lack of firmness in the application of the principle of natural interpretation, the greater part of our difficulties had sprung. There was no reason for making any exception in regard to the Scriptures. And herein lay Eichhorn's imagined triumph and vindication of the Higher Criticism. He had saved the Bible! Reimarus's charge of imposture falls at once to the ground! No one thinks of setting down Herodotus as an impostor because certain things are attributed by him to the direct action of the gods. Why then should imposture be attributed to the Biblical writers? It was their way to think and to say such things. It was a characteristic of the times, and the things were thought and said in all sincerity! The second principle was—that we must not treat Oriental hyperbole as a literal statement of fact. Up to that time, Eichhorn imagined, this had not been clearly seen, and Semitic genius had been misunderstood. It had not been perceived that the Semites by nature and custom exaggerate everything. We must, therefore, make due allowance for this peculiarity, and reduce their statements to ordinary proportions.

The ancient commentators on the Bible have perpetually placed a wrong construction upon the sacred books. and we must henceforth avoid falling into the like mistake!

Lastly, the Hebrews, seeing God everywhere and referring to His direct action all the phenomena of nature, have omitted, in their historical narratives, essential details to which they attached no importance, but which in reality proved, that what they judged to be supernatural, were among the most natural things in the world.

These were the principles of the Higher Criticism as established by its founder. We need not trouble to separate the grains of truth which they contain from the mountains of error. Eichhorn himself will show us whether any man of common sense or of common honesty can accept and apply his "principles." He applied them to the three first chapters of Genesis. The first chapter of the Bible is only, he says, a poetic description of the universe. It is a symbolic painting, not a history. The history of the creation of Adam is only a coloured picture of his appearance upon the earth. Eve had appeared at the same time as Adam, but in a different place. "Adam," he says, " had lived but a short time in the company of the beasts, when he observed a blank in the universe. He saw two creatures of the same kind among the animals; he only of all that God had created was solitary and isolated. Then there arose within him the desire for a companion. He wandered here and there in Eden—the author of our primitive history has passed over this detail in silence —in search of a creature who bore some resemblance to himself. Wearied with his wanderings, he fell into a profound sleep and dreamed that he was divided into two. When he awoke and was examining this hitherto unexplored part of his appointed abode, Eve presented herself before him, and God led her to him. It is quite true that the text says that God "took one of his ribs"; but this expression can only mean what we have just said: he dreamed, and it seemed to him during his slumber that God had taken one of his ribs."

Here the literal sense of the sacred narrative is set aside as incredible. But, we are assured, there is no attempt on the part of the Biblical writer to impose upon his readers or even to misinform them. He saw God's hand in this transaction from first to last, and therefore the narrative was cast in this mould. It was not only the writer's way; it was the way of the time. Nobody, therefore, was misled. It is only we Western, prosaic people, who must take everything, as the French say, "at the foot of the letter"—who impose a meaning upon the writer's words which they were never intended to bear! It was of no use, therefore, to remind Eichhorn that the Scripture distinctly says that Eve was created *after* Adam. That, also, is dismissed as part of the writer's mannerism. He explains, in the same way, the expulsion from the Garden of Eden and its cause. The tree of the knowledge of good and evil was a tree which he has no doubt still exists. Its fruit, good for the serpent, is a slow poison for men. The serpent never had any conversation with Eve. She observed the animal eat and enjoy the fruit, and this spectacle formed the temptation which the writer, following the Eastern method, has placed before us so dramatically. Eichhorn tells, or rather translates, the rest of the story as follows: "Eve and Adam ate the forbidden fruit and their eyes were opened. . . . Towards evening of the same day, there occurred a violent storm. It was possibly the first which man had witnessed since his appearance upon the earth. *They heard the voice of God as He walked in the Garden. The voice of God!* Who does not know that this magnificent expression is used a thousand times to designate thunder? . . . The noise of the thunder is *the voice of God;* and because the rolling of the thunder resounds for a long time in Adam's ear, *God walks in the Garden.* A new thunder-clap breaks out behind the trees, and Adam believes that he hears: "*Adam! where art thou?* Excuses then follow excuses; Adam puts the blame upon Eve, Eve upon the serpent. . . . The dialogue of God with Adam and Eve is nothing else, as I believe, than the compunctions which torment the evil conscience of the guilty. As the thunder continued to growl, the guilty pair fled from Paradise. We read that '*God drove out the man;*' this simply signifies, in the language of uncultivated people who make God intervene in everything, that *they fled.* And can one imagine a more natural cause for their flight than a tempest?"

Vigouroux remarks upon this interpretation that the poison must indeed have been a "slow" one, since it suffered Adam to live 930 years after it was eaten! * But like many another vagary of criticism, this theory which formed its first attempt, walks no more among living things. The critics desire only to forget it. Eichhorn was merely one of the many physicians who rushed to the help of German Protestantism (suffering from the wounds inflicted by a bold and aggressive infidelity), on whom she spent her living; but with regard to all of whom the confession had to be made that she was nothing bettered but rather grew worse. The narration of the methods followed by the Physicians has little value for science, but is of the utmost importance for British Christianity, whom the successors of these men desire to treat like her German sister. Eichhorn applied his method to the great transactions of the deliverance from Egypt, of Sinai, of the Wilderness, and of the entire Old Testament History. These were, all of them, natural events, narrated by the writers as if they were direct interventions of God. He halted at the New Testament. Reverence for Christ forbade him to lay his hand upon the Redeemer's story and to drag *that* down to the level of ordinary every-day events.

But the halt was only temporary. Eichhorn had led the way; others soon followed who went further. Paulus (1761-1851) had an unfortunate early experience which may, in some measure, explain his

---

* *Les Livres Saintes et la Criticque Rationaliste*, Vol. ii., p. 381.

extraordinary theory. He was only six years of age when he lost his mother. His father was so overwhelmed with grief that his mind became unhinged. He lived in another world—a world of phantoms. He imagined himself surrounded by spirits of whom his late wife was Queen. On account of these aberrations he was deposed from the sacred office which he held at Leonberg. These early experiences left marks on the lad's life that were never afterwards effaced. He has himself told us how he took advantage of his father's credulty and made him believe what he wished, and how these hallucinations led him to doubt the reality of the supernatural. It seemed to him that on the narrow stage of his own poor home, the whole tragedy, or comedy, of supposed Divine communications and answering beliefs and superstitions was re-enacted.

He carried this conviction with him when he went to study Theology at Tübingen, and it retained, unshaken and unchallenged, its sad supremacy during his long life of 90 years. It seemed to him more and more a triumphant solution of the great problem presented by the Scripture. It entirely removed the ugly element of fraud, while it made equally unnecessary the hollow theory of Eichhorn that the sacred writers said what they did not mean. They did mean, said Paulus, to write a record of genuine miracles. They intended to tell us that they saw angels, that they heard the voice of God, and that they or others were witnesses of the most wonderful interposition of Divine might. They wished us to believe these things for the best of all reasons—they themselves believed them. They were just such experiences as his father would have written, not only in all good faith, but also with the fullest conviction of their reality and importance.

With this master-key, Paulus does not hesitate to approach even the mysteries of the New Testament. The story begins with illusion. The aged priest Zacharias, the father of the Baptist, is the first victim. Excited by the unwonted honour of being permitted to offer incense in the Holy Place, he believes that he sees in the undulations of the smoke, rising in the dim light of the sanctuary, the form of an angel. He has long desired a son, and it seems to him that the angel assures him that his desire will be fulfilled. As the Gospel story begins, so it proceeds. The great army of the faithful, among whom and by whom the Kingdom of God was founded, are only a host of pious visionaries. As Zacharius took the contortions of the ascending incense fumes for the bright form of the Angel of God, so Mary mistakes an unknown visitor for Gabriel. The voice that came from heaven at the baptism of Jesus was simply the embodiment of an emotion common at the same moment to Jesus and John. " Were not their emotions too intense to permit them to discern clearly," asks Paulus, "whether the voice which they had heard came from without, or only spoke within their own hearts?" The transfiguration was merely the reflection of the light of a glorious sunrise upon Jesus, and two strangers clothed in white with whom our

Lord had an interview on the mountain top. Just as Peter rushed to a wrong conclusion regarding the appearance of Jesus, so Matthew, Mark, and Luke are misled in regard to the healing of the leper. The leper did not ask Jesus to *heal* him, he only wanted advice as to whether his leprosy had not worked itself out. Jesus saw from the abundant eruption that the crisis of the malady was past, and signified this in the words "be clean." The disciples, ready to see the marvellous in everything that Jesus did, misunderstood the matter; but a little reflection enables us to see what they missed, and to recover the fact from the midst of their excited fancies. In other instances Jesus only gave similar proofs of his ability as a physician. He cured blindness by anointing with a special eye-salve, and deafness by pouring a powder into the ear. These natural methods were passed over by the thronging crowds and by the disciples. The cures, as they imagined, were effected by a touch or by a word—in short, by the finger of God, and not by ordinary means!"

The studies of Paulus thus only gave depth and stability to the doubts planted in his mind through the unfortunate events of his childhood. The thoughts of others, with which he became acquainted, crystallized, so to speak, around that thread. He was swayed for a short time by Eichhorn's theory that the miraculous was only the natural represented in Oriental forms of speech, and he began his literary career by contributions to a publication under Eichhorn's editorship. But he soon perceived that it was impossible to continue the application of Eichhorn's theory to the Scriptures, The hideousness of the fallacy became more manifest with every step that was taken. He studied Kant, and hailed the distinction insisted upon in his philosophy of the objective element in a narrative, or the fact, and the subjective element, or the judgment of the narrator. This distinction, coupled with "the psychological explanation" of Spinoza, led him back to the doubts of his boyhood. The supernatural in Scripture was not simply in the forms of expression, as Eichhorn believed and taught. It lay deeper. It was found in the thought and conviction of the narrators. It is not a mistake of our colder Western intellect to imagine that they are speaking of what lies outside the region of ordinary occurrences. They intended to represent these matters in this very fashion. It is still a mistake—Paulus believes that as firmly as Eichhorn—but the mistake must be shifted one step further back. It does not lie with us: it lay with them. *They* mistook the natural for the miraculous, and the business of the expositor of Scripture is to find the objective element in the midst of the subjective—to extract the needle of fact from the haystack of elated and fantastic imaginations!

## CHAPTER XI.

### DEEPER DEPTHS: ASTRUC AND DE WETTE.

ONE step more was needed to evolve the new criticism of the Bible. But, before I speak of this, a contributory stream of influence requires a passing notice. We henceforth hear much of *Elohist* and *Jehovist, Elohistic* and *Jehovistic*. I hope to deal somewhat fully with this chief corner-stone of the new criticism by and by; but a passing notice is meanwhile a necessity, These words owe their origin to Jean Astruc (1684-1766), a French physician and celebrated writer on medical subjects. His father had been a Protestant pastor; but, on the revocation of the Edict of Nantes, having no taste for martyrdom, he purchased ease and plenty by conforming to the Catholic faith. His son was brought up a Catholic, but, no doubt, owed his theological tastes to the studies with which his father was still occupied. The question of the composition of Genesis had been long debated among the learned. The most recent event mentioned in the book, as every reader is aware, happened ages before the time of Moses, while its other contents stretch back from that time to the Creation. Where did Moses obtain his information? Faith has an immediate and perfectly satisfactory answer to that question: Moses received his information from God. But theologians have always been ready to exercise the most scrupulous care of the Divine dignity. Like some Eastern monarch, our Father must dwell in stately seclusion. He must not demean Himself by appearing too often! Only in cases of the most extreme necessity must there be anything in the shape of a Divine interposition! The theological idea, in fact, is the very opposite of the scriptural, as it is of that which God has given of Himself in Creation, and which He is also constantly imparting in Providence and in Grace. These tell us that there is *nothing* beneath God's thought and *nothing* outside His care. He plans for the sparrow of the house-top and numbers the hairs of our head. We exist upon Divine interpositions that have gone beyond all counting; and the biggest miracles recorded in Scripture are only glimpses of how we ourselves are dealt with by Him in whom we live and move and have our being.

But the theologians take their own way, and they have laid down the law that there must be no miracle where the end can in any way be reached by natural means. Moses was, therefore, supposed to obtain his information from human sources. He must have possessed early documents, some of which had possibly been handed down by Abraham. Accepting this as certain, Astruc asked himself whether there was any means of detecting and separating the documents thus incorporated in Genesis. Reading the book with this problem before him, he was arrested by a feature which up to that time had hardly been noticed. In the first chapter of Genesis the word "God" (Hebrew, *Elohim*) alone occurs. The Creator has to be named again and again, but this name, and no other, is used. In other parts of the book there are sections where the Divine name is as persistently "LORD" (Hebrew, *Jehovah*). In the second and third chapters these names are combined, and we have "LORD-God" *(Jehovah-Elohim)*.

There is a simple explanation of the facts, and that explanation is got in the ordinary way—by recurrence to a dictionary. The names are Hebrew words with distinct meanings, and they can be proved to have never lost their significance for the writers of Scripture. *Elohim* describes God as the possessor of every form of power, and is well represented by our word "Almighty." *Jehovah*, again, means, "He-shall-cause-it-to-be," and describes God in His faithfulness. It is quite evident that there might be prolonged sections in which one aspect of God's nature would be manifested, and where, therefore, the same name would be constantly used. This would be exchanged for the other only when the aspect of the Divine nature indicated was succeeded by that which the other name more fitly described.

But we often find what we come to seek; and so Astruc found here his supposed documents. The persistent use of the same name in certain sections and its exchange for another in other sections could, for him, have only one explanation: *these names revealed the hands of different writers!* No man, he argued, continually uses the same expression unless he has no other for which to exchange it. "Can we cite any like example," he asks, in his now famous book, "and dare we, without proof, impute to Moses a fault which no other writer has ever committed? Is it not, on the contrary, more natural to explain this variation by supposing, as we do, that the book of Genesis is formed of two, or three, memoirs (joined and stitched together in fragments), the authors of which had always each given to God the same name, but each a different name, one that of *Elohim*, and the other that of *Jehovah*, or of *Jehovah-Elohim?*" *

Such was the origin of the now famous theory. It was accepted by Eichhorn and by others with admiration and delight, and it has been made the foundation of the Higher Criticism, which till then had the will to strike at Scripture but lacked the power. Astruc's name is revered as that of the Newton of the new science. Reuss says that the discovery that the names of God indicated the work of different writers "is still regarded as one of the most solidly established principles of this great and laborious pursuit." The reader will hardly credit the

---

* *Conjectures sur les Memoires Originaux,* &c., p. 13.

statement that this "solidly established" principle has been long disproved and discarded by the critics themselves; that they have done this silently without any confession of error or acknowledgment of change; and that they continue to talk as if the building which they had reared upon that foundation were still standing. *But such is nevertheless the fact.* They found it impossible to continue the belief that the use of the names of God indicated different writers. They give the use of both names to the same writer as their predecessors did before Astruc was born. Their Jehovist uses (they themselves believe and teach) the name *Elohim*; and their Elohist used the name *Jehovah*. But, if this is so, then Astruc's distinction was a dream, and every inference built upon it has been founded upon a delusion. In any other department of human labour—in any pursuit worthy of the name of science—this would have been acknowledged long ago. The critics, however, have allowed the public to believe that the distinction still holds good, and that everyone of the revolutionary and Bible-dishonouring deductions they have drawn from it must be received as truer than the truth of God!

We can well understand the enthusiasm with which Astruc's "Conjectures" were hailed when we note how well the book served the Rationalistic attack upon the Bible. Astruc himself applied his theory only to Genesis, and even that he believed owed its present form to Moses. The theory was no sooner transplanted to Germany, however, than it bore quite other fruit. The distinction was applied to the whole of the Pentateuch. It gave the Rationalists the very instrument which they needed. In the august name of science they were now able, as has been well said, "to divide and conquer." Once the unity of the book was destroyed, and the supposed parts were assigned to different writers, the work of discrediting the history was easy. Less and less was ascribed to Moses. The earliest portions were set down as written long after his day; the later were declared to be still more recent; while the piecing of them together was the work of a yet more modern time. How Astruc in this way served the work of demolition we shall immediately see.

De Wette (1780-1849) began his studies at Jena under Greisbach, a pupil of Semler and of Paulus, whose explanation of the miracles we noticed in the last chapter. De Wette was at first charmed with the theory of Paulus; but when he attempted to apply it, he felt that it could not be sustained. It was impossible to believe that such an assembly of lunatics, as Paulus imagined the Bible writers to have been, were ever associated together outside of a mad-house. But, if the miracles were not the impressions made upon visionaries, how could they be explained? Was it necessary to revert to the old belief that the miracles were real? There are hopeful souls who are always expecting to see the Rationalists return into the home of faith. "Have patience with them," they say, "and all will yet be well." It must be confessed, however, that history gives small encouragement to the fond belief. The churches of our own land which drifted into Arianism have never returned to the faith from which they strayed. They had gone ever further away, until they have parted with almost every conviction that once bound them to the evangelical churches of Christendom. The hope was equally falsified in the case of German Rationalism. De Wette, disappointed in Paulus, did not return to the belief from which his teacher had turned aside; he went still further from it. A new theory was then making frightful havoc in profane history and literature. Everything ancient was discredited. What had been supposed to be history was now set down as myth or fable, a parable in which some truth had been set forth, but which was afterwards accepted as fact and inserted as history. Wolff (1759-1824), a once-famous classical scholar, applied the new theory to the poems of Homer. No such man had ever existed! The poems were the work of several authors, were collected into one book in the age of Pericles, and were attributed to an imaginary blind poet with whose name they have ever since been associated. Niebuhr (1776-1831) carried the mythical theory into Roman history. Men had mistaken for historical facts fanciful allusions and mere folk-lore, which it was now the business of the sober historian to separate from the record with which they had been so long associated. The spirit of scepticism had, in fact, descended upon German thought, and a haze of doubt was settling down upon everything that had descended from ancient times.

Here, however, lay the suggestion which De Wette now appeared to need. He saw that the supposition that the sacred writers were visionaries, who had mistaken their own impressions and fancies for facts, could not be maintained. How, then, could the Bible miracles be explained? That they were real occurrences and interpositions of Divine power was still more incredible to De Wette. Astruc, Wolff, and Niebuhr pointed to the pathway. If the Old Testament contained mere traditions—if it was not a record written by contemporaries, but legends first committed to writing centuries afterwards—then the marvellous element in them was at once explained! It is the way with legends to develop in this very fashion. The snowball increases in size as it is rolled along, and the stories of ancient heroes are always marvellous by the time they have reached remote generations. Those to whom nations look back with gratitude and reverence are regarded with deepening awe as the ages roll between them and posterity. It is thus that the gods have passed into their greatness. There was no reason, in De Wette's judgment, why what had happened among other peoples should not have occurred among the Jews. Everything now depended upon the manipulation of the documents. The division of Elohistic and Jehovistic documents, each of them written long centuries after the events, and these put together by an editor at a period still later, ended the trouble and removed the mystery! The Bible was not history: it was mythology. It was Israelitish folk-lore, that had afterwards been made the basis of the Israelitish religion.

In 1805, when he was twenty-five years of age, De Wette began his partition of the Pentateuch. This first attempt was an essay, in which he maintained that Deuteronomy was not written by the author of the first four books of the Pentateuch. The essay was followed by a much more important work in 1806—his "Introduction to the Old Testament." It made a profound impression, and must always be remembered as marking a new era in the history of "The Higher Criticism." The old ideas regarding the authorship of the sacred books—ideas in many cases originated by the explicit statements of the Bible—were now completely set aside. Criticism, he maintained, must henceforth set aside tradition, and get to the facts by means of its own researches. All external sources of information, it was said, were wanting; but their loss was immaterial, and was by no means to be regretted; for it called into existence that which, after all, was the surest guide—the Higher Criticism. This belief has become the chief cornerstone of the new edifice. It is the boast and the inspiration of the critics; but they are as mistaken here as they are in their rejection of ancient testimony regarding the origin of the books of Scripture. De Wette's ignorance that the field was not his own, may be excused; for Champollion's discoveries had not then given a voice to the testimony of ancient

Egypt. But the persistence of his followers, in clinging to a principle now manifestly false, deserves the heaviest censure. External sources of information are *not* wanting. In the most wonderful manner they have been supplied just as their absence was being made the pretext of one of the most insidious attacks upon the Bible which scepticism has ever planned. Three years before the publication of De Wette's first essay, Grotefend had made a beginning in unlocking the mysteries of the cuneiform alphabet, and Champollion, though only fifteen years of age when De Wette began his literary career, already felt that it was his destiny to solve the problem of the Egyptian writing. The discoveries made in the one region and in the other have discredited the Higher Criticism on every side, and on every side have justified the Scripture.

"The Introduction" was followed by a Commentary on the Psalms, the only Old Testament commentary which he ever wrote. But it was the work of a critic, not of an expositor. He tries to show that the prophetic Psalms do not apply to the Messiah; for such distinct prophecy would have been a miracle, and Rationalism, like Atheism, has decreed that "miracles do not happen." The Davidic authorship of the majority of the Psalms attributed to "the sweet singer of Israel" is denied, and they are assigned to a later date. We are reminded in this, as in other matters, of what s now happening in English criticism. De Wette professed the deepest veneration for the Bible. But this did not hinder the work of destruction. He spoke of the Chronicles as manipulating history in the interests of the Levitical caste. In a later work, his "Historical and Critical Introduction," the same charge is brought against the whole of the Old Testament history. "The historical point of view," he says, "is that of an exclusive theocracy. Almost everything is looked at in connection with the theocracy, that is to say with the relations existing between God and the people of Israel... A divine plan dominates the history in a visible manner, and all the particular events are subordinated to this plan more or less logically; further, God Himself immediately intervenes in the history by revelations and by miracles; in other words," he adds, "*history gives place to mythology.*"

But the writers, let the reader be pleased to note, are carefully shielded from blame. Their character is saved—at the expense of their work. The manipulation of the history, in favour of the priestly caste, and of Israel's supposed special relation to God, was not theirs. *The traditions had assumed that shape in their transmission from one generation to another*, and the writers placed them on record in the most absolute good faith. The same is true of the miracles recorded. The writers did not invent them. They received them from tradition, and because they fully believed them they handed them on to us. They were victims of mistake, not authors of falsehood. As to the prophets, there has been an entire misapprehension. They were merely poets, using poetic licence, and representing facts, already accomplished, as predicted by celebrated personages. Here, then, is the third and last step of the Rationalistic explanation of the miraculous. Eichhorn taught that the Biblical writers never intended to describe any miracle at all. There has been a mistake; but the mistake is ours. We have failed to understand their style, and supposed them, in our Western, unimaginative way, to be talking of the miraculous when they were merely describing what was perfectly ordinary and natural. Then came Paulus, when that explanation broke down, and, instead of leading men back to faith, he led them further astray. The Bible did undoubtedly relate miracles: but it did so in perfect good faith. The writers were themselves imposed upon through their own ardent or unbridled and diseased imaginations. It was a mistake; but a mistake that lay one step further back than where Eichhorn placed it. It was not with us; it was with the writers. And now came De Wette, when Paulus could no longer be believed in. But neither did he lead us back to the place of faith any more than Paulus had done. The face of Criticism was turned away from God, and "advance" was simply further extension of the distance which was separating from Him. There was certainly mistake, said this new authority; bu the blunder lay neither with us nor with the writers. It lay in the material with which they dealt. Eichhorn, and even Paulus —let the reader note it well—had *left us history in the Bible.* De Wette now took even that away; we had only myth, the misunderstandings and the grotesque imaginings of barbaric men. *That* was the foundation on which we had been building for time and for eternity! It was from that puddle—that stagnant, stinking pool—we had been seeking to draw the pure streams of the water of life!

De Wette was made for better things. While studying at Jena he had become a convert to the Pantheism of Fichte. "For some time," he says, in a paper published after his death, "I was happy in this error. I was proud to think that I had the power to be virtuous without relying upon any faith. But this illusion soon disappeared, and I felt myself wretched. Robbed of all belief in an immaterial world, I saw myself isolated, abandoned to myself, and, in common with the whole of humanity, I was launched into the world without an object. My soul was filled with contradictions and uncertainties; no breath of life came to warm the coldness of my heart, and death, like a bad genius, hovered over my existence. No reasoning was able to bring me peace; my feelings revolted against the convictions of my intelligence." He tried one spiritual physician after another—Schleiermacher among them—but with no lasting benefit. Baron Bunsen tells how he met him in Switzerland, looking old and weary, and with a look on his face of unsatisfied longing. He was attending the meetings of a Moravian convention, probably with the desire of learning something of their happy secret. Lines were found among his papers after his death, which told that, with all his seeking, he had found no rest. They run thus:—

> I have sown the seed,
> But where is now the yellowing harvest?
> How seldom is it that we comprehend
> And that we well apply what we have learned!
> I have lived in a troubled time;
> The unity of the faith was broken;
> I threw me into the conflict;
> In vain; I did not make the struggle cease!

He had destroyed the possibility of rest: he had crushed belief in the supernatural, in the manifested love of God: and for man's heart there is no home but that. If *De Wette's* soul was wrung with a sense of loss, will they who follow in his steps find a table in the wilderness?

De Wette, like Eichhorn, refrained from applying his system to the New Testament. But the principles laid down for the Old Testament could not be confined to any one portion of the Bible; they must also apply to the New. Yet this self-restraint imposed upon many people. They said, "It is only the Old Testament that is taken. We do not rest upon that, and it need not trouble us much what is done with it so long as the New Testament is left to us." A rude awakening, however, awaited those that were at ease in *Zion*, and that were comforting themselves with the delusion that there was no danger. To David Frederick Strauss (1808-1874) must ever be assigned the honour, or the infamy, of proving to mankind what the Higher Criticism must ultimately mean. Strauss's home, like that of Paulus, was unfavourable to deep and lasting belief. His father was a firm believer in the facts of Christianity, but failed to carry its maxims into his business and his life. He presented daily before the eyes of his observant son a picture of religion without principle. His mother, on the contrary, proved to him that, within certain limits at least, there can be principle without religion. She manifested daily the uprightness which her husband lacked, and she was as opposed to him in his beliefs as in his practices. She saw nothing more in Christ than a good and pious man.

Strauss has left behind him many details of his early years which show that the faith with which he started in life's journey was dragged through one abyss of credulity after another, so that when it finally emerged there was no more life left in it. It was a time when the marvels of revived magic, of mesmerism, and of clairvoyance seemed to obliterate the boundaries between the seen and the unseen. Young Strauss was the dupe of one pretender after another; and the discovery of his folly blighted the very capacity for belief. From the mesmerists Strauss proceeded to place himself in the hands of the philosophers, and passed with a changeful but ever ready enthusiasm from one to another. He was touched also by Schleiermacher's attempt to restore faith through an appeal to the feelings. It was not necessary, Schleiermacher maintained, that men should accept a Book, or even believe in historical facts, in order to pass from Atheism to Christianity. God and Christ revealed themselves in the hearts of those who sought the truth. Christianity was a mystic union with the Divine, and not an acceptance of dogmas. This met Strauss's position admirably. "With Schleiermacher," he himself says, "God was restored only by losing his personality. In the same way Christ, to re-ascend His throne, had to lay aside all His supernatural prerogatives." The unbeliever, who refused to accept a single Biblical statement, could still be a Christian! Christianity was no longer a full acceptance of the Gospel, and a Spirit-given joy in its pardon, its reconciliation, and its hope; it was a mystic union of the soul with God, of the soul with the Saviour—with a God of whom we know nothing—and with a Saviour in whom there is no help!

The emptying of Strauss's soul was completed by his study of Hegel's "Phenomenology." This was carried on in company with a number of his fellow-students. Each read privately the portion appointed for discussion at the next meeting. When they met the passage was read aloud, and each gave his idea of Hegel's meaning. The result for Strauss of this combined study was the loss of every vestige of faith in the historical character of the Bible and of Christianity. He had become a Pantheist.

I regret to have to add, that honesty perished as well as faith. In 1828, two years before he completed his theological studies, a prize was offered for the best essay on "The Resurrection of the Body." Strauss engaged in the competition, and shared the prize with another competitor. In a letter to a friend he says, "I proved with full conviction, both by exegisis and by natural philosophy, the resurrection of the dead. But, when I had completed my last phrase, it was clear to me that there was not one word of truth in the whole paper." He nevertheless sent it in, and accepted the prize. Worse remains to be told. Two years longer he persisted in the attempt to qualify himself for the ministry. He closed his college career with the highest honours, and was appointed to a parish at Kleiningersheim, near Ludwigsburg. Although every article of the Christian faith had been cast away, he preached and catechised with as much success as had attended his theological studies. A friend, Christian Märklin, who shared his unbelief, and who was also in the ministry, was disturbed by scruples. Strauss tried to argue him out of them. "It is the development of theology," he wrote to Märklin, "which has led us into this strange situation; it is no fault of ours that we were not able to escape. And now what is the remedy? To abandon our ecclesiastical position may appear to be the simplest means; but will it be the most reasonable and the wisest? That would be to act like a prince who should refuse to govern his country because he was unable to introduce natural rights; it would be to act in accordance with the absolute and the ideal, and not in agreement with experience and with history." These arguments did not convince Märklin; but they were good enough for Strauss.

He continued his studies of Hegel and of Schleiermacher. A hearer of Schleiermacher's lent him notes of a series of lectures by the great preacher on the life of Christ. These notes suggested the idea to Strauss of his *Life of Jesus*. But Hegel's doctrine of the Divine development in Creation troubled Strauss. God, according to Hegel, is fully manifested in humanity—that is, in humanity as a whole, *but not in any individual man*. It was impossible for Strauss, therefore, as a consistent Hegelian, to give to Jesus the place assigned to Him—especially in the Gospel of John—the place of "God manifest in in the flesh." While Schleiermacher's lectures originated the idea of *The Life of Jesus*, Strauss's Hegelianism gave it its substance and its mission. The authenticity of the Gospels, and that of John especially, must be disproved. It must be shown that they were of late origin and of no authority. To prove their late origin, he had to show that they were full of contradictions and mistakes, which showed them not to be history, but mere collections of legends and myths which grew up in the interval between our Lord's death and the composition of the Gospel history as we now have it.

Strauss went to Tübingen in 1832, where he became a private teacher in connection with the University. While lecturing there on the Hegelian Philosophy, he wrote his now famous, or infamous, book, which saw the light in 1835. Its publication made the mightiest literary sensation ever felt in Germany. The style is marked by a cold imperturbability that might pass for fairness, and by a clearness and merciless decision which give it everywhere the stamp of heartless ability. The destruction, which it worked in the inmost shrine of Christianity with such calmness and such unrelenting thoroughness, caused the book to be received by almost all parties with mingled indignation and terror. Even the Rationalists were filled with dismay. They had freely admitted the existence of myth in other parts of Scripture. They had dragged down the Inspiration even of the New Testament to admit of contradiction and of error. But they had consoled themselves with the belief that, though they had sacrificed much to the spirit of the age, everything of value remained. Christ was still left—the most commanding figure in history. But now the Master also had disappeared! A dim figure, moving in a haze, through which no man could see aught clearly, was all that was left to them! There was no such thing as Gospel *history*. The resurrection was a myth! The Christian Church had not been able to brook the idea that Jesus became a placid victim of death and of the grave. Hence there arose, more and more distinctly, the conviction that He *must* have burst their bonds. By-and-bye the conviction took shape. The story became circumstantial. One detail was, added after another, till, when the Gospels were written, it had assumed the form in which we now have it. The same easy explanation was given of every other part of the miraculous narrative. Instead of Divine interposition and a Divine gift of a Redeemer for our race, we have only the dreams of pious souls. The majestic plan of salvation is not God's answer to man's need: it is only the embodiment of man's unanswered longings!

One asks what object any man could have had in setting himself to prove such a hypothesis true. It was the purpose of all Rationalism to bring down the miraculous in the Scripture to the level of ordinary events. The Bible must be made capable of belief. *That was also the main object of Strauss.* According to him, his purpose was not to *attack* the Bible; it was to sweep away the misconceptions which prevented the Bible from being rightly understood! To this another endeavour was added—to save the character of the Scripture and of the writers of the Scripture. They were not impostors, and their work was not open to the accusation of falsehood or of fraud! They never conspired to forge a lie and to impose upon the credulity of mankind. On the contrary, they were among the most upright of men. The beliefs were already formed when they wrote. They accepted them fully, and out of the fulness of their faith they wrote these things with a glowing conviction that they were handing on highest truth, and not falsehood, to posterity. That was Strauss's service and tribute to the Gospel history! But, like all Rationalistic service, it slew what it thought to save. It was the kiss of Judas that handed over the Master to His foes. Under the amputating knife of Rationalism, which professed to remove the miraculous excrescences, the patient died! There was no longer any Gospel to declare. In Christ there was no divinely provided satisfaction for sin, and no Forerunner had, in Him, entered into the heavens to prepare a home for us on high. The character of the Evangelists was saved. They were not liars or impostors. But the reputation of the men was saved at the expense of the history. *It* was, nevertheless, a lie, though they believed it true. According to Strauss, they did not intentionally impose upon us. They themselves were imposed upon; but they, nevertheless, handed on a delusion, in the midst of which we search in vain for any satisfying glimpse of the Christ of history.

Strauss was obliged to confess that his rejection of the Gospel of John could not be sustained. His attack has long since been repelled. But the lesson of his book remains; it revealed the abyss to which the "steep place" of Rationalism leads, and to which it is leading multitudes now.

CHAPTER XII.

THE LAST STATE WORSE THAN THE FIRST:
VATKE, GRAF, KAYSER, KUENEN.

THE attack made by Baur (1792-1860) and the "Tübingen School" upon the New Testament need not detain us. It died some time ago without hope of resurrection. Strauss was a pupil of Baur's, and was helped by suggestions supplied from the wider learning of his master. Some of my readers may remember hearing the terms, "Petrine" and "Pauline," the "Petrine Party" and the "Pauline Party." These were the watchwords of Baur and his school, and they threatened at one time to become as famous as Jehovist, Elohist, Jehovistic, and Elohistic. Christianity, according to Baur, owed its present form not to Jesus, but to a struggle between Peter and Paul and their respective followers. Peter believed that Christianity was for the Jew; Paul maintained that it was for the Gentile also. Some parts of the New Testament sprang, Baur said, from the efforts of the Petrine party to spread their views, and others originated in similar attempts of the Pauline party; while a third part, like the Book of Acts, owed its existence to a later effort to unite the two contending parties in one church. Hence the writer of the Acts labours to give equal honour to both leaders. Peter raises Dorcas from the dead; Paul must, therefore, have an equally marvellous work assigned to him; and so we have the account manufactured of the falling of the young man from the open window at Troas, and his awakening to life again in the embrace of Paul—and so on. The ingenuity of the theory may disguise the blasphemy, but it cannot palliate it.

With Strauss and Baur the Rationalistic attack upon the New Testament has been temporarily exhausted. The strength of criticism is meanwhile concentrated in the attempt to discredit the Old Testament, and especially the Pentateuch. Hartmann, who died in 1838, maintained that Moses could not have been the author of the Pentateuch, for the sufficient reason that he could not write! The art of writing, it was said, was unknown to the Hebrews till after the death of Moses, and that it was only in the time of Samuel that they learned to compile histories. These assertions, we shall afterwards see, were nothing less than hideous blunders. The oldest parts of the Pentateuch, he maintained, were later than Solomon, and the book was made up of fragments which came into existence at intervals extending from the separation of the ten tribes to the times of Jeremiah and Ezekiel. This fragmentary hypothesis has been discarded for others which were not so palpably ridiculous. But, as I propose to deal later on with these theories of the Higher Criticism, I shall at present confine myself to a rapid sketch of its later history, and of the results which it now asks us to accept as the findings of "Science."

Ewald and others followed in the steps of De Wette. Nothing that can be called a new path was struck out. The changes were rung on original documents, supplements, editions, and revisions; and "criticism" has had again and again to reconstruct itself as well as the Bible. Throughout all these changes there runs one distinguishing feature which gives each of the theories a strong family likeness. It is the intolerable amount of theorising and the infinitesimal modicum of fact which make up their stock-in-trade. This absence of fact is noted not only when we look at the basis of "the Higher Criticism": it is still more remarkable when we look at its so-called "results." There ought surely to be some things in actual experience—there should be something, either visible now or traceable in history, to keep those boasted "discoveries" in countenance. If they are *discoveries*, they must be discoveries of things that exist, or that have existed. How, then, does the matter stand? We are told that there have been endless makings-up of the Bible—that the Old Testament has been put forth first in this shape, then in that, then again in this other. But where, we ask, are those editions? Who can find them? Who has given the slightest hint that he ever saw them or ever heard of them? The demand for the missing link is slowly, but surely, killing Darwinism. The Higher Criticism has to cope with a similar trouble. It supposes changes which have left no trace, and, in that very absence of trace, experience declares that these supposed changes have never happened and are only dreams.

The last development of "the Higher Criticism" was introduced by Vatke, whose book was published in 1835, the same year as Strauss's *Life of Jesus*. But, while Strauss's work attracted the whole world's attention, Vatke's was almost unnoticed, and was neglected for many years even by the learned. It was nothing less than Hegelianism, pure and simple, applied to the Bible; and the philosophical form of the book might have proved its sepulchre. Only a few had the courage to read and to study the contents. Reuss, of Strassburg, who has made himself one of the chief apostles of the new school, says: "On the appearance of the book, the table of contents, with its Hegelian formulæ, of itself terrified me to such an extent that I remained at the time unacquainted with it. A speculative treatment of history I trust no further than I can see. Since then, indeed, I have seen that theory and formulæ in this book were really only an addition which might be dispensed with, and that my inquiries might have been materially assisted if I had not let myself be deterred by them." *

To measure the distance to which the new school,

---

* Pfleiderer. *Development of Theology*, pp. 252, 532.

introduced, if not established, by Vatke, now takes us, we have to recall what the older school attempted to do. De Wette and the rest were harassed by the presence of miracle in the Bible. They might have remembered that there is no possible escape from belief in miracle—that is, from recognition of Divine intervention. Life is a miracle. We know that there was a time when life was not, and could not have been, on the earth. We also know that there is nothing earthly now by which life can be produced, and we have therefore the best reason for believing that there was nothing earthly then from which it could have sprung. The presence of life is, therefore, one incontestable proof of the creative touch of a higher Power. In the same way, Christ was a miracle, and the Bible is as palpably a miracle. There is nothing now, and there was nothing then, that could have begotten Him, or it. But Rationalism, in its haste to remove from Christianity what seemed a blemish in the eyes of unbelief, denied the possibility of miracle and tried to explain how the miraculous narratives of Scripture were consistent with the honesty of the writers. They saved the credit of Evangelists and Apostles by denying their enlightenment or their capacity, under the idea that with this limitation unbelievers would be persuaded to accept them as spiritual guides!

That was the one aim of the elder school of the Higher Criticism. The aim of the new school is far in advance of this. Its purpose is—not to explain the presence of the miraculous in Scripture—but to account for the origin of the religion of which the Scripture is the fruit and the expression. The miraculous must not only be banished from the sacred books; *it must be banished also from the religions with which they are identified.* Judaism and Christianity have in them, they tell us, nothing that is specifically Divine. They are as purely human growths as Confucianism and Budhism. "For us," says Kuenen, "the Israelitish is one of those religions; nothing less, but also nothing more." \*

Hegel was the Darwin of history and of religion. He set himself the task of showing how human society and human beliefs must have been developed; and, of course, beneath that attempt there lay the supposition that religion, like society, has developed through merely human endeavours and by purely natural processes. The evolution favoured by Hegel, like that taught by Darwin, virtually dispenses with God. Religion has been a steadily persistent and ever onward growth. There are no breaks in the story. There have been no abysses in the pathway which required miraculous bridges. Everything has been natural, gradual, and constantly progressive. These imaginary "laws" of human development were applied by Vatke with unfaltering hand to the sacred history. It was not simply the miracles of Moses which had now to disappear; the very work of Moses was alleged to be impossible. "He finds," says Pfleiderer, "that the notion of Moses having given the people its civil law and *a pure belief in God*

---

\* *The Religion of Israel*, Vol. i., p. 5.

is irreconcilable with later history. For he holds it to be impossible that a whole nation should suddenly sink from a high stage of religious development to a lower one, as is asserted to have been so often the case in the times of the judges and kings, and equally impossible for an individual to rise all at once from a lower to a higher stage, and raise a whole nation with him with the same rapidity." Individuals, Vatke maintains, do not rise much above or fall much below the standard of their age. "This is particularly the case," Vatke writes, "with Moses, since on the assumption of the truth even of only the greater part of this tradition as to his work, both his own person and the whole course of Hebrew history become inexplicable; he would have come when the time was not fulfilled, and would thus be far more miraculous than Christ Himself."

Here the cloven foot plainly reveals itself. A prophet of God, coming to an idolatrous people with a clear revelation of the Creator, is a miracle; and, therefore, as "miracles do not happen," the mission of Moses is a fable! This is the deep essential error of the later criticism. It does not come *to ascertain and to interpret facts*. It comes to the facts armed with a theory into which everything must be made to fit. The theory is laid upon the facts. Whatever can be crushed into the mould is spared, whatever cannot be crushed into t is remorselessly cut off and cast away. Hegel proved to his own satisfaction that only a certain number of planets could exist in our solar system. But Astronomy refuses to be cut and carved into shapes to suit philosophic dreams; and, as the Hegelian number of the planets has long ago been exceeded, Hegelians are prudently silent upon that subject. An unprejudiced mind would be open to consider the question whether it is a well-established fact that there appeared in Israel a conception of God which has brought light and health to the soul of man, which has harmonised the universe, and which, by its own innate truth and majesty, has shamed and swept away degrading misconceptions and hoary idolatries that had enthroned themselves in religions and sent their roots down into institutions, laws, customs, and literature. An unprejudiced mind would say whether that is not the mightiest fact in history, and whether a fact so utterly unparalleled can be explained apart from miracle. But Vatke, because it cannot be explained without miracle, denies the fact, and re-models the history!

The contention that no man can rise above his environment, and that the religious life of nations cannot decay, are equally nonsensical. But my business now is history—not refutation. Vatke admits that somehow Moses was a true prophet, but that the teaching now attributed to him was only possible about the time of the exile, when long ages had cleared men's conceptions regarding the Divine Being.

The spark sent forth by Vatke slumbered for thirty years. Meanwhile Reuss was lecturing at Strassburg, and quietly filling his pupils' minds with similar views. He refrained from publishing, as he had no desire to draw public attention to his work. Controversy was inevitable, however, and it was at last precipitated by two of his pupils. Graf, in his book on the Old Testament, published in 1866, maintained that the body of laws in the middle books of the Pentateuch was a very late production, and that it was manufactured and placed in its present position only after the Babylonian exile. The legislation was too elaborate, in Graf's estimation, for such an early period as that of Moses; and, as the account that it was Divinely given must be utterly set aside, time must necessarily be allowed for its elaboration. It is impossible, however, to fix any later date for any part of the Pentateuch than the period immediately succeeding the Babylonian exile; for we then come upon facts which say even to this sea of Rationalistic dreams and fancies, "Thus far shalt thou come and no farther." The books of Ezra and Nehemiah, the Samaritan Pentateuch, the early Greek translation of the Old Testament, called the Septuagint, and the history of the Maccabees, have all to be reckoned with. They prove that the idea of any remodelling of the Pentateuch after the close of the exile is absolute insanity.

"The Grafian hypothesis," as it was called, did not at first commend itself to German Rationalists. It was viewed by them very much as Reuss himself had regarded Vatke's theory. It had too palpable an appearance of history made to order, and even Rationalists had to wait till its air of unblushing misrepresentation was familiar enough to be tolerated and accepted. There was also another cause for hesitancy. Graf committed a blunder which played into the hands of his opponents and dismayed his friends. The body of laws, the origin of which he brought down to the times after the Babylonian exile, formed part of what till then had been declared by the Rationalists to be the oldest part of the Pentateuch. Besides the laws there was a large body of history. The critics had professed that the whole of this part was so marked by special characteristics that they were forced to consider it a separate work. These characteristics were found *in the history as well as in the laws*. Surely, then, said Graf's opponents, the history must belong to the same time, as it is somewhat of a stretch to imagine that a man who wrote a history in the 9th century B.C. would return to write, with the same style and phrase, a body of laws 500 years after he was dead! The critics were trying to flee from miracles, but this oversight of Graf's seemed likely to land them in a bigger miracle than any they had cast away!

Graf and his friends felt the difficulty keenly. He published an essay shortly before his death in which he bowed to the inevitable, and, as the Elohistic narrative, or, as it was also called, the *Grundschrift*, that is, "the fundamental document," must move altogether if it moved at all, the history was made to take a big leap over the yawning gulf of five centuries and to take its place beside the laws. This was upheld by another pupil of Reuss's, Professor

Kayser of Strassburg, whose book was published in 1874. It has now become a leading article in the creed of the new criticism. But the stone is too heavy, and will help by-and-bye to grind their theories to powder. This "Elohistic narrative," "*Grundschrift*," or "Priests' Code," contains "history" which no man with the fear of God, with common honesty, or with common-sense, could possibly have written after the Babylonian exile. For instance, it embraces the whole story of the erection of the tabernacle contained in the last six chapters of Exodus. Every reader is aware of the minute details with which these chapters are filled. Every little thing is named, described, and its story told. The measurements of great things and of small are recorded. We are repeatedly told that all these things were made in obedience to fully detailed instructions given directly by God to Moses. "According to all that the Lord commanded Moses, so the children of Israel made all the work." And we are further told that "Moses did look upon all the work, and, behold, they had done it as the Lord had commanded, even so had they done it; and Moses blessed them" (Exod. xxxix. 42, 43). If the Tabernacle be (as we know it is) emblematic of the Lord Jesus and of His work, we can understand all this elaborate detail, and this zealous carefulness in things small and great. But if no such Divine directions were given, can the reader imagine any man sitting down to plan this erection, and elaborating all these details, just to palm off a lie and to lay that lie upon God? Could the reader do it? Could Wellhausen himself do it? And yet the critics regard this hypothesis of theirs as cumbered with no mental or moral difficulty, and calmly assume that this gigantic piece of imposture and of blasphemy was done as a matter of ordinary course! The weight of that enormous absurdity is too heavy to be sustained by the strongest theory man ever built. Learned treatises and big names will fail to keep it up. It will crush them all.

But notwithstanding Kayser's advocacy, the new theory still lagged. The popular gifts and intellectual mastery of Julius Wellhausen were needed to obtain for it the wide acceptance which it has long ago received. Kuenen's book, published in 1869-70 in Dutch, on *The Religion of Israel*, prepared the way among the few German scholars acquainted with that language. Kuenen accepted Graf's theory, but made the addition to it which was afterwards found to be necessary; the history was thrown into the same abyss of legend and of lie as the laws. Kuenen begins with the prophet Amos. There is nothing earlier, he believed, in the Old Testament than the prophecy of the herdsman of Tekoa. Everything else is later than the eighth century B.C. With this new position, the veracity of the Old Testament, its miraculous character, and its importance as a revelation, were consciously and completely surrendered. Here is how Kuenen himself puts the matter: "The great question now is," he says, "with what period are we to begin? As early as possible, of course.

But how far back can we go with safety? The answer, which perhaps will surprise some, must be: 'Not further than the eighth century before our era (800-700 B.C.)'" The consequences of this are plain enough, but Kuenen leaves his reader in no doubt; he states the consequences quite frankly. The early history of Israel is completely swept away. "The account of their forty years wandering," he writes, "must be put aside as unhistorical. . . . Indeed, the representation of Israel's earliest history, presented to us in the books named after Moses and Joshua, must be rejected as in its entirety impossible. . . . how can a whole series of the wonderful events rest upon the testimony of writers who were evidently so far removed from the period and the circumstances of which they wrote that their account of them is quite misty?"* Disbelief in Israel's mission and in God's manifestation of Himself in His dealings with that people must, logically, follow disbelief in the history. Kuenen tells us that he quite acknowledges the justice of the remark, and that he has made the necessary sacrifice. He asks whether "the belief in Israel's selection (is) still tenable in our days?" And he adds: "We do not hesitate to reply in the negative." The idea that God, in order eventually to reach all nations, first made a selection of one, is called "a childish fancy." "Israel," Kuenen continues, "is no more the pivot on which the development of the whole world turns, than the planet which we inhabit is the centre of the

* Vol. i. (English Edition), 21, 22.

universe. In short, we have outgrown the belief of our ancestors."\*

The marvel is, that any reader of the Bible could state these views and not be immediately confronted by a startling difficulty. That destiny of Israel was taught in Scripture—even according to the critics—long centuries before our Lord appeared or the Gospel was preached. *Where* did that extraordinary, and indeed unparalleled, thought come from? What other nation ever lived in the hope that light was to spring from it that should scatter the world's darkness? And there is a bigger question. *The thought has been fulfilled.* The nations have been blessed from Israel's fulness. Kuenen himself wrote amid Christian light, and he had a Bible to operate upon, simply because it had been proved in the conversion of his country that "salvation is of the Jews." These things are facts, and demand some explanation; and until criticism has reached a reasonable solution, it may rest assured that it has yet done nothing.

---
\* *Ibid*, pp. 8, 9.

## CHAPTER XIII.

### PRESENT POSITION OF RATIONALISM: WELLHAUSEN, REUSS, RITSCHL, ENGLISH CRITICISM.

NOTWITHSTANDING the publications of Graf, Kayser, and Kuenen, and the influence steadily exercised by Reuss upon his pupils at Strassburg, the development theory still hung fire. It was a departure taken by the few only; and it was still a possibility that the movement might perish in its birth and be remembered only as one of many similar extravagances. This was the position of matters up to the year 1876, when all was suddenly altered by the intervention of one man. Julius Wellhausen, Professor of Oriental Languages at the University of Marburg, published his views on the origin of the Pentateuch in that year in the *Jahrbücher für Deutsche Theologie*. He included the Book of Joshua in his survey, and named the whole the *Hexateuch*. It is one of several indications of the immense effect of Wellhausen's work that this term has been widely and definitely adopted by the new

Theology, and that many have ceased talking of "the Pentateuch"—the five-volumed Book, and, imitating this master in the new Israel, henceforth know only the six-volumed Book—"the Hexateuch." There was a good and sufficient reason why the books should be separated: they are chronologically distinct. But, now that it has been decreed that both are "pious" fictions of a later era, there is no reason why they should not be bundled together and be covered by one and the same label!

One striking characteristic of recent historical work is its breadth of view. The trend of the age is toward wide and brilliant generalisations. Science has revealed the prevalence of law in almost every domain of observation. The Copernican theory has simplified astronomy, and the child of to-day has a sense of mastery in a region where the most successful observers were once "in wandering mazes lost." The Newtonian theory of gravitation, the laws of chemistry, and similar generalisations in other sciences have given us a like endowment of comprehension and of power. Where to others there seemed only a multitude of unconnected facts, the eye of some acute observer has distinguished connecting links that at once revealed a magnificent spectacle of order. The touch of genius has changed a confused crowd into an army, and what seemed a mere heap of stones into a gorgeous palace or a grand harmonious Temple.

We have been elated with these modern triumphs, and have imagined that everything is possible to our new-born science. Human affairs, like the processes of nature, must be subjected to the yoke of all pervading laws. Hence we have had such a book as Buckle's *History of Civilisation*, and other kindred, but less successful, attempts. When such a work presents itself, we feel as Eve did, that the tree is "pleasant to the eyes and a tree to be desired to make one wise," and so we pluck, eat, and mightily enjoy the fruit. We are uplifted by the deceitful sense of a new insight and a new mastery. We have an immediate and complete understanding, we imagine, of events which we have not even begun to comprehend.

Hegel is the great master in this cheap imitation of science, where preconceived ideas are made to do duty for patient observation. Wellhausen has applied the methods of his master to theology with Hegelian brilliancy and with a power of popular exposition which Hegel never had. His style is marked by a grasp of detail, a broad comprehensiveness, a closeness of reasoning, and an incisiveness and decision, which have taken German rationalism by storm and ensured the triumph of Graf's hypothesis. He issued his *History of Israel* in 1878, a second edition of which appeared in 1883 under the title of *Prolegomena to the History of Israel*. His views have also been published in the ninth edition of *The Encyclopedia Britannica*. I shall hope to deal more fully afterwards with the details of his criticism; meanwhile it is enough to say that he distinguishes three main sources of the Hexateuch.

But, in addition to these, there are smaller fragments and still later additions. There are in all eight distinct writers whose productions have been so cunningly dove-tailed together that only the lynx-eye of the later, and especially the Wellhausean, criticism can detect the joinings. Four of these are original writers, and four are editors who have, with strange and affecting unanimity, laboured on, age after age, in the "pious" endeavour to deceive all succeeding times. It will not do to use plain English and to call these creatures of the German brain by the name which their alleged conduct so richly merits; for their creators have already canonised them every one. These are the saints of the new rationalistic calendar, and all of them are reverently referred to as "pious" men who had the best of motives, but, strange to say, followed the most rascally devices.

But there is a small difficulty in the way of dealing with them individually, and, indeed, of thinking of them with any definiteness. They have left neither name nor address behind them! Of these eight men—the makers of Israel's law, religion, and institutions—*no man knows anything whatever!* They have done the mightiest work ever attempted in any age or in any land; but nobody knew they did it! They have made Moses and Joshua famous, but they themselves have escaped all notice and have wrapped their personalities in eternal oblivion! We may surely, then, be pardoned for doubting whether they ever existed outside the brains of their critical creators. Such characteristics suit dreams but do not harmonise with realities. Facts leave a deeper impress behind them, and it may safely be said that eight men never laboured at such a work as the Pentateuch and yet managed to conceal themselves with such complete success from their own and from all after times.

But this last stage of rationalistic criticism has other lessons for us. God is now ruled out of the Bible by "Christian" scholarship as relentlessly as He is ruled out of the Universe by Atheistic Evolution. Wellhausen's achievement is the supposed triumphant proof that natural development accounts for everything in the Bible. Rather, I should say, it is assumed that this was the only possible source of its contents; and then the Bible is taken to pieces, and reconstructed on that basis. Whatever is imagined to be too clear, or too advanced, for a certain age is confidently assigned to a later time. The very history of Israel is cut and carved according to this rigid rule. The monotheism of Moses, and the elaborate ceremonial given by God through him to Israel, were too advanced for that supposed rude period, and are therefore at once stamped as the forgeries of the Babylonian exile.

Pfleiderer, whose rationalism is indistinguishable from the blankest infidelity, speaks in the warmest terms of this feature of Wellhausen's work. "Personally," he says, " I welcomed this book of Wellhausen's more than almost any other; for the

pressing problem of the history of the Old Testament appeared to me to be at last solved in a manner *consonant to the principle of human evolution* which I am compelled to apply to the history of all religion."*
This confession goes right to the heart of the matter and supplies the key to the latest development of criticism. The earlier critics toiled hard to explain away the miracles of the Old Testament. But what of the giving of the Law, and what of that pure thought of God which we find in the earliest writings of Israel? Were not these quite as miraculous as any event recorded in the entire history? That pure monotheism and elaborate and eminently typical ceremonial are unparalleled. Their existence among this small and uninfluential people cannot be explained upon any natural principles. They had received this light from no other people; for no other people possessed it. They themselves were utterly incapable of originating it. Whence, then, did it spring? That was the problem which harassed the more clear-headed rationalists. They saw plainly that till this new problem had been grappled with and solved, nothing had been done. The only possible solution was hit upon by more than one among them. It was to dispose of that miracle *by denying its existence*. The purer light in which ancient Israel had rejoiced was only a fiction!

Kuenen had cut the Gordian knot in this fashion before the advent of Wellhausen. Reuss tells us that he himself had done the same thing. In the

---

* *Development of Theology*, p. 259.

preface to his *Geschichte der heiligen Schriften Alten Testaments*, published in 1881, the latter says that he had had a glimpse of this way out of the difficulty as early as 1834, when he delivered his first course of lectures at Strassburg. The idea had not taken full shape in his own mind, and it was so bold and revolutionary that he shrank from giving it publicity. Even rationalists had still some regard for historical testimony. "Those who remember," he says, "the literature of that period, not the conservative merely, but particularly the critical, will be able to understand my unwillingness at once to challenge the learned world to look upon the Prophets as earlier than the Law, and the Psalms as later than both. For these propositions, which were the main pillars of my conception of Hebrew history, were as yet rather a distant vision than a solid fabric." "He tells us," adds Pfleiderer, that "he hit upon this idea in the study of the legislation of Israel in hope of finding the thread of Ariadne, which might guide him out of the labyrinth of the current hypothesis into the daylight of a psychologically possible process of development of the people of Israel. While in his youth much effort was wasted in explaining miracles as natural occurrences, *the most unnatural miracles were left unexplained.*"

Here the secret of the latest attempt is openly confessed. Among "the most unnatural miracles is," says Pfleiderer, "the commencement of Israel's education with the developed Levitical ritual." That we know was a commencement made by God, otherwise there never would have been any commencement at all. But the latent infidelity of Rationalism must perfect itself, and so now, in the end of days, it cannot admit of any Divine intervention whatever!

The law was not given by God: it could only have been originated and slowly developed by man! The history of its introduction must, therefore, be denied, and the whole story of the Israelitish religion must be re-written to suit rationalistic ideas. The fruits of this last stage of Rationalism are as evil as its roots. There was never any revelation, we are now told, in which the living and true God disclosed Himself to a chosen people. We have hitherto believed that monotheism sprang up in this miraculous way among the idolatries of the nations, and that the light, kindled by the revelation given through Moses, and fed by kindred interpositions of God in the ministry of his servants the prophets, was intensified by the fuller revelation of God in Jesus Christ, until idolatries have bowed their heads in shame and have disappeared.

That is what the Scriptures have taught us, and what we have hitherto believed. But, says Rationalism, "miracles do not happen;" and, consequently, this belief must be abandoned. It is superstition, we are told, not science. Moses neither taught nor knew that there was only one God. It was too early for such a belief to be possible to any man. What he did was to gain Israel's consent to choose *one* of their idols and to cleave to him, or to it, only. He had some idea apparently that indiscriminate worship was confusing and unprofitable. It would be much more simple to have but one object of devotion, and if all the affection and zeal of which Israel was capable were concentrated upon one object there might be better results. That is the invention with which Moses is credited by the critics. He is the inventor of "monolatry," the worship of one God only, but not of monotheism, which teaches the existence of one God only. One god was selected as the object of national worship: the rest were left to look after themselves. From this seed-thought, everything else developed naturally. Israel came to say by-and-bye: "our God is stronger than the gods of the other peoples." Then they afterwards went further. They said: "Our God is the only God; the gods of the nations are vanity and lies; they are no gods." Monotheism is thus simply a fruit on the wondrous "bean-stalk" which has sprung from the seed dropped into the fertile German intellect by the Darwinistic Hegel. It is merely a glorious evolution. "Jahve," says Wellhausen, "was not at first the God of the Universe, who became afterwards the God of Israel; but he was first the God of the house of Israel and only became afterwards—long afterwards —the God of the entire universe."

Every sacred thing is degraded and polluted in the same fashion. The ark of the covenant, we are told, was originally an idol, which was probably box-shaped, and from that circumstance received its name. Moses never made it and never received any commandment to make it. The Tabernacle itself, the

Aaronic priesthood, and the Levitical ritual of the desert, are only dreams, and were invented bit by bit after the erection of Solomon's Temple. The same thing is affirmed of the entire Mosaic history. "The Tabernacle," says Reuss, "is a pure fiction. The same is true of the circular camp, the march in the desert, the enormous figures of the pretended censuses of the people, the unimaginable riches in precious metals and in all sorts of stuffs in a solitude destitute of water and poor in men, the daily hecatombs offered by people who had for themselves no food save the manna, of which they were tired even to loathing, the making of a land register for Canaan by a handful of employés in a country which is regarded as entirely depopulated, the forty-eight Levitical towns with their outskirts geometrically measured, and many other things which far surpass the ancient legends, and which are, properly speaking, not legends of the past, but the dreams of a miserable race."

The blasphemies of Wellhausen make still more painful reading than even those words of the Strassburg Professor. Israel's religion, he tells us in his article "Israel," in *The Encylopedia Britannica*, was a purely natural growth, and that its belief concerning God was purified by a process of forgetting and of wise reticence. "Whatever Jahve's real nature," he says, "may have been—the God of thunder, or whatever he was—it retreated more and more into the background as something secret and transcendent, and no questions were asked concerning it. The whole emphasis was laid on his action in the world of men, whose aims he made his own. . . . As the God of the nation, Jahve became the God of law and of righteousness, and as such grew (! !) to be the highest, and finally the sole power in heaven and earth." That is how the Israelites manufactured their god. Just as the sculptor of a heathen divinity took the rough block from the quarry, and by long toil and many skilful touches shaped it into a god or goddess, so did the Israelites first rough-hew and then finish their teaching about Jehovah. It seems that they were equally given to the manufacture of heroes. "David," he says, "became the founder of the united Israelite kingdom, whose military power remained always the proudest memory of the nation. Later Jewish tradition, however, was wrong in making him a Levitical saint and pious psalmist." The same thing happened, it seems, with Elijah, "the most striking heroic figure," says Wellhausen, "in the Bible, towering solitarily above his time, and whose memory was preserved by legend and not by history."

The reader will see that it is quite impossible to impose upon Wellhausen, and that he knows better than to believe his Bible. If we are so far left to ourselves as to ask the impertinent question how he knows that David never wrote psalms, or that Elijah never worked his miracles or rose superior to his age, the answer is that he is an "expert," and as such sees right into the heart of all these mysteries and can unwind every device. The reader will not perhaps be surprised to learn that, while David and

Elijah are degraded, Israel is justified. Instead of God having borne long with *them*, they were most indulgent to Him! "Jahve," says Wellhausen, "had incalculable moods; he caused his face to shine, and he was wroth, it was not known why; he created good and evil, punished sin and tempted to sin. *Satan had not then robbed him of some of his attributes. In spite of all this, Israel did not doubt him.*" The prophets, instead of being the mere messengers of Jehovah, as they have hitherto been believed to have been, were really the saviours of God's honour and the creators of the Law and of the purer conceptions of God which, according to Wellhausen, displaced older and cruder notions. The troubles with the Assyrians and the fall of Samaria were a crushing blow, he says, to the belief that Jehovah was the God of Israel. "Jahve," he says, "decided from heaven the struggle carried on on earth. He was always on the side of Israel; his interest was limited to Israel." Here, then, was a terrible danger to Israelitish beliefs. The memory of Jehovah might have perished in the disasters of his people! But Amos and his successors were equal to the crisis. "The prophets, of the line of whom Amos was the first, did not," he says, "proclaim a new God, but they preached that the God of Israel was primarily and above all the God of righteousness, and Israel's God only in so far as Israel satisfied his righteous demands. They therefore reversed the traditional order of the two fundamental articles of faith. *This delivered Jahve from the danger of coming into collision with the world, and suffering shipwreck.*" "This," Wellhausen continues, "is what constitutes their (the prophets') importance, not their being the forerunners of the Gospel. Least of all are they the latter *on account of their Messianic prophecies.* In them they really fall back upon the patriotic but illusive hopes of the common people and of the false prophets, whom they on other grounds assail. . . . It was due to the prophets that the fall of Samaria did not injure but strengthened the religion of Jahve; *they saved the faith by destroying the illusion; they also immortalised Israel by not involving Jahve in the ruin of the nation.*" \*

This shameless misrepresentation of facts will enable the reader to gauge the scientific value of the new criticism, and its blasphemy will help him to estimate the ignorance or the unblushing impudence which asks him to accept this as the unassailable conclusion of "Christian" (!) scholarship. Every Bible student knows that, not the Assyrian troubles only, but all the earlier ills that had fallen upon Israel, were punishments that came upon the people because Jehovah was the God of righteousness. That has been the unfaltering testimony of Scripture from the first. But the new criticism decrees that this cannot have been. And why? Because it would, forsooth, interfere with their development theory that God was first of all the God who was always on the side of Israel, whatever Israel did and whatever character it bore, and that only gradually the notion grew up that really Israel must be good if it expected

---

\* See Pfleiderer. *Development of Theology*, pp. 264-272.

Jehovah to be for it and not against it. It was, of course, impossible on this theory that the Law which demanded righteousness from Israel could have been given by Moses. It was a late invention, intended to embody the truths to a knowledge of which Israel had attained only in the latest stages of its history. Priests and prophets laid their heads together, and forged the books of the Law and made a history to suit, giving us an imposture so daring and so gigantic in its rascality and blasphemy that it stands unmatched in the realms of fact and of fiction. By a strange fate Rationalism has thus been brought back in this, its latest stage, to the very midst of the infidelity from which it sought to save the Christian faith, and has been plunged in the deepest mire of the unbelief to which it has sacrificed so much.

Rationalism is the child of panic, and it inherits the loss and the shame of its parent. Fearing the foes of faith, it has become their slave. It set out with a desire, honest enough though mistaken, to save the Bible and the character of the writers of the Bible. There was nothing in the Scripture, said the Rationalists, that had not been put down there in absolute good faith. That was the thesis which the earlier rationalism set itself to prove in the face of the infidelity which branded the Bible as an imposture. But Criticism has now assumed the position of its ancient enemy, and it is carrying on the warfare of the old infidelity with all the strength and all the prestige of so-called "Christian" scholarship! It now tells us that the foundation of the Scriptures—

its early history and its legislation—is one continued fraud, and that the prophets themselves deliver as the express messages of God what are really the outcome of their own reflections and the forecasts of their own political sagacity!

Much is looked for in some quarters from the attempt made by the late Professor Ritschl, of Göttingen, to find a new foothold for Christian belief. His system, like its predecessors, will have its little day and cease to be. Meantime there is small promise of help in it. A system which puts aside the authority of the New Testament and bids us walk in the light of "the Christian consciousness," will do little to heal the wound of rationalistic Christianity. But what of our English rationalism? The reply is, that we have no *English* rationalism. The home article is merely an importation; and it ought in fairness, like other importations, to bear the label "made in Germany." Perhaps the only man who added any fresh feature was Bishop Colenso, in his arithmetical calculations, and in the piling up of fallacies which have been swept away by the Government Survey of the Sinaitic Peninsula. From the days of Bishop Marsh and of Samuel Taylor Coleridge, German rationalism has striven hard to leaven the theology and the literature of our land. Matthew Arnold has done more than any other to spread its desolating doubts, and to induce that suspicion and contempt for earnest Christian belief which now gives the Higher Criticism its opportunity. Maurice and many another have also helped to prepare the way. The battle for the Bible has to be waged against heavy odds. The Midianite is in the land. The vantage-ground in our universities, colleges, divinity halls, and even in our great public schools, is largely in the hands of the foe. The learning, which ought to have protected us, has here, as in Germany, surrendered to the foe. But Midian met its death-blow in the land of its supposed triumph. And there are two foes with which criticism has yet to reckon. There is the clear-eyed, strong-souled British faith that can and that will test the new teaching. That faith *knows*, because it has believed. It has tried the Book and found in it the way to God and the way to power; and, when the Scripture comes to be judged, this faith will have something to say. It never has been brow-beaten: it will not be brow-beaten now. Emperor and Pope, king and bishop and priest, could not silence it. There is no charm in the words "scholar" and "expert" to hush its voice; for, in the bosom of its meekness, there is the majestic consciousness that it judgeth all things and is itself judged of none.

That is one foe which criticism, when it leaves the school and comes to the pulpit and the platform, has still to reckon with. The other is the testimony of FACT, which God in His Providence has strengthened mightily in these last days. How Criticism will fare in its inevitable encounter with this combatant, we shall now see.

BOOK III.

CRITICAL RESULTS TESTED BY
MODERN DISCOVERY.

# CRITICAL RESULTS TESTED BY MODERN DISCOVERY.

## CHAPTER I.

### THE TEST OF CRITICISM:

CHAMPOLLION; GROTEFEND; SAYCE ON THE MINUTE ACCURACY OF SCRIPTURE.

WE have now to bring the conclusions of criticism to the test. The new views of the Bible have certainly a suspicious origin. They are the product of panic. Fear is seldom a good judge of what ought to be surrendered or cast away, and a man who is overcome by terror will frequently give up what in his cooler and saner moments he would strenuously retain. But if the motive of Rationalism is questionable, its principles and methods are still less adapted to restore our confidence. This I hope to show in a succeeding volume; but He that is higher than the highest has intervened in this controversy regarding His Word, and I hasten to set before the reader what is nothing less than the decision of God. The critics have applied the principles of their so-called science to the books and to the statements of Scripture. They have reached conclusions regarding these that are as definite as they are startling. They tell us that in those conclusions they are all agreed, and that, viewed as results of criticism, these are absolutely certain.

Now, in God's merciful Providence, we are enabled to check these results, and so to test the new science. If any body of men should assert that they had discovered certain novel and startling Astronomical principles; and if, in addition to stating what these principles are, they should still further oblige the scientific world by themselves applying these to the determinations of the places of the heavenly bodies, they would make the testing of their alleged discovery a very simple matter. If the places agree with Astronomical observations, the new principles have amply justified themselves. But if, on the contrary, all these determinations are manifest errors, then principles and results will perish together, and the new Astronomers will leave their names as laughing-stocks to after generations. Euclid has made us all familiar with this queen of tests. It is his famous *reductio ad absurdum*. He proves a geometrical truth by disproving its opposite. The conflicting statement is supposed, for the moment, to be true. Consequences are then drawn from it that are so ludicrously untrue that the onlooker cries "hold! enough!" The opposing error is slain by *its own results*, and from the dust in which it lies neither lover nor friend will ever lift it again.

Let us now mark how this overwhelming disproof has fallen upon the Higher Criticism. The reader will not fail to mark how strangely it has been timed. The Protestantism of Germany and of other lands had its death struggle with the foe, and no such aid was brought to *it*. But now, just as the attack is made upon English-speaking Protestantism, this mighty aid is given. It deepens our praise; but let us also remember that it adds to our responsibility. The people who have helped so greatly to evangelise the earth, have this additional mission given to them —to strengthen their brethren and to re-establish the churches. May God pour out His Spirit upon us that the mission may be fulfilled. We now have our Olivet; may we have our Pentecost!

The present century has been signalised by two of the most wonderful discoveries that have ever fallen to the lot of any age. A hundred years ago Egypt was practically an unknown land. Travellers, it is true, passed through it from time to time and published the results of their observations; but Egypt to the European imagination was a kind of Oriental fairyland, where the incidents of "The Thousand and One Nights" were almost ordinary events, and where Alladin and his compeers still found a home. The year 1798 was destined to sweep out the old and to bring in the new *régime*. Napoleon set out on his expedition to Egypt. His dream was to conquer Egypt and Syria and Mesopotamia, to follow the steps of Alexander the Great, push on to India, and there to pull down the pillars of British greatness.

His counsel perished; but he served a greater purpose than he knew. He took out with him quite a little army of *savants*, scientists, and artists. The *élite* of the French Institute accompanied him. The real wonders of Egypt were for the first time laid bare to the astonished eyes of modern Europe. Those marvels of art which beggared description, and by the side of which our own ancient glories shrank into insignificance, were copied by the first artists of the time, and described by the pens of the literary princes of the period. Drawings and descriptions were published in a magnificent work by the French Government, and the wave of astonishment, felt by those who had first come into contact with those gigantic relics of Egyptian art, swept over all Europe.

But out of this astonishment there sprang an inquiry which was to develop into one of the noblest of our sciences. The monuments were covered with figures of birds, of animals, and of other objects. Inside the tombs, and on the temple walls, the same strange characters were met in the same striking profusion. On temples and tombs they accompanied pictorial representations which it was natural to imagine they explained. Those figures were doubtless the letters of a language, and the question that now pressed itself upon the attention of the learned was—what was the language and what was the information it had so long preserved and was now waiting to reveal?

Providence, which had directed attention to the problem, now supplied the material for its solution, and by-and-bye produced the man to use it. In 1799 a stone was turned up at Rosetta, while the French soldiers were digging the foundations for a fort. The French were soon driven from their position by British troops, and the stone, like some other things, was left behind them. It is now in the British Museum. This Rosetta stone has on it an inscription in three kinds of writing. There is one in hieroglyphics—the figure-writing of the monuments; there is a second in a later form of the ancient writing, called the Demotic, or writing of the people; the third was a Greek translation. This last was easily read, and the inscription was found to be a vote passed by the priesthood to set apart a day to commemorate the birth of Ptolemy Ephipany. Another stone was afterwards discovered at Philae, in the south of Egypt, which had also the three kinds of writing, and was a similar memento of the celebration of Cleopatra's birthday.

Here, then, were the materials, and now God sent the man. Champollion seems to have felt from his early years that it was his mission to penetrate this mystery. He had been prepared for the work by the study of Oriental languages, and especially of the Coptic, the ancient speech of Egypt, which had died out about 200 years before, but information about which had been Providentially preserved by a French priest, who wrote a learned work upon it just as it was expiring. *Without a knowledge of the Coptic, the Egyptian could never have been read.* The place, too, where the key might be inserted—in other words, the point at which an entrance might be made into this mysterious region—had also been mercifully pointed out. The names of Ptolemy and Cleopatra were known from the Greek translations. These names, it was natural to suppose, must appear in the same form, and letter for letter, in the hieroglyphic inscriptions. But where were they to be looked for? This was the exact spot where the key would fit, and it had already been determined. It was seen that certain characters in the hieroglyphic inscriptions were always inscribed within an oval. This oval was, on the face of it, a mark of distinction, and it was concluded that the words which the ovals enclosed were the names of the sovereigns. The ovals were now looked for, and the beginning of the alphabet was immediately discovered. In "Ptolemy" and "Cleopatra" certain letters re-appear. There is a *p* in each. Each also contains the letters *t, o, l,* and *a*. By observing what symbols were used in the two names for each of these letters, a beginning was made with the alphabet. Each step taken in this initial work, simple as it seems, was a fresh illustration of Champollion's genius. Other inscriptions were tried, and the alphabet was extended.

These results were published in 1827. They were followed by marks of royal favour, a place at Court, and the applause of the learned. But nothing could turn him aside from his great life-work. To escape from the demands upon his time, by Paris engagements and interviews with the learned of all lands, he withdrew into the country. He laboured at his *Egyptian Grammar* and *Hieroglyphic Dictionary.* He was still engaged with his grammar when he died in 1832, at the age of 42. He had returned to Paris and was seized with fever. Stretched upon his dying bed and racked with pain, he still pursued his toil, and dictated to his brother the concluding pages of his great work on the grammar of the old Egyptian tongue—a book which is still authoritative. Since that time every year has brought us the translation of monuments and of ancient papyri, till we now know more of the antiquities of Egypt than we know of the antiquities of our own country.

That is one of the discoveries to which I referred. There was a second, and still more stupendous, task awaiting European scholarship. Away in the further East a problem had been beckoning to Europe for 200 years. The ruins of Persepolis, in Persia, had been frequently visited and described. On those monuments, among the most graceful to be found anywhere upon the earth's surface, inscriptions, in a still stranger character than the ancient Egyptian, covered the walls of staircases and of buildings. The letters were made by the grouping together in various positions of a figure like a long wedge, or arrow-head. Its wedge shape gave it the name of the "cuneiform" character, by which it is now known. The inscriptions were copied with great care by Carstens Niebuhr, the father of the Roman historian, and were published in 1774, at the cost of the King of Denmark.

Scholars everywhere were studying these strange inscriptions—but without result. It seemed as if those monuments would retain their secret until all things earthly had passed away. But in the year 1802, a chance conversation led to a happier issue. A young man, named Grotefend, was studying at Göttingen. The librarian of the University knew that he was fond of such studies, and suggested to him that he might give this problem a trial. He supplied him with Niebuhr's inscriptions, and with other material. By one of those rare inspirations which we associate with genius, Grotefend divined where the key could be inserted. He knew that on later monuments found at Persepolis, the inscriptions on which were in languages that could be read, one form was always used. The inscriptions always ran thus: "A, great king, King of kings, Son of B, great king, King of kings," etc. He concluded that the inscriptions in the cuneiform character would run on in this very fashion. It was evidently the ancient style; for there was nothing about those later kings to lead anyone to ascribe such supereminent greatness to them. The later monarchs were plainly, like our own sovereigns, who still call themselves "Defenders of the Faith," following the mode of an earlier time. Grotefend picked out from beneath the portraits of what appeared to be two successive kings two inscriptions which gave a series of three names.

The inscriptions ran thus:

**A,** Great king, King of kings, Son of **B,** Great king, King of kings.

**B,** Great king, King of kings, Son of **C.**

The name represented by B was thus repeated in the second inscription, indicating that B was father in the first inscription and son in the second. A, B, C were, therefore, the names of son, father, and grandfather. But, while it was important to get three names thus in succession, it did not seem at first sight as if there was much hope in the discovery. Who was to say what three names these were? There was small chance of success, if one had to run through a long list of kings to find three that would suit this pair of inscriptions; especially when not a single letter in any of the names was known. But genius has an eye for much that escapes the ordinary observer. Did the reader notice any peculiarity about C, the last of these distinguished personages? The usual formula is wanting in his case. There is no repetition here of the phrase "Great King, King of kings." That omission was everything to Grotefend, and it revealed the remarkable Providence of God that his attention was drawn to *this* pair of inscriptions. It showed that C had not reigned. He was a private individual. B was, therefore, *the founder of a dynasty*. That was certainly something to begin with.

The three names were limited by this one circumstance to certain points in Persian history. It was well known that Persepolis, where the inscriptions were found, was built during the Persian monarchy founded by Cyrus. Was Cyrus, then, the B of the inscriptions? That supposition was soon disposed of. The son and the father of Cyrus bore the same name of Cambyses. A and C would, therefore, have been repetitions of the same word. But a glance at the inscriptions showed that A and C were *not* the same there. Another founder of a dynasty had consequently to be sought for, and Darius was the next. His father was Hystaspis, a private nobleman, and his son and successor the famous Xerxes. Here all three names were different, and so far agreed with those in the inscriptions.

It was now that Grotefend's work really began. He had to get back to the old Persian forms of these names, so that he might read correctly the name of A and the rest. If A was really Xerxes, then the letters common to that name and the other two would appear in their right places in the names of Darius and Hystaspis. The test succeeded, and about half-a-dozen letters were correctly ascertained. This discovery was made in 1802. For the next thirty-four years, no advance was made beyond the discovery of an additional letter or two. As one has said, a man gave his life for a letter of this ancient alphabet. Many applied intellect, learning, and genius to the study, but the soil was stiff and the harvest was poor, It seemed as if the door, which had been opened a little by Grotefend, would

## Further Discoveries. 283

never open far enough to allow us to enter the past into which the inscriptions were waiting to guide us. But success came eventually, and came suddenly. The door, against which so many had been pushing, gave way at last with a bound. In 1836, the entire alphabet of the Persian writing was discovered independently and almost simultaneously, by Burnouf in Paris, by Lassen in Germany, and by our own countryman, Sir Henry Rawlinson, in Persia.

Great as this triumph was, however, it was only the preparation for greater achievements. There was a still more difficult form of writing upon the monuments—the Assyrian, the characters of which represented not elementary sounds, as in our own alphabet, but syllables. There was an immense number of these characters, the power of which had all to be determined. The importance of this second class of inscriptions was proved by the discovery of Assyrian Palaces with numerous monuments and inscriptions during the excavations made by Layard and Botta. Then there was another, and still more difficult form of writing, the Accadian, which takes us back to the very beginning of the art of writing and to the dawn of human history. Both these writing-systems have been deciphered, and the languages have been recalled from the dead. Every year adds to our knowledge of the dynasties and of the triumphs of their kings, of their trade and commerce, of their laws, customs, superstitions, religion, and daily life. The times, the places, and the men live before us. We read their writings; they themselves speak with us.

Now all this has the closest bearing upon what is at present the greatest question of the time for English-speaking Christianity. The critics tell us that they must "re-construct the Bible." We have got so much legend in the Scriptures, they say, and so much late and unreliable history, and so much actual fraud, that in the sacred name of truth they must clear it away. Horrified at the blasphemy which dares to vilify the Word of God, and at the impious attempt to cast to the ground that pillar of cloud and fire which God has given to guide us in life's journey, we hasten to intervene. But God Himself prevents us. There are those whose intervention is weightier than ours can be. This is a question, *not of opinion but of fact.* The reliability of the Scripture history is challenged, and now from Egypt, from Persia, Assyria, and Babylonia, these witnesses, *whose testimony criticism is compelled to admit*, step forward in the face of the world of to-day and say: "We know these things to be true." Books are being set aside by criticism on the ground that they are not authentic. These witnesses again arrest the critic's outstretched hand. They testify: "We are here to prove that the books *are* authentic. They bear on every page the stamp of the place and the time, and every lineament is that of truth."

Let me take one out of the multitude of these testimonies. The critics have much to say in correction of The Books of Kings. These Books, they tell us, have suffered much at the hands of some imaginary compiler. They contain exaggerations, etc., etc. Let us now hear God's witnesses. Professor Sayce, in that marvellously inconsistent book of his, will act as court interpreter. There is a difference in the Books of Kings, in the spelling of the name of Rezon, King of Syria. In 1st Kings it is Rezon; in dealing with a period some 300 years later it is Rezin. "A small matter!" says the reader. But wait a moment. In our Law courts a great deal is sometimes found to hinge upon a small matter. "The spelling of the name of Rezon, in the Books of Kings," says Mr. Sayce, "is rendered noteworthy by a discovery recently made in Northern Syria. At a place called Sinjerli, to the North-east of Antioch, German explorers have found the remains of ancient palaces, as well as monuments which bear inscriptions in the letters of the Aramaic alphabet. Two of them record the name of Panammu King of Sama'la, who, as we know from the Assyrian texts, was a contemporary of Tiglath-Pileser iii., and mention is more than once made of "Tiglath-Pileser, king of Assyria." The names, both of the king and of the country over which he ruled, *are written in precisely the same way as they are in the Books of Kings.* The name of Assyria has the vowel *u* expressed in the second syllable, contrary to the usual custom of early Semitic writing, in which only the consonants are written, while the first syllable of the name Tiglath-Pileser ends with the letter *g*, just as it does in the Old Testament. What makes this remarkable is the fact that such a spelling testifies to a mispronunciation of the name. In Assyrian the name is Tukulti-Palêsar, where the guttural is $k$, and not $g$.

"An inference of some moment," continues Mr. Sayce, "can be drawn from the agreement between the representation of the name at Sinjerli and in the pages of the Old Testament. The misspelling of the name of the king and the notation of the vowel in the name of Assyria could not have originated independently in Northern Syria and in Judah. We know the age to which the monuments of Sinjerli belong; two of them at least were erected by Bar-Rekeb the son of Panammu, and consequently a contemporary of Tiglath-Pileser, whose "servant" he calls himself. Here, then, we have a proof *that even the peculiarities of spelling in the historical annals of the Books of Kings go back to the period of the events recorded in them.* The document or documents from which the account of Tiglath-Pileser is derived must have been coeval with the Assyrian king. But this is not all. We have a proof that the spelling of these documents was followed even where it was inaccurate.

"Nothing," he adds, "can put in a more vivid light *the trustworthy character of the Books of Kings.* If the Biblical compiler reproduced faithfully the mere spelling of the documents of which he made use, we may conclude that he reproduced their contents with equal fidelity. Moreover, Oriental Archaeology has shown us that in one instance, at all events, this spelling goes back to the age of the events described in the narrative to which it belongs, and that this age is anterior to the Babylonian captivity by more than a century. The fact raises the presumption *that in other instances, where as yet we cannot check the verbal accuracy of the Biblical writer, he is equally trustworthy*, and that in reading the records he has preserved for us we may feel confident that we have before us the actual words of a contemporaneous authority."\*

To this almost endless testimonies might be added, all of them enforcing the same conclusion that the Bible is, as we should expect it to be, the most exact and the most literally accurate of books. But the critics have directed their assault, not at isolated statements merely; they have attacked the authenticity and the historical character of entire books of the Bible. How Divine Providence has met these assaults, and has reinstated the books which the critics believe themselves to have overthrown, I shall now ask the reader to mark and consider.

---
\* *The Higher Criticism and the Monuments*, pp. 412-414.

## CHAPTER II.

## THE BOOK OF ESTHER:

ABSENCE OF THE NAME OF GOD.—WHO WAS
AHASUERUS?—XERXES' FEAST.

I BEGIN with a part of the Scripture in regard to which the Critics are perfectly certain—the Book of Esther. This book has always been highly valued by the Jews. Maimonides, the great mediæval Rabbi, is reported to have said: "In the days of the Messiah the prophetical books and the Hagiographa (the Psalms, Proverbs, &c.) will be done away, excepting only Esther, which will endure together with the Pentateuch." We can easily understand how appreciation of the book became so intense among the Jews. To a people so oppressed and persecuted this record of providential rescue must have been specially dear; and many an agonising prayer must have been sent up to the God of Esther and of Mordecai in the awful times through which they have had to pass in every land under the sun.

But many in the Christian Church have looked at

the book with a colder and more critical eye. They have been offended at the apparent absence of any recognition of God, and at the presence of what has seemed to them a vengeful spirit. Luther, especially, has spoken of this with that absence of self-restraint which formed an occasional but painful feature in his after-dinner utterances. There can be little question that these doubts, arising entirely from a superficial view of the book, prepared the way for the critics, and perhaps sowed the seeds of the unbelief which we deplore to-day.

Let me, then, first of all, say a word about this alleged absence of a religious spirit in the book of Esther. It is quite true that the name of God is not once mentioned in it. The absolute silence maintained on this point is remarkable, and attracted notice, as we shall see immediately, from the earliest times. In all this thrilling story of danger, and of terror, there is not one word to indicate that the Jews had any sense that their peril was owing to God's anger, or that they hoped for deliverance through God's mercy. Is it possible to believe that this was the true state of the case—that the Jews throughout the Persian empire should have been threatened with destruction, and that not a man or woman was found among them all to think of the God of their fathers? And could a book so utterly atheistic in spirit ever have found an unquestioned entrance into the canon of the Old Testament as this book undeniably did?

There is surely matter for reflection there. If this

book was *not* written by one who had forgotten God, then there is only one conclusion possible: the silence was intentional. It was the Spirit's purpose, for some good and sufficient reason, that in this record God's name should not be mentioned. When this is once noted, other characteristics of the book confirm the inference. *There is no mention in it of prayer.* We are told that "in every province, whithersoever the king's commandment and his decree came, there was great mourning among the Jews, and fasting, and weeping, and wailing, and many lay in sackcloth and ashes" (iv. 3); but it is not said that anyone *prayed to God* or mourned *before God*, or flung himself down with breaking heart *before God*. It is absolutely impossible to believe that no tear-blinded eyes were raised to heaven; or that Israel's bitter cry was not lifted to the only Helper whom they had ever known. It will also be noted by the careful reader that there is as absolute exclusion of any mention of praise to God. The Jews are visited with one of the most marvellous deliverances in all their history. But to the record of that deliverance there is joined no thanksgiving nor any recognition of Him from whom the deliverance has come. It is as if, like the maid in "the Romaunt of the Brown Rosarie," they had made a vow neither to seek God in their woe, nor to praise Him in their weal. But that such was the case is, as we know, an utter impossibility. The Jews did cry to God in their distress, and they did praise Him in their joy. The feast which they ordained, and which they bound upon themselves and upon their seed to observe for ever, was simply a memorial to all time of their indebtedness and their gratitude to God. But how is it that there is no mention of this in the book? What means this persistent silence, this Divine "hush!" whenever the sacred penman approaches the mention of anything that will link the names of Israel and of God together?

This silence, so peculiar, so passing strange, in a book given by inspiration of God, has not been understood. The Alexandrian Jews, who translated the Old Testament into Greek some 300 or 200 years before the Christian era, to enable the learned among the Egyptians and among other nations to judge what the Bible was, apparently felt that they could not let the book of Esther go out in this condition. They, therefore, put a long prayer into the mouth of Mordecai, and a still longer one into the mouth of Esther. That is how *man* would have written the book. Let us now ask whether we can gather any lesson from the Divine silence.

More than fifty years previously, the day of deliverance had been Divinely brought to Israel. Cyrus ended their captivity, as God had promised. The proclamation had been made: "Thus saith Cyrus, king of Persia, The Lord God of heaven hath given me all the kingdoms of the earth; and He hath charged me to build Him an house at Jerusalem, which is in Judah. Who is there among you of all His people? his God be with him, and let him go up to Jerusalem, which is in Judah, and build the house of the Lord God of Israel (He is the God), which is in Jerusalem" (Ezra i. 2, 3). This recall to Palestine bore God's seal upon it, because both the agent and the time had been predicted. Cyrus had been named as the deliverer before he was born, and seventy years had been fixed as the limit of the captivity. What Jew, then, ought to have remained in Persia when the door had been opened for escape? When God called, who should have lingered? When He brought deliverance, who should have spurned the gift? But every soul of those who remained in Persia had done these very things. They, in effect, told God that the deliverance which He had wrought had no attraction for them. They were abundantly content to remain where they were. Other men might spurn the fatness of Persia; others might become wanderers once more, settle amid the desolations of Judea, toil for scanty harvests, and spend their strength in rearing the walls of Jerusalem and in rebuilding the Temple. They were quite sure that such things ought to be done, and they would be among the readiest to praise the self-sacrifice it all entailed—but, as for them, they had no vocation that way.

The truth is that these Persian Jews were *types*, and *there can be no doubt that they are used as types in the book of Esther*. They represent all who reject God's salvation; and, more specially still, are they the representatives of those who bear the Christian name, but who love the world too well to endure any sacrifice for Christ's sake. It is in vain that God calls upon *them* to separate from the world, or to seek first the kingdom of God and His righteousnesss, trusting that all other things will be added to them. These are also led into tribulation; they cry, and they are delivered. But God's name and theirs will never be bound together in the story of the earth's salvation. He is with the poor, rich in faith, who went joyfully when God called them, and who are bearing in that land of promise the burden and the heat of the day. God's name and theirs will be bound up together. Their strength and His are being put into that which shall endure, and which shall be for men's good and for God's glory. But, with those who live to themselves, God will not be associated. He will deliver them, "for He maketh His sun to rise on the evil and on the good, and sendeth rain on the just and on the unjust." But they have toiled for time, and not for eternity; and they, their prayers, and their deliverances are among the things whose memory shall perish. There is no record of them on high; *their* names are not written in the Lamb's book of life.

That is one evident meaning of the Divine silence. But it seems to me that this significant absence of the name of God takes us still farther. It is prophetic. These Persian Jews are the types of their fellow-countrymen who were afterwards to reject God's salvation in Christ, and who, scattered among the nations, were again and again to be threatened with destruction. God's name and theirs have not been bound together for eighteen hundred years.

God has been working marvellously in these centuries; but those rebellious Jews and He have not been found together. God's Temple has been reared; it is being reared now; but the work is done by other hands than theirs. God's battles have been fought and won, but *their* names have not been inscribed in the glorious story. That side of the story has been repeated, and the other has been repeated also. He has watched over His rebellious people, and He watches over them still. Haman may plot their destruction; but he plots against his own life and the lives of all that are dear to him. Let Russia and every other foe of that apparently God-forsaken people take heed to it. God will avenge the wrong done to His people even though they have despised their heritage. Their unbelief cannot make God forget His word: "I will bless them that bless thee, and curse him that curseth thee" (Gen. xii. 3).

The truth is that the absence of the name of God is one proof of the inspiration of *Esther*. The absence of it is perfectly inexplicable on the supposition that the book has had a purely human origin. The apocryphal additions to Esther in the Septuagint show how *man* would have written the book. Our own astonishment at the absence of all reference to God is another indication. Had the writing of the book been left to us, we should never have cast it into that form. The silence regarding prayer and the intervention of God is simply unnatural. But when we see the Divine purpose in this painstaking, unchanging, and resolute silence, the book of Esther is suddenly brought into line with the whole of Scripture. The Spirit of God declares the same truth in that silence which the other books declare in their speech; and we need go no further to see the Divine stamp. We feel assured that this book is God's book, and not man's.

But we have to note how God's witnesses have silenced the critics. De Wette's condemnation of Esther was very pronounced. "It violates," he said, "all historical probability, and contains the most striking difficulties, and many errors with regard to Persian manners, as well as just references to them." His translator, Theodore Parker, as usual, goes further. "For a long time," he says, "this book was considered a history of actual events. Some writers at this time hold such an opinion, but it is involved in numerous and inexplicable difficulties; for the book does not bear the marks of a historical composition. . . . It seems most probable the book was written," he adds, "as a patriotic romance, designed to show that the Jews will be delivered out of all troubles, and he that seeks to injure them shall himself be destroyed. The narrative may have some historical facts for its basis, or be purely fictitious. This, at least, is certain, that it is impossible, at this day, to determine where facts begin and fiction ends." *

There is a smack of genuine satisfaction in that last sentence. Criticism had not then reached the re-constructive stage. It was, as yet, only in the

---

\* *De Wette on the Old-Testament* (Boston, 1850), Vol. ii., pp. 337-345.

destructive; and in this ruin, in which no one could tell "where facts begin and fiction ends," some capital work seemed to be done. There was one point, however, on which De Wette was quite positive. The book was not written till long after the events. "The language belongs," he said, "to a very late period." It is highly characteristic of the so-called "scholarship" of the critics that De Wette rests this conviction largely upon his ignorance. He refers to the presence of "Persian words." The ignorance of the learned world of the ancient Persian was at that time most profound. It knew nothing of it; and ever since the veil has been lifted, and men have become acquainted with the language spoken by Ahasuerus, by Haman, and by Esther, De Wette's judgment of the Book has been more and more abandoned.

By the time Dr. Driver's book came to be written, the critics had been taught some things after the fashion in which Gideon taught the men of Succoth. He is not so certain as his forerunners were as to the late date of the Book. The language, instead of being so very late as De Wette pronounced it to be, is now acknowledged as "superior to that of the Chronicles, and more accommodated to the model of the earlier historical books."* The critical position, as to the historical character of *Esther* has been quite as completely riddled. De Wette had no hesitation in assuring his dupes that the Book "violates all historical probability"; and Theodore Parker was

---

* *Introduction*, &c., p. 455.

equally resolute in trampling faith under foot by the assurance that it could no longer be "considered a history of actual events." Dr. Driver now admits that those who believed these things, and who, believing them, cast away their former faith in God's Word, believed a lie. They accepted them on the ground that they were the mature decision of competent scholarship; but now he has to admit that the supposed scholarship was simply a delusion. "The writer" (of Esther), he says, "*shows himself well informed on Persian manners and institutions; he does not commit anachronisms* such as occur in Tobit or Judith, and the character of Xerxes as drawn by him, is in agreement with history!"\*

Let us now see what it is that has led Dr. Driver so far, and that should lead us and him further still. So long as ancient Persia was practically unknown to European scholars, the verdict of the critical school was accepted by many. But, with the knowledge of that old civilisation which has dawned and brightened during the present century, the difficulties and objections have melted away like morning mist. As soon as ancient history began to be studied with thoroughness, it was felt that *Esther* must be replaced among the books that are thoroughly historical. Heeren, one of the greatest historical scholars the world has ever seen, says that *Esther* "contains a true picture of the manners of the Persian Court,"† and he places it among the

---
\* *Ibid*, p. 453.
† *Heeren's Historical Researches. Asiatic Nations*, Vol. i., p. 53.

books which are authoritative upon that subject. The significance of this judgment will be felt when it is remembered that it was passed in the face of all that was then said against the book by the Critics. But time had still more painful surprises in store for them. No sooner had Assyriology begun to bring back the ancient civilisation of Persia to the light of day, than the same verdict was repeated with emphasis. Lenormant wrote: "We find in the book of Esther a most animated picture of the Court of the Persian kings, which enables us, *better than anything contained in the classical writers*, to penetrate the internal life and the details of the organisation of the central government established by Darius." \* The most recent and reliable work published on the subject impresses the same verdict afresh. Mr. Evetts says: "Perhaps no book of the Bible has received so many elucidations from secular sources as the book of Esther. . . . . Since the beginning of this century the cuneiform inscriptions have contributed their share to the elucidation of this book." †

Let us now listen to God's witnesses, and hear what fact has to say in reply to critical fictions. There was one objection to the Book which used to be strongly urged. The picture presented of Ahasuerus was confidently pronounced to be purely imaginary. No such conglomeration of insane pride and unbridled caprice could ever have dwelt, it was said, in a human bosom. We shall now see how

---

\* *Ancient History of the East*, Vol. ii., p. 113. † *New Light on the Bible*, p. 254.

## The Book of Esther. 299

this objection was suddenly changed into a startling proof of the historical character of the book.

When the Greek translation of the Old Testament was made (300-200 B.C.), the learned Jews of Alexandria were quite in the dark as to who Ahasuerus was. But they had to translate the name; and, as it would never have done to insert in the translation a name utterly unknown to their Greek readers, they were compelled to make a guess as to who he was. They guessed and missed. They put him down as Artaxerxes. The significance of that blunder should be noted. In the end of the fourth century before Christ, the Greek empire had replaced the Persian; the persons and the doings of the Persian kings rapidly became ancient history; and now, in the third century B.C., learned Jews are unable to say which of the Persian kings Ahasuerus was. That is in itself a strong proof that the book must have been already ancient in the third century before our era, and that it could not possibly have originated at the late date assigned to it by the critics.

Later scholars were equally at fault. Some said he was Astyages; some, Darius the Mede; some, Cambyses, the son of Cyrus; others, Darius Hystaspes; and one or two suggested Xerxes. This last guess was the most fortunate, for the very first name which Grotefend deciphered in 1802, and the very first word of ancient Persian which modern scholarship brought back from the dead, was the name of this king. It was *Kshayarsha*, the name rendered into Greek by Xerxes, and faithfully represented, letter by letter, in the Hebrew Bible by *Akhashverosh*, or Ahasuerus. The initial A, though it does not occur in the Persian, is met with in the contract tablets of Babylonia. "We meet with the forms, *Achshiyarshu*, *Akkashiyarshi*, and a very corrupt form, *Akohiakarshu*."*

Among the few scholars who suggested the identity of Ahasuerus with Xerxes were some of great name. The suggestion arose, of course, out of their belief that *Esther* was true. But this afforded too triumphant a reply to De Wette's objections for him to admit it. "The main point on which," he said, "the authenticity of the Book has been rested, namely, that Ahasuerus is the same with Xerxes, is very doubtful."† De Wette felt that if this point were yielded the objection would melt away. The fear was prophetic. That Ahasuerus was Xerxes is now one of the certainties of science, and with this one discovery, the argument raised against the book on account of the king's pride and caprice was for ever hushed. The truth was suddenly recognised that here the Scripture had been presenting to believer and unbeliever alike a real historic figure. Dr. Samuel Davidson, in his rationalistic "Introduction to the Old Testament," says: "What most favours the identity of Xerxes with Ahasuerus is *similarity of character*." The italics are the Doctor's own. "The conduct of Xerxes," he proceeds, "was capricious, and in some cases that of a madman. His disposi-

---

* *New Light on the Bible*, p. 255.  † *De Wette on the Old Testament*, Vol. ii., p. 337.

tion was sensual and cruel. He was prone to indulge in riotous living. His measures were often sudden and arbitrary. All this is reflected in the person of Ahasuerus better than in that of any other Persian monarch we know."* Canon Driver is also compelled, as we have seen, to acknowledge the force of this discovery. After stating that "to many critics . . . the narrative as a whole seems to read as a romance rather than as a history," he adds, in words already quoted, that signs abound of full acquaintance with Persian manners, and in particular that "the character of Xerxes, as drawn by him, is in agreement with history."

There has, in fact, seldom been a more magical transformation. With the discovery of the name of Xerxes, *Esther* passed in one moment from the realm of supposed romance into that of history. How true the picture of the Persian monarch is may be seen from the following. Mount Athos projects into the sea, and has to be circumnavigated by vessels following the coast. Xerxes, Herodotus tells us, resolved to save this detour by undertaking a work enormously greater. He determined to cut a canal, along which his ships could go, and so make Mount Athos an island. Herodotus says: "The motive of Xerxes in this work was, as far as I am able to conjecture, the vain desire of exhibiting his power and of leaving a monument to posterity." Plutarch has also preserved a letter which it is said the king addressed to the mountain while the work was in

---

* Vol. ii., pp. 156, 157.

progress. The letter ran: "O thou miserable Athos, whose top now reaches to the heavens, I give thee in charge not to throw any great stones in my way, which may impede my work! If thou wilt do this, I will cut thee in pieces and cast thee into the sea."

Similar incidents are not wanting. Passing through Asia Minor, he was struck by the beauty of a plane-tree, and had it adorned with gold chains, and guarded by a detachment of the choicest corps in his army.* He resolved to throw a bridge of boats over the Hellespont. It was destroyed by a tempest as soon as completed. Here is the account left us by Herodotus of what followed:—"When Xerxes heard of what had happened, he was so enraged that he ordered three hundred lashes to be inflicted on the Hellespont, and a pair of fetters to be thrown into the sea. I have been informed that he even sent some executioners to brand the Hellespont with marks of ignominy; but it is certain that he ordered those who inflicted the lashes to use these barbarous and mad expressions:—'Thou ungracious water! thy master condemns thee to this punishment, for having injured him without provocation. Xerxes the king will pass over thee, whether thou consentest or not; just is it that no man honours thee with sacrifice, for thou art insidious and of an ungrateful flavour. After thus treating the sea, the king commanded those who presided over the construction of the bridge to be beheaded." †

Here we have the very man whom the Scripture

---

* Herodotus, viii. 31.   † *Ibid*, 35.

has shown us. The incidents are different, but the personality of the actor is the same. The return of the price paid by Haman for the lives of the Jews, and the king's sudden and deadly displeasure with that favourite, have also, strange to say, their parallels in the history of the expedition against Greece. A Lydian presented Xerxes with about five and a half millions sterling towards the expenses of the expedition. The king was enraptured, returned the money, and added a very handsome present to it. Shortly afterwards, the Lydian, alarmed by an omen and fearing that all his sons, who were with Xerxes, would perish on the expedition, begged the king to allow the eldest to remain at home. Xerxes was furious. He ordered the eldest son to be cut into two pieces. The pieces were laid one on each side of the road, and his army was made to march between them.

The book of Esther opens with the account of a great festival. "In the third year of his reign," we read, "he (Ahasuerus) made a feast unto all his princes and his servants; the power of Persia and of Media, the nobles and princes of the provinces being before him: when he showed the riches of his glorious kingdom, and the honour of his excellent majesty many days, even an hundred and fourscore days. And when these days were expired, the king made a feast unto all the people that were present in Shushan, the palace, both unto great and small, seven days in the court of the garden of the king's palace" (i. 1-5). Was there anything to account for this gathering and for such prolonged festivities? The discovery that Ahasuerus is Xerxes has shed a flood of light upon this and upon many other incidents in the narrative. It was in this very third year that the plans were fixed and the preparations made for the invasion of Greece. Herodotus has given us a long account of that conference. "After the subjection of Egypt," he says, "Xerxes prepared to lead an army against Athens, but *first of all he called an assembly of the principal Persians*, to hear their sentiments, and to deliver without reserve his own."

Here, then, we have a vivid picture in *Esther* of the great gathering of the Persian nobles. It was impossible for Herodotus in mentioning it to be silent regarding the Grecian expedition. For the Greeks the whole history of Xerxes practically began and ended with that disastrous, but epoch-making campaign. But to the sacred writer it was a mere incident in a long career, and it fell no more within the scope of his purpose to mention what was to be attempted in Greece, than to recount what had just been accomplished in Egypt. What is to follow hinges upon this festival, and therefore it is that the story begins there. Vashti is summoned to appear on the great day of the prolonged feast, and sends her lord and the world's master a blank refusal. That is the real beginning of the narrative. Vashti is to be deposed and another is to reign in her stead, and, therefore, we must first of all hear what was Vashti's fault. But, while the Bible confines itself to its own purpose, discovery and history unite in the assurance that this is not romance, but fact. That great gathering *was* held, and it was held in the very year which the Scripture names!

Here, then, at the very outset the critical fabric is shaken and shattered. These crushing blows are repeated as the evidence proceeds, till not a vestige of the structure remains. That this assembly of notables was called, we know from Herodotus as well as from *Esther*. But it is well to note that it was quite in accord with Persian custom. "In extraordinary cases," says Lenormant, "when, for instance, it was intended to make a great expedition, and to call the privileged race of the Persians to arms for any distant warfare, an assembly was called, the last remains of the free deliberative institutions of that nation. It was composed of satraps, commanders of the forces, the chief officers of the crown, and the heads of the military Persian aristocracy; that is, the tribe of the Pasargadae. He whose advice was followed had to answer with his head for the success of the enterprise, an arrangement that very soon put an end to the reality of deliberation, and suppressed all liberty of speech."\*

Objection has been taken to the form which the festivities take. De Wette calls it "a Bacchanalian carousal." But had the Scripture narrative been in accord with critical notions in this matter, it would have been out of accord with truth. "They are accustomed," says Herodotus, "to debate upon the

---

\* *Ancient History of the East*, Vol. ii., p. 113.

most important matters when they are drunk; and whatever they approve in their debate is proposed to them the next day, when they are sober, by their host, in whose house they happen to be deliberating, and if they still approve the matter when they are sober, they finally decide upon it. But if they have a preliminary consultation upon any matter while they are sober, they debate it afresh when they are drunk."

Such was the custom of the people. No doubt, also, the court traditions of the Empire which they had overthrown would be retained in the palace, and in these, as the sculptors show, the use of wine occupied a large and important place. Heraclides, another ancient writer, gives us the following picture of a Persian banquet. "Those who wait upon the kings of the Persians at their chief meal all wash themselves before they serve, and wear fair garments, and busy themselves about half the day over the meal. Some of the king's guests eat without; and others eat within, with the king. But the latter do not sit at the same table with him, for there are two rooms next to one another, in one of which the king takes his meal, and in the other the guests (take theirs); and the king can see them, through the curtain which hangs over the door, but they cannot see him. Some, however, if it is a feast-day, eat in the same room with the king, in the great house. And when the king has a drinking party (and this he often does), he generally has twelve boon companions. When they have finished their meal, the king sitting by himself and the guests without, one of the eunuchs calls the latter in; and when they enter they drink with the king, but not the same wine; and they sit on the ground, but he reclines on a couch with golden feet; and when they are drunk they go away. Generally the king breakfasts and sups alone; but sometimes his wife and some of his sons sup with him, and the ladies of the harem sing and play the harp during the meal." "At some of the royal banquets, however," adds Mr. Evetts, "it is said that fifteen thousand men were present, and that the expense of the meal amounted to four hundred talents, or about £1 7s. a head in our money." *

The long continuance of the feast has also been said to be improbable. It is supposed by our critical friends that the council would have been hurried through, and the nobles packed off with all haste to their distant homes. But there were many arrangements to be made for the gathering of the troops and for the provisioning of the mighty hosts at various points along the way. And, besides, it was not the custom of the court, and above all of Xerxes, to grudge hospitality. Even in the diminished splendour of the later dynasties, the traditions of royal hospitality were preserved. "Many ancient customs of the Persian court," says Evetts, "have been preserved during the different dynasties down to modern times; and Anthony Sherley . . witnessed a series of banquets at the Court of Shah Abbas, which recall to the reader the scenes described in the first chapter of the Book of Esther: 'For thirty

---

\* *New Light on the Bible*, p. 252.

days continuallie the king made that feast in the great garden of more than two miles compasse, under tents pitched by certain small courses of running water, like divers rivers, where every man that would come was placed according to his degree, either under one or other tent, provided for abundantlie with meate, fruite, and wine; drinking as they would, some largelie, some moderatelie, *without compulsion*. A roialty and splendour which I have not seene, nor shall not see againe but by the same king: our princes abhorring such vaine expence, desiring rather to have the power of dominion than to make those sorts of ostentation."* To all this add the wealth and the studied display of Xerxes, and we shall have no difficulty in seeing how the thirty days of Shah Abbas would easily be swelled to the one hundred and eighty days of the great king.

The above testimonies also prove the accuracy of Scripture in two of the very minor details of the Bible picture. We read that there was "*Royal* wine in abundance. according to the state (or bounty) of the king" (Esther i. 7). Here it is indicated that there was a special wine for the king's use. This is confirmed by the above statement of Heraclides, that the king's boon companions drank with him, "but not the same wine." The reader will also have noted another parallel in Anthony Sherley's account. The Scripture says: "The drinking was according to the law; none did compel; for so the king had appointed to all the officers of his house,

---

* *Ibid*, pp. 252, 253.

that they should do according to every man's pleasure." Anthony says the law at Shah Abbas's banquet was that the guests *drank "as they would, some largelie, some moderatelie, without compulsion."* It is in such small matters that we generally find the clearest impressions of truth.

## CHAPTER III.

### XERXES AND ESTHER.

IN chapter ii. 16, we are told that it was only in the tenth month of "the *seventh* year" of the king's reign, that Esther was invested with the honours of the disowned Vashti. It will be remembered that Vashti had been divorced in the *third* year of Xerxes' reign. The lapse of this long interval necessarily leads to inquiry. Why were four years suffered to intervene between the dethronement of Vashti and the choice of her successor? I have said that the matter naturally leads to inquiry. If the statements had been met with in any other book they would have done so. An explanation would have been patiently sought, and any probable solution of the difficulty would have been thankfully accepted. It might well be cited as one proof of the great Scripture doctrine regarding the attitude of the natural mind towards God, that, when the Bible is concerned, such a circumstance seems to immediately arouse slumbering, but when awake, lynx-eyed suspicion and distrust.

Like the statements of a witness watched by a counsel who holds a brief for the adversary, these two statements in *Esther* about the third and the seventh year have been pounced upon and been branded as a contradiction. The critics have confidently placed them in the very forefront of "the historical improbabilities," which, they maintain, reveal the book to be manifest fiction. But, just as in the case of the mention of "the third year" as that in which the notables were assembled at Shushan, so here again, the very thing upon which the critics have insisted as a mark of fiction, is one of the most signal proofs that the book is dealing with absolute fact. Xerxes had set out meanwhile upon his ever memorable expedition against Greece, and he did not return to Susa till *the spring of the seventh year of his reign.*

It would be difficult to conceive a more complete answer than that. Davidson tries to break its force by citing the statement of Herodotus that during the Grecian expedition Xerxes was accompanied by his queen, Amestris. But Herodotus makes a mistake in stating that Xerxes returned to Persia in his *tenth* year instead of the seventh, and he may have mixed events here. This very queen Amestris, who is Xerxes' *second queen,* and whose name greatly resembles "Esther," the Persian name of Hadassah, will probably be discovered to be no other than the niece of Mordecai. The one thing which has hitherto prevented commentators from admitting the identification is the character which Amestris bears in history for cruelty. But to me, this tells the other way. The events which took place at the rescue of the Jews and the vengeance which fell upon the house of Haman would naturally be so represented by native Persians; indeed, the character of Esther is read in that very way by our critical friends. The other features in the story tally remarkably with what the Scripture tells us of the relations between Xerxes and Esther. Amestris possessed the greatest influence over Xerxes during the last years of his life, and seems to have been a woman of decided character.

Special objection has been taken to the representation given in *Esther* of the formality of Persian Court customs. I cannot do better than let Dr. Samuel Davidson present these objections in his own way. "The description," he says, "of Ahasuerus's sitting on his throne when he did not give audience to anyone, and so exhibiting his royal pomp when there was no occasion, is, incongruous. And that the queen could only approach to speak to her husband at the risk of her life is improbable, unless she had fallen under the monarch's displeasure. Who can think it agreeable to Persian manners that the king should have continually a golden sceptre at hand to reach forth to anyone whom he might allow to speak to him without being summoned?" *

The above is amusing in its unconscious assumption that English middle-class manners must be the

---
* *Introduction to the Old Testament*, Vol. ii., p. 161.

standard by which to judge what was natural in the splendid and tyrannic Court of Persia. Dr. Davidson would have fared badly had he lived in that age, and had he attempted to carry his ideas into practice. Court ceremony was at its very highest in the days of Xerxes. Spanish Court rules were nothing in comparison with the rigorous ceremonial of the Persian Court. On the monuments of Persepolis, which have preserved the pictures of this very Court of Xerxes, the king is always represented as bearing in his hand a long staff with a golden knob. It was the symbol of a power which was never suffered to be forgotten even for a moment. The objection as to Xerxes sitting on his throne when he did not give audience to anyone is quite gratuitous. The times of audience were arranged and known, and when should Esther seek an interview but at such a time? There is a passage in Herodotus, describing some things which happened at the very gathering in the third year referred to in *Esther*, which might have taught Dr. Davidson caution. Xerxes had had a terrifying vision. It was repeated. He desired to know whether it would appear to any other who should take his place. He, therefore, commanded one of his counsellors, and a relative of his own, to assume his clothing, sit on his throne, and then occupy the royal couch. To sit on the king's throne was a capital offence, and Artabanus, the courtier referred to, was alarmed. "Artabanus," says Herodotus, "was at first unwilling to comply, alleging that he was not worthy to sit on the throne of the king." But, being persuaded by the king, " he accordingly put on the robe of Xerxes, *seated himself on the royal throne*, and afterwards retired to the king's apartment." Here it is plain that sitting on the throne was as much part of the routine of the king's life as wearing his robes or occupying his bed.

To sit upon the throne was essential, indeed, to anyone who assumed, and who sought to maintain, the royal dignity. This is shown in the following anecdote related of Alexander the Great by a Greek historian. The circumstance occurred in this very city of Susa. When he had captured the city, "Alexander took his seat upon the royal throne, but it was too high for his stature. One of the slaves, seeing that his feet did not reach the footstool in front of the throne, brought the table of Darius and placed it under Alexander's feet, which were hanging in the air; and as it fitted his requirements, the king accepted the good suggestion thus made. But one of the eunuchs who stood by the throne, moved in his spirit by the changes of fortune which he beheld, wept: and when Alexander asked him: 'What harm have you seen done that makes you weep?' the eunuch said: 'Now I am your slave, but formerly I was the slave of Darius; and as it is my duty to love my master, I am pained by seeing a piece of furniture, which he put to an honourable use, now dishonoured.'" "When Alexander," says Mr. Evetts in quoting the above, "afterwards captured Persepolis, he took his seat in a similar manner on the throne of the great king in the Persepolitan palace."\*

The stateliness of the Persian court ceremonial was assumed by Cyrus, and seems to have been increased rather than diminished by his successors. It was regarded as essential to the maintenance of their power. This is shown in the monuments of Persepolis. They present the picture of what the Book of *Esther* describes in words. Speaking of these sculptures, Heeren says: "The king is here represented in grand costume in the act of giving audience to an ambassador. He is seated on a throne with a footstool of gold at his feet, which was always borne after him; his golden sceptre is in his right hand; and in his left the sacred vase, or cup *Havan*, used in sacrifice, and betokening a worshipper of Ormuzd." After describing the body-guards and the ambassador standing at a respectful distance "with his hand before his mouth, not to offend the king's majesty," Heeren adds: "Everything bespeaks grandeur and magnificence."† The care and severity by which, according to *Esther*, these regulations were guarded were another striking feature of the place and time. "The palace, among the Persians," says Lenormant, "as now among the Turks, had the name of *Gate (duvara)*, and was quite inaccessible to the multitude. A most rigid etiquette guarded all access to the king, and made it very difficult to approach him. The ministers and courtiers employed in the interior of the palace were

---

\* *New Light on the Bible*, p. 254.  † *Hist. Researches*, Vol. i., pp. 114, 115.

stationed, according to their rank and duties, in the outer courts. The number of these servants, attendants, and masters of ceremonies was very large. It was necessary to apply to them in order to reach the king, so that some of them were called the ears and the eyes of the king. *He who entered the presence of the king without having previously obtained permission, was punished with death."* *

Thus in every detail of the history and in every allusion, the Book of *Esther* brings us face to face with fact, and sets us down amid the life and the scenes of that long since vanished past. The reader will remember how frequently reference is made in *Esther* to the courtiers "standing in the courts," and to others sitting in the gate of the king's palace. Xerxes asks, while it is apparently still night, "Who is in the court?" And it is added, that "Haman was come into the outward court," waiting for an interview with the king (Esther vi. 4). It is evidently taken for granted that some of the king's ministers would be in waiting there, even at that untimely hour; and here we have another reflection of Persian customs, so surprising in its accuracy and vividness that we see the Court of Xerxes with our own eyes. In the sculptures of Persepolis we have a picture of the portico of the palace, and groups of courtiers are represented standing. "They are meant," says Heeren, "to represent 'the friends,' or, in the language of the East, the 'kinsmen of the king,' 'those who stood in the king's gates;' or, as we

---

* *Ancient History of the East*, Vol. ii., pp. 113, 114.

should express it, the courtiers and great officers of the king. According to the customs of the Persians, the majesty of the king required that a number of such courtiers should be at all times found before the gates, or in the courts and ante-chambers of the palace, to be ready to attend the least signal of his pleasure."

What is said also as to the fatal import of the king's displeasure, paints the terror of the time to the very life. Speaking of the great officers of the empire, Lenormant says: "The least disobedience on their part was looked upon as rebellion, and almost always led to the death of the culprit."* The casual reference to the seven princes of the king's council shows the same full and minute acquaintance with the place and time. But I have now to mention another confirmation—a confirmation which is perhaps the most striking that has up to the present moment been accorded to any book of Scripture. The very palace has been recovered whose halls were inhabited, and whose floors were trod by Xerxes and by Esther. It was well known that *Shush*, in Persia, was the ancient Shushan. There were three conspicuous mounds in the immediate vicinity of the modern town, which travellers believed to contain the remains of its ancient splendours. This belief was fully confirmed by the researches of Loftus in 1852. One of the mounds was opened, and the foundation of a large hall was uncovered. On the bases of some of the columns an inscription of

---

* *Ibid.*

Artaxerxes Mnemon (B.C. 406-359) was found which ran as follows:—"My ancestor Darius built this *Apadana* in former times. In the reign of Artaxerxes, my grandfather, it was consumed by fire. By the grace of Ahuramazda, Anaitis, and Mithras, I have restored this *Apadana*."

This inscription is of priceless value. It shows that the first palace built by Darius, the father of Xerxes, perished in the reign of Xerxes' son, Artaxerxes Longimanus (B.C. 464-425). It passed away, therefore, from the knowledge of men within forty years, possibly within ten or twenty years, of the death of Xerxes. This fact has a most momentous bearing upon the pretensions of criticism; for, if we find in the Book of Esther references to that very palace which prove it to have been fully and minutely known, what conclusion is forced upon us? Is it not that, *if this book is of merely human origin*, it must have been written by one who knew the palace, and who was acquainted with it *in the lifetime of Xerxes*, or at the very latest *in the early years* of his immediate successor? There is, consequently, no possible escape from the conclusion that the book must have been written by a contemporary and an eye-witness of the events it describes.

But was the palace so minutely known? The facts will give the answer. Loftus was unable to carry his explorations further, and the mounds remained undisturbed till the year 1885, when M. Dieulafoy, a distinguished French architect, explored the ruins, having obtained permission from the Shah of Persia. Let me here acknowledge how great the debt is that we owe to French genius and learning and self-sacrificing labour. Other nations have been nobly represented in the fields of Assyriology and of Egyptology. Our own country has won undying honour there. But it is hardly an exaggeration to say that we owe as much to France as to all the others put together. M. Dieulafoy had long cherished the desire to subject the mounds of Susa to a thorough search. He had paid a hurried visit in 1882 to the spot, and then resolved to return, if possible, and to explore the ruins. In 1884 he prevailed upon the French Government to lend their aid. The Persian Government refused at first, however, to sanction the undertaking. But the Shah had a European physician who had considerable influence with him. His good offices were asked for and obtained. He represented to the monarch that by encouraging the exploration his reputation would be raised in Europe as a promoter of learning.

We live in days when the praise of a learned society is almost as good as a victory, and the Shah's consent was secured. There were other difficulties and discouragements, however, to encounter. Local fanaticism was peculiarly strong even for Persia. The supposed tomb of the Prophet Daniel rests upon one of the mounds, and the anticipated violation of that sacred shrine raised Mohammedan fanaticism to frenzy. The little band of explorers narrowly escaped annihilation at the hands of an excited multitude; but, notwithstanding the threats of the populace and the opposition of officials, operations were begun on March 1st, 1885, the work being inaugurated by Madame Dieulafoy, who accompanied her husband and who shared his dangers and his labours. They spent two seasons at the spot. Trenches were dug, and a wall encircling a building of vast proportions was traced.

"Dieulafoy's thorough knowledge," says a writer in *Art and Literature*, 1890, "of Persian architecture, as exhibited by the ruins at Persepolis and elsewhere, aided him in fixing upon the general distribution of the apartments of which such a palace was composed. He devoted himself more especially to that portion of it where he conjectured the grand reception or 'throne-room' to have been situated, which promised a particularly rich return. His expectations were not disappointed. The trenches being widened, they came into the 'throne-room' itself, where hundreds of glazed tiles in various states of preservation still bore witness to its former glory. Each tile, as it was taken out, was carefully numbered, and upon piecing them together, it was found that they formed part of a large frieze representing a series of lions, whose fierce aspect, as they stand to-day in the Louvre, is still well-calculated to inspire terror. These glazed tiles constituted the decoration of the palace walls, corresponding to the alabaster slabs which was the ordinary material employed by the Assyrian kings in their palaces.

"It may be imagined," continues the writer, "into what ecstasies of joy this discovery threw the Dieulafoy party. Still greater surprises, however, were in store for them. From other sources it was known that Artaxerxes had erected his dwelling on the ruins of an older building, the work of his predecessor, Xerxes, which had been destroyed by fire. Upon digging below the foundations of the *Apadana* of Artaxerxes, as this 'throne-room' of the palace was called, M. Dieulafoy came upon abundant traces of this older building. The glazed tiles found there form, perhaps, the most brilliant pieces in the 'Susa' collection. Upon entering the gallery in the Louvre, the first thing that will strike the eye of the visitor are the enormous friezes to the right and left of the entrance, showing a procession of archers. These friezes once graced the walls of Xerxes' palace, and what is most remarkable about them is that now, after a lapse of 2,000 years, they have been restored to view, the colouring on the tiles is almost as fresh and as gaudy as though the glazure had been put on within a few years."

During the second season's diggings, Madame Dieulafoy stumbled over some stones which turned out to be a wall supporting an enamelled brick staircase. It is now the most prized object in the Louvre Susa Gallery. "It is a most gorgeous piece of workmanship. The design, consisting of a series of rosettes, is delicately executed, and, as in the case of the friezes, blue, green, and yellow are the predominating colours. With the whole palace fitted up in the fashion of which the friezes and the staircase may be taken as examples, the effect must indeed have been startling in its grandeur." "For my part," says M. Dieulafoy, "when I try to restore these grand structures in my fancy: when I seem to see those porticoes of marble on porphyry columns: those double-headed bulls, the horns, feet, eyes, and collars of which must have been overlaid with a thin sheet of gold: the cedar beams and rafters of the intablature and the roof; the designs in brick work like heavy lace standing out upon the walls; the cornices covered with enamelled tiles of turquoise blue glittering in the sunlight: when I think of the draperies hung before the doors, the delicate open work of the *Mashrabiyehs*, the thick carpets laid upon the pavement; I ask myself sometimes whether the religious monuments of Egypt, or the very temples of Greece itself, ought to produce upon the imagination of the visitor so strong an impression as the palaces of the great king."*

M. Dieulafoy was enabled, through his architectural knowledge, aided by the results of the excavations, to draw up a plan of the palace. It consisted of three wings—the *Apadana* (or public reception rooms), the harem, and the king's apartments. This plan yielded somewhat startling results. "What adds," says the writer we have just quoted, "to the interest of M. Dieulafoy's discovery is the remarkable agreement, to which he himself has called attention, between the references

---

* *New Light on the Bible*, p. 249.

to the palace of Ahasuerus in the Book of Esther and the very building which he has unearthed. The three wings just referred to are distinctly mentioned by the Biblical author under their proper designations as "bithan," which corresponds to the Persian *Apadana*, the "house for the women," which is the harem, and "the house of the king," which represents the third quarter. Moreover, the position of these three quarters tallies with the picture of the palace which we would necessarily form had we the Book of Esther alone to guide us. Adjoining the bithan, or apadana, was the harem, and immediately to the south of the latter were the royal apartments, the three forming together an inverted letter L. The Book of Esther, it will be remembered, opens with a magnificent description of the festival which King Ahasuerus gave in the bithan, and it is worthy of note that in the delineation of the splendours of the palace, the colours of the draperies singled out for special mention are the very ones which appear most prominently in the decoration of the friezes and the staircase. Again, the scene where Queen Esther approaches his majesty becomes all the more vivid now that we know that the king's throne was stationed at the back of a hall in the centre of his apartments facing a corridor which led into the harem. He was so placed, accordingly, that he could see anyone approaching from a distance, and could, by raising his sceptre, indicate that he granted the visitor permission to step before him. There was a second entrance to the king's rooms by a fortified gate to the left, and it is by this gate that the king's minister, Haman, is represented in the book as coming to the king. The terms used to denote these small details are all so exact that the conclusion is well-nigh forced upon us that the Biblical writer who, it will be remembered, places his narrative in the city of Susa, must have had before him the very building which Dieulafoy has found, and it is in accord with the general conditions reflected in the book to suppose that it was written at Susa during the reign of Artaxerxes."*

* *Art and Literature* (1890), p. 40.

## CHAPTER IV.

## THE BOOK OF ESTHER:

### Further Confirmations.

WE have seen that the absence of God's name from the book is an indication that the Lord had a controversy with the Jews in Persia. Further light is, strangely enough, poured upon this in the very names borne by the two chief actors in the history—Esther and Mordecai. "The names of Mordecai and Esther," says Professor Sayce, "are Babylonian in origin. Mordecai is the Babylonian Mardukâ 'devoted to Merodach,' Esther is 'Istar,' the name of the great Babylonian goddess, who became Ashtoreth in the West. More than one inference can be drawn from this fact. On the one hand, it is clear that Jews who still held fast to the worship of their national God, were nevertheless not averse to being called after the names of the Babylonian deities. In the contract-tablets which have been discovered under the soil of Babylonia we occasionally find the names of Jews, and in some instances these Jews are associated with persons evidently of the same nationality but who have adopted, if not the beliefs, at all events the divine names of the Babylonian religion. Thus we have the name of Bel-Yahu, 'Bel is Yahveh,' a very pronounced assertion that the national gods of Babylon and Judea were one and the same. Bel-Yahu was the ancestor of Nergal-ebus, 'the god Nergal has made,' the father of Ea-Bani 'the god Ea has created.' At a later date we meet with the names of Gamar-ya'ava, Natanu-ya'ava, Subunu-ya'ava, and Aquabi-yava, in which Mr. Pinches was the first to point out that we have the full form of the name of Yahveh, Gamar-ya'ava or Gamariah is associated with Barikia or Berechiah, Samas-iriba ('the sun-god has descended') and others as witness to the sale of a slave by Sa-Nabu-duppu ('Nebo's is the tablet'), the son of Nabu-sarra-utsur ('O Nebo defend the king'), and it is a curious coincidence that the scribe who drew up the deed of sale was called Mardukâ or Mordecai."\*

The spirit of these Jews was plainly not that of him who said: "Their drink-offerings of blood will not I offer, nor take up their names into my lips" (Psa. xvi. 4). There may be some doubt, as we shall immediately see, as to the Babylonian origin of the name of Esther. It may be Persian. But these two names *stamp the Book as belonging to the time*. It was an impossibility for any Palestinian writer in the second century B.C. to have invented such words, or even to have written them with correctness. Increasing knowledge is unveiling

---

\* *The Higher Criticism and the Monuments*, pp. 469, 470.

fresh testimony of the Book's authenticity. Assyriologists were at first somewhat reticent with regard to the names of the Persian courtiers and officials named in *Esther*; but Sayce now says: "The names of those about him (Ahasuerus), as far as they can be interpreted, are all Persian." \* Where the learned Professor *keeps to facts*, he finds himself on the side of the Book. Words are employed in it with a knowledge of the Babylonian and Persian languages which is startling. "In ix. 26," he says, "we meet with the word '*iggereth*, a letter.' '*Iggereth*, which also occurs in the Book of Nehemiah, is the Assyrian *Egirtu*, the term applied to 'a letter' as opposed to a *duppu*, or 'tablet.' It is probable that it made its way into Persia after the Persian conquest of Babylon, as we know that *duppu* did. From Persian it would have passed to the language of the later books of the Old Testament. *How largely this language was affected by Persian, is illustrated by the Book of Esther.* Numerous words of Persian origin are to be found in it. Apart from the mysterious Purim, the etymology of which is still an unsolved problem, we come across words like *pathshegen* 'a copy' (iii. 14; iv. 8; viii. 13), the Persian *pati-thagana* 'correspondent,' and *akhashteranim* 'royal' (not 'camels' as in the Authorised Version of viii. 13, 14)." † He also mentions *kether* 'a crown' (i. 11, ii. 17, vi. 8), and *karpas* 'cotton' (i. 6).

Here everything is in striking accord with the belief which holds the book not only to be veritable

---

\* *Ibid*, p. 469. † *Ibid*, p. 472.

history, but also history written by Divine inspiration. *Esther* is the one book of Scripture which deals with Persian life, and it accordingly bears the marks of its origin in the use of Persian words, just as we have seen it does in its references to Persian customs and to the very arrangements of the Palace in which so many of the events, which it records, occurred. But Professor Sayce, in the pursuit of what seems to be his ambition to preserve an even balance in this controversy, having said so much to establish the authenticity of *Esther*, tries next to fashion an argument against it. "Esther," he maintains, is the same as *Istar*, the name of the Babylonian goddess. Names, *compounded with* that of the goddess, were common in Babylonia; but the name of the goddess was never transferred simply as here. It would have been the ascription of divinity to the individual so named, and would have been regarded as blasphemy. He therefore holds that the application of the name to the queen of Xerxes proves that the writer of the book belonged to a late period. He "could not have had," he says, "a very distinct idea of what these names actually meant. They must have come to him through the mist of antiquity, it may be through oral tradition, and of the Babylonian language he himself could have known nothing." *

The identification of *Esther* with Istar is premature. It is believed to be the Persian çtare, (modern Persian, *sitarch*), a star. But even if we admit

---
* *Ibid*, p. 472.

## Other Confirmations of Esther. 329

the Professor's contention, his conclusion and his premises will not hang together. He admits that the names Mordecai and Esther show a close acquaintance with the Babylonian language, and even with Babylonian orthography. How it is possible to admit that, and at the same moment to say of the writer that "of the Babylonian language he himself could have known nothing," we must leave Mr. Sayce to explain. What kind of composition we should have had from a writer whose information came "to him through the mist of antiquity" can be seen by turning to the Apocryphal additions to Esther which appear in the Septuagint version. Ahasuerus is made to think and write and speak like a Greek Jew of the writer's own time, evidently about 100 B.C. A perusal of the Apocryphal books, held in such favour by Prof. Sayce and the critics, will emphasize the lesson. Blunders of the most stupendous character abound. The writers, when they attempt to impart information, betray their ignorance alike of geography and of history. In *Tobit*, Sennacherib's father is said to have been one "Enemessar," whom Assyriologists will search for in vain. The writer was ignorant of the fact that Sennacherib was the son of Sargon. The same dense ignorance, natural to a time when the empires of Assyria, Babylon, and ancient Persia had long been things of the past, is displayed in other references. Sennacherib is said to have perished 55 days after he returned from Syria, whereas he survived 17 years. Xerxes is made to be the contemporary and companion in arms of Nebuchadnezzar, though the Babylonian king had gone to his grave long before Xerxes was born. The river Tigris, which flows past Nineveh, and to the west of that city, is placed far to the east of it and set between Nineveh and Ecbatana. In *Judith*, Nebuchadnezzar is made to reign in Nineveh, which was then lying in its ashes, and which, had it still stood in its glory, would have been nothing to the great king in comparison with his beloved Babylon. But worse than this, he is spoken of as dwelling in Nineveh *after the Jews returned from their exile*, and when the Babylonian empire had been swept away by Cyrus. But perhaps the crowning blunder is the situation assigned to Mesopotamia. As every reader is aware, and as its name implies, it lies *between* the Euphrates and the Tigris, the Euphrates being its western, and the Tigris—its eastern border. But the writer of *Judith* places it on the *west* of the Euphrates.* These inaccuracies are natural and unavoidable for a writer who deals with things that "have come to him through the mist of antiquity," and of which "he himself could have known nothing." But they are *not* the marks of the writer of *Esther*, Professor Sayce himself being witness. The writer, then, according to his own showing, and judging from the accuracy of these very names, could *not* have written of matters which came "to him through the mist of antiquity," and of which "he himself could have known nothing."

---

* See *The Speaker's Commentary*, Vol. iii., note p. 472.

Strange to say he supplies us, before we have read further than his next page, with another and more striking argument. The Greek historian, Ctesias, who resided in Persia *at the end of the fifth century* B.C. wrote his account of Assyria and of Persia after consulting the Persian royal records. He mentions a name *which is an exact parallel* to this of Esther, if it is identical with *Istar*. "Just as the name of the Babylonian goddess Istar," writes Mr. Sayce, "becomes the personal name Esther, so the Babylonian moon-god Nannar appears in the fragments of Ktesias as the satrap Nannaros." Now what is the natural, and indeed the only reasonable, inference from that fact? Is it not that, while *to the Babylonians* such a use of the names of Babylonian divinities would have been impious, *it was not so to the Persians?* Though an ancient Greek might not have done it, there is nothing to hinder an Englishman naming his infant daughter Diana. The reverence natural to a Babylonian would be quite wanting to a Persian; and this use of the names is entirely in accordance with the facts. It speaks of a place and a time when the Babylonian names and legends were intimately known, and of a people by whom the Babylonian idols were neither worshipped nor revered. This was the very time, place, and people that Mordecai and Esther were associated with.

I close this survey of the unlooked-for evidence which so completely swept away the aspersions of a criticism as self-confident as it was ill-informed, by glancing at some other discoveries which lift the same testimony. As investigation proceeds, astonishment deepens at the marvellous literal accuracy of the Scriptures. We are prepared in a Greek account, for example, of Persia or of Babylon to see Persian and Babylonian names assume more or less surprising shapes in transcription. We do not expect accuracy, and are quite content if the names are still recognisable. Turning to the Hebrew Bible, we expect that the law which holds good in other literatures will also prevail in this, and that the names will suffer in similar fashion. But the law does not hold, and the names do not suffer when transliterated into the inspired writings. We have already seen one proof of this in the name of Ahasuerus, or rather Achashverosh, which alone, in all the world's literature, has handed down the name of the Persian monarch whom the Greeks knew as Xerxes. Another instance is found in Shushan, the Scripture name for the city known as Susa. *Shushan* is the name in Assyrian, a sister language to the Hebrew, which is carved upon the monuments. The reader will also remember the phrase "Shushan the palace." This is another indication of the minute accuracy of the Bible. The palace was a huge structure which stood apart, forming a division of the city by itself. It was built upon an elevation at the foot of which lay the town.

An incidental allusion is made in chapter i. 7 to the kind of drinking cups used at Xerxes' banquet. They displayed an almost endless variety of invention. *This diversity was a feature of the people and the time.* "The Persians were also celebrated," writes Mr. Evetts, "for the variety of their drinking vessels, diverse one from the other, in the words of the Book of Esther. Several forms are mentioned by Greek authors: one kind of cup resembled a golden egg, out of which the king drank. Alexander found many gold, silver, and jewelled cups among the treasures of the Persian kings; and he himself gives a list of such, naming the various sorts of drinking-vessels, which cannot all now be identified. There were 'three silver-gilt *batiacæ*; one hundred and seventy-six silver *condya*; thirty-three of the same gilded; one silver *tisigites* . . . twenty-nine other small drinking-vessels of every shape," &c.\* There are many allusions in *Esther* to Persian customs. Mention is made more than once of letters being sent by post into all the king's provinces (iii. 13, 15; viii. 14). This arrangement was a special feature of the time. "To ensure rapid communication," says Lenormant, "between the distant provinces of the empire, couriers were established, stationed a day's journey from each other, who bore the orders of the king to the satraps, and their replies. This institution, so useful to the central power, was one of the improvements of Darius."† *Darius was the father of Xerxes.* These arrangements were, therefore, in full activity during the reign of the latter.

Mention is made more than once of "the king's scribes" (iii. 12; viii. 9). These were a special

---

\* *New Light on the Bible*, p. 252. † *Ancient History of the East*, Vol. ii., p. 112.

feature of the Persian court. They were always at the king's call, and were employed in the compiling of the archives of the kingdom and in preparing and copying the royal decrees. They even accompanied the king upon his campaigns. Herodotus tells us that they were with Xerxes in his invasion of Greece. During the sea fight at Salamis, Xerxes, says the Greek historian, "was particularly observant of the battle, and when he saw any person particularly distinguish himself he was minute in his inquiries concerning his family and city; all which, at his direction, his scribes recorded." We find the same minute correctness wherever we turn. The details are many. Every detail is clear and definite; and every detail brings out some feature of Persian civilisation and of the court customs. The couches, for example, on which Xerxes and his nobles recline at the banquet, are "of gold and silver" (i. 6). Some of those very couches were carried with Xerxes into Greece, and their description has been left us on the pages of Herodotus. Mardonius, to whom the Persian king left the conduct of the Grecian campaign, was defeated and slain by Pausanias. "It is further recorded," writes Herodotus, "that when Xerxes fled from Greece he left all his equipage to Mardonius. Pausanias, seeing this *composed of gold and silver*, and cloth of the richest embroidery, gave orders to the cooks and domestics to prepare an entertainment for him as for Mardonius. His commands were executed, and he beheld couches of gold and silver, tables of the same, and everything that was splendid and magnificent."

The description of *the extent* of the dominion of Xerxes is strikingly exact. "This is that Ahasuerus who reigned from India even unto Ethiopia." The Persian empire was then at its very greatest. Darius, the father of Xerxes, had annexed India, and Xerxes himself had just then thoroughly subdued Egypt. The vastness of the kingdom could not possibly have been put more exactly and impressively than by simply naming these countries which formed its limits on the east and on the west. The Persian words also, which, as we have already seen, abound in the book, are enough in themselves to overthrow all the assertions of the critics about its having been written at a late date. It must have been composed when the Persian sway was at its full, and when Persian words had entered into the languages of that vast empire, and were kept alive in them by the presence of Persian officials, troops, and institutions. These Persian words were used for one reason alone; their meaning was known to the generation for whom the book was written. As soon as the Persian empire was overthrown, these words died, and their meaning was forgotten. It is only now, when the old Persian has been partly recalled through recent discoveries, that we begin to understand some passages of the book. There is a word *karpas*, which our translators did not understand, but which they translated "green"—"white, green, and blue hangings" (i. 6). We now know that the word means "cotton." It is the same as the Sanscrit *karpase*, cotton-shrub. The description in *Esther* runs: "Where was an awning of white cotton and violet." White and violet were the Royal colours of Persia. Light has been shed in a similar way upon another passage. In viii. 10 we are told that the letters are sent "by posts on horseback, riders on mules, camels, young dromedaries." I have omitted the conjunction "and," which is not in the original, but with which our translators, usually so exact, and in all cases painstaking, tried to make their rendering here hang together. It will be seen, however, that the posts could hardly be said to be on *horseback*, if all those animals were employed. A word occurs in the verse which is also found on the Persian monuments. It means "Royal," and the Revisers, using this hint, have now rendered: "Posts on horseback, riding on swift steeds that were used in the king's service, bred of the stud."

Again, the king takes his signet from his hand and gives it to Haman, and Haman calls the royal scribes together, appends the royal seal to the documents and sends them forth (Esther iii. 10-12). The signet was probably a cylinder. The cylinder of Darius, the father of Xerxes, is now in the British museum. Herodotus records an incident of this monarch's reign, which shows how thoroughly the Scripture record reflects, both in this matter and in the use of the lot, the customs of the time. Darius has need of an emissary for a peculiarly perilous mission. Thirty nobles offer themselves and strive for the appointment. "As they strove together," says Herodotus, "Darius interfered, and bade them have recourse to the lot. Accordingly lots were cast, and the task fell to Bagaeus, son of Artontes. Then Bagaeus caused many letters to be written on divers matters, and *sealed them all with the king's signet;* after which he took the letters with him, and departed for Sardis."

The rationalists have objected strongly to the Book of Esther on account specially of the levity with which the taking of human life is regarded. But the *absence* of that feature would have rendered the Book an untrue reflection of the times. Persian rule was essentially cruel. Rawlinson speaks of the "lurking danger which must have thrown a shadow over the lives of all the nobler and richer of the nation, unless they were utterly thoughtless. The irresponsible authority and cruel dispositions of the kings, joined to the recklessness with which they delegated the power of life and death to their favourites, made it impossible for any person of eminence in the whole Empire to feel sure that he might not any day be seized and accused of a crime, or even without the form of an accusation, be taken and put to death, after suffering the most excruciating tortures. To produce this result, it was enough to have failed through any cause whatever in the performance of a set task, or to have offended, even by doing him too great a service, the monarch or one of his favourites. Nay, it was enough to have provoked, through a relation or connection, the anger or jealousy of one in favour at Court; for the caprice of an Oriental would sometimes pass over the real culprit, and exact vengeance from one quite guiltless —even, it may be, unconscious—of the offence given." *

There is no side, in short, on which the Book can be tested, where its marvellous accuracy is not manifested by research. Xerxes and other Persian monarchs have themselves shown us in the monuments of Persepolis what the Court life and its customs were. The Book of Esther has also presented a picture of the same things. The manner of representation is different. The incidents are different. But the identity of the things is undeniable. Every feature is distinct and clear. Xerxes has left an impress of himself upon the page of history. We gather the man's character from the accounts left by Herodotus and by other Greek authors. We have the man appearing again in the Book of Esther. It is the same man we see—only in the latter he is respected and feared—while in the former he is not seldom wondered at and mocked. We can well understand how Lenormant was led to say that this Book enables us better than any other in existence to understand ancient Persian court-life, and how Dean Stanley had to admit that the whole of it is "thoroughly characteristic," and that all the various scenes are "full of the local genius of the empire, as we know it alike through the accounts of the earliest Greek travellers and the latest English

---

* *Ancient Monarchies*, Vol. iii., pp. 244, 245.

investigators."* But this verdict, which more recent discoveries have heavily emphasized, is the condemnation of the Higher Criticism. The critics in their inflated self-confidence believed their verdict final. There was no need to wait for fresh light. The Book was judged. The critical instinct could not possibly be at fault, and it declared that every page of the Book was stamped with improbability and, therefore, with falsehood and fraud. More than that, its admission into the Canon proved that the Canon was a myth. When such a Book had been admitted, it showed that the judgment which selected the Books of Scripture was not infallible. The whole of the Old Testament was thus shaken in the supposed triumphant refutation of the claims of Esther.

What, then, are we now to say of the arrogant ignorance and of the daring impiety of these men, who, notwithstanding the exposure of their blunders, still ask us to acknowledge them as "experts," forsooth, and call upon us even now to register their verdicts, and enthrone themselves above the Apostles and even above the Lord Jesus? In the face of this gigantic failure, can any man trust them? Remembering the thousands whose faith they have shattered, and whose eternal happiness they have imperilled if not destroyed, by what is now known to be false witness, can any man fail to abhor their work and to condemn them?

---

* *Lectures on the Jewish Church*, pp. 173, 174.

## CHAPTER V.

### THE BOOK OF DANIEL.

WE shall now test "criticism" again by another of its supposed irreversible verdicts. If the critics can be said to have been entirely unanimous in anything, that one thing is their common judgment regarding *Daniel*. Their supposed exposure of the late date and of the unhistorical character of this book has been confidently pointed to as a proof of the certainty of their methods and of the usefulness of their labours. *Daniel* had long been a stumbling-block, on account of the superabundance in it of the miraculous element; but now, the critics imagined, it was cleared out of the path, and would no longer trouble the rationalistic wayfarer. It was supposed to have been triumphantly demonstrated that it was merely a bit of well-intentioned fiction. From this decision it was asserted that there could be no appeal. The case had been tried, decided, and ended, and their work was declared by Baron Bunsen to be "one of the finest triumphs and most useful achievements of modern criticism." *

---

* *God in History*, Vol. i., p. 191.

That was the calm, assured belief of the critics and of their followers. But much has happened since then. Assyriologists find that they have a good deal to say about this very matter. They are discovering that much of what the critics had set down as fable turns out to be fact. The case is accordingly being re-tried. The critics are placed on the defensive, and are being swept from one position after another.

The miraculous element in *Daniel* is certainly most marked. A dream, which the king cannot recall, is recalled and interpreted by Daniel, to whom God makes known the dream and the interpretation in a vision. Three young captive Jews, who refuse to pay idolatrous worship to the image of Nebuchadnezzar, are thrown into a furnace, the heat of which is so intense and the flames so fierce that the men who cast them in are consumed; but these three escape more wonderfully than the heroes in a fairy tale. Though they are hurled down among flames that roar around them, they are not only unconsumed; they live and breathe. They are seen by the king walking to and fro as in a garden, at ease, and with apparent enjoyment. A fourth walks with them, of majestic mien, and radiant with a more than human glory. When they are called forth, it is seen that not a hair of their head has been singed; and it is noted that they carry with them, as they pass along, no odour of burning; the smell of fire has not so much as passed upon them. Daniel himself, in his old age, is cast into a den of lions; but the lions' mouths are closed, and they do him no injury.

All this is certainly startling; and the question has risen in many a breast—"Can these things be true?" But they were meant to be startling. Those marvellous works were done for the express purpose of awakening astonishment, and proving beyond all possibility of doubt the direct intervention of God. The experience of Egypt had to be repeated, because of a like necessity. The Israelites had been swept out of their land and were in the hands of a masterful foe. God will, therefore, interpose. He will show that, though Israel has been overborne, Israel's God has not been conquered, and that He who has smitten Jacob is able also to heal him. One is accordingly sent into the king's palace and educated there, just as Joseph and as Moses in the more ancient days of Israel's need were sent into the palace of the Pharaohs. Ezekiel carries on his work among the captives, but Daniel makes God manifest to the Babylonian king, and bows the proud spirit of the world's master by the revelation of Jehovah as the Disposer of all events; and the Babylonian conqueror is made to "know that the Most High ruleth in the kingdom of men, and giveth it to whomsoever He will" (Dan. iv. 25).

But, strange to say, some of these marvels bear upon them the Divine stamp still. The dream so miraculously recalled and interpreted is still a palpable miracle. It has set forth the entire course of the world's history, and is increasingly proved to have come from God alone. Take one feature only. It is declared that there would be, beginning with the Babylonian Empire, four universal dominions, *and four only*, till the kingdom of God should be set up upon the earth and the thrones of men should be abolished. The fourth world empire was to continue in its partition and its fragments till the kingdom of God and of His saints should be established. No *fifth* dominion of man was ever to appear. Now there have been four, and *four only*, of these universal sovereignties of man. Since the days of the Roman Empire, there has never been another. Men have hoped, plotted, warred, and shed oceans of blood to establish a *fifth*, and all of them have failed. The fragments of the Roman Empire still hold the field. This empire, too, which lay furthest from the prophet's vision is more minutely described than any other. It is described with a truthfulness that has startled those who read the words in the light of what we know about that empire. It was indeed that kingdom "strong as iron: forasmuch as iron breaketh in pieces and subdueth all things; and as iron that breaketh all these, shall it break in pieces and bruise" (Dan. ii. 40).

The presence of this prediction in the Book of Daniel is the stamp of God. No man could have foreseen these things at any date that has ever been assigned to the book. There is another strange thing, to which I shall afterwards refer. The book is written *in two languages*—in Hebrew and in Syriac. In the 6th verse of the 2nd chapter Hebrew is exchanged for Syriac. The Syriac continues till the beginning of the 8th chapter. This employment of the two languages has been a standing puzzle to the critics and to the generality of commentators. But, when looked into, and compared with later Scriptures, the arrangement is plainly prophetic. Syriac was the language and the symbol at that time of the Gentile peoples; Hebrew, on the other hand, was the language and the symbol of the people of God. The use of Syriac points to the fact that this part of the book refers to "the times of the Gentiles." The subsequent predictions in Hebrew deal with God's return to His ancient people. When we read the Book in the light of that hint, everything becomes luminous. Was that a human device or a Divine arrangement? The devout reader has but one answer. Not only the things revealed, but even the kind of language, in which these things were to be recorded, was chosen in obedience to the guidance of the Spirit of God.

It is hardly in keeping with my present subject to deal with the two objections which I am about to name, as they do not come within the scope of modern discoveries. But it may help some reader if I allude to them in passing. In the Apocryphal book of Ecclesiasticus a great many Old Testament heroes and writers of Scripture are named. There is no mention made of Daniel. The critics argue from this that the Book of Daniel was unknown at that time, that is, that it was not in existence in B.C. 200. Canon Driver sets great store by that argument.

But it proves too much. There is no mention of the twelve Minor Prophets, for the passage that refers to them is an interpolation. Nor is there anything said of Ezra, Mordecai, or of others. Unless Canon Driver is prepared to deny the accepted dates of Ezra and the Minor Prophets, he cannot press the argument from the silence of the son of Sirach, the author of *Ecclesiasticus*, regarding Daniel. The foolishness of the argument will also be apparent to any one who turns to the passage in the Apocrypha. *The writer is not giving a list of the Canonical Books.* He is only citing the names of certain Old Testament heroes. The contention that since Daniel is not there named, the Book of Daniel could not have been in existence, is simply monstrous, and shows the utter recklessness of critical methods.

The statement with which the book opens, that the expedition of Nebuchadnezzar against Jerusalem, in which Daniel was carried away captive, took place "in the *third* year of Jehoiakim," is alleged to be in distinct contradiction to other parts of Scripture. It is said that there is an utter absence of any reference to such a siege of Jerusalem, and that Jeremiah speaks of the king of Babylon smiting the forces of the Egyptians in Carchemish in the *fourth* year of Jehoiakim. Now let me ask the reader's close attention to these statements for a moment or two. I take the last first. It is said there is no record of this capture of Jerusalem in the Scripture. Will the reader turn to Jeremiah 36th chapter, verse 9? He is there told that Jehoiakim, in the fifth year of his reign, and in the ninth month, appointed a solemn fast for all his people. *Why was that fast appointed?* Why were the people to humble themselves, and to humble themselves just then? This very capture of Jerusalem is the only event that we know of which can explain it. If Jerusalem had been captured the year before, and if numbers of the people were carried away, then there was abundant reason for appointing the day of humiliation. It was the first anniversary of a terrible chastisement. It was also an unwelcome proof that all those terrible predictions against which they had been steeling themselves *might* after all find their accomplishment. The indication here is most valuable, as it fixes the capture of the city in the ninth month of the *fourth* year of Jehoiakim.

Now let us turn to the other point. Carchemish was an ancient Hittite city on the west side of the Euphrates. It lay on the road from Babylon to Palestine. The Egyptians had advanced thither in their conquering career. Berosus, the Chaldean historian, tells us of this very expedition against them. He says that the father of Nebuchadnezzar, "on hearing of the revolt of the Governor, whom he had appointed in Syria and Phœnicia, to the Egyptians, being too weak to go himself, sent his son, Nebuchadnezzar, with an army." We learn from Jeremiah xlvi. 2 that Nebuchadnezzar's victory over the Egyptians at Carchemish took place "in the fourth year of Jehoiakim, son of Josiah, king of

Judah." Nebuchadnezzar then followed the beaten army, retaking the places which the Egyptians had captured, and stamping out the rebellion of which they had taken advantage. In this expedition, according to Berosus, Nebuchadnezzar "*subjugated Syria and all Phœnicia.*" These words embrace Judea. There was, then, at this very time, a capture of Jerusalem, and good reason for the establishing of Jehoiakim's fast-day.

But, it will be asked, what of "the *fourth* year of Jehoiakim?" Daniel says that "in the *third* year of the reign of Jehoiakim, king of Judah, came Nebuchadnezzar king of Babylon unto Jerusalem and besieged it." This last rag of "the difficulty" disappears when we change one word in the above translation of the Hebrew of *Daniel*. The word *bo* is capable of two renderings. It means either "to set out" or "to arrive," "to go" or "to come." This double sense has been denied, but any reader may satisfy himself on the point. We read, for instance, in Gen. xv. 15, "Thou shalt go to thy fathers in peace," where the word translated "go" is this same word which appears in Dan. i. 1. Reuben says to his brethren when he discovers that Joseph is not in the pit: "The child is not; and I, whither shall I go?" (Gen. xxxvii. 30). Here again *bo* is translated, and can only be translated, by our word "go." It does not mean to arrive at, but to set out towards. In Jonah i. 3 we read, "He found a ship which was *going* to Tarshish." Here it is equally impossible to render *bo* in any other way. The ship had not *arrived at* Tarshish; it was only *setting out* towards it.

There are other instances which might be given, but the above are quite enough. The statement in Daniel is simply this, that Nebuchadnezzar *marched to* Jerusalem in the *third* year of Jehoiakim. The third year of that king's reign was, no doubt, within a month or two of its close. The remainder of it was spent in the advance to Carchemish and in the preparations for battle; in the ninth month of the *fourth* year of Jehoiakim the conquering Babylonians had put down the rebellion between Carchemish and Judea, had swept over Judea itself, and had taken Jerusalem. Everything is in this way more perfectly harmonious than if no apparent contradiction had existed. And the seeming difficulty is really a testimony to the absolute fidelity and the minute accuracy of the Scripture. But we have not yet exhausted the testimony of this incident. The critics have, in this case, challenged the Scripture to their own confusion. Their contention is that this book was written *in Palestine*. But in those opening words — "In the third year of the reign of Jehoiakim king of Judah, Nebuchadnezzar king of Babylon marched unto Jerusalem, and besieged it" — God has stamped this book, so that the place of its origin cannot be mistaken. The writer speaks, not of Nebuchadnezzar's arrival at Jerusalem, but of his departure from Babylon. Where, then, is he located? What is his point of observation? *It is Babylon, not Palestine.* He sees, so to speak, the army marshalled on the plain before the city, and passing out from the land in which he is writing. That "*third* year," of which the critics have made so much, wrecks their theory. Daniel writes as a resident in Babylonia.

Their conclusions are being swept away from other sides. The student of *Daniel* is struck by another phrase in the beginning of the book. We are told that Nebuchadnezzar brought the vessels of the house of the Lord "to the house of his god" (i. 2). Reference is again made to this one Babylonian deity in the same way. Nebuchadnezzar speaks of Daniel, "whose name is Belteshazzar, according to the name of my god" (iv. 8). But was not Nebuchadnezzar an idolator and a polytheist? He was a worshipper of many gods and of many goddesses. How, then, can he be spoken of as having but one god? He names Daniel by the name of him whom he calls "my god," as if he had never acknowledged, or even known, any other. He brings the holy vessels of Jehovah into the house of this same idol, as if in utter unconsciousness of the existence of a single god besides in all the Pantheon of Babylon. Is this a mark of the Palestinian origin of the book, and of the authorship of some ill-informed Jew, who imagined that, just as he himself had only one god, so must it be with everybody else upon the face of the earth?

The reply is startling in its completeness. The Scripture, in this strange representation, is shown to be absolutely correct by the testimony of Nebuchadnezzar himself. He has explained it in inscriptions of his, which still remain. He has one favourite god, Merodach, *the very god named* in the book of Daniel. It is true that he is spoken of as Bel; but this again reveals an intimate acquaintance with Babylonian ideas in the time of Daniel. Bel and Merodach were originally regarded as entirely distinct divinities. But as the worship of Merodach grew, the attributes, and even the name, of the greater god Bel, were assigned to him. He was looked upon as "another manifestation of Bel,"* and was spoken of as Bel-Merodach. "He was called 'the ancient one of the gods, the supreme judge, the master of the horoscope'; he was represented as a man erect and walking, and with a naked sword in his hand." †

To the worship of this idol Nebuchadnezzar gave himself with intense adoration and affection. He speaks of him as "the sublime master of the gods"; and he calls him "my great lord," "the joy of my heart," &c. Indeed, his inscriptions appear to have largely the one object of glorifying Bel. "The inscriptions of Nebuchadnezzar are for the most part," says Sir Henry Rawlinson, "occupied with praises of Merodach, and with prayers for the continuance of his favour. The king ascribes to him his elevation to the throne: 'Merodach, the great lord, has appointed me to the empire of the world, and has confided to my care the far-spread people of the earth;' 'Merodach, the great lord, the

---
\* *Ancient History of the East*, Vol. i., p. 455.  † *Ibid.*

senior of the gods, the most ancient, has given all nations and people to my care.'"

I shall speak more fully by and bye of the religious element in Nebuchadnezzar's character; but meanwhile let the reader note the absolute accuracy of the account which makes him speak here as a worshipper of one god only. *This is the king's way whenever he refers to Bel-Merodach.* There are other passages in *Daniel* where he speaks as a polytheist, as, for example, when he refers to Daniel as "one in whom is the spirit of the holy gods" (iv. 18). This "peculiar character of Nebuchadnezzar's religion," says Canon Rawlinson,—"at one time polytheistic, at another monotheistic — *is also evidenced by his inscriptions.* The polytheism is seen in the distinct and separate acknowledgment of at least thirteen deities, to most of whom he builds temples. . . . The monotheism discloses itself in the attitude assumed towards Merodach, who is "the great Lord," "the God his maker," "the Lord of all beings," "the Prince of the lofty house," "the Chief, the honourable, the Prince of the gods, the great Merodach," "the Divine Prince, the Deity of heaven and earth, the Lord God," "the King of Gods, and Lord of Lords," "the Chief of the Gods," "the Lord of the Gods," "the God of Gods," and "the King of heaven and earth." Nebuchadnezzar assigns to Merodach a pre-eminence which places him on a pedestal apart from and above all the other deities of his pantheon."*

---

* *Egypt and Babylon*, pp. 80, 81.

This is, however, only one trait in a character which is very fully impressed upon the Book of Daniel. Every reader of the Scripture has a very clear idea of Nebuchadnezzar's personality. That idea is due to the Book of Daniel alone. Nebuchadnezzar is mentioned elsewhere in Scripture; but had it not been for *Daniel* the great king would have been only a name to the readers of the Bible, and, we may add, to the entire world. This book is the only literature in the world which has caught and preserved the man's personality. We know from profane history that of the eighty-eight years, during which the Babylonian dominion lasted, his reign covered forty-three, or nearly one-half of the whole time. We know also that he was a successful warrior. But, when we have said this, we have summed up all the information supplied by literature outside *Daniel*.

Here, then, is a circumstance which should help us to come to a clear decision regarding the Bible and the critics. We have in *Daniel* a picture of the great king so clearly and so powerfully painted that the memory of the man still lives. Nebuchadnezzar is, for every child in our Sunday Schools, one of the great personalities of history. Has this Book conveyed a true impression of the man! If it has done so, one inevitable question follows, which sweeps like an avalanche upon the critical fabric. How did that portrait of the great Babylonian monarch get into the Book of Daniel?

Let us now look at the Bible picture. We are

## Nebuchadnezzar's Personality. 353

taken, on more than one occasion, into the king's presence. The scene that transpires is so placed upon the page that we hear Nebuchadnezzar speak and see him act. The man—for one thing—has a thoroughly regal spirit. He is masterful and determined. When his fury is roused, it is like some awful conflagration. He has had a dream, which has impressed him greatly, but the details of which he is unable to recall. His astrologers and soothsayers are summoned, and commanded to tell both the dream and its interpretation. It is in vain that they expostulate. "For this cause the king was angry and very furious, and commanded to destroy all the wise men of Babylon. And the decree went forth that the wise men should be slain; and they sought Daniel and his fellows to be slain" (Dan. ii. 12, 13). When Daniel tells the king the dream and the interpretation, we note the same regal sweep in the reward which Nebuchadnezzar bestows. No one is regarded; there is nothing stinted or measured. "Then the king made Daniel a great man, and gave him many great gifts, and made him ruler over the whole province of Babylon, and chief of the governors over all the wise men of Babylon" (verse 48).

These are two glimpses of the man: let us now take another. He has a great image set up. We shall return to this incident—meanwhile let us simply note the spirit which Nebuchadnezzar displays. The proportions of the statue are vast. It is ninety feet high and nine feet broad. The spirit of the man stamps itself upon that colossal figure. Then it is not enough that a statue be erected: divine honours must be paid to it. Even that is not enough. The great officials of his world-wide dominion must be gathered together to the dedication, and the inauguration of the worship must be made a great State ceremony. The king's will is withstood by three Jews, to whom, for Daniel's sake, he has shown great favour. They are brought before him. He wants to save them, and he will give them one more chance; but it must then be compliance or death. Woe to them if they persist, for the threat that rests over them will be mercilessly fulfilled! They do refuse, and then appears the king's fierce determination. He is resolved that no god shall deliver out of his hand, and the furnace into which they are to be cast he commands to be heated seven times, so that there shall be an end of them at once. When they are delivered, it is not enough that he himself should honour the God whom these men served. He must issue a decree "that every people, nation, and language, which speak anything amiss against the God of Shadrach, Meshach, and Abednego, shall be cut in pieces, and their houses shall be made a dunghill" (iii. 29).

Now, in the providence of God, we are able to come into this man's presence for ourselves, and to hear his own words. The pride of Nebuchadnezzar is represented in *Daniel* as displayed more in his rejoicing in his buildings than even in his victories. We shall afterwards look into the account of the king's madness more closely, but meanwhile we note one part of it. The judgment fell upon him as he gazed from the roof of his palace upon the vast city stretching away on every hand. He looked on it with no feeling of gratitude to a higher Power who had permitted him to accomplish so much. His only feeling was self-elation. "Is not this," he said, "great Babylon, that I" (the emphasis in the original is placed upon the pronoun) "have built for the house of the kingdom, by the might of my power, and for the honour of my majesty?" (iv. 30).

Here we have Nebuchadnezzar revelling in the thought that he is the constructor of Babylon, and that he has made it worthy of the place it holds as the capital of the mightiest empire the world had ever seen. Will the reader bear all this in mind, and then compare that representation with what follows? The boast was, in one sense, amply justified. The neighbouring Arabs have used for generations, and still use, the ruins of Babylon as a huge quarry. They dislodge, carry off, and sell its bricks for building purposes. *Nine out of every ten of these bricks are stamped with the* name of Nebuchadnezzar. It was absolutely true that he was the builder, at least the re-constructor, of that great Babylon.

But we are able to go still further, and to show that Nebuchadnezzar himself has borne the most striking testimony to the truth of this part of God's Word. Inscriptions of his have been found in which he speaks in this very way. In all of them he dwells with special pride upon his buildings. He tells, for example, in a long inscription, how he re-built the temple of Belus, and the temples of the other gods in Babylon. He speaks with still greater self-elation of those very buildings which, in their vast extent and with their magnificent architecture, lay under his eye as he walked upon the palace-roof. "I have adorned," he says, "no part of Babylon, that city which is the pupil of my eye, as I have the palace. That is the house which commands the admiration of men. It is the central point of the country, high and elevated. It is the house of royalty in the country of Babylonia. It stretches from Imgour-Bel to the canal Libiloubol, from the Euphrates to Meboursapon. . . . I employed in it enamelled bricks, forming incriptions and pictures, and enamelled bricks also framed the doors. I collected there gold, silver, metal, precious stones of every kind and value, a collection of valuable objects and immense treasures."

This shows the delight which he took in his buildings. The other inscriptions are of a like character. Here is a short one found on a brick now in the Zurich Museum. It contains these words: "Nebuchadnezzar, king of Babylon, restorer of the temple of exaltation and of the temple of well-being (?), son of Nabopolassar, king of Babylon, I." "By far the larger number," says Schrader, "of these inscriptions—some of which are of considerable extent—are exclusively occupied, when they are not of a religious character, with the royal buildings at Babel and Borsippa."* The Rev. J. C. Ball writes of the long India House Inscription: "The Inscription paints for us in unfading colours a portrait of the man Nebuchadnezzar; it exhibits in the vivid light of actuality his pride of place and power of greatness, his strong conviction of his own divine call to universal empire, his passionate devotion to his gods, his untiring labours for their glory, and the aggrandisement of that peerless capital which was their chosen dwelling-place."† Mr. Evetts, in his recently published book, says: "The activity of Nebuchadnezzar as a builder, illustrated by the cuneiform inscriptions already found, fully corresponds to the words of the Book of Daniel, which speak of the king as exulting over the magnificence of the city which he had himself done so much to enlarge and beautify."‡

The pride of the man speaks in the following, found in the larger inscription from which I have already quoted: "*To astonish mankind*, I re-constructed and renewed the wonder of Borsippa, the temple of the seven spheres of the world." These words complete the picture. The purpose which this vast architectural display was intended to gratify was not love either to Babylon or to the gods; it was "to astonish mankind!" The reader will observe with what wonderful fidelity the man, revealed to us in his own inscriptions, is set forth upon the page of Scripture. Every feature is there.

---
\* *Cuneiform Inscriptions and the Old Testament*, Vol. ii., p. 49.
† *Records of the Past*. New Series, Vol. iii., p. 103.  ‡ *New Light on the Bible*, p 351

Through acquaintance with the Bible, we have known this man from our infancy. His personality has been so vividly painted, so clearly defined, that the monuments bring us nothing that is essentially new. We were already so fully in possession of everything, that these add nothing to our impressions and correct nothing in them. Will the critics tell us how a book, written three centuries after Nebuchadnezzar perished, could have painted him so? We believe that Inspiration was needed for the task in any case, but, if the critical date is to be accepted, it can only be by accepting along with it a yet mightier miracle of inspired insight!

## CHAPTER VI.

### ALLUSIONS TO BABYLONIAN COURT OFFICIALS AND COURT CUSTOMS.

IT was impossible to deal with the Book of Daniel without first referring to the great Babylonian king whose memory it has so long preserved, and whose personality dominates its opening pages. But it is not Nebuchadnezzar alone that has been brought from the dead to vanquish the critics. The opening verses of the book present us with quite a cluster of confirmations. Mention is made (i. 3) of Ashpenaz, "master of his (Nebuchadnezzar's) eunuchs." The word in the original is *Rab-saris*. This title is given elsewhere in Scripture to men who are evidently of the very highest rank at the Assyrian and Babylonian courts. But till five years ago the title had not been found upon the monuments. Herr Hugo Winckler, a young German Assyriologist, and one of the critical school, pounced upon this as a proof that in some cases the monuments do not confirm the Bible, but, on the contrary contradict it. He asserted that the title was absolutely unknown to the Assyrian Court; and he explained its appearance here and elsewhere in Scripture as due to a mistake made by the Hebrew writers. The mistake was this, he said, that out of the title Rab-shakeh, they had made two, Rab-shakeh and Rab-saris.

Halevy, the Jewish Assyriologist, who writes not as a believer in an inspired Bible, but simply as an Assyriologist, has supplied one of the most crushing replies ever penned.* The fact that the title had not been found on the monuments was one of the frailest of arguments. Several of the titles of the high officials of the empire were indicated on the monuments by ideograms, the real pronunciation of which was as yet unknown. Rab-saris might very well be among them. But by a most fortunate —let us say Providential—discovery, Halevy was able to provide a still better reply. There is a conical brick preserved in the British Museum, which contains an inscription in Assyrian and in Aramean. The Aramean is a translation of the Assyrian, and is easily read, being in the usual Hebrew character. One of those ideograms, used of the high officials, appears in the Assyrian inscription. It is, of course, translated in the Aramean, and there we find this very word Rab-saris!

To this there is and can be no reply. The supposed "inaccuracy," like every other on which we have had full information, turns out to be a confirmation. It is slender and unexplained allusions

*Revue des Etudes Juives, No. 39, March, 1890.*

of this kind that yield the most conclusive proof that the so-called "critics" are utterly wrong in the late date which they assign to the book. They form the best of all date stamps, as it is impossible to imitate them. A writer of to-day refers with the greatest brevity to things and customs which it would be foolish to explain or to enlarge upon, simply because they are so thoroughly well known to everyone. But these are things which may soon pass away, and leave readers of the next century clamouring for some antiquarian editor to explain what the words refer to. Our newspapers are full of such phrases as, "The Lords and the Commons," "The Forces," "The Volunteers," "Unionists," "Radicals," "Nihilists," unknown even to Englishmen a century ago, and which will probably be matters of ancient history even to Englishmen a century later. These and kindred references to institutions and well-known facts of the present day will form the date stamp of the literature of our time, and will resist the attempt of any thirty-first or thirty-second century "critic" to prove that it belongs to a later period.

Now this mention of the *Rabsaris* is only one of many such casual references in *Daniel*, which prove incontestably that the book belongs to a time before the events and institutions of the Assyrio-Babylonian dominion had passed away from the memory of men. We are told, for example, in chap. i. 2, that Nebuchadnezzar carried the vessels of the house of God "into the land of Shinar, to the house of his god." We have already seen that the deity whom he so affectionately named, was Bel-Merodach. Is it not striking, then, to find, from an inscription left by this very monarch, that it was his custom to so dispose of the choicest of his spoils? He tells us that he made an expedition "to far-off lands, distant hills, from the Upper Sea to the Lower Sea," that is, from Lake Van to the Persian Gulf. He "fettered the rebels," and "ordered the land aright," and removed the people to new localities. He then describes what he did with the chief spoils amassed in the campaign. "Silver, gold, glitter of precious stones, copper, *mismakanna*-wood, cedar, what thing soever is precious, a large abundance; the produce of mountains, the fulness of seas, a rich present, a splendid gift, to my city of Babylon into his (Bel's) presence I brought." Could a late writer, who knew nothing whatever of Nebuchadnezzar and what he was accustomed to do, have lighted by any chance upon what was so fully in accord with his devotion to Merodach, and with the practice by which that devotion was manifested?

In close connection with this we come upon allusions to other customs and institutions of the time. Ashpenaz, the *Rabsaris*, is commanded to look out "certain of the children of Israel, both of the king's seed and of the princes, children in whom was no blemish, but well-favoured and skilful in all wisdom, and cunning in knowledge, and understanding science, and such as had ability in them to stand in the king's palace, and whom they might teach the learning and the tongue of the Chaldeans" (i. 3, 4).

Now there are four things implied in this incident: (1) Learning was a recognised, honourable, and ardent pursuit among the Babylonians. They were not only warriors; they were also scholars. (2) There was a *Palace* school for the instruction of the princes and young nobility; for we read that, besides being under the control of Palace officials, food was sent them from the royal table, so that the place of instruction could not be far distant: "And the king appointed them a daily provision of the king's meat, and of the wine which he drank; so nourishing them three years, that at the end thereof they might stand before the king" (verse 5). (3) Children of foreign princes were admitted to the Palace school. And (4) the special subject of study was the literature and the language of certain people called Chaldeans.

All this is plainly implied in the simple statement contained in Dan. i. 3-5, and every item of it is now abundantly confirmed by recent discoveries. Let us take the points in the order in which I have named them. (1) Did learning hold this place among the Babylonians? It was by no means a characteristic of every conquering race, or of every ancient civilization. It has very seldom, in fact, been a leading feature of a warlike people. Learning flees from the din of camps, and the rough, active, pleasure-loving soldier has little in common with the quiet, self-denying student. It would have been so here, but for special, and I might say extraordinary, circumstances. The Babylonians were the inheritors of the earliest and—apart from revelation—the highest learning ever attained by humanity. The cradle of the human race was also the fountain of its arts, its sciences, and its wisdom.

Some members of the critical school have said that it is extremely improbable that Daniel, a strict Jew, would have consented to occupy himself with the learning of the Babylonians, or to have accepted the presidency of its learned men, seeing that the learning of the Chaldeans was wholly concerned with magic. In making this statement they have only supplied another illustration of the adage that "a little learning is a dangerous thing." The learning and literature of Assyria and Babylon was by no means confined to magic. Mr. Layard, during his excavations, discovered the remains of the library established by King Assurbanipal in his Palace at Nineveh. These books were formed, according to the Assyrian and Babylonian custom, of square tables of baked clay, which were covered with closely written cuneiform characters. The great majority of these tablets or books are now in the British Museum. They contain the remains of an immense grammatical encyclopædia, treating of the difficulties of the ancient Accadian language and writing. "We find from them," says Lenormant, "that grammar had become among the Assyrians a very advanced science, and received much attention from them, the natural and almost inevitable consequence of the complication of their system of writing, requiring long and profound study."\* The work is of a most elaborate kind, comprising a grammar and half-a-dozen dictionaries of various sorts. The study of these, without which the ancient Chaldean language could not have been understood, must, in itself, have called for immense application. But this was only one part of the contents of the library. There were also treatises on law, with details regarding special cases. There were chronological tables and a manual of the history of Nineveh and Babylon, "arranged in parallel columns." There are also remains of a large geographical encyclopædia. There were lists of the officers of the government, and of the various provinces, with statements regarding their productions, revenues, and sums paid by tributary countries and cities. There were also lists of the public buildings of Babylonia and Chaldea, "classified according to their kind, temples, pyramids, and fortified citadels."

But even this was not all. There were works on natural history containing lists of plants and minerals, and of every species of animals known to the Assyrians, classified in families and genera. The classification is rudimentary but scientific. "We may well be astonished," Lenormant writes, "to find that the Assyrians had already invented a

---
\* *Ancient History of the East.* Vol. i., p. 445.

scientific nomenclature similar in principle to that of Linnæus." They had achieved still greater success in astronomy and mathematics. "The library of Assurbanipal contained many treatises on arithmetic, and the remains give us reason to think that Pythagoras borrowed the plan of his famous multiplication table from the Mesopotamian civilisation." There were also catalogues of astronomical observations. Their knowledge of this science was of a very advanced kind. "They were acquainted with the solar year of three hundred and sixty-five and a quarter days, and invented the division of the circle into three-hundred-and-sixty degrees, the degrees into sixty minutes, the minute into sixty seconds, and the seconds into sixty thirds, which, along with the Babylonian signs for these divisions, are still retained by the science of the present time, and are thus confessed to be incapable of improvement."

It will therefore be seen that the first of the four things implied in the opening statements of *Daniel* is fully confirmed; the pursuit of learning was one of the most prominent features of the Babylonian civilisation.

(2) The second is also established by Layard's discovery. Assurbanipal's library was *the library of the Palace school.* The king says, in a notice affixed to one of the treatises: "I have placed it in my Palace for the instruction of my subjects." The monuments contain other references to these Palace schools; but the contents of the library at Nineveh

would of themselves have abundantly proved the existence of the custom. The grammars, the dictionaries, the explanatory lists of written characters, &c., are all intended for instruction. There is, in addition, a tablet in the British Museum which contains a lesson intended to teach a young princess how to spell and read Assyrian, and which is nothing else than an Assyrian A B C. We are even able, through those remains of the Palace School Library, to obtain a clear idea of the way in which the instruction was given. The tables of signs were carefully arranged, so as to lessen as much as possible the immense difficulties connected with the reading of the ancient Accadian classics.

(3) But there might be Palace Schools in Babylon, without admission being accorded to people of a subject race. It has been the policy of some conquering nations to keep a conquered race in ignorance; and even we in England to-day show no anxiety to give a superior, or indeed any, English education to our Indian Princes. We do not select any number of them for training at our home Universities, nor locate them in our palaces so that they may be instructed along with the princes of the royal house. We should have imagined that Assyrians and Babylonians would have been equally indifferent, or equally wary. But the monuments have proved that in this matter, as in the rest, the Scripture has presented an absolutely faithful picture. The confirmation comes from no less a personage than that old foe of the people of God

—Sennacherib. He has shown in one of his inscriptions that this was the practice of the Mesopotamian kings. The inscription runs as follows: "*Belibni, son of a learned man, of the race of Babylon, who as a young child had been educated in my palace, I have established upon the throne of Sumir and of Accad.*" Here we find Sennacherib, evidently following an established custom, selecting a son of a Babylonian notability, educating him in his Palace school, and then creating him, apparently after a period of personal attendance and service, viceroy of the great province of Babylon, and therefore the highest prince and first servant of the State. Belibni, in his selection, education, and advancement, forms an exact parallel to Daniel.

Three of the four customs, the existence of which is implied in the account of the removal of Daniel to Babylon, are, therefore, fully confirmed by recent discovery. We come now (4) to what is really the most important point of all. The learning and language, which the captive princes of Judah were to occupy themselves with, is ascribed to a people named Chaldeans. Daniel and his companions are brought for the express purpose of studying "the learning and the tongue of the Chaldeans." This name confronts us with one of the most peculiar features of Babylonian history. The art of writing was invented by a people who bore this name of Casdim or Chaldeans. They were the originators of what we now designate by the name of "civilisation." They were the founders of science and art, and the organisers of government. From them, too, was handed on to the Semitic population—the Babylonians and Assyrians—what was always regarded as their classic and, indeed, their sacred literature. It was for the study of these ancient texts that Assurbanipal formed his library and established his school, and in this he followed the example of his predecessors and continued a custom which dated from the remotest times, and which was devoutly followed to the latest day of the Babylonian monarchy. These fathers of science, art, and magic were, strange to say, a Turanian people, closely connected with the Tartars, the Finns, and other peoples who have never since been much distinguished for intellectual pursuits.

So surprising was this discovery that Renan declared it was most improbable that it could be true of the Turanians strictly so-called. "We acknowledge," he said, "that it does astonish us to find the word Turanian taken in its strict sense, and to see that ancient substruction of the learned civilisation of Babylon assigned to the Turkish, Finnish, and Hungarian races; in one word, to races which have never done anything but pull down, and have never created a civilisation of their own."* But there is no escaping from the conclusion. Those very peoples whom he names are too closely associated in customs and in traditions with the first founders of human learning for anyone to doubt their relationship. The name Accadian,

---

* *Journal Asiatique*, 7th Series, Vol. ii., p. 42.

which is commonly applied to these originators of literature, science and art, means mountaineer, and only designates the locality whence they came. When we go back to these same mountains we find them long retaining this very name reported to us in various forms by the classical writers. They are called *Chaldaioi*, *Kardakes*, *Kardouchoi*, *Gordiani*, *Kardu*. They are still known by the name of Kurds.

Now there was a special reason why this name "Chaldean" should appear in the book of Daniel. Those old masters and instructors of the country were, as we have seen, earlier known as Accadians, that is, as Highlanders. They were subsequently conquered by the Semitic population. In the twelfth century B.C. their language had died out, as they had adopted, under compulsion or from choice, the speech of their Semitic masters, those whom we now know as Assyrians and Babylonians. "A little later," says Lenormant, "the tribe of Kaldi appears upon the scene. They were the Chaldeans, properly so called, who boasted that they, more than any other tribe, had preserved in all its purity the blood of 'the most ancient amongst the Babylonians,' which was considered on account of its antiquity even more noble than that of the Kushites or Cephenes." *

"In the cuneiform documents," he says in another place, "the term Kaldu or Kaldi occurs as the name of a tribe of the great Accadian nation, which was at first very obscure, but which began to be renowned

* *Chaldean Magic*, (Bagster) p. 368.

about the ninth century before our era." It established itself in the south of Babylonia, and became "mistress of the whole region bordering on the sea-coast, which was then called Kaldu, and was divided into a great many small principalities governed by the chiefs of this tribe. From the eighth century (B.C.) the tribe of the Kaldi became important enough to furnish kings of Babylon."† Their power spread over the southern part of Mesopotamia, and they directed their growing strength against their Assyrian masters till, on the fall of Nineveh, the Babylonian empire was established, of which Nebuchadnezzar's reign formed the chief glory.

It was natural, therefore, that under these Kaldi kings the ancient Accadians should be called by their own name, and that all that pertained to them should be made a subject of special study. There are evidences indeed that the Accadian, though for long centuries a dead language, underwent a partial revival. Nabonidus, the last king of Babylon, whose son, Belshazzar, occupies so large a place in *Daniel*, had another name which he also uses in his inscriptions. He was elected to the throne by the "Chaldeans," properly so-called; and his second name, *Nabu-nitug*, which is the translation in old Accadian of his Assyrian name *Nabu-nadu*, no doubt showed his love for the old Kaldi tongue. "This," Lenormant writes, "indicated a kind of renaissance of the Accadian as the sacred and classical language

† *Ibid*, pp. 339, 340.

of the time of the late Babylonish empire. It also proves," he continues, "that the Accadian is indeed the 'language of the Chaldees' in the sacerdotal sense of the name, which the Book of Daniel describes as one of the principal paths of study marked out for young people destined to a learned career."

The reader will also notice the two-fold description of the study to which Daniel and his companions were directed. The *"tongue"* of the Chaldeans is mentioned as prominently as their "learning." This is now explained by recent research, which has shown that the ancient Accadian in which the Chaldean literature is written, is the most difficult language to decipher with which the human intellect has ever had to deal. Each, therefore, of the four points implied in the statement in *Dan.* i. 3-5 is now seen to be an indication of the most perfect acquaintance with the customs and the literary pursuits of the times. Under the Persian empire the knowledge of those things rapidly disappeared; and under the Greek dominion they had subsided into oblivion. These three verses, then, constitute for the "critics" a difficulty of the first magnitude. *Daniel* cannot possibly belong to the time of the Maccabees, and it presents us, not with romance, but with statements which modern discovery has shown to be the best informed and most reliable history.

Professor Sayce has marred his recently published book by an ill-considered attack upon *Daniel*. This is the more to be wondered at that there is no book in the whole of Scripture which has been so steadily confirmed by the growing light cast upon Babylonian history and civilisation. Had he merely enumerated the points which, one after another, have been definitely settled, to the confusion of those who have assailed this Book, and to the triumph of those who have maintained its Divine origin and authority, his readers would have been amazed and his own cavils would have been hushed. He makes a point of the names assigned to Daniel and his companions. Now, the history of opinion regarding these and the other names in the book is significant. They were confidently declared by the "critics" to be Persian and not Babylonian. It was supposed that the knowledge of the Babylonian language was entirely forgotten when *Daniel* was written, and that the Persian itself had become a matter of such antiquity that its names and terms were taken as representative of the most ancient civilisation of Mesopotamia. This was certainly the case in the age of the Maccabees, as every reader of the Septuagint and of the Old Testament Apocrypha knows; and if *Daniel* had been written at that time, as was confidently declared by "criticism" to be undeniable, then nothing but gigantic blunders were to be expected. *It is now acknowledged on all hands that these names are largely Babylonian, and that those of Daniel and his friends are wholly so.* Is not that in itself a striking fact? The knowledge of the Babylonian had died out by the third century B.C. No writer of the

Maccabean period, writing in the second century B.C., knew anything whatever of it. The "critics" themselves have proved this, and, because it was incontestable, they asked that judgment should be given against the claims of Daniel. They have, therefore, really established the claims of the book. For a very full knowledge of Babylonian is now seen to be undoubtedly in it; and, if that knowledge was not possessed in the Maccabean times, nor in the century that preceded them, then the book must have had an earlier origin than either. The "critics" have really proved too much for their own comfort; and, while attempting to demolish *Daniel*, they have been cutting the ground from under their own feet.

But, apart from the names themselves, there is something implied in the very giving of them. It is no part of our customs to change the names of those who are appointed to public offices, or of those who have been received into royal favour; but it is plain that, if this book is to be believed, such was the custom in Mesopotamia. Not only is Daniel's name changed, but the names of all his companions are changed also. When we ask whether this was so, we receive another proof of the service which the Scripture (so often rejected and maligned) has been rendering to humanity when it is viewed merely as history. The Assyrio-Babylonian civilisation had passed almost completely out of sight; but here and elsewhere in Scripture it has been shown us as faithfully as one's form is reflected in a mirror. It was a custom common to Babylonian and Assyrian kings to give Assyrian names to foreigners who were received into favour and service. Assurbanipal placed an Egyptian prince, the well-known Psammetik, at the head of a province, and changed his name to Nabu-sezi-banni. In changing the names of these Hebrew princes, Nebuchadnezzar was, therefore, simply following a custom established by his predecessors.

## CHAPTER VII.

BABYLONIAN NAMES—NEBUCHADNEZZAR'S DREAM—
THE TWO LANGUAGES OF THE BOOK—
A SEVENFOLD TEST.

I TOUCHED, in the preceding chapter, upon the names in the Book of Daniel. Professor Sayce shows in this matter the unreliable side which has all along marred work which in many other respects has been valuable and admirable. *Abed-nego* is evidently a copyist's mistake for Abed-nebo. The *b* and the *g*, like so many other letters of the Hebrew alphabet, resemble each other so closely that in the faded writing of an ancient copy the one might easily be mistaken for the other. In the days when the Septuagint translation was made, every notion of the meaning of the word had passed away from Jewish learning. They transliterated the name into Greek as *Abdenago*, evidently in entire ignorance that the word *Abed* was the same as the Hebrew *Ebed*, "servant." Abed-nebo means "the servant of the god Nebo," and is stamped as pure Babylonian by its very composition. It was the fashion of that

## Names of Daniel and his Companions. 377

country to form names in which those of the gods thus appeared. Sayce is also compelled to append the following note to his antagonistic criticism of *Daniel:* "I have found the name of Abed-Nebo in an Aramaic inscription of the sixth or fifth century B.C. engraved on the sandstone rocks north of Silsilis in Upper Egypt."[*] That is, in plain English, the name Abednebo was a name in use at the very time that it is said in *Daniel* to have been conferred upon one of the young Jewish princes.

The name of Daniel himself comes in for similar treatment at the hands of the Professor. In the Hebrew alphabet there are two symbols for the letter *t*, one *(Tau)* representing an aspirated *t*, the other *(Teth)* representing the letter unasperated. "Belteshazzar," says Professor Sayce, "was the name given to Daniel after his adoption among the 'wise men' of Babylon. Now Bilat-sarra-utsur, 'O Beltis defend the king,' is a good Babylonian name. But in the Book of Daniel the name is written, not with a *tau* as would be required by the word Bilat, but with a *teth*, so that the first element in it is transformed into the Assyrian word *ballidh*, 'he caused to live.' The result is a compound which has no sense, and would be impossible in the Babylonian language."[†]

This is a big superstructure to raise on the slight foundation supplied by a shade of difference in one letter! Let us suppose that Professor Sayce is absolutely correct in his assertion that *teth* is *never*

---

[*] *The Higher Criticism and the Monuments*, pp. 532, 533.   [†] *Ibid.* 532.

used to stand in Hebrew for the Assyrian *t* in *Bilat*, still the mistake of a copyist substituting *teth* for *tau* might have caused the whole difficulty. "Abednego" has apparently suffered in one letter; Belteshazzar might equally well have suffered in another. But the Professor and the "critics" have to face one fact, and this is, that, in the second century B.C. (when they suppose *Daniel* to have been written), there was no knowledge of Babylonian in existence to enable anyone to forge names so near to true Babylonian names as these are even in their present condition. If this was such an attempt, there is absolutely nothing to explain its almost complete success; and we are forced to the only other conclusion possible—that it shows an acquaintance with the language which takes us back to the time of Daniel.

His note on the name Arioch is curious, but is a capital specimen of the gratuitous rashness of his attack upon *Daniel*. "Though 'Arioch' (ii. 15) is found," he says, "in the cuneiform inscriptions, it would not have been used in Babylonia in the age of Nebuchadnezzar. It was . . . a name of Sumerian origin, and it had passed out of use centuries before Nebuchadnezzar was born. It may have made its way into the Book of Daniel from the fourteenth chapter of Genesis; it certainly did not do so from the Babylonia of the Exile."

The suggestion that the writer of *Daniel* went back to the account in Genesis xiv. to help him out in a forgery, and to find Babylonian names for the characters in his religious novelette, is one for which the "critics," whom Professor Sayce, in other parts of his book, has had to handle so roughly, will no doubt be duly grateful. But when they come to utilise it, they will encounter some difficulties. Why did this pious forger fix upon *one* name only? Why did he not pick out of Gen. xiv. names for Daniel and his companions? It seems, upon the face of it, exceeding strange that he should have recourse to this ancient quarry only for the name of an obscure official who might as well have not been named at all. And there is another strange thing. He chooses, on this theory, a name—Arioch, king of Ellasar—which the text warns him is *not* Babylonian, and passes over the name "Amraphel," which is given as the name of the king of Shinar, or Babylon. These difficulties are likely to make the Professor's gift to the "critics" an encumbrance rather than a help. But the monuments are here as distinctly against him as they are throughout against them. A much greater Assyriologist than Sayce has borne distinct testimony in favour of the Scripture upon this very point. François Lenormant, in his *La Divination chez les Chaldeens* (p. 198), says: "Many private (Babylonian) documents show us *Ariku* ('the long one') employed as a proper name."

Let us now turn to a matter of greater interest, and one that affords a broader test of the book. The second chapter of *Daniel* contains the record of a dream which must ever rank among the mightiest marvels of the book. The vision of that colossal image, with its head of gold, arms and breast of silver, belly and haunches of brass, legs of iron, and feet partly of iron and partly of brittle earthenware, has helped to make *Daniel* one of the biggest stumbling-blocks in the path of unbelief. The supernatural, which meets us on every page of *Daniel*, assumes here startling dimensions. Superstition seems stamped on the very face of this narrative, and seems to be the very stuff out of which it is woven. A dream cometh of the multitude of business, and a man ought, we say, no more to concern himself with these wandering thoughts of the night than with the dimensions or the motions of his shadow during the day. There is as much substance, and as much significance, we imagine, in the one as in the other.

It would be no strange thing, however, if God met this man just where he expected to find a Divine message; and the question which the dream raises is just this, whether it was *natural* for him to expect a message from God through such a medium? That the dream *was* a message from God I hope to show by and bye. It is stamped, more than almost any other part of Scripture, with the Divine seal. But what we have to do now is to see whether "the date stamp" is upon this second chapter as legibly as we read it upon the opening chapter. Let me first, however, clear away a misconception which has misled Professor Sayce and many another.

In Daniel ii. 4 we read (according to both Authorised and Revised Versions), "Then spake

the Chaldeans to the king in Syriac" (the Revised—
"in the Syrian language"). On this Professor Sayce
writes: "An almost equally clear indication of date
is furnished by the statement that 'the Chaldeans'
spoke to Nebuchadnezzar 'in Syriac' or Aramaic.
It is true that their words are given in Aramaic, and
that after the age of the Exile the common language
of the Jews was Aramaic both in Palestine and in
Babylonia. But it never was the language of the
'Chaldeans,' unless it were in those later days when
'Chaldeans' told fortunes to Syrians and Greeks.
The statement, therefore, that the King of Babylonia
was addressed by his native subjects in Aramaic,
proves that its author was unacquainted with the
real language of the Chaldeans."

This entire argument is founded upon a blunder
for which Professor Sayce is not alone responsible.
He is only repeating a mistake which others ought
to have corrected long ago. The word *Aramith* is
certainly translatable in the way in which both
versions render it, though it is well to notice that
the preposition "in" is wanting in the Hebrew.
But the word is also capable of another rendering,
which the slightest inspection of what follows
imperatively demands. It is not the speech of the
Chaldeans only that is given in Aramean, but
chapter after chapter—on till the end of the seventh
—is written in the same language. The Aramean
portion occupies, indeed, one-half of the book, and
the word is simply an intimation to the reader
that *he now comes to another language than that which*

*the writer has so far used.* Put the word in a parenthesis and all is plain—"Then spake the Chaldeans to the king (Aramean), 'O king, live for ever,'" &c. The word is thrown in as a necessary explanation to the reader of the strange fact that an entirely different language is used in the portion of the book that is to follow. It is a plain intimation also that the change is due not to accident but to design, and this intimation of deliberate purpose was no doubt meant to awaken inquiry as to what the purpose was. The book is prophetic; it is full of symbols; this is only one symbol more, and one that covers much, and that can doubtless tell us some things that will instruct and comfort.

Can we, then, detect the purpose, or shed any light upon the mystery? An inspection of the contents of chapters ii. to vii. shows that they deal with the long period of the Gentile supremacy, ending with the vision of the Antichrist and the triumph of God and His saints over the Gentile power in that, its latest, cruellest, most blasphemous and most daring development. Those six chapters form a complete panorama of the world's history from that time to the end of the present dispensation. But this panorama shows us the changes of the political arena *without any reference to Israel.* It is the world's history from the Gentile point of view. The first chapter of the book shows us the tree of the Davidic sovereignty of Israel cut down to the roots. Of it and of Israel we hear nothing more till the eighth chapter is reached. There the

Antichrist appears *in his attack upon Israel.* He is "the little horn which waxed exceeding great," who "magnified himself even to the Prince of the host, and by whom the daily sacrifice was taken away, and the place of His sanctuary was cast down" (verses 9-11). In each of the chapters which follow increasing light is thrown upon this last struggle and upon the fortunes of Israel during the Gentile domination.

Now we can at once see a fitness in the Hebrew language—the speech of God's people and the tongue in which God's Book was written—being used for the first portion of Daniel and for the last. The Hebrew, the sacred language, is the symbol of God's chosen people. Was there any corresponding fitness in using Aramean for the middle portion? Was it, in other words, a speech representative of the Gentile peoples? Professor Sayce has partly indicated the answer. "The Aramean," he says, "had become to a certain extent the language of international trade, and it is very probable that it was commonly used as a means of intercourse with foreign populations like that of the Jewish exiles who inhabited Chaldea."* This understates the fact. The Aramean was the *lingua franca* of the time. It was, like Greek in the time of our Lord, the language of trade and of international intercourse. There are distinct traces of its use in this way in inscriptions, for example, of the time of Sennacherib

---

\* *The Higher Criticism and the Monuments,* p. 536.

—two centuries before the Book of Daniel was written—in which the Assyrian is accompanied by an Aramean translation. It was the representative Gentile speech of the time.

No fitter emblem, then, could have been found for the period of Gentile supremacy. But the use of this tongue instead of the Hebrew, in which the Old Testament oracles are given, meant more. It seems to me that two things are indicated by it. (1) *Israel will be apparently forgotten during this long period.* That intimation has been abundantly fulfilled. God's work has been carried on, but not by it. (2) The kingdom of God, however, will not be established in the earth apart from God's ancient people. When the time of the end draws near, the language of the Gentiles is exchanged for the language of Israel. We know how fully these indications are borne out by other portions of Scripture, and we can only admire the wisdom and the love which have written the lesson again so clearly, and which have, so to say, given us in these two portions of the book of Daniel a *coloured* map of the world's entire history.

The change, then, from Hebrew to Aramean is prophetic, and this very fact stamps the book as Divine. It is an indication of a prolonged Gentile supremacy, and of "the times of the Gentiles," when the Jewish people will be so completely set aside that their ministry and language shall no longer be used for the service of God. This Bible "difficulty," therefore, takes its place in the very first rank of Bible confirmations.

We now come from the language to the contents of the second chapter, and here we meet quite an array of fresh tests, which it would be simply impossible for a book of an unhistorical character to sustain. (1) It is assumed that a dream would be received by the Babylonian king as a message from God, to which he would attend, and by which he would be haunted and troubled till the message was understood. (2) The subject of the dream will have some bearing upon the question whether this book really belongs to the time and place of which it speaks. Our Lord's parables have the mark of time and place woven into their very texture. It is the same with Jotham's parable, and with the illustrations and the allegories of the Prophets. Pharaoh's dreams are also distinctly Egyptian, as are those of his servants in the prison. What, then, of Nebuchadnezzar's? (3) Certain men are represented as making the interpretation of dreams their sole occupation. (4) These occupy a high rank in the State. (5) They are divided into classes. (6) The classes bear certain names. (7) A certain official is mentioned who is charged with their destruction. Here we have a sevenfold test, which will in itself be more than enough to prove whether we have here a book of the time of Daniel, or a forgery, trying to obtain currency under his name, but really written 370 years after he was laid in his grave.

1. Let us now look at the first of these, which takes it for granted that dreams were regarded among the

Babylonians as a medium of communication between them and the gods. Nebuchadnezzar is sure that some Divine intimation has been sent him, and at every risk and cost he is resolved to know what the message is. All this is implied in the events recorded in the second chapter. Is it borne out by what we now know of the land and of the time? Diodorus of Sicily has told us that the Chaldeans explained dreams, like prodigies, in a prophetic sense. This is fully confirmed by the inscriptions. Some of the clay tablets of an ancient work, a copy of which Assurbanipal placed in his library at Nineveh, show that the interpretation of dreams was reduced to a science. A fragment of one of the tablets runs thus:—

If a man in a dream
Sees a cock . . .
Sees a body of a dog . . .
Sees the body of a bear with the feet of another animal . .
Sees the body of a dog with the feet of another animal . .

&c. Women used to spend the night in the temple of Aphrodite, or Zarpanit, in order to have dreams which were afterwards registered, and from which the diviners drew predictions regarding their future. There were certain men named "seers," who appear to have been attached to some of the temples and who were supposed to be favoured with prophetic dreams. In one of his inscriptions Assurbanipal tells a long story of comfort once sent him in a dream. Certain princes were residing with him belonging to the family of Te-Oumman, king of Elam. Te-Oumman demanded their extradition, and, his request being refused, he invaded Assyria. Assurbanipal goes to worship Istar, and one of the seers of her Temple has a dream. He beholds Istar and the king, and listens to their conversation. Istar promises victory, and Assurbanipal proceeds with good heart to meet his foe. He also narrates, in another inscription, that to Gyges, king of Lydia—a district, "the name of which the kings my fathers had not heard—the account of my great kingdom was related in a dream by Assur the god, my creator," and that, moved by this dream, Gyges sent a messenger the same day to plead for Assurbanipal's friendship.

But a crowning proof of the Babylonian character of this incident is afforded by a cylinder of Nabonidus (the father of Belshazzar) discovered by Mr. Hormuzd Rassam in 1881. Nabonidus tells how he was commanded by Merodach in a dream to restore the temple of the Moon at Sippara. "O Nabonidus, king of Babylon," Merodach is represented as saying, "bring bricks with the horses of thy chariots, build the temple, and let the Moon-god, the great lord, take up his abode therein." Here, as in all the preceding instances, we meet the same deep and constant conviction that in every case the dream is sent from heaven. Belief in the Divine origin of dreams was therefore a leading characteristic of the place and of the time.

2. The first test has thus shown that the book takes us right into the midst of the Babylonian life and thought. Let us apply the second, and ask whether

that matter is also Babylonian. Nebuchadnezzar sees a colossal statue of imperious mien and startling splendour. It is composed of various metals. There is gold and silver and brass and iron in its structure. Now, it need hardly be said that our dreams are built up out of our experiences. The arrangement may alter, but the materials are those with which we are familiar during our waking existence. A dreamer of the last century would not have seen in the visions of the night a modern railway train darting through the land, nor a steamboat ploughing its way through the sea. And it is just as unlikely that a dreamer of to-day will have a vision of a stage-coach or of one of those lumbering vehicles in which rank and beauty were drawn along to the court of the Stuarts. Dreams, in short, like most other things, bear the stamp of their place and time.

Does the dream, then, bear the stamp of Palestine in the year 160 B.C., or of Babylon in the year 600 B.C.? No one who knows anything of the Grecian Empire in the East can possibly see the slightest reflection of it in Nebuchadnezzar's dream. But in the land of gigantic sculptures we see at once the origin of the dream. Layard has given a vivid description of the overwhelming astonishment and awe of his labourers, when they unearthed the first of the gigantic human-headed bulls that guarded the gateway of an ancient palace. He tells us that even he shared the impression. It was impossible to look upon the sculpture and not be conscious of the majesty with which the sculptor's art had clothed his work. These figures were everywhere. Nebuchadnezzar had reared them in scores and hundreds in his palaces and in his temples. Occasionally in the inscriptions of an Assyrian king we read that he had made "an image of his sovereignty." The Egyptian kings had for long ages tried to equal, if not to surpass, their precedessors by the erection of immense statues of themselves. There was nothing more natural than that the conqueror of Assyria and of Egypt should try to enforce the recognition of his supposed vast superiority in the same way.

But the image was not only colossal, it was made of *metal*. We know that images of stone were a feature of the time; was this also true of *metal* images? One quotation from the annals of Assurbanipal will give the answer. The Assyrian king describes the booty he brought back with him from Elam, and among it were "thirty-two statues of kings—of silver, of gold, of bronze, and of alabaster." Here we have three of the metals used in the composition of "statues of kings," which appear in the colossal image of the dream—the gold, the silver, and the bronze, or brass. The additions are in metal, which was known but not hitherto used in this way, and the clay thoroughly well known, but—for such a purpose—quite as thoroughly despised. The introduction of these elements had therefore a plain significance. The iron was *a new kingdom*—differing from all that went before it in this very feature of hard, uncompromising strength —while the clay spoke of the baseness with which in its later developments it should be allied.

The first two, then, of our seven tests emphatically assign the book to the age of Daniel. What the others have to say we shall see in the next chapter.

## CHAPTER VIII.

### THE WISE MEN OF BABYLON.

WE proceed with the remainder of the sevenfold test supplied by the second chapter of *Daniel*. (3) Certain men are represented as making the interpretation of dreams their sole occupation. Is this borne out by what we now know of the ancient Babylonians? The reply is distinctly—"Yes." We have already seen that there were "seers" attached to the temples, whose occupation it was to obtain communications from the gods. "In Assyria," says François Lenormant, "and probably also in Chaldea —for in all these things the Assyrians were only disciples and imitators of the Chaldeans—there were, as certain texts testify, seers *(sabru)* who had the special privilege of being favoured by the gods with prophetic dreams. Without doubt, like the seers and the diviners of an infinitude of other peoples, even the most savage, they procured them by the aid of artificial means, such as narcotic potions and intoxicating fumigations."

The place occupied by the seer is, as Lenormant indicates, strikingly illustrated in the poem of Gilgamesh, or Nimrod, the great epic of Chaldea. Gilgamesh is accompanied by his seer Ea-bani, whom he rescued from the power of a monster who had held him captive. Ea-bani explains the dreams of Gilgamesh. When Ea-bani is afterwards slain by another monster, Gilgamesh is in despair at the loss of his spiritual guide. It is to supply this lack that the gods send him another dream, in which he is told to go and consult Khasisatra (evidently Noah). But, whatever may have been the position of the seers in Babylonia, there is no doubt about the existence of a class of men whose sole business it was to interpret dreams and prodigies. The recovered literature of Babylon shows that they were the learned of the time. We now know that they devoted to this subject an immense amount of thought and labour. "They gave," says Vigoroux, "a scientific form to the interpretation of all presages, reduced to writing their observations, collected as in a kind of encyclopædia all the rules relating to astrology, necromancy, auguries, indications of the entrails of beasts offered in sacrifice, explanation of atmospheric phenomena, chance meetings, monstrous births—in a word, whatever might serve as food for superstition.*

(4) This will become still clearer as we look at the next point—that they occupy a high rank in the State. That this is the representation in *Daniel* is

---

\* *La Bible et les Decouvertes Modernes*, Vol. iv., p. 459.

evident from the reward conferred upon the prophet by Nebuchadnezzar. The dignity of chief ruler over the wise men is apparently a superior position to that of "ruler over the whole province of Babylon." In ii. 48, three things are named in which the king expressed his gratitude. "Then the king made Daniel a great man, and gave him many great gifts, and made him ruler over the whole province of Babylon, and chief of the governors over all the wise men of Babylon." The appointment of Governor of Babylon was more than the "many great gifts," and it is natural to suppose that the highest place among the wise men was a still greater mark of the king's favour. In any case, it is worthy of special mention, and of being set alongside the ruling of the great home province of the Babylonian Empire.

That here again we have a statement that shows the fullest acquaintance with Babylon as it was in the time of the great king, will appear from the following:—"They became," continues Vigoroux, "the most powerful body in the kingdom, and they acquired such a reputation that, for long afterwards, 'Chaldean' was a synonym for magician and diviner."* Lenormant says: "The superior and dominant caste, entirely exclusive, was composed of the Chaldeans properly so-called, who, as we have already attempted to show, were strangers and conquerors of the Turanian race. They had obtained exclusive possession of all priestly functions, and used them so as to govern the State. Classical

* *Ibid*, p. 460.

writers give us some details on their organisation, functions, and power. 'The Chaldeans,' says Diodorus Siculus, following Ctesias who had seen them at Babylon, 'are the most ancient of the Babylonians; they formed in the State a body resembling the priests in Egypt. Set apart for following up the worship of the gods, they passed their whole life in meditation on philosophical subjects, and had acquired a great reputation in astrology; they especially devoted themselves to the science of divination, and to predictions of the future; they attempted to avert evil, and procure good fortune either by purifications, or by sacrifices, or by enchantments. They are accomplished in the art of predicting the future by observing the flight of birds; they explained dreams and prodigies. Skilled in the art of inspecting the entrails of victims, they were accounted capable of giving the true interpretation. But these branches of knowledge were not taught as among the Greeks. The learning of the Chaldeans was a family tradition; the son who inherited this from his father was exempt from all taxes. Having their relations for instructors, they had the double advantage of being taught everything without reserve, and that by masters in whose statements they could put implicit faith. Accustomed to work from infancy, they made great progress in the study of astrology, partly because learning is easy at an early age, and partly because they received a long course of instruction. . . . The Chaldeans always remained at the same point in science, maintaining their traditions without alteration; the Greeks, on the contrary, thinking of nothing but profit, were constantly forming new schools, disputing among themselves as to the truth of the most important doctrines, confusing the minds of their disciples, who, tossed about in continual doubt, ended in believing nothing at all!

"We see by the Book of Daniel (Dan. i. 4; ii. 2; v. 7) what were the functions of the Chaldeans; they composed many distinct classes, of more or less elevated rank, in the hierarchy. Some of them were the sacred scribes, decipherers of writing; others the constructors of horoscopes, or interpreters of the stars, magicians who pronounced magical formulæ, conjurors who had power to avert malign influences. Their power of divination assured them great influence, as it made them, so to speak, masters of everyone's destiny. They usually foretold in almanacks, a custom that seems to have lasted to our own times, all that our common almanacks now predict, fluctuations in the temperature, physical phenomena, and historical events. The Chaldeans were not confined to Babylon, but were spread over all Babylonia. They had schools in various places, more or less flourishing; according to Strabo, that at Borsippa was the most celebrated. That at Orchoe, or Erech, was also well known, and maintained its reputation down to the times of the Romans. In the period of the Seleucidæ, the doctrine of the unity of God was distinctly taught there; as we know from tablets with cuneiform inscriptions, dated in the reign of several Greek kings, found at Warkah, and now in the British Museum. The only name of a Deity found in them, and this is many times repeated, is 'God One.'

"But the Chaldeans did not confine themselves to the duties and positions of priests and astrologers, and to the unbounded influence derived from this position both over the State and over individuals. They became the absolute governing class in politics. Members of this caste commanded armies, and held all the chief offices of the State. From them came all the Royal families who ruled Babylon, whether vassals of Assyria, or, after the time of Phul, completely independent. At the head of the hierarchy and caste was an Archi-Magus, whose national and proper title we do not yet know; he was, next to the king, *the chief personage of the empire*; he accompanied the sovereign everywhere, even in war, to direct all his actions according to priestly rule and presage. When the king died and the legitimate successor could not immediately assume the reins of power, this personage administered the Government in the interim, as in the instance which occurred between the death of Nabopolassar and the arrival of Nebuchadnezzar."\*

I have given this passage entire, although it touches upon more than one point, on account of its great importance. The headship of all the wise men of Babylon was the greatest position in the Babylonian State.

---

\**Ancient History of the East*, II. p.p. 493-495.

Let us now turn (5) to the next point. The wise men are divided into classes. These are carefully enumerated. In verse 2, for example, we read: "Then the king commanded to call the magicians, and the astrologers, and the sorcerers, and the Chaldeans, for to show the king his dreams." The same enumeration is made in verse 27: "Daniel answered in the presence of the king, and said, The secret which the king hath demanded cannot the wise men, the astrologers, the magicians, the soothsayers show unto the king." Years afterwards, when they are summoned before Belshazzar, "The king cried aloud to bring in the astrologers, the Chaldeans, and the soothsayers" (Daniel v. 7.) Is it a matter of fact that they were divided in this way, or is this one of those mistakes into which a late writer, picturing a vanished state of society after his own imagination, is sure to fall?

The reply has been spontaneously furnished by the leading Assyriologists of the time. This very division of the wise men of Babylon into sections, each of which has its distinctive work and name, has formed for them a crowning proof of the historical character of the Book of Daniel. Lenormant tells, in his work on *Chaldean Magic*, of the "scientific generosity" displayed by Sir Henry Rawlinson in sending him proofs of the *fac-simile* plates of his fourth volume of *The Cuneiform Inscriptions of Western Asia*. These were copies taken from the remains of a great Babylonian work on magic, which Lenormant thus describes:—

"The great work on magic, many copies of which had been executed by the scribes of Assurbanipal, according to the pattern placed centuries since in the library of the famous school for priests at Erech in Chaldea, was composed of three different books. We know the title of one of the three, 'The Wicked Spirits,' for we find at the end of each of the tablets, which come from it, and which have been preserved entire, 'Tablet No.—of the Wicked Spirits.' As the title shows, it was filled exclusively with formulæ of conjurations and imprecations, which were designed to repulse demons and other wicked spirits, to avert their fatal action, and to shelter the invoker from their attacks. Portions of a second book exist, and, judging from what remains of it, it would seem to be formed of a collection of these incantations, to which was attributed the power of curing various maladies. Lastly, the third book contained hymns to certain gods. A supernatural and mysterious power was attributed to the chanting of these hymns, which are, however, of a very different character from the regular liturgical prayers of the official religion, a few of which have been preserved to us. It is curious to notice that the three parts composing thus the great work on magic, of which Sir Henry Rawlinson has found the remains, correspond exactly to the three classes of Chaldean doctors which Daniel enumerates, together with the astrologers and divines (*Kasdim* and *Gazrim*), that is, the *Khartumim* or conjurors, the *Chakamim* or physicians, and the *Asaphim* or theosophists. The further we advance in the knowledge of the cuneiform texts, the greater does the necessity appear of reversing the condemnation *much too prematurely pronounced by the German exegetical school* against the date of the writings of the fourth of the greater prophets."

The above testimony is conclusive. The distinction constantly made in *Daniel* between the various classes fits in so completely with the indications in the magical books that we are compelled to admit that the language of Daniel is that of one who was in close contact with the life of the time. Our fifth test is consequently triumphantly conclusive. Let us now look at the sixth. The classes bear certain names in the book of Daniel. The book has shown accurate knowledge in dividing the wise men into *classes;* let us now see whether the inscriptions have anything to say as to the correctness of the *names*.

(6) The correctness of all of them is vouched for either directly or indirectly by the monuments. The *Kasdim* (the Chaldeans) were the astrologers who imagined themselves able to foretell the future by means of astronomical observations. They made careful notes of the conjunction of astronomical phenomena and terrestrial events which they used as a foundation for their predictions. Here are some of these records gathered with so much painstaking diligence. "In the month of Elul (August), the 14th day, an eclipse happens; in the north it begins, and in the south and east it ends; in the evening watch it begins, and in the night watch it ends. To

the king of Mullias a crown is given. . . . There are rains in heaven, and in the channels of the rivers floods. A famine is in the country, and men sell their sons for silver.

"An eclipse happens on the 15th day. The king's son murders his father, and seizes on the throne. The enemy plunders and devours the land.

"An eclipse happens on the 16th day. The king of the Hittites plunders the land, and on the throne seizes. There is rain in heaven, and a flood descends in the channels of the rivers.

"An eclipse happens on the 20th day," &c.* Here the month and day on which eclipses occur are carefully noted along with the terrestrial events. By consulting these records, they were no doubt enabled, on the foundation of a supposed but misleading "science," to say what an eclipse on any month and day denoted. The *Gazrim* (the soothsayers) were the diviners. The name is connected with *gezer*, a "piece or part of a sacrificial animal," and the *Gazrim* foretold events and destinies by the inspection of the entrails of the sacrificial victims. The great work on magic, to which Lenormant refers, and the fragments of which have been recovered from the ruins of the palace of Assurbanipal, relate, not to these divisions of the wise men, but to the following three. It contains, indeed, the incantations and the formulæ which were necessary for the carrying on of their arts. The *Khartumim* (the magicians) were the conjurers who

---

* Rawlinson's *Egypt and Babylon*, pp. 55, 56.

believed themselves to have power over evil spirits.
The first part of the three books bears the title of
"Evil Spirits," and contains the conjurations
repeated by the *Khartumim* to repel the evil spirits,
and to avert or to neutralize their evil influences.
The second book was designed for the service of the
*Chakamim*, or doctors, and contained a collection of
incantations for the healing of diseases. The third
book was taken up with hymns to certain gods. A
supernatural and mysterious power was attributed
to the singing of these hymns. All of them—strange
to say—conclude with the old Accadian word *kakama*,
which the Assyrian translation renders by *Amana*,
our "Amen!" This shows from what hoar antiquity
the concluding word in our daily supplications has
come down to us. It was the accompaniment of
man's first approach to God, and, in all likelihood,
was heaven-taught. These hymns were used by the
*Asaphim* ("Enchanters," translated wrongly "Astrologers"), and seem to have been employed in the
endeavour to gain responses from the gods. The
name *Asaphim* has a close relation to another which
appears in the Babylonian inscriptions. The gate of
the higher chapel of the pyramid of Borsippa, which
was consecrated to Nebo (or the "prophet" god),
was called *Bab Asaput*, "the gate of the oracle,"
that is, the gate of the divine response. The
inscriptions also speak of a "*bit asaput*" in the
pyramid of the royal city of Babylon, that is, of a
"house or a chamber of the oracle." Into this
chamber the *Asaphim* were no doubt accustomed to

go in the attempt to obtain responses to their appeals for guidance.

The last point relates to (7) the official who is charged with the destruction of the wise men. He is called in the sacred text *Rab Tabbahayya*, and bears the name of Arioch. I have already referred to the name. Professor Sayce, in his zeal to surrender *Daniel* to the critics, has pounced upon "Arioch" as a proof of the unhistorical character of the book! The name, he says, was not used among the Babylonians of Daniel's time, and has been copied from Genesis xiv. 1. The Professor's knowledge of the private life of Babylon about 600 B.C. would surely require to be very complete before he could pronounce with such certainty as to whether anyone did or did not then bear the name of Arioch. But he is directly contradicted, as we have seen, by the distinct statement of Lenormant (*La Divination chez les Chaldeens*, pp. 133, 134): "Many private Babylonian documents show us *Ariku*, 'the long one,' used as a proper name."

The confirmation of the description of his office is as striking as the confirmation of his name. *Rab Tabbahayya* is correctly translated in the margin of the Authorised Version as "Chief of the executioners," or "slaughtermen." The Babylonian and Assyrian title was *Rab Daiki*, "chief of the slayers." An enamelled brick, discovered at Nimrud by George Smith, represents one of these *Daiki*, or executioners. He is standing beside the king's chariot, and holds a dagger in his right hand. His left hand rests on the string of his bow, which is slung over his back. The figure is accompanied by an explanatory legend which describes the office of this official. Sir Walter Scott represents Louis XI. of France as constantly accompanied by his hangman. The kings of Assyria and of Babylon seem to have been almost as constantly accompanied by similar grim functionaries.

## CHAPTER IX.

### NEBUCHADNEZZAR'S GOLDEN STATUE.

THE third chapter of Daniel is the record of one of the most wonderful miracles related in Scripture. We can scarcely wonder, therefore, that it has proved to be so great a stumbling-block in the path of unbelief. That God should intervene to keep men uninjured in fierce flames that would have melted iron, and should have enabled them to walk to and fro and to breathe as if only the sun's genial warmth was about them—this must startle even the strongest faith. It is only with reflection that assurance returns. Was there anything here *beyond* the power of God? If He could have preserved them unharmed for *one* moment among those roaring waves of fire, why not, then, for a thousand moments? And was not the very stupendousness of the miracle just what was needed to arrest at the very outset this persecution of God's helpless people? If God is to appear for them at all, He must appear in His glory; and so the more that is said about the improbability of the miracle, the more do we see the effect it must have had upon Nebuchadnezzar and upon his court; and the more glorious becomes that wisdom of God which the miracle displays.

The "New Criticism," like its predecessor the old Infidelity, makes its stand here. One of the critics has lately said that Daniel iii. 5, is sufficient to convince him, though it stood alone, of the late date of *Daniel*. Professor Driver also makes that verse his chief argument against the authenticity of the book. It mentions several musical instruments by name. The names are said to be Greek, and not Babylonian, or even Persian; and the "critics" rush at once to the conclusion that this is certain proof that the book was written during the Grecian empire. We shall immediately see how, just here, on ground which they themselves have chosen, they have been utterly routed. But there have been, and there are, other objections. Everything, we are told, bears the stamp of regardless exaggeration. The proportions of the statue are said to be enormous—105 feet high if we calculate the cubit at 21 inches, and 90 feet if we take it at 18 inches. The quantity of gold it must have taken shows, it is said, that we have fable before us and not history. A furnace is prepared before it is known that there will be any offenders. The heating of it "seven times," and the gathering of *all* the notabilities to the inauguration of the new idol, are referred to as additional proofs that this is merely a romance. Where was Daniel, too, it is also asked. How was it that nothing was said of him when his three friends were accused? But this is a question which we would press home upon the "critics" themselves. If the book *were* a romance, the absence of any mention of Daniel would be inexplicable. The theory of the "critics" is that the book is written to extol Daniel, and set *him* up as an example for every Israelite during the terrible persecutions under Antiochus Epiphanes. It is, then, a very natural inquiry how they explain that Daniel, in this moment for heroic confession of God, is not placed upon the stage at all. Has he hidden himself? Has he run away? Has he quailed in the day of trial, and found it expedient to be absent on "important business?" And, if he has, will the "critics" explain how this book can nevertheless have been written with the one design of holding up Daniel for the admiration and the imitation of posterity? Is *this* a thing to be admired and imitated by a Jew in a time when there is danger of a universal apostasy?

The critical theory is thus wrecked by an incident which shows that the book is *recording* events, and not fabricating them. The probability is that Daniel was present, and that he was too powerful to be touched. His friends are first dealt with by the Babylonian priests and nobles. If they are successful with them, they will by and by deal with Daniel himself. There is nothing said or suggested to this effect; but it is so much in accord with what we know of Eastern diplomacy and intrigue that we can read between the lines. Meanwhile, the very silence of the Scripture is the proof of its veracity. A forger would have put Daniel in the forefront; and a writer compiling the book "with a view" would, even though dealing with facts, have inserted an explanation.

This cluster of difficulties thus presents another series of tests, and will issue, as we hope to show, in a cluster of confirmations. I take first of all what we are told about the statue. There is (1) the work to which the king had given himself; was it a likely thing for Nebuchadnezzar to think of? (2) Was it at all probable that its erection should have been attended with such an imposing ceremony? (3) Was the quantity of gold used excessive, or even impossible? And (4) was there anything in the circumstances of the time to account for the erection of the image?

(1) Applying the first of these tests, we find that the result is a rapidly increasing confirmation of Scripture. As discovery proceeds, as the mounds are excavated and the inscriptions are read, one "find" after another steps out and ranges itself by this statement in Daniel. From the very earliest times the rearing of a statue was a favourite mode of celebrating victories and asserting superiority. For a king to erect a statue of himself seems to have been the natural expression of his right to command the obedience and the admiration of men. It seemed at one time, however, as if Chaldea and Assyria presented very few traces of this practice. Though bas-reliefs are frequently discovered, statues

are rare. But as the excavations have proceeded, the number of statues has increased. A statue of Assurnazirpal was unearthed by Layard at Nineveh, which, along with another afterwards found by him, is now in the British Museum. A statue of Sargon, the father of Sennacherib, was found in the island of Cyprus, and is now in the Berlin Museum. A statue representing Shalmaneser II. is also in the British Museum. But from 1876 to 1881, all doubt was removed as to this being an ancient Babylonian custom, through the discoveries made by M. de Sarsec at Tell-Loh, the ancient Sirtella. Ten statues were found in the mounds of ruins. They are of an exceedingly hard and dark-coloured stone. Nine of them represent an ancient Chaldean king, named Gudea, and these prove that this custom goes back *to the earliest times of Babylonian civilisation.*

It was a custom which lived on through age after age. To the instances noted above, I may add that of Samas Rimmon, whose father was a contemporary of Ahab. He describes himself in his annals as raising a statue of himself at the close of a victorious campaign. "An image," he says, "of my magnified royalty I made." Now, if there was enough in Babylonian custom and tradition to make it natural for the proud-spirited Nebuchadnezzar, who could not suffer the thought of being exceeded in any direction, to erect a statue of himself, his recent expeditions must have numbered this purpose among his most dearly cherished plans. In Egypt, the rage for fame had forced Egyptian art into its

## Nebuchadnezzar's Statue. 409

highest and most extravagant achievements. The erection of colossal statues became the serious pursuit of almost every reign. Rameses II. had reared an enormous statue of himself, which towered above surrounding obelisks and temples, and was visible for miles on every side. Nebuchadnezzar had been in Egypt. He had conquered the country and rooted out its people. Egypt was trampled in the dust. What, then, could have been more certain than that he would determine to rear in his own land a statue of his "magnified royalty," which should bear witness to the fact that he was master, not only of Egypt, but of the world?

(2) Let us now glance at the pomp with which the erection of the statue was celebrated. The triumphs which ancient Rome accorded to her successful generals were only a perpetuation of more ancient customs. The Egyptian records have made us familiar with similar scenes. The king is expected to make his triumphal entry, and the streets are thronged with the Egyptian youth. Every face is bright, every form radiant with spotless and shining white garments. The toilet of each has been performed with the utmost care, and from the shining locks sweet odours are flung till it becomes a delight to inhale the scented atmosphere. Every right hand grasps a palm branch, and as the royal procession comes in sight, the air is rent with shouts that hail the victor, and the branches wave, swept to and fro in a tempest of delight. Now, if that was Egyptian as well as Roman, is there any reason for believing

that it was not also Babylonian? The monuments bear abundant testimony that the removal or the installation of the statues of the gods was celebrated in this very way. The Assyrian sculptors have left us representations of these spectacles; and here is an inscription in which Nebuchadnezzar himself lifts up his voice to confirm the Bible. It refers to the erection of a statue to the god El, and a solemn surrender or dedication of the booty which the king had accumulated during his conquests. "The abundance of the treasures," he says, "which I have accumulated around the city was placed there as an ornament, when at the feast of Lilmuku, at the beginning of the year, on the 8th day and the 11th day, the divine prince, the divinity of heaven and earth, the lord-god, was there uplifted. (The statue) of the god El, the beauty of the sphere, was borne with reverence; the treasures were set forth before him." Here a great and imposing ceremony is plainly intimated. We are not left, therefore, to depend merely upon inferences drawn from the customs of earlier and later times. Nebuchadnezzar himself testifies to the fact that it was a custom of his own day.

I have taken it for granted that the monument which Nebuchadnezzar erected was a statue of himself. There have been various opinions ventured as to its character, some maintaining that it was an obelisk, others a pillar with a statue, or at least a bust, on the top. The Aramæan word employed in the original may be taken as settling this very subordinate question. It means a "likeness." The statue was, as Assyrian kings had described such an object, an image of his "magnified royalty." The very vision given him at the beginning of his reign may have contributed to the suggestion. He was now the world's master, and he no doubt judged that the time had come when the fact should be duly acknowledged. He had yet to learn that that mastery was God's gift, that its possession was no mark of inherent greatness, but that God giveth it to whomsoever He will.

(3) The next point we have to deal with is the enormous quantity of gold required for such an image. This, strange to say, has excited the incredulity of learned men, although it is one of those very characteristics that should have impressed them with the truthfulness of the narrative. Had the proportions of the image been anything short of extraordinary, where would have been the call for display? The very marvellousness of the structure was that which had been aimed at, and which was relied upon for impressing the king's contemporaries, and for ensuring the admiration of posterity. It is in keeping also with everything we know of the great king. Whatever he did was colossal. His aim was to leave upon everything which he touched the mark of a greatness that would rebuke the idea of imitation. And he succeeded. The stupendous walls of Babylon have never been equalled. Herodotus, Ctesias, and Diodorus Siculus unite in describing them as three hundred feet high and

seventy-five feet thick. This must have taken 18,750 millions of the largest Babylonian bricks known to us.* The mounds of his ruined palaces astonish travellers now by their size, just as the structures themselves once amazed mankind by their immensity and their magnificence. Alexander the Great rashly resolved to rebuild one of Nebuchadnezzar's Temples. His army was engaged for months in an attempt to clear away the rubbish of the fallen edifice, so as to make a beginning with the work of restoration. But even that first step was too much for Grecian ability. The labour seemed interminable, and the design was abandoned in despair.

The marvellousness, then, of the description of the statue, both as to proportions and as to material and value, is a testimony to its truth. He delighted, as he himself has said, "to astonish mankind." But it has appeared to many that the amount of gold required was so enormous that it could not, in that age, have been supplied. Recent discoveries have proved abundantly that the riches and splendour of those times put our own completely in the shade. The magnificence of Egypt and of the contemporaneous Eastern kingdoms has never been exceeded anywhere, or at any time, and Nebuchadnezzar was now master of the whole. He had found an immense booty in the land of the Pharaohs. He had been baffled at Tyre. Thirteen years did the Babylonian armies encircle that city, and when it was at last taken, Nebuchadnezzar found only an

---

* Canon Rawlinson, *Egypt and Babylon*, p. 92.

empty shell. The precious treasures had been removed. And so God said that he would pay Nebuchadnezzar for service at Tyre out of the riches of Egypt. These, therefore, to which attention is so fully directed by the Scripture, must have been immense. There was certainly gold enough for the statue.

This appropriation of the treasures of conquered countries was in complete accordance with what we know of Babylonian customs. Herodotus, in his description of the Temple of Belus in Babylon, says: "On the topmost tower there is a spacious temple, and inside the temple stands a couch of unusual size, richly adorned, with a golden table by its side. . . . . Below, in the same precinct, there is a second temple, in which is a sitting figure of Jupiter, all of gold. Before the figure stands a large golden table; and the throne whereon it sits, and the base on which the throne is placed, are likewise of gold. The Chaldeans told me that all the gold together was eight hundred talents in weight. Outside this temple are two altars, one of solid gold." Gold was thus the very metal which, in accordance with Babylonian custom, would be applied to this purpose; and its very abundance is so in keeping with all we know of Nebuchadnezzar that what may seem like exaggeration bears all the more clearly the stamp of truth.

(4) Our last inquiry in regard to the statue itself is whether there was anything in the circumstances of the time that made its erection likely. Was there

any occasion or call for such an undertaking? An old tradition, mentioned by the Septuagint, gives the date as the eighteenth year of Nebuchadnezzar. It is plain from the position of the narrative that the event occurred some considerable time after the king's dream and Daniel's accession to power. The promise of supreme greatness given in that vision has been fulfilled, and the monarch is intoxicated with the sense of power. He has no longer any equal, or, indeed, any foe. The world lies at his feet, and with chastened and awed spirit it owns him as its one master.

Now, the Scripture has indicated a time when such a display may be said to have been natural. It brings us, however, to a later date than that mentioned in the tradition. In Ezekiel xxix. 18-20, we read: "Son of man, Nebuchadnezzar king of Babylon served a great service against Tyrus; every head was made bald, and every shoulder was peeled: yet had he no wages, nor his army, for Tyrus, for the service that he had served against it. Therefore thus saith the Lord God: Behold I will give the land of Egypt unto Nebuchadnezzar king of Babylon: and he shall take her multitude, and take her spoil, and take her prey; and it shall be the wages for his army. I have given him the land of Egypt for his labour wherewith he served against it, because they wrought for Me, saith the Lord God." Here was a triumph, then, more complete than Nebuchadnezzar ever dreamed of. It came after a time of great depression. Thirteen years had been spent in the siege of Tyre, and the strenuous and gigantic efforts put forth by himself and his armies had been rewarded only by a barren victory. They got hold of Tyre, but it was, as I have said, an empty shell. The treasures of the city had been borne away to the neighbouring island, and possibly to still more distant places of safety. When, therefore, the defence of Egypt collapsed so suddenly and completely, we can hardly wonder that the Babylonians were intoxicated with joy, and that Nebuchadnezzar's pride selected this as the right moment to assert his unchallenged supremacy. He had just become lord of the land of colossal statues, and his must needs be as gigantic and more precious than any Egypt had ever borne. The Pharaohs had carved their effigies in stone; his shall be cast in gold. And no better moment could have been chosen for the assembling of the governors of the subject provinces, many of whom, like Gedaliah in Judah, were princes chosen from among the nobles of the conquered countries. The chains already placed upon their spirits would now be rivetted by a display, on the one hand of the might and glory of the new Empire, and on the other of the terrific punishment which awaited the first indication of rebellion.

The Book of Daniel is, therefore, in fullest accord with all that we now know of the time; and this is so, without the slightest attempt being made to adapt the narrative, or even to explain why the things which it narrates were done. It is the simple, grand, and, I might say, *unconscious* coherence of truth. We might well ask whether this is possible in a forgery; and how a writer—*imagining* events four hundred years after the Babylonian empire had passed away, and had been over-laid by the two resplendent civilisations and gigantic achievements of Persia and Greece—could by any chance have hit upon an action which so happily interpreted the deepest feelings and the most pressing political necessities of the time?

A most remarkable confirmation of this much contested part of Scripture has been afforded by a discovery made by Oppert, the great French Assyriologist, during his researches in Babylon. The discovery has shown, for one thing, the perfect exactitude of the Scripture. Has the reader noticed the concluding words of the first verse of the third chapter? They read: "He set it up in the plain of Dura, in the province of Babylon." Why are these last words "in the province of Babylon" added? When I say that we *now* know there were other two Duras much to the north of Babylon, we see at once that *this knowledge was shared by the writer of the book,* and that *he* could not have been an ignorant Jew writing in Palestine four centuries after these events. Captain Selby, of the trigonometrical survey of Mesopotamia, reports that a plain in the neighbourhood of the ruins of Babylon bears the name of "Dura" at the present day. Oppert entirely confirms this statement, and has announced a still more striking discovery. Passing from Babylon to the south-east, after crossing several

## Nebuchadnezzar's Statue. 417

canals now dry, the traveller reaches, after a journey of five miles, an ancient watercourse, called *Nahr Doura*, or "the river of the wall." Continuing along the same route, a series of mounds is reached, which extend for more than a league. "Almost all these mounds," says Oppert, "are in a south-southeast direction, and bear the name of *Toloul Doura*, 'hills of Doura.' Here the *Nahr Doura* empties itself, after having run from north to south along a course of over six miles. We then reach land which bears traces of Babylonian cultivation; near two large hills, placed close together, but which have no special names, we see one smaller but sufficiently elevated to be seen from a distance.

"This mound is called el-Mokattat, 'The rectilinear mound,' and it really deserves this name, because it presents, with a height of about 20 feet, an exact square of about 46 feet at the base. The mound faces the four cardinal points, and is higher at the corners than in the middle, so that, when one is on the top, he finds himself surrounded by four blocks of masonry, which are part, however, of one solid mass. The whole is built of unbaked bricks. . .

" On seeing this mound," continues Oppert, "*one is immediately struck with the resemblance it presents to the pedestal of a colossal statue*, as, for example, that of Bavaria, near Munich, and *everything leads to the belief that the statue mentioned in the book of Daniel* (chap. iii. 1) *was set up in this place*. The fact of the erection by Nebuchadnezzar of a colossal statue has nothing in it which can cause astonishment."

Oppert adds: "There is nothing incredible in the existence of a statue sixty cubits high and six cubits broad; moreover, the name of 'the plain of Dura, in the province of Babylon,' agrees also with the actual conformation of the ruin."

Before passing from this subject, I may mention another recent confirmation. In the colossal statues of the Egyptian kings the monarchs are seated. The base of Nebuchadnezzar's colossus, it has been urged, is too small (according to the measurements given) for a figure of *that* kind. Here, then, was another difficulty; for the base and the height indicate clearly that the statue was not a seated, but an erect, figure.

But here also recent research has supplied a most satisfactory reply. Remains of a colossus raised by Rameses II. at Tanis have been discovered by Mr. Petrie. It is an *erect*, and not a seated, figure. It weighed 1,200 tons, and was 100 feet high, the pedestal making an additional 15 feet in height. When the statue was in position, it must have been 65 feet higher than the surrounding statues and obelisks, and must have been visible for miles across the plain. *That statue was no doubt standing* when Nebuchadnezzar invaded Egypt, and may well have suggested to him the conception and the details of his own undertaking.

## CHAPTER X.

### THE MUSICAL INSTRUMENTS MENTIONED IN DANIEL.

WE now come to what the "critics" imagine to be the one utterly indefensible portion of the Book of Daniel. The reader will notice the mention made of musical instruments in the beginning of the third chapter. "An herald cried aloud, To you it is commanded, O people, nations, and languages, that at what time ye hear the sound of the cornet, flute, harp, sackbut, psaltery, dulcimer, and all kinds of music, ye fall down and worship," &c. (Daniel iii. 4, 5). The same enumeration occurs again in verses 7 and 10.

The mention of these instruments has greatly disturbed the serenity of many devout but somewhat suspicious readers of *Daniel*, and has inspired the enemies of the book with confidence and joy. The names enumerated are declared to stamp the book as the product of a late age. Some of these instruments bear designations which seem to be of Greek origin. Everybody knows that Babylon and the East were conquered by Alexander the Great in the end of the fourth century before the Christian era, and that, under one form or another, the Greeks continued their dominion and influence for centuries afterwards. These Greek names, it is argued, could not have been used by any writer at the time in which Daniel lived. It is further insisted upon that they could not have been used by any Eastern writer before the second century B.C., and that, consequently, those writers are completely justified (by the very presence of those names) who have maintained that the book is a forgery of the period of the Maccabees.

Davidson sums up the argument thus:—"It is improbable that the reception of Greek words into the Aramean took place before Alexander the Great. All the influence exerted by the Greek over the Babylonian till then was comparatively unimportant; whereas Greek instruments with Greek names presuppose very considerable influence over the upper Asiatics. The writer, whoever he was, must have got the names of these instruments from the Greeks either directly or indirectly. Is it at all likely that Daniel would have done so? But a Palestinian Jew, living in the period of Alexander's Hellenic successors, might very naturally use the words in question. They suit his age and position much better than that of a Jew in the Babylonian captivity, when the influence of Greek or Aramean must have been small." *

* *Introduction to the Old Testament*, Vol. iii., pp. 193, 194.

This is cautious. Davidson evidently felt that it was possible that the edge of the argument might be turned aside. But Dr. Driver, who is spoken of as a "moderate critic," and who has publicly dissociated himself from the "advanced" school, shows no moderation here. He goes further than Davidson. Referring to two of the names, he says: "These words, it may be confidently affirmed, could not have been used in the Book of Daniel unless it had been written *after the dissemination of Greek influence in Asia through the conquests of Alexander the Great.*" \*

The italics are Dr. Driver's own. The words themselves are emphatic enough, and in this double emphasis Dr. Driver may be understood as here nailing his colours to the mast. In his critique on Professor Sayce's Book, "The Higher Criticism and the Verdict of the Monuments," he endeavours to show that, while the monuments are undoubtedly adverse to the "advanced" critics, they leave his own positions quite untouched. In the face of that disclaimer, let me ask the reader to note carefully the verdict of the monuments, to which we shall by and bye listen. Let us first of all, however, inquire what words are in question. A large claim was at first made by the critics. Six names of musical instruments are given in Dan. iii. 5 and 10. At first the critics asserted that these were "almost all Greek." This claim they have been obliged to modify. They were quite sure some forty years ago,

---

\* *Introduction to the Literature of the Old Testament*, p. 471.

however, that the Greek origin of *four* of the names could not be denied. These were *Kaitheros, Pesanterin, Sumphonyah, and Sabkah.* Here, it was argued, were undoubtedly the Greek names Kitharis, Psalterion, Sumphonia, and *Sambuke.* But in making that claim their learning was shown to be faulty. The Grecian origin of the *Sambuke* is disclaimed by the Greeks themselves! Athenæus and Strabo both testify that the instrument was introduced into Greece from Syria. The mistake was, in this case, the more unpardonable that the word *Sambuke* has no relationship to any other in the Greek tongue, and is plainly an importation. There is also some shade of doubt about *Sumphonyah*, and even the Grecian origin of the word Kitharis has been questioned.

The boasted array would thus dwindle till we have only the word *Pesanterin* left. The probability, however, is that the three last words *are* Greek, and that the instruments *may* have been imported into the East from Greece. But this by no means obtains a verdict for the critics. Their argument breaks down under its own weight. They say that the names could only have got into the book in a time when Greek speech, civilization, and art had flooded the East, and had long become the prevailing speech, civilization, and art of the time. Now, if this is admitted, that stamp on the book of Daniel will not be a small one. It cannot have diminished itself until it became a mere speck like this. The book will be pervaded and saturated with Grecian thought and speech. But, *outside these two, and at the very most three, Greek names,* there is no other Grecian stamp in Daniel! There is not the slightest trace of Grecian thought, and not the slightest reference to Greek civilization or to Greek institutions. If Greek influence had entered so far into the book as to contribute three Greek instruments, how did it not come further and do more? That one unanswered and unanswerable question is sufficient proof of the precipitancy with which "critical" results are reached. If they had tested their so-called discovery, it would have been evident that it proved too much, and that, if these Greek names placed the book down in the midst of the Greek dominion, the absence of every other trace of Greek civilisation and of Greek speech must have inevitably put it back again into a period earlier than that in which the Greek dominion began.

We have now to press our critical friends for the reasons which have led them to assert that two, or at the most three, Greek names of musical instruments prove *Daniel* to be later than the time of Alexander the Great. It is quite true that, in the period *after* Alexander, Greek instruments would be brought into the East. But their argument needs a broader basis than that, if it is not to be put to the blush before the bar of honest inquiry. The critics must go further and show that *at no earlier time* was it possible for Greek instruments to be brought into Babylonia. If the doors of the East were hermetically closed against Greece till they were burst open by Alexander the Great, then the foundation of their argument is broad enough to sustain their conclusion. But if the doors of the East were not so closed; if they were ever so little open that a Greek instrument or two could have been carried through a century or two before Alexander the Great was born; then their argument is in the dust. More than that, they have unwittingly disclosed another proof of the genuineness of *Daniel*. I have already shown that the absence of any consciousness in the book of Greek art, institutions, life, or thought, will not accord with the theory of a late date. But if there was restricted intercourse between Greece and Mesopotamia at and before the time of Daniel, this would be in perfect accord with the presence of just these two, or three, Greek names, and also with the utter absence of any further trace of Greek civilisation. Whether this last is the truth or not we shall now see.

Now, within the knowledge of everyone acquainted with even the rudiments of Greek history, there *was* a connection between Greece and Mesopotamia centuries before the time of Alexander the Great. What about Themistocles and other Grecian statesmen who got into trouble in their own land? Whither did they run for refuge when Greece grew too hot for them? Have the critics forgotten the fact that they made for the court of Persia? When they fled to the court of the Persian king, we may be certain that they did not go to a place that was utterly strange. We may be quite sure that they went by roads of which something was known. This one circumstance, therefore, overthrows their boasted argument. If Greek statesmen found their way to the Persian court long ages before the conquests, or the birth, of Alexander the Great, then, surely, one or two Greek instruments might have got there also!

But this only the beginning of my reply, and I mention it merely to show how inexcusable the objection is. An explanation of the blunder may be possible; but to me it is inconceivable that any man, whose aim was to discover the truth and not merely to forge an argument, could have put this objection into words, and have suffered it to be published. He must have known *that it was utterly untrue* that no connection existed between Greece and the East before the time of Alexander the Great; and, knowing that, how could he in common honesty build up an argument and urge a conclusion which ignored undeniable fact? Dr. Driver owes an explanation to the public, which, I trust, will not be withheld.

I repeat, however, that my reply has only begun. There were other ways in which Greek instruments might have come into the East three or four centuries before that wonderful age of the Maccabees, which, according to the critics, originated so much of the Old Testament, but which managed to make or mend so little besides. Xerxes was in Greece in 480 B.C. Darius warred with it in 492 B.C. The Persians took many things back with them; might not two or three Greek instruments, and even Greek musicians, have well been among the spoils of an invaded country? The Persians held Cyprus in 518 B.C. They occupied Asia Minor (which was filled with Greek thought and Greek art) in 537 B.C. The book of Daniel does not claim to have been written earlier than 534 B.C. Plainly, therefore, Greek instruments might easily have arrived in time for mention by the sacred writer.

But it may be urged that all this applies only to the *Persian* period, whereas *Daniel* credits the use of these instruments to the time of Nebuchadnezzar, about 70 years earlier. I might reply that 70 years is a small margin to fight about. If Greek instruments could have got to Babylon in 534 B.C., it will be hard to believe that they could not have been there in 600 B.C. But there is no necessity for argument over this. I shall still let *facts* reply. So overwhelming is the answer furnished by these that what I have already stated is quite unnecessary, except to show the terrible recklessness of critical methods. Flinders Petrie, by his discovery of two Greek cities in Egypt, has, as he himself pointed out, blown this critical argument to atoms. He has unearthed in Egypt the ruins of the ancient Naukratis and Daphnae. Those cities were inhabited by 30,000 Greek troops, besides other settlers from Greece, as well as women and children, about 665 B.C. These mercenaries were the main reliance of the Pharaoh Psammetik for protection against foreign and domestic foes. Daphnae, or as it was named by the Egyptians and the Bible, Tahpanhes, was situated on the eastern border of Egypt, and was, so to say, the gate of Egypt which looked towards Palestine. "We cannot doubt," says Mr. Flinders Petrie, "that Tahpanhes—the first place on the road to Egypt—was a constant refuge for the Jews during the series of Assyrian invasions; especially as they met here, not the exclusive Egyptians, but a mixed foreign population, mostly Greeks. Here, then, was a ready source," he continues, "for the introduction of Greek words and names into Hebrew, long before the Alexandrian age; and *even before the fall of Jerusalem the Greek names of musical instruments* and other words may have been heard in the courts of Solomon's temple."\*

Here, then, was a source from which those few Greek instruments might have found their way to Babylon long before the time of Nebuchadnezzar. If it were my object merely to riddle the critical argument, what has now been advanced would be amply sufficient. But we want to know the truth about this, and I am thankful to say that, if there ever was any darkness on the subject, God has now showed us abundant light. He has enabled us to carry our reply still further. We are now acquainted with facts which grind this boasted critical argument to powder, and sweep it to the winds.

But, before I mention what I may call the crowning reply, I should like to make the reader acquainted with an argument which must have been known to Dr. Driver. Dr. Pusey, in his priceless volume on

---

\* *Ten Years' Digging in Egypt.*

*Daniel*, published in 1864, says that the presence of two or three Greek musical instruments in Babylon "would be nothing more remarkable than the corresponding fact that Greeks imported Syriac or Hebrew names of instruments, together with the instruments themselves, as *kinura, nabla*. We know that the Babylonians loved foreign music also, and that they saddened their Hebrew captives by bidding them *sing* to their harps some *of the songs of Zion* (Psalm cxxxvii. 2). Isaiah, foretelling the destruction of Babylon, says, "*Thy pomp is brought down to the grave, the noise of thy viols*" (nebaleica) (Isaiah xiv. 11). Babylon was a *city of merchants*;\* she *exulted in her ships*.† Her manufactures found their way to Palestine in the days of Joshua (vii. 21). The Euphrates connected Babylon downwards with India, and above even with Armenia and the line of Tyrian commerce, and, through Tyre, with Greece. Nebuchadnezzar had himself, at enormous expense, connected it with the Persian Gulf by a gigantic navigable canal. We know the rival lines of commerce—that from Sardis by land across to Armenia, and, beyond, to Susa; and that from Petra to Babylon, a transit both from Egypt and Tyre. Tyre again had its own northern line, through Tadmor (Palmyra) to Tiphsach (Thapsacus) and thence southward to Babylon. Thapsacus ‡ was the north-eastern extremity of the kingdom of Solomon; and the line of commerce, for which doubtless he built or re-built Tadmor, § was at least more than four centuries

---

\* Ezekiel xvii. 4.  † Isaiah xliii. 14.  ‡ 1 Kings iv. 24.  § 1 Kings ix. 18.

anterior to this date. The intercourse of Greece with Tyre, in ante-Homeric times, is evidenced by the use of a Phœnician or Hebrew word to designate 'gold.' Asia, from the Tigris westward, was systematically intersected with lines of commerce. Sardis and Babylon were proverbially luxurious. It were rather a marvel if *the golden* music-loving *city* (Isaiah xiv. 4) had not gathered to itself foreign musical instruments of all sorts, or if, in a religious inauguration at Babylon, all the variety of music which it could command had not been united to grace the festival and bear along the minds and imaginations of the people.

"The Greek names are but another instance of the old recognised fact that the name of an import travels with the thing. When we speak of tea, sugar, coffee, chocolate, cocoa, cassia, cinnamon, tobacco, myrrh, citrons, rice, potatoes, cotton, chintz, shawls, we do not stop to think that we are using Chinese, Malay, Arabic, Mexican, Hebrew, Malabar, South American, Bengalee, Persian words, and we shall continue to use them, even though they were originally misapplied, and we know that the word tobacco was the name, not of the plant but of the vessel out of which the natives smoked it. When Solomon's ships brought him the peacocks, apes, ivory, almug or algum wood, they brought with them also the Sanskrit and Malabar names of the ape (which passed thence into Greek and our European languages) and of the algum-wood; the Tamul name of the peacock, and the Sanskrit of the elephant. There is nothing stranger in our finding Greek instruments of music in Nebuchadnezzar's time at Babylon than in the Indian names of Indian animals and of an Indian tree having reached Jerusalem under Solomon. Perhaps there is a trace of trade in the female slaves, for which Phœnicia was early infamous, 900 years before Nebuchadnezzar, in the Pentateuch, there being no etymology for the Hebrew word "concubine," "pilegesh," or "pillegesh," in any Semitic or other Eastern language, while it does correspond with the Greek *Pallax* 'maiden.'" \*

"I have treated this question of the mention of Greek instruments," adds Dr. Pusey, "on what I believe to be the only philosophical ground, the fact of an old and extensive commerce between Babylon and the West. 'The name travelled with the thing,' is an acknowledged principle of philology. It needed not that a single Greek should have been at Babylon. Tyrian merchants took with them the names of the wares which they sold, just as our English merchants transmitted the names of our East Indian imports with them into Germany, or the Spaniards brought us back the American names of the products of the New World, or as at this day, I am told, some of our Manchester goods are known by the name of their eminent manufacturer in Tartary, where the face of an Englishman has probably been scarcely seen. Yet the actual intercourse of the Greeks with the East is now known to

---

\* *Lectures on Daniel, the Prophet,* p.p. 25-27.

## Greek Instruments in Daniel. 431

have been far greater than was formerly imagined. Brandis thus opens his book on the historical gain from the deciphering of the Assyrian incriptions:

"'Long before the Greeks began to write history they had, as friends and foes, come into manifold contact with the empire of the Assyrians. That Assyria took part in the Trojan war, as Ctesias and others related, no one would give out for an historical fact; but the battle and victory of Sennacherib in the 8th century B.C. over a Greek army which had penetrated into Cilicia is fully attested by a relation out of the Babylonian history of Berosus. On the other hand, the extensive commerce of Greek colonies must not unfrequently have led Greek merchants into Assyrian territory. Did they not penetrate even to the inhospitable steppes of Russia on the Dnieper and the Don? The most important, however, must have been the intercourse with the Assyrian provinces of Asia Minor, especially with the countries bordering on the Black Sea and the Mediterranean, and certainly with Lydia also, which, as appears, for above five hundred years, until near the end of the eighth century B.C., was dependent upon Assyria. In Cyprus too, where the Greeks traded, and the Assyrians had established themselves even in earlier times, these nations must have come into manifold contact. That Greeks came to Assyria itself as merchants must remain conjecture only, but certainly Esarhaddon, who, first of the Assyrian rulers, had a paid army, was accompanied by Greek soldiers also on his marches through Asia. Be this as it may, Anaximander's map of the world (he was born about 610 B.C.) implies an accurate acquaintance with the East. That the Westerns generally took more part in the revolutions of the East than we should have thought appears from the fragment of a poetical address of Alcæus to his brother Antimenides, who had won glory and reward under the banner of Nebuchadnezzar. The name of Javan, or Greece, occurs in the inscriptions of Sargon among those from whom he received tribute. We know that articles of luxury formed part of the tribute to Assyria. Sargon's statue found at Idalium commemorates an expedition against Cyprus. More recently, Labynetus I., of Babylon, had been present at the great invasion of the Lydians by Cyaxares. It was no great matter for monarchs who transported a monolith obelisk from Armenia and moved those colossal bulls, and brought cedars from Lebanon, to import a few Greek musical instruments. Either way, then, whether as spoils of war or articles of commerce, Greek instruments of music might easily have found their way to Babylon. In the monuments even of Sennacherib, the Assyrian generals, says Layard, are represented as welcomed by bands of men and women, dancing, singing, and playing upon instruments of music. We find from various passages in the Scriptures that the instruments of music chiefly used on such triumphant occasions were the harp, one with ten strings (rendered viol or lyre in some versions, but probably a kind of dulcimer), the tabor and the pipe; precisely those represented in the bas-reliefs. First came five men; three carried harps of many strings, which they struck with both hands; a fourth played on the double pipes, such as are seen on the monuments of Egypt, and were used by the Greeks and Romans. They were blown at the end like the flutes of the modern yezidis, which they probably resembled in tone and form. The fifth musician carried an instrument not unlike the modern santour of the East, consisting of a number of strings stretched over a hollow case or sounding-board. 'The santour of the East' was recognised by Gesenius as the *pesanterin* of Daniel. Even the two ways of spelling, which occur in Daniel, recur in the modern Arabic instrument. The psaltery, as described by S. Augustine, corresponds with the 'santour' as recognised by Layard on the bas-reliefs of Babylon."\*

Now all this, I repeat, *was published in* 1864. There is quite enough in it to demolish the argument from the Greek instruments. How did it happen that an argument like this, backed up by so many statements of alleged fact, was neither dealt with nor acknowledged? Its existence could not have been unknown to Dr. Driver. Will any reader ask himself whether *he*, knowing what I have now quoted, could have written and published in 1894: "These words, it may be confidently affirmed, could not have been used in the Book of Daniel, unless it had

---

\* *Ibid.* pp. 30-33.

been written *after the dissemination of Greek influences in Asia through the conquests of Alexander the Great?*" I have again to explain that the italics are Dr. Driver's. They may be taken to emphasize the value which should be attached to the statements and conclusions of the "Higher Criticism." But the progress of discovery has been still more unkind to Dr. Driver and his friends. Their contention is that a Greek musical instrument could not have got even to Palestine, not to speak of Babylon, before the time of Alexander the Great. The Tel-el-Amarna tablets refer to an Ionian who was on a mission to the country of Tyre before the time of Moses.* The writing and the language which was at that time used in Palestine for political purposes, were the Babylonian, so closely had the Palestinian and the Mesopotamian peoples been brought together even in that early time. What becomes now of the critical judgment that the East was hermetically sealed, so far as concerns Greek influence, till the time of Alexander the Great?

But we have the most positive proof that one Greek instrument at least got to Nineveh some forty or fifty years before Nebuchadnezzar began to reign. The *cithara* (or harp), with seven strings, was invented by Terpander, a Greek musician and poet, about 650 B.C. This event and date are fixed by Greek testimony. But that same seven-stringed harp is sculptured upon a monument erected by Assurbanipal, king of Assyria, about this very time.

---

* Sayce, *The Higher Criticism and the Monuments*, p. 20.

"This invention," says M. Lenormant, "is ascribed to Terpander about 650 B.C.; and on the Assyrian monuments this *cithara* with seven strings appears only from the time of Assurbanipal (668-625). The coincidence of these dates," he adds, "is striking." With that observation even Dr. Driver must agree. Here is an undoubted proof that *one* Greek instrument found its way to Mesopotamia at least thirty years before Daniel was born. We might argue that, if *one* did so, there was nothing to hinder others finding their way there, too. But, as Lenormant says, the *coincidence* of the dates is striking. *No time was lost* in carrying Terpander's invention to the Assyrian Court. This proves that an enterprising commerce was at that time in full activity between Assyria and Greece, and that Greek musical instruments were purchased and valued by Assyrians and Babylonians before the time of Daniel.

This contention, then, which has wrecked the faith of so many, and which is even now the confidence of scholarly men in their rejection of this Book, has been completely overthrown by that one discovery. But *all the instruments named* are found upon the monuments of Babylon and Assyria. These sculptures show us, indeed, not the instruments only, but even the manner in which they were played. And here we are forced to carry the war into the enemy's camp. They have attacked us, and they have been defeated; we have now to pursue their retreating forces, for, as honest men, they are bound to deal with the facts which have been disclosed.

and to give some rational account of them. Here we have in *Daniel* a minute description of Babylonian music. We are told that certain specified instruments were used by the court musicians in the time of Nebuchadnezzar. We are also told that a large number of musical instruments of many kinds was employed. Both statements are found to be minutely and absolutely correct. These statements are consequently proved to be the result of a full and accurate knowledge of the place and time. They are not chance hits; they are pictures of fact. Was that knowledge possible to a Palestinian Jew writing four hundred years after the Babylonian civilisation was overthrown? Does it not plainly and unmistakably speak of a knowledge possible only to one who was personally acquainted with the things of which he speaks?

There is another fact which makes this knowledge still more remarkable, and which, therefore, gives a still sharper point to my questions. It was first of all imagined that it was only a childish invention to give music this place in a Babylonian state ceremony. The discoveries in Chaldea have shown that here so-called learning was only self-confident ignorance. The employment of music has that very place in the great state ceremonials of Babylon at that very time. This is abundantly proved by inscriptions and by sculptures. So essential a feature was the employment of music in the great state functions of the period, that Assurbanipal mentions the presence of musicians at his triumphal entry into Nineveh at the close of one of his campaigns. It will be seen also that he counts foreign musical instruments and instrumentalists among his chiefest spoils. He says: "I brought alive Dunan and his brethren from the midst of that city (Sapibel); his wife, his sons, his daughters, his concubines, his male musicians, and his female musicians, I led forth, and as booty I counted. Silver, gold, furniture, and the instruments of his palace I carried away, and as booty I counted. With the booty of Elam and the spoils of Gambul, which my hands had taken by commandment of Assur, *with musicians playing music, I entered into Nineveh in the midst of rejoicings.*" In another of the same monarch's inscriptions he speaks of having received a command from the goddess Istar "to glorify her divinity" by a musical solemnity.

But the reply which we are now enabled to give, is still more complete. The part assigned to music was *a comparatively new feature*. It would not have been true of a *much* earlier period. "Under Assurnazirpal," says M. Lenormant, "musicians occupy a small place in the representations of festivals, and they are in possession of only three instruments, a kind of harp, held horizontally and played with a plectrum, a lyre played with the hand, and the cymbal. Under the successors of Sargon, on the contrary, the troops of musicians figure every moment in the bas-reliefs, just as their presence is frequently mentioned in the inscriptions. The musicians of that time use a dozen different instruments." Can we wonder that this great Assyriologist turns upon his critical friends with the remark: "An author separated from the events by four centuries would have been a veritable scholar such as his age could hardly parallel if he had known this circumstance, attested by the texts and by the figures on the monuments, that instrumental music, little used by the first Assyrian kings, had become, *precisely at the opening of the seventh century,* a chief element of all religious and public ceremonies in Assyria and at Babylon."* This also the critics have got to explain. For us the explanation has long ago been found. *Daniel* is not only the word of truth: it is the word of God.

---
* Fr. Lenormant, *La Divination chez les Chaldeens*, p. 190.

## CHAPTER XI.

### Babylonian Traits in Daniel.

THE much-debated question of the musical instruments has detained us long, but there are some other matters in the third chapter of *Daniel* which will repay notice. We have an incidental allusion, for example, to the kind of dress worn at that time in Babylon. The king's command that the Hebrew martyrs should be burned alive was so urgent that there was no time to undress the victims of his wrath or to make any change whatever in their attire. This made the miracle the more astounding; for, when they were brought out, these garments showed how perfectly God had preserved His servants from injury. Not only had the fire "no power" upon their "bodies," but "neither were their coats changed, nor had the smell of fire passed upon them" (verse 21).

It is in this way that we have the mention, to which I refer, of the martyrs' dress. In verse 21 we read: "Then these men were bound in their coats, their hosen, and their hats, and their (other) garments, and were cast into the midst of the burning fiery furnace." *Sarbalehon*, the word rendered "coats," means "mantles," long robes which formed the upper garments. "Hosen" *(Patishehon)* turns out to be a mistranslation. The *Patish* seems to have been the same as the *Petasos* of the Greeks —a covering or decoration for the head. The word translated "hats," *Karbelathon*, on the other hand, is an Assyrian word for the under garment or tunic "which was kept close to the figure of the wearer by the girdle or belt so essential to the Babylonian costume. It is probably the same as the *Kulubultu* of the Assyrian inscriptions (Norris, 'Assyrian Dictionary,' II., 560)."\*

Here, then, we have a description of the dress worn by Babylonian nobles on a great festive occasion. There is an outer and an under or shorter garment specified, as well as an adornment or covering for the head. In such a matter it was the easiest thing in the world for an author writing in a late age to go wrong, and an almost impossible thing for him to give an exact description. On the other hand, it would have been as easy for Daniel to have described the dress of his friends with unfailing exactness as it would be for us to indicate the ordinary dress of people of our own time or rank in society. If the book is of the late time, that the critics say it originated in, here is a place, then, where the writer will give himself away. His disguise will be thrown aside; for the Palestinian

---

\* *Speaker's Commentary*, Vol. vi., p. 280.

Jew of the time of the Maccabees, who (they say) is trying to pass himself off as Daniel the prophet, will betray the notions and the customs of his place and time.

Now, there is one most significant fact which no critic can ignore or explain. The Aramean of Daniel was not understood when the Septuagint translation was made. The "seventy" who rendered *Daniel* into Greek did not know what to make of the first word *sarbalehon*—mantles or long robes. They translated it in verse 21 by *hypodemata*, sandals, and in another place by *sarabara*, that is, the loose Persian trousers. They were evidently quite "at sea," and whether *sarbalehon* meant sandals, trousers, or something else, they were unable to say. Such was the state of uncertainty of these learned Jews at the very time when the critics say *Daniel* was written in Aramean and in Hebrew! How, then, could the alleged forger have used with such appropriateness a word of the meaning of which the most learned of his own people had not the slightest knowledge?

But the writer of *Daniel* not only used the word correctly, he also takes us back into the midst of the time. He presents, in this incidental allusion, a correct picture of the Babylonian costume. We have two sources of independent information regarding the usual array of the people among whom Daniel's lot was cast. "The dress of the Babylonians," says Herodotus, "is a linen tunic reaching to the feet, and above it another tunic made in wool, besides which they have a short white cloak thrown around them, and shoes of a peculiar fashion, not unlike those worn by the Bœotians. They have long hair, wear turbans on their heads, and anoint their whole body with perfumes."

The other source of information is the monuments, "The dress of the Babylonians," says Rawlinson in a note on the above passage, "appears on the cylinders to be a species of flounced robe, reaching from their neck to their feet. In some representations there is an appearance of a division into two garments; the upper one being a sort of short jacket or tippet, flounced like the under-robe or petticoat. This would seem to be the *chlanidion*, or short cloak of Herodotus. The long petticoat would be his *kithon podenikes lineos* ('linen tunic reaching to the feet'). The upper woollen tunic may be hidden by the tippet or *chlanidion*. . . . There are several varieties of head-dress; the most usual are a low cap or turban, from which two curved horns branch out, and a high crown or mitre, the appearance of which is very remarkable." * But in any case the fact stands thus; Herodotus notes what the cylinders also indicate. There are *three* portions of Babylonian attire that specially attract attention. One is a mantle or long robe, the second is a shorter garment which fits close to the body, the third is the Babylonian head-dress. There are other parts of the ordinary attire, but they do not call for special mention. How is it that the Scripture has mentioned

---

* Rawlinson's *Herodotus*, Vol. i., p. 269.

these three specially? Is there not an evidence there of a knowledge of the period which no man could have had after the Babylonian civilisation had passed away, unless he possessed an acquaintance with antiquities which is a feature only of the age in which we live? Even in so small a matter as this we have to acknowledge the stamp of the time.

A similar testimony is supplied by the enumeration of the great officials of the Empire. "Then Nebuchadnezzar the king sent to gather together the princes, the governors, and the captains, the judges, the treasurers, the counsellors, the sheriffs, and all the rulers of the provinces" (*Dan.* iii. 2). "There is not one of the titles," writes Fr. Lenormant, "of this enumeration which does not correspond to a genuine Assyrian title, mentioned in the documents of the kings of Nineveh and of Babylon. It would be an easy task to point out their correspondence with certainty. But it is to be noted that for two only of these titles—*Pahat* and *Sakan*, nearly corresponding to those of *Pacha* and *Kihaya*—has the Assyrian form been preserved. For all the others the Aramean text gives equivalents. . . . If this book," he continues, "had been invented at the time of Antiochus Epiphanes we should have had it in some Greek words . . . we should have had at least the title of *strategos* (general), which was received without delay into the Semitic languages as we see it in Aramean inscriptions."[*] It will be difficult to escape the force of that observation. It

---

[*] *La Divination chez les Chaldeens*, pp. 198, 199.

is contended that the book was written at a time and in a land where thought had been saturated with Greek ideas and where speech had been filled with Greek words for nearly 200 years. And yet this writer completely detaches himself from the thought, speech, and institutions of his time; he soars above them all, casting off every particle and trace, and he rises into the speech and thought and institutions of a time long passed away, and of which he could have known nothing; and he so writes that every word recalls that buried past! Is it conceivable that such a feat should be done?

Other confirmations of the absolute genuineness of the book meet us in this third chapter; but before I pass to these, let me direct the reader's attention to an instance of critical mistake which will point its own moral. In the fourth verse, we read: "Then an herald cried aloud, To you it is commanded, O people," &c. Here a great discovery was formerly supposed to be made. The Aramean word for herald here is *karoza*. Upon this the critical finger descended with prompt decision and exceeding jubilation. Here was, without the slightest doubt, *kerux*, the *Greek* word for herald! Now, there is certainly a close resemblance, and it might have been regarded as quite enough to lead to inquiry. It was within the limits of possibility, for example, that the Greek word might have been derived from the Oriental root. But the shameful thing about these "difficulties" of "pious men," and "sanctified scholarship," is that, instead of inquiry, there has been suspicion, and even loud-voiced and jubilant condemnation. What should we say were any friend of ours treated in such fashion? And what will God say of such treatment of that Word which should be trusted beyond all else, and on whose honour no breath of suspicion should be cast?

But the folly of this attack has been made as manifest as its impious temerity. The word *karoza is found to be a Semitic and not a Greek word! Karoza* occurs in the Assyrian and Babylonian inscriptions in the sense of "edict." "It is also found on an Assyrian coin of the 7th or 8th century B.C. (De Vogue *Melanges d'Archeologie Orientale,* p. 125). 'Our engraved gem,' says M. de Vogue, 'proves to us the use of the root *karaz* at an epoch not only earlier than *Daniel,* but prior to any intervention of Greece in Aramean affairs.'" *

Let us now mark several other incidents in this third chapter of Daniel on which light has been cast by recent discoveries. There is nothing said in the book about Nebuchadnezzar's veneration for the gods; but his expressions, his zeal, and his repentings all bear the stamp of exceeding devoutness. Every reflecting reader of Scripture has been astonished by this feature in the heathen king's character. His words not unfrequently glow with the fire of profoundly earnest, though uninstructed, devotion. This characteristic appears in the great solemnity on the plain of Dura. It is when the representation is

---

* *Speaker's Commentary,* Vol. vi., p. 279.

made to him that the three friends of Daniel serve not his gods, nor worship the image that he has set up, that "Nebuchadnezzar in his rage and fury commanded to bring Shadrach, Meshach, and Abednego" before him (Dan. iii. 12, 13). And when the reply was given, "Be it known unto thee, O king, that we will not serve thy gods nor worship the golden image which thou hast set up, then was Nebuchadnezzar full of fury" (verses 18, 19).

Though evidently an image of himself, the erection and the worship of the statue was in some way connected with the worship of the gods of Babylon: Nebuchadnezzar claimed to be descended from the gods and to share their divine nature. His own worship might thus be closely associated with that of the national gods. But what I ask the reader to note is the king's religious zeal. His deepest indignation is aroused by this Jewish insult flung upon the divinities of the land. He is so concerned for their honour that every consideration of friendship is cast away. He knows the value of these men's service, and the loss which their death will cause to the State. But nothing can restrain him. His gods are so dear to him that the refusal to worship them can only be atoned for by death in its most terrific form. Even the ordinary furnace, flaming fiercely though it be, is not terrible enough to meet the necessities of the occasion, and so the order is given that it be heated seven times, till every stone glows like molten metal, and the men who are charged to cast the victims into the mouth of the furnace perform their service at the cost of their lives.

We turn then to the monuments, and ask, have *they* anything to tell us of this man, and can they say whether this pronounced religious devotion was a feature in the great monarch's character? It so happens that several inscriptions have been recovered in which Nebuchadnezzar speaks for himself. What is called "The India House Inscription" is of great length, and is in good preservation. Mr. Ball says of it *(Records of the Past,* New Series, iii. 102), "The inscription paints for us in unfading colours a portrait of the man Nebuchadnezzar; it exhibits, in the vivid light of actuality, his pride of place and power of greatness, his strong conviction of his own divine call to universal empire, *his passionate devotion to his gods, his untiring labours for their glory,* and the aggrandisement of that peerless capital which was their chosen dwelling-place."

Nebuchadnezzar's words fully support this testimony. He says that he "daily bethought him" of the great temples of Babylon. "The holy places of the god" (Merodach), he continues, "I regarded, the way of the god I walked in. Of Merodach, the great lord, the god my creator, his cunning works highly do I extol. Of Nebo, his true son, the beloved of my majesty, the way of his supreme godhead steadfastly do I exalt; with all my true heart I love the fear of their godhead, I worship their lordship. When Merodach, the great lord, lifted up the head of my majesty, and with lordship over the multitude of peoples invested me; and Nebo, the overseer of the multitude of heaven and earth, for the governing of the peoples a righteous sceptre placed in my hands; for me, of them I am heedful, I have regard unto their godhead."

The inscription is full of such expressions, but I confine myself to one more extract. It is a prayer presented by Nebuchadnezzar to the king of the gods. "To Merodach, my lord, I made supplication, prayers to him I undertook, and the word which my heart looked for, to him I spake: 'Of old, O Prince, lord of all that is! for the kingdom thou lovest and whose name thou callest, that to thee is pleasing; thou leadest him aright, a straight path thou appointest him. I am a prince obedient unto thee, a creature of thy hands; thou it was that madest me, and with sovereignty over the multitude of the peoples didst invest me; according to thy goodness, O Lord, wherewith thou crownest all of them. Thy lordship supreme do thou make loving, and the fear of thy godhead cause thou to be in my heart; yea, grant that to thee is pleasing, for my life truly thou makest."

Here, then, Nebuchadnezzar reveals himself. He himself comes and tells us what he was, what thoughts lived in him, what motives swayed him. There can be no doubt about the reality of the disclosure. We see the man, and, when we have looked, we find the Nebuchadnezzar of reality, *the Nebuchadnezzar of the Bible*. Was it possible for any writer of "pious," or other fiction—separated by centuries from the time in which Nebuchadnezzar lived, and writing at a period when the great king was only a name—so to recall him from the dead? Archæologists have drawn attention to another incident in the Scripture narrative—the accusation laid before the king by intriguing courtiers. The monuments show that this was a danger attending court life in Assyria and Babylonia. An official, for example, presents a memorial, which is still in existence, accusing certain other officials of misappropriating gold intended for a statue of king Assurbanipal. It was quite in keeping, therefore, with the usages of the time and place that the officials should seize this occasion when their malice could assume the form of zeal for the gods and for the most sacred feelings of the king.

Professor Cheyne has made a remarkable admission with regard to *Daniel*. In an article in Vol. vi. of the last edition of the *Encyclopædia Britannica* he says: "There are three undoubted points of agreement with Babylonian customs, viz., the punishment of burning alive (Dan. iii. 6); the description of the dress of the courtiers (iii. 21); and the mention of the presence of women at feasts (v. 2)." We have already noted what has compelled the admission in regard to the second point. We shall by and by see what necessity exists in regard to the third, and I hope now, in closing the present chapter, to show that there is equal urgency for admission in regard to the first. But the significance of Canon Cheyne's words should be closely marked. It is a confession which is quite new in critical notices of *Daniel*. The book was at first supposed to bear everywhere the stamp of a late origin. But the unveiling of the Babylon of Daniel's time has proved that, even in what must have been unstudied references and details, the book bears the stamp, not of the late period and of the place where and when the critics believed the book to have been written, but of Babylon, and of the Babylon of Daniel's day.

The punishment threatened by Nebuchadnezzar's proclamation is of a very special kind—burning in a furnace of fire. There is another reference to the same thing in Scripture. In Jer. xxix. 21-23 a fearful end is predicted for two false prophets who added to their impiety unbridled immorality. "Of them," says the Scripture, "shall be taken up a curse by all the captivity of Judah which are in Babylon, saying, the Lord make thee like Zedekiah and like Ahab, whom the king of Babylon roasted in the fire." Here is clearly an indication that either for crimes of a special character or among the tortures inflicted upon captured enemies, the Babylonians employed that of burning alive. But *Daniel* carries us further than this. The punishment of burning alive has been inflicted in historical, we might almost say recent, times in our own land. It has, however, been administered in one definite fashion. It has been burning "at the stake." The victim was securely bound by chains to a stake or post, and fagots or other combustible materials were heaped up around. When the moment came for execution the torch was applied, and the mass was fired. From the account which has been preserved of the martyrdom of Polycarp, this was the practice among the Greeks of Asia Minor during the Roman Empire. Burning by fire was also practised in the case of the deceased and of widows down to our times in India. We have a reference to the same custom in what is told us of the punishment at first assigned to Crœsus, the king of Lydia, by Cyrus. But in these latter instances a pile of wood was erected on which the dead or the living was placed. There is no mention of *the furnace* which forms so peculiar a feature in the description contained in the third chapter of Daniel. "Whoso falleth not down and worshippeth," the Babylonian herald proclaimed, "shall the same hour be cast into the midst of a burning fiery furnace" (verse 6). Reference to this furnace is made again and again, as if its employment added terror even to this fearful form of capital punishment. The description is consequently as definite as it is unique. If we have in this, as Professor Cheyne admits, a distinctly Babylonian trait, it will carry us a fair way to a conclusion in this controversy that will set our judgment on the side of those who refuse to believe in a late origin for this book of Scripture.

That the trait *is* Babylonian will be seen from the following. Assurbanipal, the Sardanapalus of the Greeks and one of the last kings of Assyria, tells in his Annals of a terrible vengeance which he took upon a prince named Dunanu. On the march to

Nineveh, apparently, he hung round the captive's neck the decapitated head of his friend and ally, Teumman, king of Elam. His tongue was afterwards pulled out, and he was flayed alive. We should have imagined that even the most fiendish ferocity could not have gone further than this. But Dunanu had been guilty of what, in the eyes of Assurbanipal, was one of the greatest possible crimes, and he must needs suffer yet more. "Dunanu and Nebonzalli, men who were over Gambuli," says the inscription, "who against my gods uttered great curses, in Arbela their tongues I pulled out. I flayed off their skin. Dunanu in Nineveh over a furnace they placed him, and consumed him entirely." *

This happened about fifty years before Daniel was carried to Babylon. The punishment of burning alive in a furnace was, therefore, one known to the Assyrians and Babylonians, and was practised by them at this very time. Another confirmatory feature is that burning alive in a furnace of fire was the punishment specially allotted to impiety. Dunanu is burned for the specified reason that he had uttered great curses against Assurbanipal's gods. This is the very offence, be it remembered, with which Shadrach, Meshach, and Abednego are charged. Nebuchadnezzar puts it to them: "Is it true, O Shadrach, Meshach, and Abednego? Do not ye serve my gods, nor worship the image which I have set up?" And it is when they reply, "Be it

---

*Records of the Past*, Vol. ix. (1st series), p. 56.

known unto thee, O king, that we will not serve thy gods, nor worship the golden image which thou hast set up," that the decree is issued, and the furnace heated to sevenfold intensity.

The case of Dunanu does not stand alone. On the palace walls of this same king, Assurbanipal, at Koyoundyik, the punishment itself is depicted. Two men are being burned alive after their tongues are plucked out, and the accompanying inscription informs us that they are being punished for their impiety. "The celebrated 'Inscription of Khorsabad,'" says the Rev. J. M. Fuller, M.A., in the *Speaker's Commentary* (Vol. vi., p. 272), "records burning and flaying as punishments inflicted on the king of Hamath and his allies (B.C. 714), and a similar fate befel Assourlih (B.C. 712)." But we have a more striking instance still. It is that of a great State execution, by burning in a fiery furnace, in Babylon itself. Assurbanipal records the revolt of Saulmagina, his younger brother, whom he had made Viceroy of Babylon. Saulmagina became the leader in a great revolt, not only in Babylonia, but over a large part of the conquests of Assyria. In the beginning of the war Assurbanipal was encouraged, he tells us, by a vision. "In those days, then, a seer in the beginning of the night slept, and dreamed a dream thus: Concerning the matter which Sin was arranging, and of them who against Assurbanipal, king of Assyria, devised evil. Battle is prepared; a violent death I appoint for them. With the edge of the sword, the burning of fire, famine, and the judgment ôf Ninip, I will destroy their lives." The inscription afterwards relates: "Saulmagina, my rebellious brother, who made war with me; in the fierce burning fire they threw him and destroyed his life" *(Records of the Past,* 1st series, Vol. i., pages 76, 77, 79). The words "fierce burning fire" may mean that, as in the case of the three Jewish martyrs, the furnace was heated to an unwonted intensity.

The narrative implies a certain form of furnace, which is also in accord with ancient remains. The king sees four men walking about in the flames. This implies that he was able to see the furnace floor. There must, therefore, have been an opening in front, as well as one at the top, where the criminals were usually thrown in. An old Roman furnace for baking earthenware, found in Northamptonshire, and described in Smith's *Dictionary of Antiquities,* may give us an idea of the usual structure. "The dome-shaped roof has been destroyed, but the flat circular floor on which the earthenware was set to be baked is preserved entire. The middle of this floor is supported by a thick column of brickwork, which is encircled by the oven. *The entrance to the oven is seen in front.*"

One point more remains to be noted. It has been objected that the keeping of a furnace burning before it was known that anyone would dare to disobey the decree, is extremely improbable. We need not argue the point, as the customs of "the unchanging East" make argument needless. The punishment of burning alive in a fiery furnace was in existence during the seventeenth century, and this very precaution of keeping the furnace burning to enforce a decree was then exemplified. Chardin, in his "Travels in Persia," published in 1711, says that Ali Kooli Khan, commander-in-chief of the Persian army, "caused one large furnace to be built before the palace and another in the public square, and commanded the criers to proclaim that those who sold their bread at a higher than the fixed price, or who concealed their wheat, should be cast alive into them. These furnaces burned continually for a month, but no one was thrown into them, because no one chose to risk the experience of such rigorous punishment by his disobedience." The burning of the furnaces emphasized the decree, and invested the threatened punishment with the desired terribleness.

## CHAPTER XII.

### NEBUCHADNEZZAR'S MADNESS.

THERE is one striking feature in the present controversy which should be pondered. If believers in the Bible were conscious of weakness they would be struck with doubt or fear whenever the monuments unfolded a piece of real history that enables us to check the Bible account, or when they presented us with the actual portrait of some Bible character. There would be a shrinking from the test and a fainting of heart amid the broadening challenge of modern discoveries. But, as everyone knows, there is no one who so rejoices in the increasing results of these researches as the believer in the Bible. The various societies, under whose auspices and with whose resources these researches are pushed, are almost wholly sustained by believers in the Bible. They rejoice in every fact brought to light that has the remotest bearing on the Scripture. The growing popularity of these archæological enterprises may be said to be due to this deepening interest of theirs. The detractors of the Bible, on the other hand, find themselves increasingly hampered, corrected, and confuted by these discoveries. The sweeping condemnation which they have passed upon certain books, such as Chronicles and Esther, has had to be modified and in large part withdrawn.

This fact, I repeat, is one to be pondered. The monuments have corrected the critic, and comforted and strengthened the believer. Could any book stand these repeated and unexpected tests that was not absolutely true, and could men welcome with joy any new opportunity of having a book they love tested, whose faith in it had not cast out fear? This fourth chapter of *Daniel* gives us another chance of submitting the claims of the book to the arbitrament of facts. It is a chance which my readers and myself hail with gladness. To have to pass over this chapter would have been a disappointment, and it is with relief that we recognise that here also the glories of the Word of Truth are to be again disclosed.

The fourth chapter is a Babylonian State document. It is a proclamation of the great king to his subjects. He tells how he dreamed of a great tree which spread out its branches over the earth, giving shelter and food to "all flesh." As he looked he heard the command given from on high to cut the tree down, but to leave the stump of his roots in the earth; "let it be wet with the dew of heaven, and let his portion be with the beasts in the grass of the earth; let his heart be changed from man's, and let a beast's heart be given unto him; and let seven times pass over him." The dream is interpreted by Daniel, and the king testifies that the prediction was literally fulfilled. "He was driven from men, and did eat grass as oxen" (Dan. iv. 33).

Critics, in reading this document, have found doubts grow upon them at every step. Assyriologists, on the other hand, are impressed by the Babylonian character of the document, and are surprised by references to facts that are now well known, and which could not have been known to anyone not well acquainted with the times. But the malady of Nebuchadnezzar is of so strange a nature that the Babylonian traits in the narratives must be postponed till I have dealt with it. Critics have argued as if this one thing were quite enough to prove that the book is a collection of fables. "The seven years' malady of Nebuchadnezzar is strange and improbable,"* writes Dr. Samuel Davidson.

Modern investigation has shown that the malady though strange is not improbable. "It is now conceded," says Dr. Pusey, "that the madness of Nebuchadnezzar agrees with the description of a rare sort of disease called lycanthropy, from one form of it, of which our earliest notice is in a Greek medical writer of the fourth century after our Lord, in which the sufferer retains his consciousness in other respects, but imagines himself to be changed into some animal, and acts, up to a certain

---

* *Introduction to the Old Testament*, Vol. iii., p. 184.

## Nebuchadnezzar's Madness. 459

point, in conformity with that persuasion. Those who imagine themselves changed into wolves howled like wolves, and (there is reason to believe falsely) accused themselves of bloodshed. Others imitated the cries of dogs; it is said that others thought themselves nightingales, lions, cats, or cocks, and these crowed like a cock. It was no dissimilar form of disease, that others imagined that their bodies were wholly or in part changed into some brittle substance, whence they avoided contact, lest they should be broken. Others had similar delusions, varying incidentally from each other.

"The monotony of the descriptions of the disease seems to imply that it was very rare. Marcellus (fourth century) mentions two sorts. 'They who are seized by the kynanthropic or lycanthropic disease, in the month of February go forth by night, imitating in all things wolves or dogs, and until day especially live near tombs.' Aetius (end of fifth century) quotes the exact statement; giving his account also of the symptoms, and of remedies. Paulus of Aegina (latter half of seventh century) omits only kynanthropy. Further, Galen, I believe, only mentions one case, of one who acted like a cock. 'Another, hearing cocks crow, as they, before they crow, clap their wings, so he, flapping against his sides, imitated the noise of the animals.' Trallian, again (in the sixth century), mentioned the same form of disease only; 'others think they are a cock, and imitate its crowing.' The notices, moreover, in the Middle Ages are rare. Mostly, one only occurs in an author, writing on the subject of melancholic alienation; and the repetition of the same stories in modern writers shows how little, in addition, modern experience furnishes. The disease is one from which there have been recoveries. Mercurialis says: 'The disease is horrible, yet not destructive to life, even if it last for months; nay, I have *read* that it has been thoroughly cured after years.' The exact form of the disease, which would be Boanthropy, I have not found any notice of; perhaps because the howling of wolves, or dogs, or the crowing of cocks, are most heard by night, and are more piercing sounds, and so make most impression on a diseased brain. The remarkable expressions, *his heart was made like the beasts, let a beast's heart be given him*, fit most naturally with this form of disease. This would be its most literal and exhaustive explanation. The rest of the description would be in conformity with this, that Nebuchadnezzar, when affected with this disease, ate grass as an ox, and allowed his hair and nails to grow, unshorn and unpared, as if he was the animal." *

Dr. Pusey, who has treated this question with such thoroughness that his book is likely to long remain the one authority on the subject, points out several additional confirmations of the narrative. It is said, for example, that during Nebuchadnezzar's madness, his nails became "like birds' claws" (Dan. iv. 33). "The growth of the nails described, is exactly that which modern physiologists have stated

---

* *Daniel the Prophet*, pp. 425-428.

## Nebuchadnezzar's Madness. 461

to be their growth, when so neglected. ... 'The nails,' says Kölliker, '*so long as they are cut*, grow unremittingly; when this is omitted, their growth is confined. In this case, as may be observed in the sick when long bedridden, and in the people of Eastern Asia, the nails become one-and-a-half or two inches long, and *curve* round the fingers and ends of the toes. The principles which regulate the excessive growth of hair are, Dr. Rolleston tells me, less ascertained. Both being, I believe, called excremental, the excessive growth of both would probably be simultaneous. But both may have been the result of that personal neglect, which is so strangely humiliating, a part of the most distressing form of mental disease, and which I have seen as the result of disappointed pride."

Another very remarkable part of the narrative is that Nebuchadnezzar is said to have prayed *before* his reason returned. His prayer was not the result, therefore, of a sane interval. The return to sanity was, on the contrary, the consequence of the prayer. Here, it might be imagined, was a direct departure from all that is probable. Can the insane pray? Dr. Pusey has replied to this question also. "Whichever was the form," he says, "of Nebuchadnezzar's disease, not even the extreme form of insanity interferes with the inner consciousness, or, consequently, with the power to pray. Altomar gives an instance of lycanthropy, which he had himself witnessed, in which neither consciousness nor memory was at all impaired. The person who had thought himself a wolf, asked him afterwards whether he was not afraid of him. An eye-witness has related to me how, when visiting an asylum, one accompanied him, who made such acute observations on the several forms of insanity of the other patients severally, that the visitor expressed his surprise how he came to be confined there. 'Oh, I am a cock,' was the instant answer, and he began crowing and flapping his arms; just as the disease is described by Galen."

He also details the experiences of the Père Surin, who for several years was afflicted with a severe form of madness, who all the while not only prayed, but enjoyed communion with God. I have quoted largely from Dr. Pusey, but must also add the following:—" Dr. Browne, who has done more, I am told, than any other of our day for mental disease, tells me, as the result of the experience of above thirty years, ' My opinion is that of all mental powers or conditions, the idea of personal identity is but rarely enfeebled, and that it never is extinguished. The Ego and non-Ego may be confused. The Ego, however, continues to preserve its personality. All the angels, devils, dukes, lords, kings, 'gods-many,' that I have had under my care, remained what they were before they became angels, dukes, &c., in a sense, and even nominally. I have seen a man declaring himself the Saviour or St. Paul sign himself *James Thomson*, and attend worship as regularly as if the notion of Divinity had never entered into his head.'

## Nebuchadnezzar's Madness. 463

"I think it probable—because consistent with experience in similar forms of mental affection—that Nebuchadnezzar retained a perfect consciousness that he *was* Nebuchadnezzar during the whole course of his degradation, and while he ate 'grass as oxen,' and that he may have prayed fervently that the cup might pass from him.

"A very large proportion of the insane pray, and to the living God, and in the words supplied at their mother's knee or by the Church; and this, whatever may be the form or extent of the alienation under which they laboured, and whatever the transformation, in the light of their own delusions, they may have undergone. There is no doubt that the sincerity and the devotional feeling is as strong in these worshippers as in the sane." \*

In this particular also, therefore, the description in the fourth chapter of *Daniel* is in striking agreement with fact. Now, how is all this to be accounted for? Nebuchadnezzar is afflicted with a disease so extremely rare that critics believed its existence to be incredible. The description is, nevertheless, found to be so much in accordance with fact that no physician, writing on the subject, would hesitate to include Nebuchadnezzar's malady among historical instances of it. The detail also about the form assumed by the nails is equally correct, though equally removed from ordinary observation. Must we not come to the conclusion that here again the critics have been wrong, and

---
\* *Ibid*, p. 432.

that the Scripture has been assailed in ignorance and with a rash confidence that are among the most deplorable exhibitions of human foolhardiness and incompetency?

Let us now inquire what recent exploration has to say upon this matter. While critics had found doubts grow upon them as they pondered the 4th chapter of *Daniel*, Assyriologists, on the contrary, found certainty deepen the longer they studied it. The very form of the document is no mean argument for its genuineness. English history affords no instance in which sovereigns take their people into their confidence regarding either their maladies or their dreams, and issue such a proclamation to their subjects, although they have had this of Nebuchadnezzar's before them for centuries. It was no part of the Imperial customs of Rome, or of the dominions which sprang from the Empire of Alexander the Great. More than this, it was not customary among the Jewish or Israelitish peoples. Hezekiah is sick, and is marvellously healed; but, while the Scripture records a *song* of thanksgiving to God, it is silent regarding any proclamation to Hezekiah's subjects. David is in straits and is delivered. Again, the story is told in Psalms as well as in sacred history; but we have nothing at any time like this edict of the Babylonian king.

Now, this is the thing that strikes the Assyriologist—that, while such a proceeding was not in accord with Jewish, Grecian, or Roman antiquity, it is quite in keeping with the Court customs of Assyria and of Babylon. We find this very thing done by Assyrian and Babylonian monarchs. In solemn communications to their contemporaries and to posterity they relate their dreams and other connected incidents. Both Assurbanipal of Assyria and Nabonidus of Babylon tell their dreams to their people.

Assyriologists also find in the record of Daniel the very style of Nebuchadnezzar. He has left inscriptions in praise of Merodach which strikingly resemble this chapter. Let the reader compare the following with the sacred narrative: "O Merodach the lord, chief of the gods, a surpassing prince thou hast made me, and empire over multitudes of men hast entrusted to me as precious lives; thy power have I extended on high, over Babylon thy city, before all mankind. No city of the land have I exalted as was exalted the reverence of thy deity; I caused it to rest, and may thy power bring its treasures abundantly to my land. I, whether as king and embellisher, am the rejoicer of thy heart, or whether as high priest appointed, embellishing all thy fortresses, for thy glory. O exalted Merodach, a house have I made. May its greatness advance."

Here, as one has said,* it is impossible not to recognise the analogy of style which exists between these words of the king of Babylon and those which are reported in the Book of Daniel. We have the same conceptions and expressions. The only difference is that in the inscription the king exalts his favourite god Merodach, while in

---

* Vigouroux, *La Bible et les Decouvertes Moderne's*, Vol. iv., p. 507.

the Scripture he exalts, after his healing, the God of Daniel.

The Babylonian stamp of the document is further patent to the Assyriologist in expressions that recall others with which the inscriptions have made us familiar. Daniel's reply to the king, "My lord, the dream be to them that hate thee, and the interpretation thereof to thine enemies" (verse 19), is evidently moulded by the formulas which were in regular use for dissipating the consequences of evil dreams. Only in this case we have a careful avoidance of the magic with which these were associated. But, though the wish is pure from all stain of witchcraft, the form of it is distinctly Babylonian. The same thing is true of other expressions which are met with in the chapter.

It will be observed that the pride against which Nebuchadnezzar is warned springs up in overmastering strength in certain specified circumstances. He is walking on the roof of his palace —"in the palace of the kingdom of Babylon"— and the words burst from his lips, "Is not this great Babylon that I have built for the house of the kingdom by the might of my power, and for the honour of my majesty?" Here, again, we have an allusion thoroughly impossible to the most acute and capable forger that later times could produce. The man made known by his own inscriptions is set before us with a fidelity and vividness that are startling. It may be safely said that no other words which could 'possibly be put together could so picture him.

They sum up his mightiest achievements, and lay bare his inmost thoughts. "Babylon 'the great,'" says Rev. J. M. Fuller, M.A., referring to this passage, "is now but 'a possession for the bittern and pools of water' (Isa. xiv. 23), for miles 'an uninterrupted line of mounds, the ruins of the vast edifices collected together, as in the heart of a great city.' But even as Herodotus saw it, after much suffering from the Persian conquest, there is evidence enough of what must have been its 'glory' a century earlier in the days of its full splendour. Babylon was traversed in the middle by the Euphrates, surrounded by walls three hundred feet in height, seventy-five feet in thickness, and composing a square of which each side was nearly fifteen English miles in length. On one side of the river, in a circular place surrounded by a lofty wall, rose— a central and commanding object—the royal palace, with its memorable hanging gardens or terraces, on the other the temple of Bel. Subsidiary to these, yet each of them great in their way, rose palaces and temples with their dependent buildings, court-yards, and gardens. Around and among all were the common dwellings of the people, with their palm-groves, their orchards, and their small plots of corn-land. . . The completion of many of the works begun by his father, Nabopolassar, the actual commencement and erection of others, occupied Nebuchadnezzar's attention during the 'twelve months' which elapsed after the interpretation of the dream. In the 'Standard Inscription' there is a detailed acccount of what he did for gods and men; how he restored the 'Pyramid'—the sepulchre (or temple) of Belus (the modern 'Babel') and the tower of Borsippa (Birs-Nimroud), the temple of the 'seven spheres of heaven and earth;' how he built temples to Mylitta, to Nebo, to Sin, to Samas, to Nana, sometimes in Babylon, sometimes in Borsippa; how he completed the suburbs or quarters of Imgour-Bel and Nivit-Bel, supplying them with conduits, forts, and gates. Much of this work could only have been done in time of peace.

"Yet great as was the magnificence, satisfactory as was the result of the above works, there was one work, not yet mentioned, upon which Nebuchadnezzar (according to the Standard Inscription) especially prided himself. It was that work to which the Book of Daniel refers in the text. 'I have adorned no part of Babylon—that city which is the pupil of my eye—as I have the palace. That is the house which commands the admiration of men; it is the central spot of the country, high and elevated; it is the house of royalty in the country of Babylonia; it stretches from Imgour-Bel to the canal Libil-ouboul, from the Euphrates to Meboursapon.' The inscription tells how Nebuchadnezzar —working upon Nabopolassar's foundations—reared the palace anew, building it of brick and bitumen, using cedar and iron, and decorating the brickwork with inscriptions and painting, 'silver, gold, metals, gems nameless and priceless, objects of rare value, immense treasures have I heaped together,' to ornament 'that tower, the abode of my majesty, which contained the treasures of my imperishable royalty.' Tower and palace were connected. 'In a month of happy significance, and in an auspicious day' that work was begun. 'In fifteen days I finished its magnificence; I embellished the seat of my royalty.' Of this glorious building—known to modern travellers by the name *Kasr*, but called by the Arabs by the significant name Mujelibe, 'the overturned '—nothing is now left but a ruin of loose bricks, tiles, and fragments of stone, from the centre of which rises a solid mass of masonry, still entire and retaining remains of architectural ornament. It was the terrace, perhaps the hanging gardens, of this royal palace which Alexander the Great sought when the hand of death was upon him; it was within its walls that he died; it was around that death chamber that hundreds of Macedonians sought and found their graves. But a prouder—though not greater—monarch than Alexander had lived and died there before him. As Nebuchadnezzar 'walked in the palace of the kingdom of Babylon,' as he paced these terraces and hanging gardens, and looked upon all that he had begun and ended—that fifteen days' marvel, above all—the proud thought within him found expression in proud words: 'The king answered (his thought) and said, Is not this Babylon the great which I have built for the house of the kingdom ('the house of royalty,' inscription), by the might of my power (*cp*. the original of vv. 11, 12, ii. 37) and for the honour of my majesty?' ('the abode of my majesty,' inscription). The dream, the interpretation, the counsel, were all forgotten in that moment of exultation and self-glorification." \*

This speaks for itself. The inscriptions reveal the man. They bear the stamp of his mind and character. When we take up the Scripture narrative the very same stamp is there. We see and hear the same man. The phrases so peculiar to him are repeated—repeated not with the slavish imitation of a copyist, but with the freshness and freedom of actual life. If any man say that this could have been done by a forger writing four centuries after the events, when two empires and civilizations had overlaid and blotted out the Babylonian, we despair of changing opinions which refuse to be affected by the most stupendous facts. When Herodotus visited Babylon, only one hundred years after the great king's death, Nebuchadnezzar, even for an inquiring Greek traveller, was not even a name in the city that he had built. The Greek traveller heard nothing of him. And yet it is supposed that a Palestinian Jew, writing after other two centuries had deepened the oblivion, could so recall the past, that this man should be set before us just as he lived and thought and spoke!

There remains one other question before we pass to the *fifth* chapter of *Daniel*. Is there any trace, outside the Bible, of Nebuchadnezzar's malady and recovery? It is quite true that the monuments

---

\* *The Speaker's Commentary*, Vol. vi., pp. 292, 293.

record no reverses; but an event of this magnitude must have left some trace, we should think, either on the monuments or in the Greek narratives which has been handed down to us of the history of Assyria and Babylon. Of the history by Berosus we have only fragments. The work itself has long since perished, and we know of it merely by chance quotations made by one writer and another. His notice of Nebuchadnezzar seems to have been very meagre, and to have given only a brief summary of the achievements of the real founder of the last Babylonian dynasty. He uses a phrase, however, in speaking of the king's death, which appears to point to some such fact as is recorded in *Daniel*. His words are that, "having *fallen into a weakness* he died, having reigned forty-three years."

It was pointed out long ago that these words were unusual, and that they indicate that *a period of inactivity* preceded the death of the king. The reply was made by the critics that the same phrase is used by Berosus concerning Nebuchadnezzar's father, Nabopolassar. This answer was supposed by some even of their opponents to be so complete that they judged that the point should not be further pressed. Fuller consideration has, however, made our position stronger. It is quite true that a similar (though not the same) phrase is used regarding Nabopolassar. But it escaped the critics and the others that the phrase was fully justified. It covered a most important fact. Towards the end of his reign Nebuchadnezzar's father did fall into feeble health, and was no longer able to go forth at the head of his armies. It was on that very account that Nebuchadnezzar was made co-regent with him during the last years of his reign, and conducted the campaign against the Egyptians, who had marched to the Euphrates, driving them back from their Eastern conquests, and taking Judea and Jerusalem. It was when this war had nearly reached its completion that Nabopolassar died, and Nebuchadnezzar had to return with haste to Babylon to secure his possession of the throne.

When Berosus, then, said of Nabopolassar that, "having become feeble, he died," he is not using words at random. He has carefully chosen a phrase which indicates the fact that the end of the king's reign was preceded by a cessation of his former activity. Now, the words applied to Nebuchadnezzar are stronger. When he says that he "*fell into a feeble state of health,*" it is to be presumed that he is choosing his words with equal care, and that a more remarkable cessation of active participation in the affairs of the kingdom characterised the end of the son than had marked the end of the father. What caused the cessation in Nebuchadnezzar's case Berosus does not say. But he plainly indicates a fact which is, so far, in accord with the statements of the Scripture. Both agree as to a period of suffering, and both place that period near to, or at, the end of Nebuchadnezzar's reign.

Another writer, however, who is supposed by some to have been an Egyptian priest, and to have lived

## Nebuchadnezzar's Madness. 473

and written under the Ptolemies at the same time as Berosus, left a similar work which, fortunately, takes us farther. One writer stated some centuries ago that a complete copy of the works of Abydenus was contained in an Italian library. But it has never seen the light, and we only know the work, as we know that of his contemporary Berosus, through quotations made by ancient authors. One of these has massed together a number of things which the Scripture account of Nebuchadnezzar's madness alone enables us to understand. The passage professes to describe some remarkable circumstances which preceded the death of Nebuchadnezzar. It runs thus: "After this, as the Chaldeans relate, on ascending to the roof of his palace, he became inspired by some god, and delivered himself as follows: 'Babylonians! I, Nebuchadnezzar, foretell you a calamity that is to happen, which neither my ancestor Bel nor Queen Beltis can persuade the Fates to avert. There shall come a Persian mule* having your own gods in alliance with him, and shall impose servitude upon you, with the aid of a Mede, the boast of the Assyrians. Rather than this, would that some Charybdis or sea had engulphed him in utter destruction, or that he had been forced some other way *through the desert, where there are no cities, and no path trodden by man, but where wild beasts feed, and birds roam, where he must have wandered among rocks and precipices!* and that I had found a

---

* That is, one whose parents are of different countries. Cyrus was of mixed Median and Persian parentage.

happier end before becoming acquainted with such a disaster!' Having thus said, he immediately disappeared."

Here there are several things which will strike a reflecting reader. (1) The mention of Nebuchadnezzar's ascending to the roof of the palace. This visitation, according to Abydenus and the Chaldeans, whose accounts he summarised, fell upon him there. Is not this in itself a confirmation of the Bible history? There *was* some marked experience in the great king's life connected with this special place—the palace roof—and any reader, turning, for the first time, from Abydenus to this Scripture, would naturally feel that fuller light was given him here as to what that experience was. Then (2) prophecy and madness were closely connected together. Eusebius had long ago remarked: "We are not to be surprised if the Greek historians or the Chaldeans conceal the disease, and relate that he was inspired, and call his madness, or the demon by which he was possessed, a god. For it is their custom to attribute such things to a god, and to call demons gods." The change, in fact, consisted of some form of possession, and this again is a confirmation of the Scripture. (3) The reference to Cyrus and the Persian dominion overthrowing the Babylonian is a distinct reflection of the prophecies in Isaiah and Daniel; and, though they are mixed up here, it is evident that they had left their mark upon the minds of the Babylonians. But (4) the curse which he would fain invoke upon the head of Cyrus is a graphic representation *of his own fate.* He was "driven into the desert, where there are no cities, and no path trodden by man, but where wild beasts feed and birds roam, where he must have wandered among rocks and precipices." Why this kind of fate rather than slaughter in battle, or pining in a prison, should have been invoked upon the coming Persian prince, it would be hard to say. The Bible history enables us to understand the whole, and to bring order out of confusion.

There is, so far as discovery has yet gone, only one sentence upon the monuments which has any bearing upon the king's trouble. Neriglissar, one of Nebuchadnezzar's successors, but a usurper, gives to his own father Bel-sum-iskun, the title of king. Now, there is no record of his reign, and no place in the list of kings which can be assigned to him. Oppert and Lenormant solve the problem in this way. Bel-sum-iskun, like his son Neriglissar, was chief of the Magi; for the office was hereditary. As chief of the Magi, he would practically assume the sovereignty during Nebuchadnezzar's madness. His son, wishing to strengthen his own position, would naturally recall the fact to the Babylonians, and hence the epithet which has exercised Assyriologists so much. Here, again, we have one of those chance indications which are worth even more than fuller and more evident confirmations.

## CHAPTER XIII.

### WHO WAS BELSHAZZAR?

THE fifth chapter of Daniel takes us suddenly to the closing scenes of the Babylonian empire. There is nothing told us about Nebuchadnezzar's death, nor about those who succeeded him on the throne; nor is anything said as to how Belshazzar has come to be king. Is there any explanation of this silence, or of the sudden leap from Nebuchadnezzar's edict to Belshazzar's feast?

The omission has been utilised to discredit the book. "If the author," says Bleek, "had intended these narratives to be really historical, we must necessarily expect that he would have placed the separate narratives in some sort of connection with one another, by forms of transition at least, and would have somehow knit them together in an historical whole." But criticism of this sort has a painful air of presumption. It takes for granted that the purpose of the Scripture must either be that which the critic imagines it should have been, or it cannot exist at all. Now, there is not the slightest indication from first to last that the Book of Daniel was intended to be a history of Babylon; and to look for the sequence and connection which we find in such a history is to expect what never apparently entered into the purpose of the book. But to any reader who will give the matter a few minutes' quiet thought it will soon be evident that a very high purpose has set its seal upon every page. These chapters on Babylon are nothing else than an account of how God was striving to lead it from its pride, self-will, and ignorance of Himself. Chapter iv. has told us of the warning given to Nebuchadnezzar, of his punishment, his contrition, his healing, and his gratitude. And now in chapter v. we see how the goodness of Babylon has been like the morning cloud and the early dew. Belshazzar defies Him before whom for a moment Nebuchadnezzar humbled himself, and then the punishment falls: Babylon is judged!

There is thus a very real and significant connection between chapters iv. and v., a connection which any additional historical details would merely have broken or obscured. The Scripture has itself pointed to this in chapter v. 18-24. The prophet recalls the very incident recorded in the fourth chapter, and sets the hardihood and the blasphemy of Belshazzar's act in the light of the revelation of God which was then given. "O thou king, the most high God gave Nebuchadnezzar thy father a kingdom, and majesty, and glory and honour. . . But when his heart was lifted up and his mind hardened in pride, he was deposed from his kingly throne, and they took his glory from him; and he was driven from the sons of men; and his heart was made like the beasts, and his dwelling was with the wild asses; they fed him with grass like oxen, and his body was wet with the dew of heaven; till he knew that the most high God ruled in the kingdom of men, and that he appointeth over it whomsoever He will. And thou his son, O Belshazzar, hast not humbled thine heart, though thou knewest all this; but hast lifted up thyself against the Lord of heaven; and they have brought the vessels of His house before thee, and thou, and thy lords, thy wives, and thy concubines, have drunk wine in them; and thou hast praised the gods of silver and gold, of brass, iron, wood and stone, which see not, nor hear, nor know: and the God in whose hand thy breath is, and whose are all thy ways, hast thou not glorified." In the light of that terrible indictment who can fail to see the connection between chapters iv. and v., or fail to understand why the events they record were thus sharply set the one against the other? There is also another question which one is forced to ask. How did this purpose (which is surely worthy of the Word of God) escape the observation of the critics? Are men so blind fit guides for those who wish to know what they ought to think about the Bible? Or are they competent to judge a Book which confessedly they cannot understand?

Let us now leave Belshazzar a moment, and try

to obtain some clear notion as to the successors of Nebuchadnezzar, so that we may understand allusions which must be made in dealing with the questions which are to come before us. The information is also called for in answer to a question which will here naturally occur to the reader. The narrative brings us to the close of the Babylonian empire. Daniel appears here, and enjoys Court favour till the first year of Cyrus (i. 21). One of the after prophecies is dated in the 3rd year of Cyrus. Was this possible? Were all these reigns capable of being compressed within the limits of an ordinary lifetime? In matters of this kind, a late writer, necessarily ignorant of many facts, would be sure to stumble. Does this book, then, display such stumbling, or have we here again evidence of absolute truthfulness, and of perfect mastery of facts?

Nebuchadnezzar reigned 43 years, and died 561 B.C. If Daniel was 12 years old at the beginning of Nebuchadnezzar's reign, he would be 55 when the king died. Nebuchadnezzar was succeeded by his son, Evil-Merodach, who reigned only two years. He fell a victim to a Court conspiracy. He is said to have been intemperate, and to have shown contempt for the laws. He was succeeded by Neriglissar, or Nergalsharezer. This name occurs in Jeremiah xxxix. 13, among the list of the Babylonian princes whom Nebuchadnezzar sent to conduct the siege of Jerusalem, while he himself remained at "Riblah," in the land of Hamath. He is there called "Rab-mag," or chief of the magi, a title which Neriglissar, who succeeded Evil-Merodach, assumes in his inscriptions. It has been supposed, therefore, that he is the person named by Jeremiah as being in Judea some thirty years before. It is more likely, however, that the Nergal-sharezer of Jeremiah was Neriglissar's grandfather. His father, as we have seen, was Bel-sum-iskun, who appears to have been regent during Nebuchadnezzar's madness, so that the office of Rab-mag, possessed also by Bel-sum-iskun, could have come to him only after his father's death. The office was hereditary, and the facts seem to indicate that Bel-sum-iskun's father and son bore the same name.

Neriglissar, who now succeeded to the Babylonian sovereignty, had married a daughter of Nebuchadnezzar, and no doubt he owed his elevation to this relationship as well as to the high office which he held. He reigned three years and some months, enjoying peace with the surounding peoples and occupying himself in the building of a great palace in the western portion of the city. He left behind him an infant son, whose name has come down to us under the portentous, and to Assyriologists unrecognisable, form of Laborosoarchod. Lenormant thinks that the child was probably named Bel-sum-iskun, or "Bellabarisruk, after his grandfather." If this should prove correct, it will be somewhat of a confirmation of our suggestion that Neriglissar himself was named after *his* grandfather. This child reigned only a few months. The turbulent Babylonian nobles desired another

## Who was Belshazzar? 481

change, and the child's life was brought to a sudden termination. It was said that he betrayed vicious and cruel instincts, the only remedy for which was the extinction of the child's life! The nobles then proclaimed one of their number, Nabonahid, king. Nabonahid, whose name has been handed down to us by the Greek historians as Nabonidus, or Nabonadius, had been raised to the dignity of Rabmag, or chief of the magi, probably by Neriglissar, and was, no doubt, on this account elevated to the throne by the conspirators. He reigned during the last seventeen years of the Babylonian empire.

We are now in a position to say what the answer is to the question whether all these changes could have been embraced in the compass of a lifetime.

|  |  |
|---|---|
| Daniel was (say) at Nebuchadnezzar's death... | 55 |
| Evil-Merodach reigned ... | 2 yrs. |
| Neriglissar ,, ... | 3 ,, |
| Laborosoarchod ,, (say) ... | 1 ,, |
| Nabonidus ,, ... | 17 ,, |
| So that Daniel would have been ... | 78 |

years of age when the Medes and Persians took possession of the country, an advanced age certainly, but one by no means improbable, and certainly quite in keeping with the narrative. If we add to Daniel's age when carried into captivity five years more, this would make him, when Cyrus captured Babylon, not more than 83 years, an age which is still within the limits of possibility.

Here, then, where any late writer would certainly have stumbled, the Scripture walks surely. But what was supposed to be one of the greatest difficulties of the book now confronts us. This fifth chapter was long regarded as one of the securest strongholds of the critics. Other chapters, such as those containing the miraculous dreams, the preservation of the three martyrs in the fire, and that of Daniel in the den of lions, had certainly stones enough of stumbling and rocks enough of offence; but in the fifth chapter the critics seemed to be on surer ground, and imagined themselves triumphant. There was a distinct historical blunder—a blunder, in their judgment, so patent, and so stupendous that no ingenuity could clear it away. The Scripture here says that the last king of Babylon was slain in the capture of the city. Both Berosus, the Chaldean historian, and Abydenus unite in saying that he was not in Babylon at all when it fell; that he had taken refuge in the stronghold of Borsippa, where he was subsequently besieged and captured; that even then he did not die; for Cyrus not only spared his life, but gave him estates in Carmania (according to Berosus), and even made him governor of the district (according to Abydenus). Berosus says he there ended his days in peace; Abydenus tells us that he offended Darius, and was deprived of his place in Carmania. But, whatever their differences in details may be, both unite in the testimony that the last king of Babylon did not die when Babylon fell, but, on the contrary, lived for many years after his sovereignty had passed away.

There were two other points which seemed to strengthen the critical position greatly. Scripture

## Who was Belshazzar? 483

was wrong, they said, in the name as well as in the fact. There was no trace anywhere of a king called Belshazzar. Every name among the successors of Nebuchadnezzar was known, and his had no place among them. He was certainly, also, not the last king of Babylon, as Herodotus spoke of Labynetus, and others of Nabonidus or Nabonadius, but no one knew anything of Belshazzar. As if all this were not enough, the Scripture was supposed to have embarrassed itself with another historical inaccuracy. It distinctly states that Belshazzar was a lineal descendant of Nebuchadnezzar. The queen speaks to Belshazzar of "the king Nebuchadnezzar, thy father" (verse 11); and Daniel, referring to the same monarch, says: "And thou, his son, O Belshazzar, hast not humbled thine heart, though thou knewest all this" (verse 22). Now Berosus is very explicit on this matter, and tells us that Nabonidus was not of Royal descent, but was chief of the magi, and was placed upon the throne by the Babylonian nobles.

Here, then, was a threefold cord which could not easily be broken. The replies given by orthodox scholars form not altogether pleasant reading. They were certainly able to show that the historical authorities were not in agreement. Herodotus and Xenophon, for example, both represent the last king as a descendant of Nebuchadnezzar, and Xenophon states that he was killed fighting, sword in hand, when the city was surprised on the night of a festival. These statements of men, who wrote before the Persian empire fell, were certainly grave enough to call for an arrest of judgment; and if they had contented themselves with this, the defenders of the Scripture would have fulfilled their duty and have arrested the advance of the foe on this side. But they allowed themselves to indulge in theories that have stood the test no better than the theories of their opponents.

The manner in which light has dawned and brightened upon these dark problems, forms one of the most astonishing chapters in the story of Modern Discoveries in their relation to the Bible. It was perfectly true that Nabonidus was the last king of Babylon; that he was not of royal lineage; that he was raised to the throne by the Chaldean nobles; and that he did not die when the city was captured. But the book of Daniel was also absolutely correct in all that it has told us of Belshazzar. The earliest confirmation was furnished by a discovery made by Sir Henry Rawlinson, in the year 1854 at Mugheir, the ancient "Ur of the Chaldees." At the four corners of the ruins of the temple to the moon-god, four terra-cotta cylinders were found. They were duplicate copies of an account by Nabonidus of his building the temple. The former structure had fallen into decay. It was originally begun by "Urukh, a king who lived long ago," and completed by Ilgi, his son. Nabonidus continues—

    In my days that tower
    had disappeared entirely.
    . . . . . . .
    Unto the moon, chief of the gods of heaven and earth,

> King of the stars upon stars
> which dwell in heaven great, Lord of that temple of "the great tree"
> in the city of Ur, my Lord,
> from its foundation
> I raised it anew.

The inscription concludes with a prayer—

> Like heaven may their foundations stand fast!
> Myself, NABO-NID, King of Babylon,
> in the fear of thy great divinity preserve me!
> My life unto distant days
> Abundantly prolong!
> and of BEL-SAR-USSUR,
> my eldest son,
> the offspring of my body,
> the awe of thy great divinity
> fix thou firmly in his heart
> that he may never fall
> into sin
> and that his glory may endure!

This mention of Nabonidus's son, Bel-sar-ussur, a name which is identical with the Belshazzar of Daniel, astonished many, and delighted lovers of the Bible. These last never doubted that the Scripture was a better authority than even Berosus, and had wisely concluded that, as discovery had hitherto steadily borne witness to the accuracy of God's Word, it would also eventually speak out in regard to this part of its testimony. One would have thought that the Assyriologists would have been with the believer in this matter. Sir Henry Rawlinson, indeed, at once declared his opinion that this was the Belshazzar of the Bible, and that Nabonidus had associated him with himself in the government of the country. But it was not so with others. H. F. Talbot, who gave a translation of the tablet in *Records of the Past* (vol. v., 145), prefaced it with the following observations: "Several writers have maintained that the Prince Bel-sar-ussur, who is named in the inscription as being the eldest son of Nabonidus, is identical with the Biblical Belshazzar. As I am, however, of a different opinion, I will state some of my reasons for doubting it. I willingly admit that Belshazzar is the same name as Bel-sar-ussur, but this proves nothing; because Bel-sar-ussur, meaning *Bel protect the king*, is not an unfrequent name in the cuneiform inscriptions. Again, the book of Daniel presents to us Belshazzar as a reigning king, and gives not the least hint (?) of his having a father still alive and on the throne. Yet this is maintained by some writers, who say that Bel-sar-ussur was co-regent with Nabonidus his father. But of this there is not the slightest evidence in the inscription (?) or elsewhere. He may have been a mere child when it was written. His father merely asks the gods to bless him. Again, Belshazzar was the son of Nebuchadnezzar and not the son of Nabonidus (?) (Dan. v. 2)."

Mr. Fox Talbot has not been alone in his opposition. Schrader's rationalism will not permit him to own defeat even now, and Professor Sayce's wild attack on Daniel and misrepresentation of the testimony of the monuments will engage our attention further on. It is enough to say, meanwhile, that here, as elsewhere, the Scriptures have risen in the esteem of Assyriologists, and this mention of Belshazzar has made them depend upon it more than ever as reliable history. Even Sayce admits that "the cuneiform inscriptions have proved that the Belshazzar of Daniel is no figment of the imagination."

The reader will note that I have questioned several of Mr. Fox Talbot's statements. Whether the challenge is justified the reader shall judge. (1) He says that the book of Daniel "gives not the least hint of his (Belshazzar's) having a father still alive and on the throne." What, then, of his promise to Daniel to make him the "third" ruler in the kingdom? Why does he not offer the *second* place? Why merely the third? Was he trying to make a hard bargain with Daniel, or was he saving the second place for anyone else? It is perfectly evident that, in his terror and eager desire to know his fate, he was offering the highest reward that it was in his power to bestow; and this, indeed, suggested the true solution of the difficulty to Christian students both in this country and in France. They said, "He offers the highest place which any subject is able to fill; and if that is the third and not the second, it must be because there are *two kings* and not one upon the throne; Belshazzar's own place is the second and his father's is the first." Mr. Fox Talbot, therefore, could not have read his Bible carefully, or he could not have said that the Scripture record "gives not the least hint of Belshazzar's having a father still alive and on the throne." There was a hint there in that word "third" which was sufficient to lead scholars widely separated, to a correct idea of Belshazzar's position before the monuments had told their story.

He is not more fortunate in his second assertion when he says (2), "There is not the slightest evidence in the inscription or elsewhere" that Belshazzar was co-regent with Nabonidus. My readers will note the air of absoluteness and omniscience, which is unfortunately too common with scientists of every kind. No men hate dogma more, and no men present better examples of its most offensive characteristics. It will be remembered that Nabonidus names Belshazzar in the foregoing inscription. There was evidence enough in that very fact to lead Sir Henry Rawlinson to say that Belshazzar reigned jointly with his father. "On reading this," says Canon Rawlinson,* "the learned decipherer at once declared it to be his opinion that Bel-shar-uzur had been associated in the government by his father, and possessed the kingly power. If this were so, it could scarcely be disputed that he was Daniel's Belshazzar. Sir H. Rawlinson's inference from the inscription has, however, been denied. Mr. Fox Talbot has maintained that the inscription does not furnish 'the slightest evidence' that Bel-shar-uzur was even regarded as co-regent with his father. 'He may,' he says, 'have been a mere child when it was written.' The controversy turns upon What was the Oriental practice in this matter? Sir H. Rawlinson holds that Oriental monarchs generally,

---

* *Egypt and Babylon*, p. 151, 152.

and the Assyrian and Babylonian kings in particular, were so jealous of possible rivals in their own family, that they did not name even their sons upon public documents unless they had associated them. Kudurmabuk mentions his son Rim-agu; but he has made him king of Larsa. Sennacherib mentions Asshur-nadin-sum, but on the occasion of his elevation to the throne of Babylon. Apart from these instances and that of Bel-shar-uzur, there does not seem to be any mention made of their sons by *name* by the monarchs of either country."

The force of these remarks is increased when we note again that Nabonidus speaks of "Bel-sar-ussar, my eldest son." This proves that *Nabonidus had other sons.* Why does he not pray *for them*? Why does he not even name them? The co-regency would amply explain this; will anything short of it do so? Mr. Fox Talbot is not more happy in his assertion that (3) the Scripture, in saying that Belshazzar was the son of Nebuchadnezzar, excludes the possibility of his having also been the son of Nabonidus. To this the following triumphant reply has been furnished by Canon Rawlinson.* I give the quotation entire, for its completeness consists in the multitude of the testimonies as to Scripture usage. "In Scripture," he says, "'father' stands for any male ancestor, 'son' for any male descendent. Jehoshaphat is called 'the son of Nimshi,' though really his grandson; Jesus of Nazareth is 'the son of David,' who is the 'son of Abraham' (Matt. i. 1).

---

* *Egypt and Babylon*, p. 155-158.

Ezra is 'the son of Seraiah' (Ezra vii. 1), the 'chief priest' of the Captivity (2 Kings xxv. 18), who died B.C. 586 (verse 21), of whom Ezra therefore (B.C. 460-440) must have been really the grandson or great grandson. Conversely, Abraham, Isaac, and Jacob are the 'fathers' of the Israelites after they have been four hundred years in Egypt (Exodus iii. 15, 16); Jonadab, the son of Rechab, the friend of Jehu (II. Kings x. 15), is the 'father' of the Rechabites, contemporary with Jeremiah (Jeremiah xxxv. 6), and Jehoram, King of Judah, is the father of Uzziah (Matt. i. 8), his fourth descendent. The *rationale* of the matter is as follows:—Neither in Hebrew nor in Chaldee is there any word for 'grandfather, or grandson.' To express the relationship it would be necessary to say 'father's father' and 'son's son.' But 'father's father' and 'son's son' are, by an idiom of the language, used with an idea of remoteness—to express distant ancestors or descendents. Consequently, they are rendered by this usage unapt to express the near relationship of grandfather and grandson; and the result is that they are very rarely so used. As Dr. Pusey has well observed, * 'a single grandfather, or forefather,' is never called 'father's father,' always 'father' only. This is so, alike in early and in late Hebrew; and the Chaldee follows the idiom. Jacob says, 'The God of my father, the God of Abraham, and the fear of Isaac' (Gen. xxxi. 42). God says to Aaron, 'The tribe of Levi, the tribe of thy father'

---

* *Lectures on Daniel*, Lecture vii., pp. 405, 406.

(Num. xviii. 2). The confession to be made at the offering of the first-fruits began, 'A Syrian, ready to perish, was my father' (Deut. xxvi. 5); and in the same sense, probably, Moses says, 'the God of my father' (Exod. xviii. 4). David said to Mephibosheth, 'I will surely show thee kindness for Jonathan thy father's sake, and will restore to thee all the land of Saul thy father' (II. Sam. ix. 7). And Asa is said to have 'removed Maachah, his mother, from being Queen,' though it is said in the same chapter that she was the mother of Abijam, his father (I. Kings xv. 2, 13). Maachah herself, who is called 'daughter of Abishalom' (I. Kings xv. 2), was really his grand-daughter, he having left only one daughter, Tamar (II. Sam. xiv. 27), and her own father being Uriel (II. Chron. xiii. 2). Again it is said, 'Asa did right in the eyes of the Lord, as did David his father' (I. Kings xv. 11), and in like way of Hezekiah (II. Kings xviii. 3). Contrariwise, it is said that 'Ahaz did not do that which was right like David his father' (xvi. 2); that 'Amaziah did right, yet not like David his father; he did according to all things as Joash his father did' (xiv. 3). Here, in one verse, the actual father and the remote ancestor are alike called 'his father'; as before the father and grandfather Mephibosheth were called, in the same verse, 'his father.' 'Josiah,' it is said, 'walked in the ways of David his father, he began to seek the God of David his father' (II. Chron. xxxiv. 2, 3). In Isaiah there occur 'Jacob thy father' (Isa. lviii. 14); 'thy first father' (xliii. 27)—

*i.e.*, Adam; and to Hezekiah he said, 'Thus saith the Lord, the God of David thy father' (xxxviii. 5). So, on the other hand, there is no Hebrew or Chaldee word to express 'grandson.' In laws, if the relation has to be expressed, the idiom is 'thy son's daughter' (Lev. xviii. 10), or 'thy daughter's daughter' (Ibid); or it is said, 'Thou shalt tell it to thy son's son' (Exod. x. 2); 'Rule thou over us, thou, and thy son, and thy son's son' (Judges viii. 22). The relation can be expressed in this way in the abstract, but there is no way in Hebrew or Chaldee to mark that one person was the grandson of another, except in the way of genealogy —'Jehu, the son of Jehoshaphat, the son of Nimshi.' And so the name 'son' stands for the 'grandson,' and a person is at times called the son of the more remarkable grandfather, the link of the father's name being omitted. Thus Jacob asked for 'Laban, the son of Nahor' (Genesis xxix. 5), omitting the immediate father, Bethuel; Jehu is called 'the son of Nimshi' (I. Kings xix. 16; II. Kings ix. 20) omitting his own father, Jehoshaphat. The prophet Zechariah is called 'the son of Iddo' (Ezra v. 1; vi. 14), his own father being Berachiah (Zech. i. 1). Hence the Rechabites said, as a matter of course, 'Jonadab, the son of Rechab, our father, commanded us; we have obeyed in all things the voice of Jonadab, the son of Rechab, our father' (Jer. xxxv. 6-8); although Jonadab lived some one hundred and eighty years before (II. Kings x. 15). And reciprocally God says, 'The words of Jonadab, the son of Rechab, that he commanded his sons, are performed' (verse 14); and 'Because ye have obeyed the commandments of Jonadab your father, and kept all his precepts' (verse 16)."

There is really, therefore, no more force whatever in this objection than there is in the others. If Nabonidus had married a daughter of Nebuchadnezzar, it was quite in keeping with Scripture usage to speak of Belshazzar as that great king's son. Let us now look at another of Mr. Fox Talbot's statements. It was possible for him to write as late as 1875 that there was nothing to show that Belshazzar was not a mere child when he was named by his father on the inscription found at Mugheir. But since that time inscriptions relating to Belshazzar have become so numerous that he is now as much a personage to Assyriologists as he is to readers of *Daniel*. This is largely owing to a most remarkable "find" which has greatly enriched Assyriology. In 1876, the very next year after that in which Mr. Talbot's unfortunate paper saw the light, news was sent to England by Sir Henry Rawlinson, that the natives had discovered a large number of cuneiform tablets at Hillah, that part of ancient Babylon which was the abode of the poor and the outcast, and, strange to say, is the only part of it which has been spared. During the rainy season the front of one of the mounds of ruins had fallen down, disclosing several large earthenware vases, which till then had been buried in the rubbish. These vases bore the shape of the ancient jars of the country. The mouth was covered with a tile which

was carefully cemented with bitumen. When the
jars were opened they were found to be filled with
Babylonian documents, and contained from three to
four thousand contracts of all sorts. Mr. George
Smith, acting on orders received from the British
Museum, bought the greatest part of them (about
2,500 tablets) and sent them to London, where they
arrived in November, 1876.

"The tablets vary in size," says Mr. Pinches, of
the British Museum, to whose care they were
confided, "from three-quarters of an inch by half an
inch to nine inches by twelve. They are usually
covered with writing on both sides, and sometimes
on the edges as well. Many contain no date, and
these, on examination, prove to be either rough
memoranda, lists of objects or produce, or letters.
The more important transactions were re-copied on
larger tablets with great care and elaboration of
details. These larger tablets usually contain impressions from cylinder seals, and nail-marks, which were
considered to be a man's natural seal."\* These
turned out to be the securities held by a large
banking house, calling themselves "Sons of Egibi,"
or, as we should say, "Egibi and Sons." The firm
seems to have continued for about 600 years at least,
since their documents take us down to the fourth
century B.C., and there are notices of them in
inscriptions about 1,000 B.C. The discovery has
proved to be one of the most valuable ever made.
The documents are carefully dated, and this fact,

---

*Records of the Past* (First Series) xi., 89, 90.

## Who was Belshazzar? 495

combined with the large number of transactions, supply us with a regular chronology of the last kings of Babylon.

They are specially precious to us, however, on account of the new light which they shed upon Belshazzar. Professor Sayce published in 1890 *(Records of the Past,* new series, vol. iii.) a translation of three tablets relating to him. These show that as early as the fifth year of Nabonidus (and thirteen years, therefore, before the end of his reign and the night of the fatal banquet) Belshazzar was old enough to have a household of his own, and to require the services of a secretary. A house belonging to one of the Egibi is let on a three years' lease (I quote the document) "to Nebo-yukin-akhi, the secretary of Belshazzar, the son of the king, for one-and-a-half maneh of silver, sub-letting of the house being forbidden, as well as interest on the money. Nebo-yukin-akhi undertakes to plant trees and to repair the house." The money was to be repaid when the house was vacated, so that the consideration appears to have been the use of the money for trading purposes. In another contract, dated six years later, we find Belshazzar possessed of a sheep-farm, a steward, and "secretaries" It opens thus: "The sum of 20 manehs of silver for wool, the property of Belshazzar, the son of the king, which has been handed over to Iddin-Nerodach, the son of Basa, the son of Nur-Sin, through the agency of Nabo-tasabit, the steward of the house of Belshazzar, the son of the king, and the secretaries of the son of the king."

It is evident, then, from the Egibi Tablets that Belshazzar was not a mere child, but was a personage of the time. Inscriptions discovered at a later date have shed further light upon this dark place in Scripture history. One of these is of a most important character. It is an account, authorised by Cyrus himself, of his invasion of Babylon. He tells us that Nabonidus remained in Teva, that is, in a quarter of Babylon which lay on the west side of the Euphrates. But in this year—the seventh of the reign of Nabonidus, and, therefore, eleven years before the end, "the king's son," says Cyrus, "the nobles and his soldiers, were in the country of Akkad," that is, in the northern part of Babylonia. No one doubts that "the king's son" is Belshazzar. For some reason the command of the army was assigned to him, and he was watching the movements of Cyrus, while his father remained in Babylon. Cyrus was conquering one power after another on the frontiers of Babylonia; and, though the Babylonians, apparently, made no attempt to succour the assailed, they kept a large army of observation upon their own borders. The inscription further says that the same thing was done in the ninth, the tenth, and the eleventh years of the reign of Nabonidus. It is only when the crisis of the war arrives that Nabonidus takes the field. He is defeated, flees, and is afterwards taken prisoner.

The following is Cyrus's account of the close of the struggle (I give Professor Sayce's translation):—

"At the end of the month Elul the gods of the country of Accad, which are above the sky and below the sky, entered Babylon; the gods of Borsippa, Kutha, and Sippara did not enter. In the month Tammuz (June), when Cyrus had delivered battle against the soldiers of Accad in the city of Rutu (?), on the banks of the river Nizallat, when the men of Accad also had delivered battle, the men of Accad raised a revolt. Some persons were slain. On the fourteenth day of the month, Sippara was taken without fighting; Nabonidus fled. On the sixteenth day Gobryas (Ugbaru), the governor of the country of Kurdistan (Gutium) and the soldiers of Cyrus entered Babylon without fighting. Afterwards Nabonidus was captured, after being bound in Babylon. At the end of the month Tammuz, the javelin-throwers of the country of Kurdistan guarded the gates of E-Saggil; no cessation of services took place in E-Saggil and the other temples, but no special festival was observed. The third day of the month Marchesvan (October) Cyrus entered Babylon. Dissensions were allayed before him. Peace to the city did Cyrus establish, peace to all the province of Babylon did Gobryas, his governor, proclaim. Governors in Babylon he appointed. From the month Chisleu to the month Adar (November to February) the gods of the country of Accad, whom Nabonidus had transferred to Babylon, returned to their own cities. The eleventh day of the month Marchesvan, during the night, Gobryas was on the bank of the river. . . . The wife of the king died. From the twenty-seventh day of Adar to the third day of Nisan there was lamentation in the country of Accad; all the people smote their heads. On the fourth day Kambyses, the son of Cyrus, conducted the burial at the temple of the Sceptre of the world. The priest of the temple of the Sceptre of Nebo, who up-bears the sceptre [of Nebo in the temple of the god], in an Elamite robe took the hands of Nebo. . . . the son of the king (Kambyses) [offered] freewill offerings in full to ten times [the usual amount]. He confined to E-Saggil the [image] of Nebo. Victims before Bel to ten times [the usual amount he sacrificed]." *

The importance of this inscription has been obscured by Professor Sayce in one most important particular. When a translation of the inscription was first published by Mr. Pinches, his rendering of the passage regarding the death of the person, at whose obsequies Cambyses presided, was "the king died." The significance of that translation will be at once apparent. What king was it? It is not Cyrus; for he lives to tell the tale. Neither was it Nabonidus; for he is a captive and long enjoys the conqueror's favour. *It must have been Belshazzar.* Schrader, whose resolve to admit nothing in favour of the book of Daniel that can be set aside is a serious blot upon an otherwise fair fame, pronounced the reading to be, "the wife of the king," and Professor Sayce has adopted the suggestion with characteristic precipitancy, and, as we have just seen, has such

---

* *The Higher Criticism and the Monuments, pp.* 502, 503.

confidence in it as the only true translation that he does not give his readers the slightest hint that any other rendering has ever seen the light. In reply to an inquiry of mine, Mr. Theo. G. Pinches writes: "The characters cannot be *u assat*, 'and the wife of,' but must either be *u*, 'and,' or *u mar*, 'and the son of.' This last improved reading I suggested about four years ago, and the Rev. J. C. Ball and Dr. Hagen, who examined the text with me, accepted this view. Dr. Hagen wrote upon the subject in Fried. Delitzsch's *Beiträge*, Vol. i."

The Babylonian characters for *u assat*, "the wife of," are entirely different from those which occur in this part of the inscription. The sign, on the contrary, for the conjunction *u*, "and," and that for the two words *u mar*, "and the son of," closely resemble each other. But within these two last translations lie the limits of the doubt. The rendering must either be "And the king died," or "And the son of the king died." In either case the reference to Belshazzar is a matter of certainty. *He was slain on the taking of the city*, as the Scripture says he was, and his death was the cause of such sorrow that "from the twenty-seventh day of Adar to the third day of Nisan there was lamentation in the country of Accad; all the people smote their heads." The presiding of Cambyses at the funeral on the fourth day of Nisan would have been quite out of place had the deceased been the wife of Nabonidus. What call was there for Cambyses to act as chief mourner at the burial of another man's wife? But, as the heir to the Babylonian sovereignty, it was a graceful act, and one well fitted to ingratiate him with the Babylonian people, that he should preside at the burial of Belshazzar.

## CHAPTER XIV.

### BELSHAZZAR'S FEAST.

THE reader will observe that the critics have been driven from one position after another. First of all, there was no trace of any Belshazzar. It was accordingly concluded that the presence of the name in Daniel was the blunder of a late writer! Historians mentioned Nabonidus, and the monuments also contained the name. It was plain, therefore, that there was no room for Belshazzar! The plea of believers that Nabonidus might have also been named Belshazzar was rightly rejected on account of the differences in their history. Belshazzar died when Babylon was taken; Nabonidus lived long after.

The critics were triumphant. But the triumph, like every other supposed victory of unbelief, came to an end. First of all, Belshazzar's name was found in an inscription left by Nabonidus. Then the assertion, that he might have been a mere child, was set aside by the transactions revealed in the Egibi tablets. He had a household of his own, with servants, stewards, and a staff of secretaries.

Afterwards appeared the inscription of Cyrus, in which Belshazzar, "the son of the king," is apparently a more important personage than the king himself. And, last of all, the information was supplied, by the same high authority, that, on the occasion when Babylon passed into the hands of the Persians, "the king," or "the son of the king," died. Here almost the last ditch was captured. Belshazzar had been at the head of the Babylonian armies; he was in Babylon when the city was taken; and he lost his life, as the Bible says he did, when the Babylonian empire fell.

Two points, however, still remain. Belshazzar, it is quite clear, was the second personage in the realm, but is there any indication that he had *ascended the throne?* The doubt which rests on the reading of the inscription of Cyrus prevents our receiving any aid in that quarter. But there is another inscription which presents a problem of which the Scripture account appears to be the only possible solution. Among the Egibi tablets there is one dated in the third year of a king who is called *Marduk-sar-uzur*. It is the record of "the sale of a field of corn by a person named *Ahi-ittaspi*, son of a man called *Nabu-malik*, to Idina-marduk, son of Basa, son of Nursin, as a partner in the Egibi firm." One of the three witnesses to this document is "Ina-bit-saggal-zikir, son of Dayan Marduk, son of Musizib."\*

---

\* Mr. Boscawen in the *Transactions of the Society of Biblical Archæology*, Vol. vii., pp. 27, 28.

The reader will immediately see what light can sometimes spring from dry details, and how much all-important truth may lie hid in a name. No king of the name Marduk-sar-uzur is known; but the form of the name at once suggested a solution of the difficulty. If we substitute the name Bel for Marduk, or Merodach, we have the now well-known name Bel-sar-uzur. "The first argument against identification," says Mr. Boscawen, "is in the names; but this does not seem very forcible, when we consider how many of the kings of Assyria had double names, in which the divine names are changed; as Sin-ahi-iriba and Assur-bani-pal and Sin-bani-pal. And in the Egibi family we have Bel-pahir and Nabu-pahir and Nabu-fir-ukin as names of the father of Sula. And when we consider the close relationship between the Babylonian Bel and the god Marduk, this similarity in the names becomes more striking. The close connection between the story of Bel and the Dragon in the Creation Tablets and the story of Bel and the Dragon in the Apocrypha is at once apparent; and the great temple of Merodach of Babylon was certainly the one which was identified as the great Temple of Belus." *

But the tablet has something more to say. There are other names upon it; do they tell anything? The purchaser is a member of the great banking firm of Egibi, and bears the name of Idina-Marduk, son of Basa, son of Mirsin. Now the tablets form

---

* *Ibid*, p. 28.

a nearly continuous series; and, by the succession of names contained in them, they tell us the story of these Rothschilds of the East. This same Idina-Marduk takes his place in the chair of the great banking firm in the thirty-third year of the reign of Nebuchadnezzar, that is 572 B.C., ten years before Nebuchadnezzar died. He continues till the third year of Cambyses, the son of Cyrus, or 527 B.C. Some time, then, between Nebuchadnezzar and Cambyses, this king Marduk-sar-uzur reigned. *But there is no vacant space into which he can be put.* He must, therefore, be identified with some one of those who are now fully known to us, and *the only one that will suit is Bel-sar-uzur.*

This conclusion is strengthened by the mention of the witness, whose name I have given—Ina-bit-saggal-zikir, son of Dayan Marduk, son of Musizib. Those witnesses whose names are found in the contracts, would seem to have been clerks engaged in the service of the firm. Their names appear in a series like those of the Egibi family, and have, like theirs, yielded important results. This witness is described as the son of Dayan Marduk, son of Musizib; that is, he is the grandson of Musizib. Now, Musizib appears as witness to some other transactions in the eighth year of Nebuchadnezzar, or 596 B.C. Belshazzar died in 539 B.C., or fifty-seven years afterwards, a space of time which seems just sufficient to bring us from the grandfather to the grandson. Some of the other witnesses also appear in contracts drawn up in the last years of Nabonidus, so that the conclusion appears to be unavoidable, that Marduk-sar-uzur is Bel-sar-uzur, and that he actually reigned as king.

There is a confirmation of *Daniel* in the very mention of this "third year," which appears on the tablet. Two of Daniel's visions are dated, "In the first year of Belshazzar king of Babylon" (chap. vii. 1), and "In the third year of the reign of king Belshazzar" (chap. viii. 1). Mr. Boscawen points out that it is plain from the tablet that Belshazzar's third year was not his last. The tablet, therefore, carries us beyond both the dates given in Scripture. The second point to which I referred is the descent of Belshazzar from Nebuchadnezzar. Nabonidus did not belong to the royal family, but it has been suggested that he may have tried to strengthen his position by marrying a daughter of Nebuchadnezzar's after he became king. But, as he reigned only seventeen years in all, it is plain that Belshazzar could not have been the offspring of such a marriage. It is far more likely that he had previously married into the royal family, and was chosen, like his predecessor, Neriglissar, because he was son-in-law to the great king. Such intermarriages between the royal house and the nobility were not uncommon. There is an inscription extant, for example, which relates the request of the high priest of Ezida on Birs Nimrod to have in marriage the daughter of Neriglissar. A passage in Herodotus may throw some light upon this matter. He represents the last king of the Babylonians, and he who perished when the city was taken, as the son of Nitocris, a queen to whom he ascribes the great defensive works which have been represented elsewhere as the work of Nabonidus. This would seem to indicate that the memory of the wife of Nabonidus had been treasured by the Babylonians when her husband had been comparatively forgotten. This would find an easy explanation if she had been the daughter of the great hero-king.

But there is another indication which leads still more definitely to this conclusion. Referring to the suggested intermarrying of Nabonidus with the royal house, Canon Rawlinson says: "It must be granted that we have no proof that he did. We have, however, some indications from which we should, naturally, have drawn the conclusion independently of the Book of Daniel. Two pretenders to the throne of Babylon started up during the reign of Darius Hystaspis, both of whom called themselves 'Nebuchadnezzar, son of Nabonidus.' It is certain from this that Nabonidus must have had a son so called, for no pretender would assume the name of a person who never existed. How, then, are we to account for Nabonidus having given this name to one of his sons? Usurpers, as a rule, have no desire to recall the memory of the family which they have dispossessed. The Sargonidæ discarded all the names in use among their predecessors. So did the Egyptian monarchs of the eighteenth and nineteenth dynasties. So, again, did those of the twenty-first, and the Psammetichi. Nabonidus must have intended to claim a family connection with the preceding Babylonian monarchs when he thus named a son. And if he was indeed 'no way related to Nebuchadnezzar,' the connection could only have been by marriage. The probability, therefore, is that the principal wife of Nabonidus, the queen (or queen-mother) of Daniel v. 10, was a daughter of Nebuchadnezzar, and that through her Belshazzar was Nebuchadnezzar's grandson."\*

We have now to notice more fully one of the latest attempts to disparage *Daniel*, and that, too, in the name of Assyriology. Professor Sayce has here supplied another instance of that impetuousness which has marred much useful and, indeed, brilliant work. In his book, *The Higher Criticism and the Monuments*, he appears to have felt it incumbent upon him to let the critics down as gently as possible. After showing that they have been wrong almost everywhere besides, he gives *Daniel* away to them, and actually tries to prove that they have been fully justified in their rejection of *it*. He has been forced to admit that the monuments have told us much about Belshazzar; "but," he continues, "Belshazzar never became king *in his father's place*. No mention is made of him in the Annalistic tablet, and it would, therefore, appear that he was no longer in command of the Babylonian army when the invasion of Cyrus took place. Owing to the unfortunate lacuna in the

---

\* *Egypt and Babylon*, pp. 159, 160.

middle of the tablet, we have no account of what became of him, but since we are told not only of the fate of Nabonidos, but also of *the death of his wife*, it seems probable that Belshazzar was dead. At any rate, when Cyrus entered Babylonia he had already disappeared from history."

"Here, then," he continues, "the account given by the book of Daniel is at variance with the testimony of the inscriptions. But the contradictions do not end here. The Biblical story implies that Babylon was taken by storm; at all events it expressly states that 'the king of the Chaldeans was slain.' Nabonidos, the Babylonian king, however, was not slain, and Cyrus entered Babylon 'in peace.'"

"Nor was Belshazzar the son of Nebuchadnezzar, as we are repeatedly told in the fifth chapter of Daniel. He was the son of the usurper Nabonidos, and Nabonidos did not even belong to the family of Nebuchadnezzar. The error is an indication of the age to which it belongs. It is an error which we find again in the pages of Herodotos, though Herodotos substitutes Labynetos, that is to say, Nabonidos for Belshazzar."\*

Now, there is hardly a single statement in this extract which is not marked by prejudice and by haste. Take the last assertion, that Daniel is marred by the same errors that characterise Herodotus. Is it fair to conceal the significance of the fact that Daniel names Belshazzar correctly, and

---
\* *The Higher Criticism and the Monuments*, pp. 525, 526.

that neither Herodotus nor any other ancient writer does so? The only mention made of him in all literature was this in the book of Daniel. Herodotus blunders, and Xenophon blunders, in this matter; the Scripture alone is accurate. Can this, then, be said to point to the same age as that in which the memory of this man's name had passed away? If Herodotus and others were unable to find it, where did the writer of *Daniel* pick it up? To any careful reader of facts, the only possible conclusion is that, since Herodotus wrote about the middle of the fifth century B.C., *Daniel* must have been written earlier still; that is, the presence of the *name* Belshazzar proves that the book was written *at the very time to which it has always been assigned!*

There are other unfortunate statements in the extract. Professor Sayce seems to think it a contradiction of the Scripture that "Belshazzar never became king *in his father's place.*" But there is no contradiction. On the very last night of his life, as we have already seen, the highest place Belshazzar has to offer is the *third*. "Whosoever," he says, "shall read this writing and show me the interpretation thereof . . . shall be the third ruler in the kingdom" (Daniel v. 7). This proves that he regards his father as still alive and as still possessed of the regal dignity. The Scripture is here, therefore, in entire accord with the monuments, for these prove that Belshazzar did not outlive his father. An equally extraordinary statement is met by the same answer. "Herodotos," says Professor

Sayce, "still knows that Nabonidos was the king who was overthrown by Cyrus; in the book of Daniel even this is forgotten " (page 527). The fact is that Herodotus does not mention Nabonidus at all. He speaks of "Labynetus," not Nabonidus. The Professor follows, indeed, the usual custom, and identifies the Labynetus of Herodotus with the Nabonidus of history; but it shows, at the least, great lack of caution to assert that " Herodotos still knows that *Nabonidos* was the king who was overthrown by Cyrus; *in the book of Daniel even this is forgotten.*" The evident purpose of the statement is to impress the reader with the belief that *Daniel* was written *after* the time of Herodotus. But here, again, the evidence points the other way. Daniel had no call whatever to mention Nabonidus. He is not writing a history of Babylon, nor even giving an account of the events which led to its fall. He is merely recounting an incident in his own history with which Belshazzar is closely connected, and with which Nabonidus has nothing whatever to do. It is only forgetfulness of the purpose of the book that can permit anyone to treat this silence as due to ignorance ; and that forgetfulness is still more astonishing in face of the fact that, while not mentioning Nabonidus, he clearly indicates his existence in that phrase "the third ruler," of which I have already spoken.

The absence of distinct mention of Nabonidus in *Daniel* is therefore fully accounted for. But what are we to say of the argument when we test the alleged knowledge of Herodotus. The Greek historian mentions a name that is known neither to history nor to recent discovery. He speaks, as I have said, of *Labynetus*. Daniel, on the other hand, does mention a name that is absolutely correct. Does not this show that, viewing *Daniel* as an ordinary literary composition, it must be earlier than Herodotus? Herodotus gives us a name that has plainly suffered by transmission. Daniel gives us one in which no trace of the changes wrought by tradition is found. The latter must plainly have written therefore at a time when the recollection of the facts was still fresh. It is extremely doubtful also whether the identification of the Labynetus of Herodotus with the Nabonidus of history can be sustained. Herodotus plainly intimates that his Labynetus was a direct descendent of Nebuchadnezzar, which we know Nabonidus was not. He was also, says Herodotus, the son of a queen named Nitocris, to whom Babylonian tradition attributed the great works usually ascribed to Nabonidus. This Nitocris must have been *the wife of Nabonidus*, the mother of Belshazzar, and a daughter of Nebuchadnezzar. The Labynetus of Herodotus would consequently be the Belshazzar of the Bible, and not the Nabonidus of the historians.

I have already dealt in anticipation with the Professor's statement that "no mention is made of him (Belshazzar) in the Annalistic tablet .... but since we are told not only of the fate of Nabonidus, but also of the death of his wife, it seems probable that Belshazzar was not dead." Now there is no mention whatever of the death of the wife of Nabonidus. The word in the inscription cannot be read as *u assat*, "the wife of." The inscription reads: "The son of the king died." *This can only be Belshazzar.* The tablet also says that he died exactly as the Scripture says he died. "In that night," says Daniel, "was Belshazzar the king of the Chaldeans slain" (verse 30). The tablet reads: "The eleventh day of the month Marchesvan, *during the night*, Gobryas was on the bank of the river . . . . And the son of the king died. From the twenty-seventh day of Adar to the third day of Nisan there was lamentation in the country of Accad; all the people smote their heads." There was, therefore, a *night entry* into Babylon, and in immediate connection with it Belshazzar died. Xenophon says that he stood in the midst of his nobles sword in hand, and intimates that he fell fighting. The statement of the tablet that Babylon was captured without fighting also bears out the Scripture. The city was taken by surprise, and the capture was in some way connected *with the river*. We read in the tablet, "during the night" of the eventful day just named "Gobryas," the general of Cyrus, "was on the bank of the river;" and then, after a break in the inscription, the next words we come to are, "and the son of the king died."

There is another "correction" of Daniel to which Professor Sayce lends his authority, on which it is needful to say a word or two. It refers to the writing upon the wall. "It has long been recognised," he says, "that the words in question are Aramaic. But it was reserved for the acuteness of M. Clermont-Ganneau to point out their philological explanation. *Par'su* or *Bar'su*, in Assyrian, means 'a part of a shekel,' while *tekel* is the Aramaic representative of the Hebrew *shekel*, the Assyrian *siklu*. *Mene* is the equivalent alike of the Assyrian *mana* or 'maneh,' the standard weight, and of the verb *manu*, 'to reckon.' In the Babylonian language, therefore, the mysterious words which appeared upon the wall would have been *mani mana sikla u bar'si*, 'Reckon a maneh, a skekel and its parts.'"

Here Professor Sayce has outdone himself! He admits that the words are Aramaic, but nevertheless tries to read them as Assyrian, with the result that they are turned into nonsense. The writing on the wall was *mene, mene, tekel, upharsin* (u-parsin), and signified "numbered, numbered, weighed, and breakings asunder." The repetition of the word "numbered" meant, no doubt, that the work was completed; and hence in the interpretation Daniel says: "God hath numbered thy kingdom and *finished it*." And not only was it brought to an end, it was weighed in the balances of the sanctuary and found wanting. It was therefore given over to judgment. The plural form, *Parsin*, has a yet fuller prophecy in it than is exhausted in the immediate fulfilment which Daniel indicates. The reader will notice that the singular only is used in the explanation. "*Peres;* thy kingdom is divided (or broken asunder), and given to the Medes and Persians" (Dan. v. 28). One wonders why the word quoted should be the singular *Peres*, instead of the plural *Parsin*, which was written by the finger of God. The answer seems to be that this breaking asunder was only the first of repeated calamities. The Scripture had declared that the breaking up and spoiling of the nations in which Babylon had delighted should be terribly avenged. These words had been written and were waiting for their fulfilment: "Many nations and great kings shall serve themselves of them also; and I will recompense them according to their deeds, and according to the works of their hands" (Jer. xxv. 14). That unexhausted plural form told the whole after history of the land. Only one of these breakings asunder was to find its fulfilment in the advent of the Medes and Persians; others would surely follow.

It is probable that the existence of these prophecies led to the profanation of the vessels devoted to God's service and to the doom of Belshazzar. Xenophon's account of Cyrus has long been set down as a romance; but the discovery of Cyrus's tablets must modify this opinion. Cyrus indicates, for example, that the war with Babylon was long continued, and that the hostilities with Babylon itself were preceded by one war after another conducted by Cyrus against the neighbouring territories. That is the very picture presented by Xenophon. This fact is quite enough to show that Xenophon's biography of Cyrus is history and not romance. He tells us that the besieged in Babylon were full of confidence even after the army of Cyrus had appeared before the walls. He dug ditches and raised turrets and ramparts; "but they that were within the walls," says Xenophon, "laughed at this blockade, as being themselves provided with necessaries for above twenty years. Cyrus, hearing this, divided his army into twelve parts, as if he intended that each part should serve on the watch one month in the year, and when the Babylonians heard this they laughed yet more than before; thinking within themselves that they were to be watched by the Phrygians, Lydians, Arabians, and Cappadocians, men that were better affected towards them than they were to the Persians."

But what, then, of these predictions? Cyrus, named by Isaiah, nearly 200 years before, had come. The same prophet declared that Cyrus would not come to Babylon in vain. God had said that He would "open before them the two leaved gates," that He would "break in pieces the gates of brass, and cut in sunder the bars of iron" (Isaiah xlv. 1, 2). These predictions appear to have been known to Belshazzar and to the Babylonians; and now the king who had laughed at the Persians would show what he thought of these things. They would also laugh at the threatenings of the God of Israel. The vesssels of His sanctuary, which Babylonian might had spoiled, were ordered to be fetched. "Then they brought the golden vessels that were taken out of the temple of the house of God which was at Jerusalem; and the king, his princes, his wives, and his concubines drank in them. They drank wine, and praised the gods of gold, and of silver, of brass, of iron, of wood, and of stone" (Daniel v. 3, 4). It was while this bravado was in process that God's answer came. "In the same hour came forth fingers of a man's hand, and wrote over against the candlestick upon the plaister of the wall of the king's palace, and the king saw the part of the hand that wrote" (verse 5). No one needed to tell Belshazzar whose hand it was. He knew that his doom was written there. Xenophon tells us what followed. It was a night of high festival, not only in the palace, but throughout the city. Gadatas and Gobryas, the leaders of the army of Cyrus and Babylonian nobles whom Belshazzar had deeply wronged, found entrance into the city by the river-bed, which they had drained. Coming to the palace gates, they found them shut. "And they that were posted," he says, "opposite to the guards, fell on them, as they were drinking with a great deal of light around them, and used them immediately in a hostile manner. As soon as the noise and clamour began, they that were within, perceiving the disturbance, and the king commanding them to examine what the matter was, ran out, throwing open the gates. They that were with Gadatas, as soon as they saw the gates loose, broke in, pressing forward on the runaways; and dealing their blows amongst them, they came up to the king, and found him now in a standing posture, with his sword drawn. They that were with Gadatas and Gobryas, being many in number, mastered him; they likewise that were with him were killed; one holding up something before him, another flying, and another defending himself with anything that he could meet with. .... When day came, and they that guarded the castles perceived that the city was taken, and the king dead, they gave up the castles."* Here, it will be noted, that he who died at the head of his nobility is spoken of as "the king." This could not have been Nabonidus, as he did not die then. It could only have been Belshazzar, and thus we have another testimony that the royal title was accorded to him, and that he did indeed reign.

Before I pass from the Scripture account of this incident, let me point to three minor touches which prove its thorough historical accuracy. Mention is made of "the plaister" on the palace wall. This detail shows the most intimate acquaintance with the Babylonian edifices. "The walls were built," says Evetts, "of baked or crude bricks. . . . The chambers of the palace were internally decorated with bas-reliefs carved on thin slabs of alabaster, which lined the walls from the floor to a considerable height..... Above the line of the bas-reliefs the Assyrian chambers were decorated by paintings on the stucco; for the bare brickwork was nowhere allowed to be seen."† The word in the original means "stucco." This is found still clinging to the

---
\* *Cyropaideia*, vii., 5.   † *New Light on the Bible*, pp. 400-404.

ruined walls of the Assyrian palaces. The very position assigned to it should also be remarked. The lower part of the wall was covered with the alabaster slabs. The stucco, therefore, occupied the *higher portion* on which the inscription would naturally be written, so as to command the attention of the king and of the revellers.

Next let us notice the feast and its character. It is a banquet in which wine occupies a prominent place. A piece of sculpture illustrating this was found by Botta in Sargon's palace which he unearthed at Khorsabad. The Assyrian and Babylonian customs were alike in these respects, so that the Assyrian artist enables us to see what passed in the palace at Babylon. The guests are divided into groups of four, who sit on raised seats facing each other. Each group has a special table and attendant. The long robes of the nobles descend to their feet, and we mark that they are shod with sandals. Their arms are bare, and are adorned with armlets and bracelets. Each holds a wine-cup of elegant shape raised in his right hand as high as his head, and are evidently engaged in pledging each other. The bottom of the cup is in the form of a lion's head. The table is richly ornamented. It is covered with a kind of tablecloth which hangs over the side. Musicians are in attendance. This is the common representation. The main part of the feast seems to have consisted in wine-drinking. The sculptures always represent the guests not eating but drinking. The servants carry the empty cups to a vase of large dimensions placed on the ground; and, after having filled them, carry them back to the guests, who drink abundantly. In perfect keeping with the representations on the monuments are the words of Daniel, which speak again and again of the drinking of wine as *the* feature of the feast. "Belshazzar made a great feast to a thousand of his lords, and drank wine before the thousand." The sacred vessels are brought in that the guests "might drink therein," &c. Was it possible for a late writer to describe with such perfect accuracy, and with such unobtrusive naturalness, the customs of a civilisation with which he had no acquaintance, and which, indeed, had perished centuries before he was born? The critics must really bethink themselves. While asking us to believe less, they must not saddle us with the burden of believing impossibilities.

The last feature makes the matter worse. It is the statement (Daniel v. 3, 23) that women were present at Belshazzar's feast. This was a distinctly Assyrian and Babylonian custom. The evidence of it may be seen in the British Museum. A slab taken from the palace of Assurbanipal at Koyoundjik represents the queen seated at a table drinking wine with the king, who is represented reclining on a couch. The freedom accorded by the Babylonians to women was not in accord with Persian customs, and still less was it in accord with those of the Greeks. This fact so embarrassed the translators of the Septuagint version, who did their work, be it remembered, at the very time at which the critics say Daniel was written—it so embarrassed them that they altered the word of God that they might not provoke the criticisms of their contemporaries. "The Septuagint translators," says Mr. Fuller, in the Speaker's Commentary, "omit altogether the notice of the women; and Theodotion (in the second century of our era) records the presence at Belshazzar's feast of 'the concubines' only; in this following the customs common at the time of the composition of their translations. Daniel's account of what took place was to them inconsistent with what they knew of Oriental habits; yet history has proved him correct." But will any one of those who argue for a late date of *Daniel* tell us how their contention and this fact can possibly agree? It was so impossible for writers in the second century B.C. to imagine that women should, in a civilised land like Babylon, be present at a banquet, that the Greek translators of the Old Testament had to suppress the passage. But, if that is so, how was it possible for the writer of Daniel at that very time to compose a statement which men of his own age dare not translate if they were to save his credit? This is quite as hard a conundrum as the other, and the only possible conclusion is that the book was written by one to whom the Babylonian customs were quite as familiar as the customs of our own land and time are to ourselves.

## CHAPTER XV.

### DARIUS THE MEDIAN.

THE fifth chapter of Daniel concludes with these words: "And Darius the Median took the kingdom, being about threescore and two years old." Had there been perfect faith in the book as a statement of facts, this notice would have been regarded as of the very greatest value. Daniel is not writing a history of Babylon, nor even giving a full account of the events of his own times. He is merely narrating certain matters which he was commissioned to place on record for our learning. In connection with these we have this reference to the succession of Darius, as we also have in the sixth chapter an incident which occurred in his reign. The notices stand alone in history. They are the only known record of a man whose memory (if we except a few indistinct echoes) has perished everywhere besides.

I repeat, therefore, that the fifth and sixth chapters of Daniel ought to be doubly precious on that account. They retain for every age a most vivid picture of a man of whom we should otherwise have known nothing. But there has not been perfect faith in *Daniel*, and its glory in this matter has been turned into shame. On the outlook for whatever may be represented to its disadvantage, unbelieving scholarship has swooped down upon every addition made in *Daniel* to our historical knowledge, and turned it into an argument against the historical character of the book. Because no other history mentioned Belshazzar, it was at once concluded that the Belshazzar of *Daniel* was a myth. A similar conclusion has been rushed at, and is still confidently persisted in, with regard to Darius. The silence of those who have given us the slender information which we have regarding this period, has been assumed to be a positive disproof of the fuller information contained on this particular point in *Daniel*. The scholars were utterly misled as to Belshazzar, the silence of all the historians notwithstanding. It may be safely said that they are equally wrong in regard to Darius.

There is no question whatever as to who was the actual conqueror of the Babylonians. It was Cyrus. It is also true that the Persian dynasty begins with him. How, then, could "Darius the Mede" take the kingdom, and who could he be? Before I cite the confirmations of the accuracy of the Scripture in this matter, it may be well to glance at some suggested explanations, which are now offered, but which are quite untenable. It is supposed that the kingship of Darius was a Babylonian vice-royalty, and that Cyrus might have conferred this upon either of two men who are mentioned as having been of special service to him during the campaign. These were Gobryas and Gadatas. Both of them were Babylonian nobles whom Belshazzar (who seems to have early developed into a savage tyrant) had foully and barbarously wronged. But this Babylonian origin of theirs entirely disposes of the theory. Neither of them could have been described as "Darius the Median."

The theory that the dignity of Darius was a vice-royalty and not a sovereignty must also be put aside. Darius was absolutely monarch of Babylon and of its conquests. When Daniel says that "Darius the Median took the kingdom," the meaning plainly is that he took the kingdom which had belonged to Belshazzar. That was a full sovereignty and not a vice-royalty. Two other statements of Scripture are equally emphatic in their rejection of the suggested explanation. Cyrus is represented as *succeeding* Darius, not as being his over-lord and as reigning contemporaneously with him. The words which conclude the historical part of the book are these: "So this Daniel prospered in the reign of Darius and in the reign of Cyrus the Persian" (vi. 28). The opening words of the same chapter are not less explicit as to the kind of sovereignty exercised by Darius. "It pleased Darius to set over the kingdom an hundred and twenty princes, who should be over the whole kingdom." Here arrangements are made for the entire dominion of the Medes and Persians.

They are made without consultation with, and without reference to, any higher authority. To adopt the suggestion, therefore, of a vice-royalty would land us in fresh difficulties of quite as grave a character as those from which escape is sought.

Was there any Median, then, to whom the conquests of Cyrus were likely to be surrendered? Herodotus tells (and in this he is borne out by Cyrus's own inscriptions) that Astyages, king of the Medes, was conquered by Cyrus at the outset of his career. Xenophon, on the other hand, gives us quite a different representation. Astyages, according to him, is succeeded by his son Cyaxares, who sends for Cyrus and his Persians to help him to repel a threatened invasion of the Babylonians. With Cyrus's response to that appeal the story of his triumphs begins. But, antagonistic as these accounts appear at first sight, there are indications of agreement. Cyrus prevails over Astyages, Herodotus says, because of a revolt of his own subjects against him and in Cyrus's favour. This would prevent Cyrus treating Media as a conquered country, and may have led to his arranging for the succession of Cyaxares. Then it is plain, even from Xenophon's account, that the dominion of Cyaxares over the Medes is largely nominal. The affection of the people and their virtual allegiance are bestowed upon Cyrus, and the wounded pride of the Median king has to be soothed by more than one device.

Can Cyaxares, then, be the monarch who ascends the throne of Babylon? Much can be urged in favour of an affirmative reply. Xenophon reports that Cyrus told Cyaxares that a "house and a dominion" awaited him at Babylon, and that Cyaxares gave his daughter in marriage to Cyrus with the succession to the Median throne, as he himself had no son. This means that he had no hope of a male heir, which would agree with the statement in Daniel regarding the age of Darius. It is also clear from other notices in the ancient historians that Cyrus, from some reason or other, was extremely solicitous to gratify the Medes. The Median robe became, for example, the State garb of the new Empire. The ordinary procedure would have been, either to have given the place of honour to the Persian costume, or to have retained the Babylonian. The adoption of that of Media points to a strong desire to propitiate that people. If the attempt to gratify them had been carried to the extent of making one of their race the first sovereign of the new dynasty, it would be at once another proof of statesmanlike policy on the part of Cyrus and a full explanation of the choice of the Median costume. For, if Darius the Median was the first sovereign, then, necessarily, the State garb of the new dominion would be that of his own nationality.

But we are not reduced to mere theories. There are statements on the pages of historical authorities which the account given by Daniel alone enables us to understand. We have already seen that Nabonidus was spared by Cyrus, and made governor of Carmania. But we are told by two authorities that

Nabonidus's tenure of the province was interrupted. Abydenus (quoted by Eusebius) says, "Cyrus, after he had taken possession of Babylon, appointed him (that is, Nabonidus) governor of the country of Carmania. *Darius, the king, removed him out of the land.*" Now, this Darius could hardly be Darius Hystaspis, the next of the name after Cyrus, for, in that case, Nabonidus must have lived to an extreme old age. But, if it is our Darius, then he acts with an authority that makes no scruple of altering an arrangement made by Cyrus himself. The statement is also made by Alexander Polyhistor, who says, " Darius, the king, removed (him) a little out of the country."

Another significant hint comes from an ancient note appended to a play by Aristophenes. The Daric was a famous coin belonging to the Persians, which circulated throughout the then known world, and which made many a bright eye sparkle among the Greeks. The scholiast says that "the Darics were named, not from Darius, the father of Xerxes, but from another *more ancient king.*" Who was this more ancient king? Darius, the father of Xerxes, that is, Darius Hystaspis, is the first Darius known to our ordinary histories. Him the author of this note sets aside, and tells us that the Persian Daric owes its name to an older Darius. Who that Darius was Daniel alone has told us. He was "Darius the Median." When the Medo-Persian empire was established, the conquerors saw the necessity and expediency of a new coinage, and the Daric thus preserves a name which has dropped almost entirely from the page of profane history.

Our last proof comes from the monuments, which will, no doubt, by-and-bye shed a fuller light upon this matter. Darius ascended the throne at the age of sixty-two (Dan. v. 31). *This was in the sixty-eighth year of the captivity of Judah.* The seventieth year of the captivity was the first year of Cyrus. Darius, therefore, according to the Scripture, reigns only two years. This fact, which we have to get at by close inspection and by inference, is strangely confirmed by a significant variation of phrase in the contracts drawn up in the reign of Cyrus. Fr. Lenormant, referring to this two years' reign of Darius, says:—
"I have found an indication of it in this significant fact, that, on the Babylonian and Chaldean contracts in cuneiform writing, Cyrus is designated 'king of Babylon, king of the nations,' only from *the third year*, counted from the capture of the city. In the contracts of the year 1, and of the year 2, he is called only 'king of the nations.'" What caused the difference during these two years? There is some reason, during the first and the second years after the capture of Babylon, for the diminished title of its conqueror. At the end of the second year the obstacle is removed, and the full title is given. Daniel's account explains this fully. During these two years Darius the Median wielded in name, and with all the insignia of royalty, the sovereignty of the ancient mistress of the world.

We now come to the closing incident in the historical portion of the Book. Daniel's old age was as full of vicissitude as his youth. His fearless prophecy on that last night of Belshazzar's reign no doubt commended him to the conquerors. But, whatever the reason may have been, Daniel was in greater favour with Darius than he had been with Belshazzar, or indeed since the days of Nebuchadnezzar. He was one of the three great President Princes of the new empire, and such was the impression made by his integrity and administrative ability upon the mind of the Median king, that it was his declared intention to make Daniel the one great minister of the new dominion.

But it was more than the Median and the Persian nobles could endure, to have a stranger placed over them amid the conquests they had just made, and whose spoils they were, therefore, entitled to share. Before the appointment is made, means must, therefore, be taken to ruin the man whose advancement they feared. They knew that there was no chance of success, unless they could turn Daniel's own integrity against him; and they accordingly so arranged matters that Daniel must make his choice between disloyalty to God and disloyalty to the king. It is the choice which persecution has often forced upon the servants of God. "Then these presidents and princes assembled together to the king, and said thus unto him: King Darius, live for ever! All the presidents of the kingdom, the governors, and the princes, the counsellors and the captains, have consulted together to establish a royal statute, and to make a firm decree, that whosoever shall ask a petition of any god or man for thirty days, save of thee, O king, he shall be cast into the den of lions." The decree was approved. Daniel was caught in the snare, and thrown to the lions. But God delivered him, and the punishment which these men designed for another, came upon themselves and upon those whose lives were dearer to them than their own.

This narrative, like most things in Scripture, has been rejected with contempt and with indignation. The decree of Darius is said to be "insane." No man, it is imagined, would ever have listened to such a suggestion, and that only an uninstructed dreamer could have attempted to pass this off as history. The objection, however, is open to this very charge of ignorance. If the Median and Persian kings were supposed to be Divine, then the suggestion that the divinity should be asserted and acknowledged in Babylon, may have had much to commend it in the eyes of statesmanship in those early days of the Medo-Persian kingdom. That this divinity was claimed and allowed is a matter of fact. "The Persians," says Dr. Pusey, "looked upon their king as the representative of Ormuzd, as indwelt by him, and, as such, gave him divine honours. Persians, Persian monuments, contemporary Greek writers, attest this. 'With us,' said Artabanus to Themistocles, 'of many and good laws this is the best, to honour the king, and worship him as the image of God who preserveth all things,' that is, Ormuzd.

Curtius says, 'The Persians worship their kings among the gods;' Isocrates 'worshipping indeed a mortal man, and addressing him as a divine being, but dishonouring the gods more than men.' Arrian relates that, from the time of Cambyses to that of Alexander, the Magi had had the hereditary charge of the tomb of Cyrus at Pasargadæ, and received daily from the king a sheep, wheat-flour, and wine, and monthly a horse to sacrifice to Cyrus.' In Persian inscriptions they are called 'offspring of the gods' and 'gods.' Representations at the royal graves at Persepolis, in whatever way they are to be explained, indicate some very close relation and identification of the king with Ormuzd. The Persians, as they borrowed other things from the Medes, so probably this. Deioces is represented by Herodotus as retiring and keeping himself out of sight. In this account of Darius itself, the unalterableness of the law of the Medes and Persians is part of the supposed relation of the king to Ormuzd, man claiming to act through a divine presence."\*

It has also been argued that religious intolerance was utterly foreign to these Eastern civilisations, and that the interference with worship which marks the decree suited a later age, but was not in accord with the time of Cyrus. This also is a palpable mistake; but it is the mistake not of Daniel, but of his critics. The Assyrian kings regarded their campaigns as religious wars. Tiglath-Pileser I. speaks of subduing "the enemies of Ashur," of

---
\* *Daniel the Prophet*, pp. 442-444.

warring with "kings hostile to Ashur my lord." The following phrases also display the same feature: "did not acknowledge Ashur my lord," "paid no worship to Ashur my lord," "foreigners hostile to Ashur," "heretics, my enemies and the enemies of Ashur," "with sixty kings victoriously I fought, and the laws and religion of my empire I imposed upon them." It is abundantly plain that religious intolerance was no invention of later times, and that the penalty of death, threatened for disobedience to the decree for the worship of Darius, was no outrage upon the notions of the period.

The nature of the punishment was also distinctly Babylonian. Lions abounded in Babylonia, were kept by the king, and are pictured on the monuments in cages, the doors of which are raised by attendants, who stand on the top and are protected by a cage-like structure. Lions were also used as the instruments of royal vengeance. Assurbanipal says in an inscription: "The rest of the men alive in the midst of the bulls and the lions—as Sennacherib, the father of my father, threw into the midst—so I (following) his steps, into the midst I threw." Objections have been urged against the representation of the lions' den implied in the Scripture. Davidson, in his *Introduction*, repeats the objection of one of his German "authorities," and grows merry over the supposed absurdity. "How did the animals live," he asks, "in a *cistern-like* den? Did an angel give them air to breathe, whose vitalising property could not be exhausted? It is difficult to see how life

could have been long supported in the place.
Lions would soon have died in it." A complete
answer to this has been furnished by Höst in the
account of his travels in Fez and Morocco. He
found lions' dens in Morocco in which the ancient
arrangement has evidently been preserved. The
dens consist, he tells us, of a large square cavern
under the ground. There is a partition wall in the
middle, with a trap-door which (as in the Assyrian
lion-cage) can be opened from above. The keepers
when they wish to clear out one division throw food
into the other and open the door. As soon as the
lions pass through, the door is closed and the now
empty compartment is cleansed. The cavern is open
at the top, which is surrounded with a wall. The
mouth of the den is a door in the wall, from which
steps go down which are used by the keepers in their
descent. "The Emperor," says Höst, "sometimes
has men cast in." This agrees fully with the indications in the Scripture. It probably continues, as I
have said, the ancient plan; but in any case it proves
that there was as little ground for rationalist merri-
ment here, as there is for the objections which
widening knowledge is sweeping aside as the dawn
rolls away the darkness.

## CHAPTER XVI.

### The Visions of Daniel.

THE book of Daniel is divided into two equal parts. The first six chapters are historical; the second contains visions and predictions. In the first part, it is true, there are two visions; but these are not Daniel's, but Nebuchadnezzar's. In the second part the visions are Daniel's, and form one of the most remarkable portions of Scripture. The 9th chapter, for instance, gives us the number of years which were to intervene between the restoration of the Jewish state and the manifestation of Jesus to Israel and His atoning death. At the latest date ever assigned to the book, at least a century and a half stood between it and that great world-transforming event. The hand that reached over even 150 years, and measured on to the point at which the Christ was to suffer, was not man's hand. The accuracy of the date proves it to have been the hand of God. It must be remembered, too, that there is no room for the suspicion that the prophecy is a Christian interpolation. The *Jews* have handed on the book and the prediction to us. They have handed it on unaltered, though they had the most powerful inducements to change it and to blot out one of God's own testimonies to Jesus and to their sin in rejecting Him. But the Jew has never dared to change even a letter of the Hebrew Bible, and the prediction stands to-day as God's seal upon a Book rejected, strange to say by so-called Christians, but revered by the Jew.

It is not my intention now to deal with the visions of Daniel, except in so far as light is cast upon them by recent explorations. Before touching upon this, however, let me note one or two minor points in the first portion of the book. In the 5th chapter we note that evidently great honour is paid to the queen mother. She comes into the banqueting-house unbidden, gives her counsel amid, evidently, respectful silence, and sees it immediately and reverently acted upon. We have one of the highest possible testimonies—a testimony which takes us into the very time—that this representation shows us the customs of the place and of the age. There is a reference in a tablet of Nabonidus, the father of Belshazzar, to the death of his mother. We are told that the court went into mourning for three days on the occasion of her death. It would seem from the Annalistic tablet of Cyrus that the event took place in Belshazzar's camp. We read as follows:—"The fifth day of the month Nisan, the mother of the king, who was in the fortress of the camp on the Euphrates above Sippara, died. The king's son

(Belshazzar) and his soldiers mourned for three days. There was lamentation. In the month Sivan there was lamentation in the country of Accad over the mother of the king."

There is a reference in chapter iii. 29 to a peculiar form of punishment. Nebuchadnezzar threatens that the man who shall "speak anything amiss against the God of Shadrach, Meshach, and Abednego shall be cut in pieces." Here again we are made to see the very place and time as recent explorations have once more shown them to us. Assurbanipal, king of Assyria, says of some offenders: 'I threw these men again into that pit; I cut off their limbs, and caused them to be eaten by dogs, bears, eagles, vultures, birds of heaven, and fishes of the deep."

The reader will also recall the very peculiar feature of the unchangeableness of the Persian king's decree. Once it is issued it must remain unaltered. This is proved to have been a distinctive feature by accounts of the times which have come down to us. "We find Xerxes, the son of Darius Hystaspis," says Rawlinson, "brought into almost exactly the same dilemma as 'Darius the Mede,' bound by having passed his word and anxious to retract it, but unable to do so on account of the law, and, therefore, compelled to allow the perpetration of cruelties whereof he entirely disapproved."

Other confirmations might be pointed out, but we turn to the visions. To rightly apprehend the testimony which these yield, a word or two must be said on one of the most marvellous features of the Scripture. We hear a great deal now of "the human element in the Bible;" but there is grave reason to doubt whether those who speak most of this understand it best, or indeed understand it at all. They speak as if the presence of the human element made the presence of the Divine element impossible, and that to show that the human element is anywhere is to prove beyond the possibility of denial that that cannot be the Word of God. Are they forgetting the mystery of the Incarnation, and that, in all that Jesus did and said and was, the human element was always present, and that the Divine element was neverthless never wanting? This mystery may present a difficulty to some minds, but it forms for the believer the foundation of a glorious hope. God will yet so fill our life and thought that every word of ours will be God's word, and every act of ours will be God's act. Christ is but the first-fruits of the new creation in him; and the time will come when the whole field of redeemed life will be alike glorious. We shall then comprehend the mystery. And this hope which is so fully given in Christ has been hinted and proclaimed in all inspired service for God. God does not put His servant aside that *He* may speak. The Divine does not sweep out the human. The Divine preserves, raises, glorifies, perfects the human. It fills the human, and lifts it up to God's great ideal. The prophets were never so much themselves as when God spake by them. Their individuality was perfected. God always works from identity or likeness to diversity; from the single to the manifold. There are stages in which many living creatures are indistinguishable from each other; but these are the stages of immaturity. As life advances, and as God's plan is accomplished, the likeness disappears, and each is clothed with that individual form which God meant it to wear. And so, in God's highest earthly creation, each perfected spirit has its own endowment, and place, and glory.

This is the reason why the diversity of the human element in Scripture is so very marked. The writings of ordinary men may not be so stamped with strong individuality that their distinctness is at once apparent to every one. But it is so in the Bible. We are at once aware of an unlikeness between David and Moses. When we pass from Isaiah to Ezekiel, or from Jeremiah to Daniel, we feel that we have passed from the influence of one servant of God to that of another. The message is God's; the ministry is man's. The same glorious melody is continued, but it is continued by another instrument.

Now, this principle is of the utmost value in the questions which confront us to-day. We are told, in the name of a much-vaunted scholarship, that this book was written by a Palestinian Jew in the second century B.C. That is, that it was written by one who never had any acquaintance with Babylon and its culture, and whose thought did not reflect in any way the institutions, manners, and customs of the time and the land of Nebuchadnezzar. Now, if the individuality of Daniel is stamped upon his book, it will have something to say about this. We shall very soon be able to note whether it is the individuality of a man whose thought is cast in a Babylonian mould. If that is the case, criticism will dash itself against this rock in vain.

Does the writer, then, display an individuality that has been moulded by the later or by an earlier time? Is he a man of Babylonian or of Palestinian culture, and is he writing for men the form of whose conceptions and ideas is due to Palestine or to Babylon? In other words, does the Book of Daniel reveal the watermark of Palestine under the Greek dominion of the second century B.C., or that of Babylon four centuries earlier? God, in communicating to Daniel His counsels, would do this by making use of the ideas with which Daniel was familiar. Wishing to reach the people through Daniel, the Holy Spirit would use conceptions, figures, and allusions through which the Jews of Daniel's time could be best informed and instructed. If the book belongs to the Babylonian period, the form of its visions will fit in with that period.

This principle is one which is not so widely recognised as it ought to be. There is a savour of offence in it. It brings the human too near the Divine, and may even seem to some to limit the Divine by the human. We forget that the Scripture is like the ladder seen by the Patriarch. Its foot is on the earth and its top is in heaven. Even our Lord's own teaching fits into the time, and is therefore, to that extent, of the time. His message is meant for all ages; but it becomes increasingly clearer as we become more familiar with the time and the place in which our Lord lived and taught. And what is true of the Master is equally true of all His servants. Let us suppose, for a moment, that the Book of God had yet to be added to, and that a prophet was raised up in this nineteenth-century England by whom God was to continue the work of Revelation. His prophecy would necessarily contain references which would be entirely new. There would be some impress of our modern modes of thought, and some reflection of, if not distinct reference to, our railroads, telegraphs, steamships, our commerce, our industries, our politics, and our national customs. The message, spoken by a man of the England of to-day, and to men of the England of to-day, would of necessity have much in it which would adapt it both to him and to them. Had a similar message come three or four centuries ago by a Frenchman, and been given through him to the French of that period, it would have had a like adaptation to the place and the time; and, should any doubt be afterwards raised as to the period when these books originated, the question would be settled by looking at the watermark woven into the work. The French prophecy would bear the stamp of its age and place; and the mark of the English prophecy would be equally distinct.

Let us now turn the light of this principle upon the book of Daniel. There are two prophecies which belong to the Captivity and to Babylon—Daniel and Ezekiel. The visions which they contain are of a character which makes them resemble each other quite as much as they separate them from the other prophetical books of the Bible. In Nebuchadnezzar's vision, for example, of the image—and to that prophecy all the rest in the latter part of this Book refer—there is, as we have already seen, a reflection of place and times and man. The same thing is true of those further explanatory visions given to Daniel himself. "The second part of the Book of Daniel," says Vigouroux, "is marked, like the first, with a strongly accentuated Babylonian colouring. It resembles in no way anything that has been written in Palestine. It has a remarkable originality. . . . We feel, in reading these majestic visions, that we have left Jerusalem, the banks of the Jordan, and the mountains of Palestine. We are in another land, under another sky, and in entirely different surroundings. The spectacles which are constantly under the eyes of the prophet are no longer those which struck Isaiah or Jeremiah. We live in a different world. Not only has the language changed and the vocabulary been modified, but the images also are new. All the symbolical forms—all the materials of the visions, so to speak—belong to Babylon. They bear no analogy to those of any other Jewish writer save Ezekiel, and he, too, lived in Babylon."

In the seventh chapter, we have one of the most magnificent descriptions contained in the whole

Bible. It is a revelation of God. "I beheld," says the prophet, "till the thrones were cast down, and the Ancient of Days did sit, whose garment was white as snow, and the hair of His head like pure wool; His throne was like the fiery flame, and His wheels as burning fire. A fiery stream issued and came forth from before him; thousand thousands ministered unto Him, and ten thousand times ten thousand stood before Him; the judgment was set and the books were opened" (verses 9, 10). This picture stands alone; and, if we exclude the prophecies of Ezekiel, there is nothing like it in the whole of Scripture. For a merely human author it would have been one of the most daring attempts man ever made. It paints and sets forth *in visible shape* the personality of the invisible God! It tells us the colour of God's robe, and it describes His hair as well as His throne! And yet we feel it to be a revelation of God. God is indeed made visible; but it is a presence of infinite majesty. It might be imagined that such a representation favoured idolatry; but we have only to look again in order to see that it blights idolatry. The vision makes imitation impossible; for we are face to face with the living God. The poverty and absurdity of idolatry were never felt as they are felt there. We seem to hear the cry, "To whom then will ye liken God, or what likeness will ye compare unto Him?" (Isa. xl. 18).

If we ask why the representation is made at all, the answer lies at hand. The four great universal empires have passed before us; we are now to look upon the Lord, *the* King. The empires of man are represented under the form of *wild beasts;* for, like these, the empires of man have come to devour and to destroy. *The only really human kingdom*—the kingdom that pities, that serves, that understands need, and that stoops to meet it—is God's kingdom. We understand now what at first shocks us. We see why God is represented as a man. It is the revelation of the kingdom of God as *opposed to the heartless dominions of man.* But when we go further and ask why this vision of man should assume the special form which it takes here, we see upon it the stamp of its origin. Every trait in the picture is Babylonian. The Jews in Babylon and Daniel himself were accustomed to look upon these very things as associated with royalty. The white garments, the hair like white wool, the throne, are all eloquent. They speak God's resolve. The Ancient of Days will yet reap the fruit of His long waiting and His ceaseless toil. His eternal purpose will be fulfilled. He will take unto Him the sovereignty over the world which He seems to have abandoned. He will reign over the nations, and the days of His kingdom will be a revelation of God that will bring Him nearer and make Him more real to men than any revelation has ever yet done. Is it not written, "They shall *see* God?" And there, in this seemingly daring picture in Daniel, is the promise of that hallowed and glad time!

But Assyriologists have been struck with the correspondence between the pictures in this seventh chapter of Daniel and the sculptures which have been excavated. Our museums and this prophecy set before us the same things! M. Longperier, a distinguished French scholar, in a description of the bas-reliefs in the Louvre, says: "The tunics of a very great number of Assyrian figures, which appear to have been painted white, and the way in which the hair is arranged in little wavelets, supply a commentary upon this passage in Daniel: 'Whose garment was white as snow, and the hair of His head like pure wool.'" Speaking of an Assyrian throne mounted on wheels, he is again irresistibly reminded of this strange description in the prophet. "The existence," he says, "of this royal throne mounted on wheels, permits us to comprehend a passage in Daniel, which, obscure as it appears, becomes a magnificent type of the reality: 'His throne was like the fiery flame and His wheels as burning fire.' We understand now what is meant by 'the wheels of a throne," and we admire in this verse the poetic image of a rapid movement."

The representations of the kingdoms are also exclusively Babylonian. The Babylonian kingdom is represented by a winged lion, the Roman by a beast with ten horns. The winged lion is a representation exceedingly common in Assyrian sculpture. And the part played by the horns in this and the following vision finds an explanation only in the Babylonian and Assyrian monuments. We can understand how it could be used as the symbol of power. The horn is the animal's power for defence. But in Babylonian sculpture the symbol is fully accepted and frequently used in that very sense. The notion of a head adorned with *ten* horns seems to us to border upon the ludicrous; but in those sculptures horns are multiplied in this very fashion, and are so disposed as to be distinctly ornamental. They are placed even upon the figures of heroes and of gods with the very symbolism used in the prophet. Referring to one of these gods, M. Longperier says, "The bull's horns which decorate the tiara of this figure are a symbol of power and of glory. The way in which the horns are ranged at the base of the tiara explains to us in what fashion the prophet Daniel conceived the disposition of the ten horns of the symbolic animal which he saw in vision."

Let me ask again, was it not in Babylon alone that such representations were called for in conveying the revelation of the things to come? And do they not stamp the book as one written in, and primarily written for, that time, and not in and for a time when such images were utterly unknown? If the authenticity of *Daniel* were to rest upon these visions alone, the proof is ample and irresistible.

There is another feature in the vision equally startling, but when rightly understood, equally confirmatory. The name "Ancient of Days" applied to God by the Holy Spirit through the prophet is new to Scripture. It is unrepeated. No writer before Daniel uses it, and no writer after him repeats it. Here, then, is a problem with which criticism should make itself familiar. If it can show that in Palestine in the second century before the Christian era—for to that date they are resolved this book shall be assigned—if in the Palestine of that age there was anything to suggest the use of this name—anything that would give it significance, or even make its use natural, the critics will have gone far to prove their case. Little more will be required to show that the book belongs to that late date and not to the time at which it professes to have been written. But if, on the other hand, there is nothing whatever to suggest such a phrase in the circumstances in which the critics say the book originated, then here is one most marked feature which they must admit they have not accounted for. They are in the position of a general invading a foreign country and leaving strong fortresses and large garrisons of the enemy in his rear. His communications may be cut off, and a disastrous retreat may be the issue.

Now it is this very thing that has happened. The name has no relationship to the time or place fixed upon by the Rationalists. But it does have a very striking relationship to the time and place to which the Scripture itself assigns the vision. Behind the idolatry of Babylon, as behind every other ancient religion, there was the light of the primeval revelation. The Babylonians were once acquainted with the true God; but, not glorifying God as God, their wisdom became folly. They worshipped and served the creature more than the Creator. The true God was once known by the name of *Ilu*, the Hebrew *El*, "the Mighty One," represented in our version by the name "God." By and bye, other deities were put in His stead, and these were said to be emanations from *Ilu*. *Ilu* faded away into distance. The newer gods had visible representations. It spoke of the older and truer notions of the Creator that He was not so represented. *He* was conceived of as "infinite, without body, parts, or passions." But, while abandoned for idols, He was still remembered, in a way, and bore the title of "THE ANCIENT OF THE GODS." *Ilu* was worshipped by Nebuchadnezzar under the name of "The Being who exists," an evidence that some notion of the nature of the only living and true God lived on amidst the darkness of idol-worship. Here, then, we have the name at once explained. *The God whom Babylon had forsaken* is He who will yet be manifested as the Lord of heaven and of earth and who shall take the dominion, which the Babylonians had believed to be the gift of their idols, and shall give it to "that Man whom He hath ordained." The gods are not mentioned—for they are vanity. But a change is made in the name which reminds Babylon, and reminds the Jews who are living in the midst of Babylonian idolatry, of the older and purer faith. The God of that earlier and purer time, is He with whom Babylon has still to do.

"The days" may refer to "the days of creation," and "the Ancient of Days" may thus designate God as the Creator. Another phrase in the description, which is equally strange, is employed to indicate the innumerable host of the angels. "Thousand thousands ministered unto Him, and ten thousand times ten thousand stood before Him" (vii. 10). Assyriologists have recognised here, also, the Babylonian watermark. Oppert says that the word expressing "ten thousands" is "a word frequent in inscriptions and expressive of repetition. It is used generally, and is indicative of an innumerable multitude according to the Babylonian mode."\* Language is thus again used which is not only natural to Daniel, but which is also full of significance to the Babylonians and to the Jews who had been brought up in the midst of Babylonian thought and in constant contact with Babylonian forms of speech. A reference of the same kind is seen in the punishment visited upon the fourth beast: "I beheld then," says the prophet, "because of the great words which the horn spake: I beheld even till the beast was slain, and his body destroyed, and given to the burning flame" (verse 11). This form of punishment had an eloquence for those acquainted with the Babylon of the time of Daniel which is lost for us, as it must have been lost for the men of any other civilisation. It was the special doom of blasphemy and of crime against the State, and its use by the prophet indicated the terribleness of the revolt which will fill up the measure of the world's iniquity, and spoke of the awful nature of that destruction from the presence of the Lord which shall fall upon the Antichrist and those who band themselves with him against the Lord and His Anointed.

---

\* See *Speaker's Commentary*. Vol. vi., p. 327.

But the critics have not only gone in the teeth of the witness of archæology; they have also called to their aid a false archæology. The doctrine of the resurrection is clearly taught in Daniel. In xii. 2 we read, "And many of them that sleep in the dust of the earth shall awake, some to everlasting life, and some to shame and everlasting contempt;" and in verse 13 it is said to Daniel, "But go thou thy way till the end be, for thou shalt rest, and stand in thy lot at the end of the days." These clear indications of belief in a future life were declared to have been impossible at the time of Daniel. It was said that the Jews received these beliefs from the Persians, and that their presence in *Daniel* is a conclusive proof of the late origin of the book. It was even asserted that "in Daniel's time they did not yet think of the resurrection," and that the doctrine "was first received by the Jews who remained behind in the Captivity, and who lived in an atmosphere altogether filled with this doctrine, and it at last passed from the Eastern Jews to the Jews, as Jewish."

This view is simply impossible to any thorough student of the Old Testament. The doctrine lies imbedded in psalm, prophecy, and history. Why did Jacob confess himself a pilgrim and a stranger? He recognised himself as belonging to another land, and his whole life as one continued journeying to it. When the Psalmist says, "God will redeem my soul from the power of the grave; for He will receive me," the Scripture plainly teaches that death will not have a lasting triumph even over the believer's body. The critics are, of course, consistent, and put down such passages, as well as Job's expression of faith that his Redeemer liveth, as later additions to the text. It is an easy way to silence testimony, and to get rid of difficulties, any one of which is sufficient to wreck their theory. But what of Ezekiel's vision of the valley of dry bones? Even if the doctrine of the Resurrection had been new and strange to the Jews before his time, it must from that time onward have been no new thing in Israel.

But when the Rationalists appeal to archæology, they deliver themselves into the hand of the enemy. The doctrine of a resurrection from the dead was the hope of Egypt. That land of mummies, which so carefully preserved the bodies of its dead against that day, must have taught the Israelites this doctrine, even if they had never heard of it before. But growing acquaintance with ancient beliefs proves beyond the possibility of denial that the hope of life after the death of the body, and even of the recovery of the body itself from the power of the grave, has always been the heritage of man. It was as much a feature of Babylonian as of Egyptian faith. "The belief of the Babylonians and Assyrians," says Rev. J. M. Fuller, M.A.,* "in the existence and immortality of the soul, in a resurrection, in a future life, and in heaven and hell, is no longer disputed. The twelfth and last tablet of the Flood series of legends speaks thus of hell and heaven. Hades is—

---

* *Speaker's Commentary*, Vol. vi., p. 396.

The house of the departed, the seat of the god Iskaka ;
The house from which there is no exit ;
The road, the course of which never returns
The place, within which they long for light ;
The place, where dust is their nourishment and their food mud ;
Its chiefs, like birds, are clothed with wings.
Light is never seen, in darkness they dwell.

Heaven, on the contrary, is—

The place of seers .    wearing crowns, who from days of old, ruled the earth,
To whom the gods Anu and Bel have given renowned names.
A place where water is abundant, drawn from perennial springs.
The place of chiefs and of unconquered ones ;
The place of bards and great men ;
The place of interpreters of the wisdom of the great gods."

These doctrines take us back into the dimmest regions of human history. The idea, too, of restoration is found in the ancient beliefs. "The tablets also speak of a god . . . who gives Ishtar drink of the waters of life, and so releases her from Hades; or of the god Hea, who similarly releases Heabani and raises him to heaven ; or of the god Silik-moulou-Khi, who possesses the same power. This tablet-teaching on the doctrine," continues Mr. Fuller, " was open to the 'wise men' of the Babylonians in Daniel's time. It needs no proof how immeasurably superior in spirituality is the truth revealed to, and recorded by, the inspired prophet."* The Babylonian inscriptions prove, therefore, that the doctrine was no novelty, and show that there is not the vestige of a pretext for assigning the book on this ground to a later date. The perfect identity, too, of the doctrine in Daniel with that of the New Testament shows

---

* *Ibid*, p. 397.

that both have come from the same source—the inspiration of the Almighty.

It will thus be manifest that the attempt to disprove the authenticity of the book of Daniel has, through a gracious Providence, been triumphantly overthrown. We have also seen that the attack upon *Esther* has equally failed. I have selected these two portions of Scripture, because "the Higher Criticism" imagines that in its attack upon them it has won its most signal triumphs. If it has failed there—if its most confident conclusions are repelled and disowned by facts, then, this so-called science is a delusion. Its initiation was a blunder: its continuance is a crime.

In taking leave of my readers, let me say that I hope at some future time to show that the overwhelming demonstration of mistake and falsehood follows "the critic" like his shadow. But there is another side to this revelation of God's watchful care. These confirmations come laden with supreme consolation. We cannot fail to ask why their arrival has been so timed as to meet us just when the faith of English-speaking Protestantism in the Word of God is subjected to the severest and most insidious attack which it has ever experienced. It seems to me that God means that faith to stand. There has been much among us to merit the Divine disapproval; there is much now. But God is not unrighteous to forget our work of faith and labour of love, and so He will keep us in the hour of temptation that cometh to try all them that dwell upon the face of the earth. The preparation for that keeping is the preservation of our faith in His word. May God grant that, unworthy though we are, the promise of these things may be abundantly fulfilled!

# APPENDIX.

## ARCHDEACON FARRAR ON DANIEL.

THE latest addition to *The Expositor's Bible* is sadly eloquent of the times into which we are passing. It is a professed exposition of the Book of Daniel, by Archdeacon Farrar; but from its first page onward it is a direct attack upon the inspiration, and even upon the truthfulness, of this portion of God's inspired Word. He, to whom the Lord Himself referred as a prophet, and to whose words He bids the generations take heed, is robbed, so far as man can rob him, of every vestige of his prophetic credentials. The same spirit of opposition to the miraculous has led Archdeacon Farrar to misrepresent and to misinterpret every prediction, and the result is a book well fitted to appal those who have hitherto imagined that the Higher Criticism comes to shed light upon the Scripture and not to deprive us of its guidance.

The book is marked by depthless contempt of everything outside the critical school. In a note, in which he censures Hengstenberg and Pusey (who, at least, brought scholarship to their task), we have the following flowers of rhetoric: "What can be more foolish"—"ingenious sophistries"—"violent ecclesiastical tone of autocratic infallibility"—"mere theological blindness and prejudice"—theirs are "assertions which are utterly baseless," and his are "assertions based on science and the love of truth." The condemnation of critical methods expressed by his opponents "are mere bluster of impotent *odium theologicum*." On the other hand, he claims that the critical judgment is "the conclusion of all the ablest and most candid inquirers." Let us see whether the epithets, the lofty superiority, and the withering contempt are justified. More than once he refers to the position which the book holds in the Hebrew Bible. The Jews make a three-fold division of the Old Testament into the Law, the Prophets, and the Khethubim, *i.e.*, the writings. These last are better known under the Greek name, Hagiographa, or, "the holy writings." It is in the last of these divisions, and not among the prophets, that the Book of Daniel appears. With the exception of the later historical books, that is, Ezra, Nehemiah, and Chronicles, *Daniel* is the *last* Book of the Hebrew Bible. Let me ask the reader to notice this in passing. It is a point I shall have to refer to later on.

From this fact, Dr. Farrar argues that *Daniel* was lightly esteemed by the Jews, and was added to the canon only at a late date. He says, "It can only have been the late and suspected appearance of the book, and its marked phenomena, which led to its relegation to the lowest place in the Jewish canon." He fixes the date a few years lower than many of the critics, and places its origin in 164 B.C. This is a date much later, be it remarked, than is ascribed to some of the Apocryphal books. *Ecclesiasticus* is supposed to have made its appearance in the Greek translation about 36 years before, while the Hebrew original was many years earlier. This raises a very awkward question for the Archdeacon and his friends. How did it come about that the Jews refused a place to *Ecclesiasticus*, and granted it so many years later to *Daniel*? If the canon was arranged after 164 B.C., how did *Ecclesiasticus*, a then comparatively ancient Book, get slighted, and *Daniel*, an entirely new production, written under their very eyes, and a manifest and known imposition, get accepted and installed as part of the Word of the Living God? If there was any enlightened and honest desire to embrace in the Canon only what was indubitably inspired, or, indeed, if there was any common sense left in Israel, this was hardly a proceeding calculated to manifest one or the other; and no one who pauses to weigh Dr. Farrar's statements will rest quite satisfied without some further explanation. The Jews have never received the Apocrypha. They have never polluted the Jewish Old Testament by putting the holy and the profane together. With an unbending integrity, and an unfaltering judgment, they drew the line between the canonical and the uncanonical writings. The former they set upon the highest pedestal that man has ever raised; the latter they rejected and largely despised. Were these the men—even if we suppose that the matter was left to the judgment of uninspired and fallible Jews—were these the men to blunder in the case of *Daniel*, who did not blunder in that of Tobit, or Judith, or the Son of Sirach? On the face of it, the imputation is one which cannot for a moment be entertained.

The critical position appears quite as unsatisfactory and irrational when viewed from other sides. The three-fold division of the Books was made at an early period, as we find reference to it in the New Testament. In Luke the Old Testament is spoken of as the Law, the Prophets, and the Psalms. The Psalms stand at the beginning of the *Khethubim*. But here we have also to notice what entirely overthrows Dr. Farrar's argument. This last division of the Old Testament is recognised as being as authoritative and as fully inspired as either of the others. The Psalms are referred to by our Lord as "Scripture," which "cannot be broken." And again and again they are quoted by Him and by the Apostles as the Authoritative Word of God, and as the utterances of the Holy Spirit. The fact, then, of *Daniel* being in the Hagiographa did not, and could not, show that any lower position was assigned to it. Being anywhere in the Scripture, it was stamped as the Word of God.

But we are, fortunately, able to go further than this. In

the Gospel of Luke, the prophecy regarding the abomination of desolation standing in the Holy Place is referred to as spoken by "Daniel the Prophet." *This shows that the position of Prophet was not refused to Daniel in the New Testament times.* We have another and independent witness as to the feeling of the Jews with regard to *Daniel* in the first century of our era. Josephus speaks of him in most emphatic terms. Not only does he place him by the side of the other prophets; he would seem to place him even above them. Here are his words—" He did not only prophesy of future events as did the other prophets, but he also determined the time of their accomplishment; and while the prophets used to foretell misfortunes, and on that account were disagreeable both to the kings and to the multitude, Daniel was to them a prophet of good things, and this to such a degree, that, by the agreeable nature of his predictions, he procured the goodwill of all men; and by the accomplishment of them, he procured the belief of their truth, *and the opinion of a sort of divinity for himself among the multitude.*" \*

These words require no comment. There is not in the mind of Josephus a shadow of a doubt as to the place occupied by Daniel. He accords him, on the contrary, a position of prominence above the other prophets, because he not only foretold future events, but determined the very time of their occurrence. He also, in the conclusion of the chapter from which we have quoted, points specially to Daniel's prophecies as proving beyond everything else, the intervention of God in human affairs. He says, " All these things did this man leave in writing, as God had shown them to him, insomuch that such as read his prophecies, and see how they have been fulfilled, *would wonder at the honour with which God honoured Daniel.*"

What are we to say, in the face of these things, and of those already quoted, to the following from Dr. Farrar's pen?—" Josephus," he says, " adopts a somewhat apologetic

---

\**Antiquities*, xi. 7.

tone, as though he specially declined to vouch for its historical exactness." A statement like this leads one to ask whether the spirit of truth has forsaken the ranks of the critical hosts. The misrepresentation is by no means unfamiliar to those who read the writings of the new school. But the practice is as un-English as it is un-Christian, and will eventually bring upon the heads of its authors the condemnation which they deserve.

It is as impossible to minimise the testimony of Josephus as it is to set it aside. Dr. Farrar and his school have also to reckon with another testimony, the importance of which they do not seem to have recognised. *The Septuagint accords the same position to Daniel. His prophecies occupy the same place in that translation as they do in our own.* They immediately follow those of Ezekiel; and Daniel is reckoned as one of the four greater prophets. This is an indication, taken in connection with those to which we have already referred, which demonstrates the opinion of the Jews before, and at the beginning of, the Christian era regarding the Book of Daniel.

Is there any reason why there should have been a change *after* the beginning of the Christian era? Those who know anything of Aquila's translation of the Old Testament are aware that it was made in the interests of Jewish controversy, and with an evident attempt to baffle the advocates of Christianity. This was in the middle of the second century. The stress of the battle, which the Jews had to wage with their own inspired writers, was felt from the very first. We have plain intimations of their helplessness in the New Testament. When Peter and Paul cite the Scriptures, their adversaries are speechless. This is the one cause of the lowered estimate among the later Jews of the Hagiographa. To afford some shield, their learned men were compelled to accord a lower degree of inspiration to the writings so largely used in Christian controversy. *They had no fewer than eleven distinct degrees of inspiration*, and it is from the

Rabbis that these rationalistic notions of degrees of inspiration have come into the Christian Church.

Basnage says that Spinoza received his infidelity from the same source. The present position of *Daniel* in the Hebrew Bible is another evidence of a late change. If we leave out of view the books of Ezra, Nehemiah, and Chronicles, *Daniel*, as we have already seen, is placed last. It comes even after the Book of Esther, and is, therefore, out of chronological order. Now, if the Book stood first of all among the greater Prophets, as in the Septuagint version, and if a change was made after the order of the other books was settled by usage, we can understand its present position. It was taken from its place as the fourth of the prophets, and put *at the end of the Hagiographa*.

These are considerations which Dr. Farrar has completely overlooked. But there seems no ground for the opinion that the Canon of the Old Testament was settled by the consent of the Jews. From Zechariah vii. 12, it is plain that the Canon was already established. We read, "Yea, they made their hearts as an adamant stone, lest they should hear the law, and the words which the Lord of Hosts hath sent in His Spirit by the former prophets; therefore came a great wrath from the Lord of Hosts." Here a two-fold division of the Scriptures is referred to—"the Law and the Prophets." To the last Zechariah applies the epithet "former," as distinguishing them from himself and his contemporaries. The Canon was, therefore, already formed, and was only waiting for the last utterances of Old Testament Prophecy. The Books were evidently handed to the Jews of the Prophet's own time, with the distinct testimony and seal of their Divine origin, and no question is ever agitated regarding their authority.

The Archdeacon's attempt to get rid of the Old Testament recognition of Daniel as a man honoured of God, will meet with no better success. We have three references in the Book of Ezekiel to the prophet. He is specially named, and is referred to in terms of the deepest respect. Every attempt, which men can possibly make, has been made to get rid of this testimony. Ezekiel is a witness whom they cannot annihilate; and it is equally hopeless to suggest that the passages are interpolations. In Ezekiel xxviii. 3, the Spirit of God says to the Prince of Tyrus, " Behold, thou art wiser than Daniel! There is no secret that they can hide from thee!" The second and third references are in Ezekiel xiv. 14 and 20. "Though these three men, Noah, Daniel, and Job, were in it, they should deliver but their own souls;" and again, "Though Noah, Daniel, and Job, were in it, as I live, saith the Lord God, they shall deliver neither son nor daughter, they shall but deliver their own souls by their righteousness."

The Archdeacon finds endless difficulties in accepting this witness. He gives us no fewer than six, specially stated and emphasised. These six reasons may safely be taken as his estimate of the strength of the testimony. He says it was very unusual among the Jews to elevate their contemporaries to such a height. The obvious answer to this is, that whatever may have been the custom among the Jews, it is by no means unusual in the Scriptures. Then Daniel was too young for Ezekiel to honour him in this way. Here, again, we have no knowledge as to what Ezekiel might or might not have done. We have to do with Ezekiel's Master, and *He* made no scruple of honouring Joseph, and Jeremiah, and even the child Samuel. Dr. Farrar is quite as unfortunate in his attempt to make capital out of the fact that Daniel is named in only *one* of the Old Testament books. If the Doctor were to carry out this new canon, what would become of Ezekiel himself? In what other book of the Old Testament is *he* mentioned? and which prophet could, or ought to, have mentioned Daniel but Ezekiel? Ezekiel is prophesying among the captives who are in Babylon, and whose affliction Daniel is sharing. Every man among those to whom Ezekiel spoke had heard of the honour which God had put upon their young countryman with astonishment and grateful joy. His name had become a household word among them. It was as natural that the Spirit, speaking through Ezekiel to these men, should have referred to Daniel as it was for our Lord to speak of John the Baptist.

Let us suppose for a moment that everything related in the second and fourth chapters of *Daniel* is absolutely true, and that the young captive had not only interpreted, but actually recalled—and that, too, in its minute details—a dream that had passed through the king's brain in the visions of the night. Had there ever been in all human history so marvellous a display of insight as that? And, when an illustration is needed, which will express to the captive Jews, who know these things, the blasphemous pretensions of the Prince of Tyrus, what more natural than the words: "Behold thou art wiser than Daniel; nothing secret is obscure to thee?" If *Daniel* is history, the reference was natural and the illustration the very happiest that could be found. This will be admitted by every unbiassed mind. But if that is so, then we have here one of the most powerful arguments that can be imagined for the truth of the earlier part of *Daniel*. Here, in the writings of an undeniable contemporary, is a reference which is pointless and meaningless, unless these miracles of insight are true which are recorded in the Book.

The two-fold mention of Daniel by Ezekiel in the fourteenth chapter is equally conclusive. The Jews left in Palestine no doubt called to remembrance one fact in connection with the destruction of Sodom. Jerusalem was denounced as having rivalled the wickedness of that ancient city. Isaiah had addressed rulers and people in these words: "Hear the word of the Lord, ye rulers of Sodom; give ear unto the law of our God, ye people of Gomorrah" (i. 10). "The implied accusation may be true," the Jews seemed to say: "but Sodom would have been saved if ten righteous men had been found in it. Ten times ten may be found any-day in Jerusalem; and will God be less indulgent to His chosen people than to Sodom and Gomorrah?" It is to this imagination that the Word of God replies. The righteous will save his own life, but not one life besides. The judgment about to fall upon Israel was an emblem of that which will eventually fall upon the world. Each will be judged apart and alone. The wicked will not be shielded by the righteousness of even him to whom he is dearest. It is a day of Divine judgment, and the sinner shall perish in his iniquity.

To emphasize this decree, three men are named for whose sake God had done and would do much—"Noah, Daniel, and Job." Were even these within Jerusalem, they should neither save it, nor a single member of their own households. Here, again, a contemporary testimony presents itself to the truth of *Daniel* which no ingenuity can explain away. There was some self-sacrifice in connection with Daniel's history, some instance, or instances, of unswerving fidelity which set him amongst the righteous ones of the earth. When we read the first chapter of the Book, we understand the reference and how the mention of Daniel's name must have told upon the men of that generation. But, Dr. Farrar argues, with the rest of his school, that *the order* of the names is against this. Daniel is mentioned before Job, and the reference must therefore be, he says, to some earlier Daniel. But is there no other order known to Scripture than that of *time?* When we meet a series of names must we always conclude that they are given in strictly chronological series? The notion is absurd, and yet it is on that very notion that critics build an argument! A little scholarly patience would have paused and questioned whether there was any reason for the grouping steadily maintained in both verses (Ezek. xiv. 14, 20). And the patience would have been rewarded. The coupling of Daniel with Noah indicates a resemblance in their history. Noah's righteousness saved his house; was there anything in Daniel's experience that formed a parallel to that? Will the reader remember what it was that first brought Daniel into prominence? We are told of his self-sacrifice for righteousness' sake, of some marks of God's approval, and then of a sudden danger into which Daniel, his companions, and all the learned of Babylon are thrown. Daniel's righteousness and faith *make a way of escape not only for himself, but for all who are threatened with destruction.* There was nothing like this in Job's history, though his three friends were saved from chastisement by his prayer. Here, then, we have a reason for Daniel being linked with Noah; but it is a reason which again vouches for the truth of the Book of Daniel.

Quite on a par with this is his assertion that there is no reference to Daniel's predictions in the prophets who follow him. That might have been true, and yet leave every prediction unchallenged. It was no part of a prophet's work to refer to every prophecy that had been uttered by those who had preceded him. But it is not true. Who can remember Zechariah's vision of the four horns, without recalling the four dominions of Daniel, and the imagery, so peculiar to Daniel, in which horns are used as symbols of the world powers? Dr. Wright, speaking of Zechariah's vision of the Four Riders, says: "Kliefoth seems to us to be correct in considering that Zechariah had before his mind the four world-empires of Daniel."* Dr. Wright may be viewed as an unprejudiced witness, as his unfortunate International Teachers' Bible shows that his sympathies are more with the critics than they are with us. But if either of these references to *Daniel* is admitted, then the critical date assigned to the Book can no longer be maintained. But the amount of consideration which Dr. Farrar has given to his task will be evident from the following. According to him, genuine predictions must not be definite; and he therefore argues that those of Daniel can not be genuine! God hides the future, he says, and teaches us "to regard all prying into its minute events as vulgar and sinful." "Nitzsch," he continues, "most justly lays it down as an essential condition of prophecy that it *should not disturb man's relation to history*. Anything like detailed description of the future would intolerably perplex and confuse our sense of human free-will." "Not one such prophecy," he adds, "unless this be one, *occurs anywhere in the Bible*." He hastens to admit an exception in regard to the Messianic prophecies; and well he may, for these will suggest themselves to every reader of the foregoing statements. The Passover fixed the very month and the very day and the very hour on which Jesus was to die. The 22nd Psalm describes the manner of His death, and the jeers and the mockery which were to be rained upon Him in His dying hour. Isaiah notes the fact that the sentence which appointed for Him a criminal's burial was to be reversed at the last moment. "They made his grave with the wicked, but He was with the rich in His death" (Isa. liii. 9). So clear indeed is the picture of Christ and of His work in the Old Testament predictions, that they form a Divine re-statement of the conclusions which we ourselves deduce from the Gospel history. We repeat, that it is well the Archdeacon should make an exception here; but the confession does not save his theory regarding the nature of prophecy. It is an admission, on the contrary, that his theory is killed as soon as it is stated. The Messianic predictions form the great bulk of Scripture prophecy. They paint a distant future, and they paint it minutely. What becomes then of the statement that "not one such prophecy occurs anywhere in the Bible?" Is it the conclusion of a man who interprets facts, or the self-delusion of a determined theorist?

It would be easy to show that this minuteness characterizes many a prediction besides, but we forbear. Dr. Farrar fashions another argument to prove that Daniel's predictions cannot be real. *They are chronological*, and he says "there is no other instance in the Bible of a *chronological* prophecy!" Even if this were so, no argument could be founded upon

---

\* *Zechariah and his Prophecies*, p. 17.

it. There is nothing in mere numbers to limit the Spirit of God. He who could foretell the events might very well be able to also foretell the time. But the statement makes us ask whether Dr. Farrar knows his Bible? " No other instance in the Bible of a *chronological* prophecy "!!! What, then, of God's prediction to Abraham that his seed should sojourn among strangers for 400 years—a chronological prophecy which, we are told in Exodus, was fulfilled to the very letter? What of the word which came through Jeremiah that the exile of Israel would endure for 70 years (Jer. 29, 10)? And of that in Ezekiel which fixed the exile of Egypt at 40 years (Ezek. xxix. 11)? And of Isaiah's prediction to Ahaz that "within three score and five years shall Ephraim be broken that it be not a people " (Isa. vii. 8)?

I have already pointed to some extraordinary features in this New "Exposition" of *Daniel*; but, in what I have now to name, Dr. Farrar has excelled himself. It would, of course, never do to allow the prediction regarding the four World-Empires, which were to arise before the dominion of Jesus, to pass unharmed. That in itself is a miracle, and is more than sufficient to re-establish faith in *Daniel* as the Word of God. Even the last feature—a dominion in the earth of the Son of Man—is startling enough. It is not the mighty reality that it will yet be; but Dr. Farrar and his school are never wearied of expatiating upon this feature of the Gospel time. But where could the writer of *Daniel* have seen any hope of this even in 160 B.C.? The Jews did not see it even when Christ came, and neither Greek nor Roman suspected Christ's coming triumph during all that long period when the attempt was made to extinguish the Gospel. By whom, then, was this calm outlook given of a dominion that should put all rule and authority under the feet of the Man Christ Jesus? The Rationalists may as well try to empty the sea as to remove the Divine stamp from the Book of Daniel.

But Dr. Farrar fights hard against the ordinary view

## His Separation of the Median & Persian Kingdoms. 565

which identifies the fourth Empire with the Roman power. He splits up the Median and Persian Dominion into two, so that the powers referred to in the vision may be (1) the Babylonian, (2) the Median, (3) the Persian, (4) the Grecian. This suits exactly the *alleged* date of the composition of the Book; for in 160 B.C. the successors of Alexander were still reigning in the East. It troubles the Archdeacon little, apparently, that he has to ignore the language of the Book which he is professing to interpret. But when he asks us to acknowledge that this is the plain meaning of the writer's words, we must enter an indignant protest. Where does Daniel ever distinguish between the Empire of the Medes and that of the Persians? No such distinction was possible. The Medes *never had* a universal Empire apart from Cyrus and his Persians, and Daniel invariably speaks of their Empire as one. Though Darius the Mede reigns, he is represented as himself bound by "the law of the Medes *and Persians*." Even then the law of the kingdom was not that of Media alone, but of the two allied powers. The union is equally represented in the breast with its two arms in the vision of the second chapter, in the bear with one side raised higher than the other (vii. 5), and in the ram with the two horns (viii. 3).

It is impossible, then, to find the shadow of a foundation in *Daniel* for dividing the Median and Persian Empire into two. The Archdeacon, no doubt, saw that it was still more hopeless to establish the contention that the Grecian Empire can be made into two. The words of Daniel are equally explicit in binding up Alexander and his successors as together composing the third dominion. "The great horn" of the he-goat is broken, but the power is maintained by the "four notable ones" which spring up in its stead. There is, therefore, no possible escape for the Rationalists. They spread the sail and they put out the oars to save their theory from striking on the rock of this magnificent and undeniable prophecy. But nothing can save them. The whole course of the world's history, from the prophet's time to the end, is summed up with a clearness, a mastery, and an ease, on which we read, as on the heavens above us, the glory of God. The very time when this was done speaks of God; for it reveals His mercy. The kingdom had passed from Israel, and God's people were henceforth to be under the heel of the Gentiles. *They needed to know that this was God's arrangement;* God wished also to turn them from that longing gaze upon past glories, to look for the appearing of Him who should be the glory of Israel and the light of the nations. And so God gives this hope, and in giving it guards them against disappointment in what will seem a long delay. Before Christ comes *there should be four*, AND ONLY FOUR, universal Empires. The fourth should be more extensive and more terrible than any of the rest. "The fourth kingdom shall be diverse from all kingdoms, and shall devour *the whole earth*, and shall tread it down and break it in pieces" (Dan. vii. 23.) This kingdom is to continue in its fragments, and in the days when these number ten, God shall set up that kingdom which shall never be destroyed. The Jews, in our Lord's time, knew that the fourth Empire was the Roman. *We* are God's witnesses that it has continued in its fragments until the present hour, and that no fifth dominion of man, though attempts have been often made, has supplanted these remnants of the fourth. What miracle could be more stupendous than this prophetic chart of the world's history? And what cause can be more hopeless than that of him who attempts to show that the book which contains it is not the very Word of God?

In Dr. Farrar's treatment of the testimony of the Assyrian monuments we are reminded of poor Mrs. Malaprop, and her attempt to sweep back the Atlantic with her broom! It is the most determined endeavour to defeat the inevitable that we have ever known. Clearer-headed critics seek safety in silence; or, like Dr. Driver, content themselves with the statement that, while the monuments have dealt hardly with the "advanced" critics, their own positions have been scarcely touched. Dr. Farrar perceives, however, that this will no longer do, and so he rushes in where critics fear to tread. The necessity for some intervention, if criticism is to be saved, will be apparent to all who know anything of the subject, and who are at all acquainted with the revolution which the discoveries have effected in learned opinion regarding *Daniel*. But the folly of the Archdeacon's intervention will be apparent when I state that he comes unarmed with a single fact. He calls to his aid not a single discovery, for there is none that will help him. Let us rapidly follow him through the xv. (!)—the Archdeacon is great in tabulations—alleged historical and other blunders of the Book.

I. "In the third year of Jehoiakim, king of Judah, came Nebuchad-*n*ezzar," &c. (Daniel i. 1). He has a fling, in passing (*a la* Sayce), at the spelling of the Babylonian king's name. It is given as Nebuchad*r*ezzar in Jeremiah, and this is the form hitherto found upon the monuments. But it is too early yet to say that this was the only form used, and to set down the *n* in Nebuchadnezzar as a blunder. It is spelt in no fewer than five different ways in the Old Testament. It is given as Nebuchad*n*ezzar in II. Kings; I. and II. Chronicles, Ezra, and Nehemiah. Is Dr. Farrar prepared to question the historical character of all or of any of these Books because they spell this king's name so? Why, then, should it be urged against *Daniel?* Was it quite honest for him to hide the fact from his readers that the spelling was *not* a peculiarity of the Book of Daniel, and what force can be attached to the reasonings of a man who argues as if it were? As to the date, when for "came" we substitute the equally good translation "marched," we have a chronological notice which falls in line with statements in the Scripture and elsewhere, and which proves that the Book is written with the fullest knowledge of the times. This mention of the third year of Jehoiakim's reign would stamp the Book as historical, if it stood alone.

II. The names given to Daniel and his three friends are subjected to a critico-rhetorical mangling. Sayce founds his objection to the name Belteshazzar upon *a single letter* (the presence of an unaspirated, where he says there should be an aspirated, T). But where Sayce reasons, Farrar can only storm. With the exception of the single letter referred to, even Sayce admits that Belteshazzar, or *Bilat-sarra-utsur*, " is a good Babylonian name." The other names, like Abed-nego (which should evidently be Abed-Nebo, "the servant of Nebo"), have probably suffered in transcription. But these mistakes of copyists have been unable to disguise the genuine Babylonian character of the names. For Lenormant, possessing an authority on those questions, at which Archdeacon Farrar will scoff in vain, says upon this very point: "It is certain that all the proper names, where the faults of copyists have not too much altered them, are perfectly Babylonian, *and such as one could not have invented in Palestine in the second century before our era*;" and he adds, "But at least one does not remark in the Book any of those proper names of other times, and of other countries," which characterise the compositions of late writers, who seek to pass off their compositions as the work of an earlier time.* Here, then, competent judges find *for* Daniel, and not against it, and Dr. Farrar's No. II. falls by the side of No. I.

III. is unworthy of notice. It is an attempt to form a difficulty out of the mention in Daniel ii. 1 of "the second year" of Nebuchadnezzar. Every one is aware that Nabopolassar had, in his last days, to commit the conduct of affairs to his son's hands, and no one has experienced any difficulty in understanding this "second year" as the second of Nebuchadnezzar's sole reign. If any one were

---

*La Divination chez les Chaldéens, p. 182.

to pursue Dr. Farrar in this petti-fogging style, the public would soon grow weary of them both.

IV. is a misleading notice of the classes of the "wise" men, referred to in Daniel ii. 2. It might surely astonish him that a Jew of 160 B.C. should be so intimately acquainted with the fact that the Chaldean wise men *were* divided into classes, and should arrange them in an order that corresponds exactly with that of the priestly books, utterly unknown in 160 B.C., and known even in Daniel's time only to the members of the sacred caste. When that fact can be explained, one huge stumbling-block in the way of believing in the late date of Daniel will be removed. Till that *is* done, the stumbling-block remains. He dwells, with Schrader and Sayce, on the mention of "the Chaldeans" among these classes, and insists that it was only in late times that the name was applied, as by the Roman writers, to "wandering astrologers and quacks." Till then, it was, he says, the name of a people and not of a class. This is regarded by Dr. Farrar, as it is by Prof. Sayce, as an irrefutable argument against the genuineness of *Daniel*. He says: "*This single circumstance has decisive weight in proving the late age of the Book of Daniel.*" The reader will now have an opportunity of judging how much real learning goes to furnish a critic and expert, and what weight ought to be attached to critical statements. This distinction, so confidently declared to be the exclusive mark of a "late age," *is found in Herodotus!* Referring to the temple of Bel, he speaks of "the Chaldeans, the priests of this god."* They were, therefore, in 450 B.C. *a class*, and not merely a nation. Other Greek writers speak in the same way, and the belief that this was the representation of only a late time is simply a gigantic blunder. Sir Henry Rawlinson and Fr. Lenormant have shown that this two-fold use of the name "Chaldeans" is borne out by indications of the time.

V. is a mixture. He touches upon "Arioch, the chief

---

* *Rawlinson's Herodotus*, Vol. i., p. 255.

of the executioners," but proceeds without raising any
objection. I may note, in passing, that the mention both
of the name and of the office reveal a perfect acquaintance
with the time. He finds himself more at home in insisting
that the statement in the first chapter, about Nebuchadnezzar
finding Daniel and his companions "ten times better than all
the magicians and astrologers that were in all his realm," is
at variance with the terms in which Arioch introduces Daniel
to the King. But he might have discovered a much more
surprising variation than that in the closing words of the first
chapter, which tell us that "Daniel continued even unto the
first year of King Cyrus," that is, in official employment.
Why, it might be asked, having taken us on to the accession
of Cyrus, should the narrative return to the times of
Nebuchadnezzar? The evident reply is, that the first
chapter is dealing with Daniel's self-sacrifice and its fruits.
*It is a summary*, and his place in the esteem of Nebuchadnezzar, like that in the employ of Cyrus, belongs to a later
time.

VI. and VII. dwell upon the impossibility of Daniel
suffering the worship paid to him by the astonished king.
The Book forms the best answer. There is no more humble-
minded man mentioned in Scripture than Daniel. With
that portrait before us, there is no chance of our mis-
interpreting the silence of the sixth chapter. But Dr. Farrar's
silence is striking. The action ascribed to Nebuchadnezzar
is in full accord with all we know of him from the
monuments. It shows us the man in his imperious decisive-
ness and deeply religious spirit. How could a writer of
pious fiction, to whom the great king was only a name, have
drawn, in these few rapid sketches, the man's exact portrait?

VIII. objects that Nebuchadnezzar *could not* have appointed
Daniel, a foreigner, to be ruler over a proud and passionately
intolerant priesthood. The priesthoods of Christendom have
shown subservience enough to have suggested that in an
autocracy like that of Nebuchadnezzar's, even more than

this was possible. His other objection, that Daniel could not have accepted the position, is founded in ignorance of what the learning of the Chaldeans really was. It embraced all the science of the time, and much of that was by no means contemptible even from a nineteenth century point of view.

In IX. we have another compound blow, which rebounds with terrific force upon Dr. Farrar and upon the cause he champions. (1) There is no mention, he complains, of Daniel in the third chapter. His name is not included in the accusation, and there is no record of his presence at the inauguration of the statue. Now, this is a matter for the Archdeacon to explain. If *Daniel* were written to glorify this Jewish hero—and that is the critical theory—then the silence is inexplicable. (2) There are Persian titles, he says, among the officials summoned to the ceremony, and in a note it is charitably suggested "that to enhance the stateliness of the occasion the writer introduced as many official names as he knew"! That is what Dr. Farrar would make of the Scriptures! But some of these so-called Persian words are now proved, to the confusion of the critics, to be Assyrian and Babylonian. One of them, *Pachoth*, is found upon a monument of Sargon's, the father of Sennacherib, and is applied by him to the viceroys of his kingdom. Schrader, a Rationalist, but an archæologist as well, declares that the word has no relation whatever to any in the Persian language, and says "there is absolutely no reason for holding the word to be foreign or Persian in origin." * Many such titles were, no doubt, borrowed from the Babylonians by the Persians. (3) There are two Greek names applied to musical instruments. On this, he touches lightly, but it is the great critical argument against the Book. Here, however, the critics have dug a pit which promises to become their grave. It is now proved that there was an active trade between Greece and Persia in musical instruments *before the time of Daniel*. The mention of one or

---

* *Cuneiform Inscriptions and the Old Testament*, Vol. i., p. 175.

two Greek instruments is, therefore, an absolutely accurate reflection of the time, as archæologists, indeed, now confess the entire chapter to be.

X. contains nothing but empty declamation about Nebuchadnezzar's madness; but XI. is a bold attempt to regain the battle long since lost over Belshazzar. "History," he says, "knows of no such king. The prince of whom it *does* know was never king, and was a son, not of Nebuchadrezzar, but of the usurper Nabunaid." This bundle of misrepresentations is immediately qualified by a confession—"There *was* a Belshazzar," &c. He says history *does* know of a prince named Belshazzar. What history? There was not one single reference to the name in any book but *Daniel*. Is it generous to omit mention of the fact that the only record of this man's existence was here? Is it honest to blur it over, and to give away the glory of *Daniel* to histories that never had any existence? Listen to the story of this question, and then sum up the value of critical methods, and estimate its bitter determination to admit no fact that upholds the Scriptures. (1) Belshazzar, outside of *Daniel*, was utterly unknown. His existence was therefore denied. (2) Sir Henry Rawlinson discovers Nabonidus's inscription, which names Belshazzar as his eldest son. It is then said that he may have died in his childhood, and that there was no ground for believing that he was the Belshazzar of *Daniel*. (3) The Egibi tablets next revealed the fact that Belshazzar had come to man's estate, had a separate establishment, and stewards, and secretaries. Driven backward, they still contested every step. (4) It was maintained, and is maintained now, that he was not a descendent of Nebuchadnezzar. Darius Hystaspis tells of two usurpers who sprang up in Babylon, each calling himself "Nebuchadnezzar the son of Nabonidus." It has been pointed out that Nabonidus would not have recalled the dynasty he displaced by bestowing such a name on a child of his, unless he was connected with Nebuchadnezzar by marriage. He, no doubt, owed the throne to his marriage with a daughter of the great king. (5) It was, and is, said that he never reigned. Among the Egibi tablets there is one dated in the third year of Merodach-sar-uzur. *This can be no other than Belshazzar.* Here, step by step, the critics have been driven back, and the absolute truth of the history, which they challenged in their self-confident ignorance, has been established by growing enlightenment.

XII. is a quotation from Professor Sayce. He concludes from Cyrus's tablet that "there was no siege and capture of Babylon." No better illustration could be found of the Professor's rashness. The inscription has an evident intention which no thoughtful reader can possibly overlook. It was the object of Cyrus to remove from the minds of the proud Babylonians every idea of a Persian conquest. He therefore represents himself as the avenger of the honour of the gods whom Nabonidus had grievously offended. But it was impossible to obliterate *every* trace of the capture of the great city, and no one can read the inscription without noting this fact. I refer to the important passage, "On that night Gobryas was on the bank of the river . . . . and the son of the king died." Why was the Persian general on the bank of the river at night, if not to surprise and assault the city? In close connection, too, with that feat, the son of the king died. Is not this almost wholly identical with the statement in Daniel—"In that night was Belshazzar the king of the Chaldeans slain"? And does it not speak of the blindest prejudice, when an Oxford Professor and a Westminster Archdeacon can read both accounts and fail to acknowledge the parallelism?

It is hardly necessary to notice his attempt to deny that Belshazzar's promise to make Daniel the *third* ruler in the kingdom proves that there were *two* kings reigning. He says, "the translation 'third ruler' appears to be entirely untenable. It means 'one of a board of three.'" This is a point on which scholarship is not yet "entirely" agreed

But, if we suppose that it does mean "one of a board of three," the Archdeacon's case is still far from being made out. The promise would then literally run "thou shalt reign one of three," which *is the very sense* given in our translation. The ruling power, according to the promise, would then have been a triumvirate, and, to make the three, we need another besides Daniel and Belshazzar—Nabonidus. But I pass on to XIII., in which the old difficulty about Darius the Mede is made to do duty as another crowning disproof of the claims of Daniel. He says that "historic monuments and records entirely overthrow" the supposition that Cyrus was preceded in the throne of Babylon by a Median prince. This is "entirely" mistaken. Cyrus, indeed, so far as the broken tablet shows, makes no mention of Darius. But silence is not necessarily disproof. There are distinct indications of a Darius before the first Persian king of that name with whom we are now acquainted, and the tablets show that for the first two years after the conquest of Babylon, Cyrus is not styled King of Babylon, but "king of the nations." It is *during these very years* that *Daniel* represents Darius as reigning. I have no doubt that future discoveries will prove that the King of Media, whose name is given in Greek history as Cyaxares, is Darius. It was the policy of Cyrus to yield the first place to him, and so to weld the Medes and the Persians together.

XIV. and XV. complete this snow-mountain of objections. Darius the Mede is said to be the son of Ahasuerus. Darius Hystaspis, the third king after Cyrus, has *a son* called Ahasuerus or Xerxes. The Archdeacon accordingly rushes to the conclusion that *these* must be the two meant. What would be said of the New Zealander who tried to pick up English History in that way, and who, finding that in one place a James is said to be the father of a Charles, corrects his authority, and concludes that these are the same as a subsequent Charles and James who were brothers? Would such petulance be either admirable or profitable? When the monuments have told their story fully, it will be time to correct the Scripture. Till then it will be wise to trust a Book which the monuments have hitherto steadily confirmed and illustrated.

The last of this long list is quite touching in its resolute blindness. He says, "In xi. 2, the writer only knows of *four* kings of Persia. These are evidently Cyrus, Cambyses, Darius Hystaspis, and Xerxes—whom he describes as the richest of them." Now, there are two things here which are quite enough in themselves to establish the age and the nature of the Book of Daniel. No writer in 160 B.C. *could have known so much about Xerxes as to designate him the richest of all the Persian kings.* This shows an intimate acquaintance with Persian history. That is the first feature to which I refer. The second shows an insight into history still more remarkable. The absurd idea that a writer, who knew so much of ancient Persia, could represent Xerxes as the king overthrown by Alexander the Great, must be rejected as utterly unworthy. But when this is set aside, we have the truest reading of the conflict between Greece and Persia anywhere to be found. Xerxes' invasion of Greece begins a struggle which, on the field of history, has for its climax and end Alexander's invasion of Persia. *We* place the two events in that order now. *Daniel* placed them in that order before either event occurred. We see, in that conjunction of Xerxes and Alexander, the Divine *insight* as well as the Divine foresight.

Step by step we have followed Dr. Farrar in his argument. Not one of his contentions can be maintained. He is also singularly silent regarding strong confirmations of the Book lately yielded by Assyriology. What of the reference to *the palace school*, and to the literary and peculiar character of Babylonian civilisation with which the Book opens? Had a *Greek* mark of that kind been stamped on the first chapter, it would have been taken as a triumphant proof of its late origin. What, then, must be said of the *Babylonian* mark?

Does not *that* prove the Babylonian origin of the Book? The same stamp is upon the visions of *Daniel*. They are visions cast in the mould of the place and of the time, as they required to be, in order that they might speak *to* the place and the time. What, then, of these? If the visions had been cast in the mould of the thought and life of 160 B.C., would not that have been enough to prove the *late* date? If reasoning is to continue to be fair and just, must not the fact which I have now named prove the earlier date? Dr. Farrar and the critics will not, of course, admit defeat. But the battle, through God's good providence, is already won. There is no British jury before whom this case could be argued, who would fail to admit that the authenticity of *Daniel* has been proved to the full.

# INDEX.

| | Page. |
|---|---|
| AHASUERUS, proved to be Xerxes | 300 |
| "Ancient of Days," the | 544 |
| Apocrypha, historical blunders of the | 329 |
| Apologetics, coldness of, in 18th century | 147 |
| Apostolic Church, the, its teaching regarding Scripture | 31 |
| Archæological testimony to Esther | 338 |
| Arioch | 378, 379 |
| Asceticism, rise of, in Christian Church | 97 |
| Astruc's theory of the composition of Genesis | 219-221 |
| ,, ,, accepted by Eichhorn | 222 |
| ,, ,, demolished by the critics, yet palmed off by them as still sound | 223 |
| Athenagoras, his view of Scripture | 27 |
| Augustine, his weak compliance with error | 99 |
| BAHRDT, the German Voltaire | 193 |
| Babylonian names in *Daniel* | 373 |
| ,, traits in *Daniel* | 439 |
| ,, belief in immortality | 549 |
| Barnabas, epistle ascribed to, its teaching regarding Scripture | 30 |
| Belshazzar, who was he? | 476 |
| ,, the first trace of, in the inscriptions | 484 |
| ,, did he reign? | 487-502 |

| | Page. |
|---|---|
| Belshazzar, was he a descendant of Nebuchadnezzar? | 489 |
| ,, did he die when Babylon was taken? | 499 |
| ,, his Feast | 501 |
| Belteshazzar | 377 |
| Bible, the, views of the Apostolic Churches regarding | 20 |
| ,, the, part played by, in the Reformation | 116 |
| Bishops, mediæval, growth of their power | 105 |
| Bolingbroke, Lord | 141 |
| Burning alive, Babylonian punishment for high treason and blasphemy | 450 |
| CAIUS, his estimate of the Scripture | 25 |
| Calixtus, rancour against | 159-160 |
| Calvin and the Bible | 127-130 |
| Chaldeans, the, their place in Babylon | 368 |
| ,, ,, a class as well as a nation | 393 |
| Champollion | 277 |
| Church, the Christian, soon secularised | 105 |
| ,, the Christian, tendency to reflect the age | 108 |
| Clement of Alexandria, his opinion of Scripture | 23 |
| Clement of Rome, his opinion of Scripture | 30 |
| Colenso, protest of Bishops and Clergy to | 15 |
| Compromise, attempts at | 62 |
| Critical Results tested by Modern Discoveries | 273 |

# 578                     Index.

| | Page. |
|---|---|
| Cyprian of Carthage, his view of Scripture | 24 |
| DANIEL, the superabounding miracles of | 341 |
|   ,, written in Hebrew and in Aramean | 381 |
|   ,, purpose of the Book of | 476 |
|   ,, cast to the lions | 529-532 |
|   ,, the visions of | 533 |
| Darius the Median | 521-532 |
|   ,, ,, ,, was not a viceroy | 523 |
|   ,, ,, ,, probably Cyaxares | 525 |
|   ,, appears to be referred to by Greek historians | 525, 526 |
|   ,, ,, ,, his reign indicated by the monuments | 527 |
| Dieulafoy's Discovery of the Palace of Shushan | 319 |
| Discoveries, Modern, and the Bible | 275 |
| Divisions of Babylonian *Literati* correctly given in *Daniel* | 397 |
| Doctrine, the, of Scripture cannot be saved by sacrificing the history | 67 |
| Drinking Cups, the, referred to in *Esther* | 332 |
| Driver, Dr., his admissions regarding *Esther* | 297 |
|   ,, ,, his contention regarding Greek Instruments in *Daniel* | 421 |
|   ,, ,, owes explanations to the public | 425, 433 |
| EGYPTOLOGY, rise of | 275 |
| Eichhorn, the father of the Higher Criticism | 207 |
|   ,, his concessions to infidelity | 209 |
|   ,, his explanation of Bible miracles | 210 |
| Empires, the four, of *Daniel* | 343 |
| "Emptying Himself," our Lord's | 74 |

| | Page. |
|---|---|
| England in the 18th Century | 131 |
| Established Church in the 18th Century | 137 |
| *Esther*, the Book of | 288 |
|   ,, its silence with regard to God | 289 |
|   ,, Dr. Driver's admissions in regard to | 297 |
|   ,, Heeren's tribute to | 297 |
|   ,, an old Book when the Septuagint translation was made | 299 |
|   ,, confirmations of | 300-339 |
| FRANCKE, J. A,, his conversion | 171 |
|   ,, ,, his labours | 172 |
| Freethinkers, English, of 18th Century | 141 |
| Frederic the Great, his hurtful influence | 179 |
| GERMAN RATIONALISM, rise of | 176 |
| Gold, the quantity used in Nebuchadnezzar's statue | 411 |
| Gospels, the variations of the | 154 |
| Graf's hypothesis | 248 |
|   ,, blunders | 249 |
| Greek instruments in *Daniel* | 419 |
|   ,, instruments could have reached Babylon long before the time of Daniel | 425 |
|   ,, instruments could have got to Babylon 1,000 years before | 434 |
|   ,, instruments *were* in Assyria before the time of Daniel | 434 |
|   ,, words in *Daniel*, supposed | 444 |
| Grotefend | 280 |
| HEEREN's tribute to *Esther* | 297 |
| Hegel, the Darwin of history and religion | 245 |
| Higher Criticism, the rise of | 206 |
|   ,, ,, absurdity of its fundamental principles | 247 |
|   ,, ,, its failure | 267 |
| Human element, the, in the Bible | 536 |

*Index.* 579

| | Page. |
|---|---|
| Huss and the Bible | 121 |
| Hymn Books, poisoned by the Rationalists... | 204 |
| IGNATIUS, his views of Scripture | 28 |
| Indefiniteness, "the happy medium" of Rationalism | 200 |
| Infidelity in Germany in 18th Century | 177 |
| Inspiration, extent of ... | 13 |
| ,, no theory of, possible | 14, 15 |
| ,, ordinary beliefs regarding ... | 16-18 |
| ,, Old Testament view of ... | 33-49 |
| ,, New Testament view of ... | 50-72 |
| ,, our Lord's witness to... | 73-89 |
| ,, illustrated by David ... | 41-43 |
| ,, illustrated by the 70 elders... | 43 |
| ,, illustrated by Jeremiah ... | 44-47 |
| ,, illustrated by Balaam ... | 47-49 |
| Investigation, necessity of ... | 9 |
| Irenæus, his views of Scripture | 26 |
| JEHOIAKIM, mention of his third year in *Daniel* | 345 |
| Jesus, the Lord, His witness to the Old Testament ... | 73 |
| ,, the Lord, did not abrogate the Old Testament | 84 |
| ,, the Lord, His teaching regarding Inspiration | 85, 86 |
| Justin Martyr's view of Inspiration ... | 27 |
| KAYSER ... | 250 |
| *Kenosis*, the Lord's | 74 |
| Kuenen ... | 251 |
| LARDNER, Dr. ... | 152 |
| Learning, place of, in Babylon | 363 |
| Lessing, his early history | 195 |

| | Page. |
|---|---|
| Lessing, his Wolfenbüttel Fragments | 196 |
| Literature, the only faultless ... | 95 |
| Luther and the Bible ... | 125 |
| MAGDEBURG, massacre in | 161 |
| Melanchthon ... | 156 |
| Moravian Brethren, the, and the Bible | 121 |
| Music, the period when it was used in state ceremonies confirms *Daniel* ... | 436 |
| Mysticism, rise of, in the Western Church ... | 113 |
| NAMES, changing of, a Babylonian custom ... | 374 |
| Nebuchadnezzar, his statue ... | 405 |
| ,, his statue, its base found by Oppert | 416 |
| ,, his religious zeal ... | 447 |
| ,, his apparent monotheism | 349 |
| ,, his devotion to Merodach | 350 |
| ,, his character | 353 |
| ,, his dream | 379-390 |
| ,, his madness | 456 |
| ,, his pride ... | 466 |
| ,, traces of his madness in history ... | 470 |
| ,, traces of his madness in the inscriptions ... | 475 |
| ,, successors of | 479 |
| OLD TESTAMENT, the, claims full inspiration | 32 |
| ,, ,, our Lord's witness to | 73 |
| Origen, his views of Inspiration | 21 |
| PALACE SCHOOL, the, in Babylon ... | 366 |
| Paper, invention of ... | 124 |

## Index.

|  | Page. |
|---|---|
| Paulicians, the | 101 |
| Paulus, his early history | 215 |
| " his theory | 216 |
| Persepolis, inscriptions at | 279 |
| Philosophy (German), effect of upon Rationalism | 191 |
| Pietism, rise of | 166 |
| " decay of | 175 |
| Polycarp's view of Inspiration | 28 |
| Postal arrangements (Persian), a feature of Esther's time | 333 |
| Printing, effect of the invention of | 123 |
| Protestantism (German) in 17th Century | 163, 169 |
| Pusey on Greek instruments in Daniel | 429 |
| " on Nebuchadnezzar's madness | 458 |
| QUOTATIONS of Old Testament in the New | 51 |
| RAB-SARIS, title mentioned in Daniel | 360 |
| Rationalism, Genesis of | 93 |
| " its conflict with the Reformation | 133 |
| " English, beginnings of | 145 |
| " preparations for Continental | 156 |
| " rise of German | 176 |
| " not in its beginning infidelity | 184 |
| " in its end worse than infidelity | 185 |
| " its panic | 185 |
| " failure of | 267 |
| Rawlinson, Sir Henry | 283 |
| Reformation (German), its rapid decay | 156 |
| " (German), injured by political arrangements | 162 |
| Reimarus | 196 |
| Reuss | 247 |
| " his testimony to the New Testament Doctrine of Inspiration | 87 |

|  | Page. |
|---|---|
| Revival of learning, its influence upon belief | 132 |
| Richard of St. Victor | 114 |
| Rosetta Stone, the | 277 |
| SACERDOTALISM, rise of | 99 |
| Sayce, Professor, on Persian names in *Esther* | 327 |
| " Professor, his admission in regard to names in Daniel | 377 |
| " Professor, his misreading of Cyrus's tablet | 499 |
| " Professor, his misreading of writing on the wall | 513 |
| Scholasticism, rise of | 109 |
| Schools, Rationalistic poison poured into the teaching of the | 203 |
| Scribes, the king's, a confirmation of *Esther* | 334 |
| Scriptures, the claim of the | 32 |
| " the, minute accuracy of the | 285 |
| " the, more miraculous than a messenger from the dead | 82 |
| Semler | 186 |
| " his doctrine of accommodation | 188 |
| " his pet theory of two parties in the Jewish Church | 189 |
| Sermon on the Mount, the | 83 |
| Sermons (English) of 18th Century | 157 |
| "Shushan the palace," discovery of | 314 |
| "Shushan the palace," phrase explained | 332 |
| Spener, Philip Jacob | 165 |
| Statue, Nebuchadnezzar's Golden | 404 |
| Strauss, his early life | 232 |
| " his duplicity | 235 |
| " his *Leben Jesu* | 236 |
| " reveals the goal of Rationalism | 239 |
| TERTULLIAN's view of the Scripture | 24 |

|                                             | Page. |                                              | Page. |
|---------------------------------------------|------:|----------------------------------------------|------:|
| Theology, the new, confession of            | 16    | WALDENSES, the, and the Bible                | 118   |
| Theophilus of Antioch, his view of the Scripture | 26 | Wall, the writing on the                     | 512   |
| Thirty Years' War, the                      | 160   | Webster, his definition of Inspiration       | 15    |
| Thomasius, his reforms                      | 173   | Wellhausen                                   | 254   |
| Tillotson, Archbishop                       | 152   | ,, his eight writers                         | 257   |
| " Traditional " view, the, not necessarily wrong | 11 | ,, an evolutionist                          | 259   |
| Tübingen School, the                        | 24    | ,, profanes and degrades everything          | 262   |
| UNBELIEF, law of                            | 95    | ,, his *Encyclopædia Britannica* article     | 264   |
| ,, early developed among the scholastics    | 112   | ,, his blasphemies                           | 265   |
| Unitarianism, rise of                       | 146   | Westcott's *Introduction to the Gospels*     | 21    |
| University of Paris, unbelief in the        | 112   | Wette, De                                    | 224   |
| Uzzah, transgression of                     | 37    | ,, his theory                                | 226   |
|                                             |       | ,, his confession                            | 252   |
| VARIATIONS of the Gospels                   | 154   | Whiston, William                             | 140   |
| Vatke                                       | 243   | Wiclif                                       | 119   |
| Verbal Inspiration, not dictation           | 12    | Wolff, Professor at Halle                    | 185   |
| ,, ,, the working theory of all Christian Theology | 18, 19 | ,, (the classicist) and Homer            | 225   |
|                                             |       | Women, their presence at Belshazzar's feast  | 519   |
| ,, ,, not an evolution                      | 31    | Xenophon's account of the capture of Babylon | 516   |
| ,, ,, absurdity of usual objections to      | 55    | Xerxes, the Ahasuerus of *Esther*            | 300   |
| Voltaire, his connection with Bolingbroke   | 142   | ,, his character                             | 301   |
| ,, his visit to England                     | 143   | ,, palace of, discovered by Dieulafoy        | 319   |
| ,, his determination to overthrow Christianity | 144 | ,, palace of, remarkable agreement of remains, with intimations in *Esther* | 323 |

www.ingramcontent.com/pod-product-compliance
Lightning Source LLC
Chambersburg PA
CBHW031935290426
44108CB00011B/561